# Transforming Leadership

## From Vision to Results

JOHN D. ADAMS, Ph.D.
General Editor

# Miles River Press

1009 Duke Street, Alexandria, Virginia 22314

DEDICATION

*To all those who have chosen to make a difference*
*with their life's work*

**ISBN** 0-917917-02-2

10  9  8  7  6  5  4  3  2

Printed in the United States of America

# Contents

# The Strategic Leadership Perspective

by

**JOHN D. ADAMS**
**SABINA A. SPENCER**

So at last the time has come
to trust the inner flame
that leads us into worlds unknown
and truth that's ours to name.
For those of us who take this step
and choose a peaceful earth
we'll know the power of mastery
a gift that's ours from birth.

*Sabina Spencer*

In many ways, this volume of readings is a sequel to *Transforming Work*, which was published in 1984. Initially there was difficulty getting that collection of readings printed: publishers were hesitant to publish an edited collection, and many of them felt the topic was too much on the fringe to be successful. However, with a conviction that the book would succeed and a strong grasp on the vision it portrayed, we went ahead with the publication. As it turned out, *Transforming Work* has been a great success, and is already in its second printing.

This collection is intended to extend and deepen the ideas presented in *Transforming Work*, with a particular emphasis on the role and the thinking processes of leaders in various types of organizations faced with complex and turbulent environments. It is written explicitly for those members of any organization who have chosen to make a difference in their lives and work; those who are no longer satisfied with *trying* to do their best and are committed to working in inspired ways that reflect their true potential.

This collection is blatantly optimistic in holding out hope for a better and more effective way to "be" in organizations. It is different from most other books on leadership in that it suggests we can achieve much more, in vastly more fulfilling ways, if we learn to focus on our visions of how we want things to be; if we inspire others to work toward these visions in ways that serve their own sense of purpose, while continually maintaining a commitment to integrity and truth. We do not view leadership as a trait or personality variable, but rather as a mind set or cognitive orientation. We explore the mental focuses that tend to be common to outstanding leaders and often overlooked by investigators of leadership. It should be noted that we are not suggesting that leaders are found only at the top of their organizations. Any organizational member can tap into his or her leadership potential at any moment simply by adopting what we are calling in this introductory chapter the "Strategic Leadership Perspective."

## THE STRATEGIC
## LEADERSHIP PERSPECTIVE

Over the past few years, there has been a tremendous resurgence of interest in leadership, especially as it contributes to performance excellence. There have been many books and articles published and a huge number of seminars and workshops offered. The bottom line has been that with special efforts, incremental performance improvements are possible. These improvements always seem to be measured against average performance standards, rather than what is *potentially* attainable. We believe that now is the time to step beyond this level of performance enhancement and begin asking the question: "What does it take to make a quantum leap from incremental performance enhancement to actually approaching that which we are capable of in our organizations?" The leadership perspective presented in this book raises this question in many forms and provides some excellent ideas for making these quantum leaps.

### The Role of Operating Premises

We refer to the various conscious and unconscious attitudes, beliefs, values, and expectations one uses to define and relate to the world as one's operating premises. These operating premises have operated during our lifetimes to get us where we are today—both individually and collectively. One of *our* operating premises is that the only way to fundamentally alter what one is "getting" in life is to alter one's operating premises. Everyone's personal operating premises are highly self-fulfilling; that is, whatever it is that one values/believes/expects/assumes will happen determines to a large extent how one acts. How one acts determines to a large extent what one "gets" from life. For example, if I believe that if I don't do "it," it won't get done, I will behave in certain ways. Over a period of time, others will react by allowing me to "do it all," fulfilling and reinforcing my belief.

Thus, a primary emphasis in strategic leadership is on adopting or stepping into a new set of premises, "experimental premises," which serve and support the results desired. One thing we have found in our seminars on strategic leadership is that, when asked to do so, participants have no difficulty in specifying what they don't like about their lives and work (e.g., impatience, crisis management, poor planning, lack of followthrough, etc.). However, they generally find it much more difficult to articulate what it is, specifically, that they do want. The reason for this is that we have all had a lot of encouragement and practice to notice what is wrong, but few of us have had much encouragement or practice in specifying exactly what we do want.

## Where Do Our Operating Premises Come From?

Cognitive psychology tells us that, for the most part, the foundations for our operating premises are created by the repeated messages (themes) we receive from the significant authorities in our lives (e.g., parents, teachers, close friends, church, the community, etc.) during our first 12 or so years. In addition, there is the continual reinforcement of Cartesian thinking (specialization, rational thinking, compartmentalization) which still dominates Western cultures, influencing and reinforcing the nature of our operating premises throughout our lives. The result of these thematic messages and cultural reinforcements is literally to hypnotize us into a socially acceptable way of relating to reality. It would be a major undertaking to reprogram permanently the operating premises we have, but if we become aware of the nature of these hypnotic suggestions, we can choose to reprogram ourselves with experimental premises from time to time to get different results. If we act "as if" a different set of premises were true, the self-fulfilling nature of these "new" premises would tend to occur, helping us to get more desirable results.

We can return to our strategic leadership seminars to illustrate the nature of the normal operating premises most of us hold. When we ask people to report on the thematic messages they recall from their first 12 or so years of life, the vast majority of their responses fall into one of three categories: No, Don't, or That Was Wrong. Most also report highly significant experiences of rejection by parents, siblings, or close friends which have left them feeling vulnerable or unworthy in some way. The outcome of this kind of programming, especially in the context of the broader Cartesian influences mentioned earlier, is a reactive style of thinking and behaving, in which the normal tendency is to:

- solve problems quickly

- maintain consistency, predictability, status quo

- reflect on the past, reacting to events after they happen to correct deviations

- think in a predominantly rational analytic mode

- break situations down into their smallest parts as the means to understanding

- be controlled by external circumstances

George Ainsworth-Land, a philosopher, consultant, and author, reports that in an investigation of innovative potential, there was a rapid decline as people went through the experience of adopting this reactive basis for their operating premises. At age five, 98 percent were judged to have high innovative potential; by age 10, the percentage had dropped to 30 percent; and by age 15, 12 percent. The predominant modes of organizing are also rooted in the same reactive bases, and both formal and unwritten rules continue to reinforce the reactive style in organizational members. For example, while one might be told to be innovative at work, he or she soon finds that the rewards are for *not* rocking the boat, *not* taking risks, and *not* making mistakes. By and large, organizations today still reward emulation rather than innovation. As a result, by age 30, only 2 percent of the subjects in the study reported by

Ainsworth-Land are judged to have high innovative potential. Perhaps not surprisingly, the percentage begins to rise significantly at around retirement age!

## Managerial Operating Premises Are Necessary

We must emphasize at this point that there is nothing fundamentally wrong with a reactive style. On the contrary, we would argue that this way of thinking is necessary in today's world and that it would be foolhardy to rebel against it. It is so characteristic of management today in most parts of the world that we could also suggest that it forms the basis for the majority of managerial operating premises. Quick problem-solving, maintaining the status quo, operating rationally, and taking corrective actions are part and parcel of what management is about. We need to "mind the store" on a day-to-day basis and be responsive to shifting conditions around us. Being reactive is a perfectly normal result of the predominant programming process through which most of us were socialized.

There are obvious limitations to adhering solely to this style of thinking. For example, most people who work in organizations can report numerous instances where the tendency to seek quick solutions to problems, coupled with the tendency to reduce situations to their component parts, has led to the treatment of a symptom rather than the real problem. Further, most of us are continually reminded that tomorrow morning's 10:00 deadline *always* takes precedence over the long-term plans we developed at the annual management retreat. Crisis management is reinforced by this style of thinking. Planning receives lip service, and the status quo is always protected from moment to moment. After years of consulting on planned change efforts, it is our strong conclusion that it is impossible to bring about major fundamental changes in organizations when a reactive style is adhered to by a critical mass of individuals in the organization.

## CHOOSING OUR FUTURES: THE POSSIBILITIES ARISING FROM ALTERED OPERATING PREMISES

Let us consider an alternative style of thinking (actually, an altered state of consciousness), which we can call "creative thinking." It is playfully instructive to note that the word "reactive" and the word "creative" are made up of exactly the same letters. The only difference between the two is that you "C" (see) differently!

We can describe the creative style used for developing experimental premises by comparing it point for point with the reactive style:

- Focus on envisioning desired outcomes without assuming limitations
- Intuitive bias, which is checked out through analysis (One should note here that few, if any, major breakthroughs have ever occurred from purely rational analysis — intuitive inspiration is needed.)
- Anticipation of trends and tendencies and adoption of a preventive stance

- Emphasis on the desired future and on catalyzing energy toward making it happen

- Holding a systemic perspective, in which one is able to see the interrelatedness of the many different parts of the organization

- These concepts, when taken together, lead to a sense of personal mastery, in which one experiences a very high degree of self- or inner control.

We have previously said that we could refer to the reactive style as being the basis for managerial operating premises. We can also refer to the creative style as being the basis for leadership operating premises. While it is the manager's responsibility to direct, control, and maintain his or her part of the organization, it is the leader who expands, crosses boundaries, innovates, and brings about changes in how the organization operates. Since these are seen as states of mind, anyone, including formal managers, can choose to adopt a creative perspective at any time.

Through history, all spiritual traditions have suggested that the true nature of the human race is to evolve toward becoming co-creators of reality. This creative state of consciousness, which any individual can adopt at any time, is therefore our natural birthright. Our normal style of thinking, the reactive, is still predominant and the style we use most of the time. We must *choose* the creative as a conscious act. Until we become more skilled and practiced, we will be able to remain in the creative consciousness for only brief periods.

## The Operating Premises of Strategic Leaders

This section summarizes the preceding paragraphs and also provides some of the criteria that guided the selection of chapters for this collection of readings. Five operating premises of strategic leadership are described which can be adopted as experimental premises by anyone at any time.

*Premise I: Leadership Is a State of Consciousness Rather Than a Personality Trait or Set of Skills.* The self-fulfilling premise states that whatever we hold in our minds as an expectation will have a tendency to occur. It is our experience that the self-fulfilling nature of premises still holds when we consciously and intentionally create desirable new expectations at any time.

Management and organizational patterns and structures nearly always encourage stability and predictability. With increasing environmental turbulence and unpredictability and with technology influencing organizations to become flatter, managers are being forced both to respond quickly to the unexpected and to accept that there is less potential for upward mobility. In this context, individuals need to develop their own sense of creativity, and organizations need to be more focused on determining their futures. The alternative is to become driven by the external circumstances with minimum control on the results achieved.

The leadership state of consciousness encourages individuals to: (1) become self-determining; (2) live with and value ambiguity; (3) create and work with alternative choices, structures, and systems; (4) encourage differences and seek the "gift" each person has to offer; (5) experience the *absence* of change as potentially disruptive to high performance; (6) reward risks taken in service of the vision; (7) develop

9

flexible temporary structures that are organized to best serve the outcomes expected of them.

*Premise II: A Primary Role of the Leader Is to Activate, Establish, and Nurture a Focus on Vision, Purpose, and Outcomes.* The self-fulfilling premise is once again important. Establishing and holding a vision of desired outcomes greatly increases the probability of realizing them. Activating and nurturing others' adoption of and focus on the results — often referred to as "creating alignment" — further increases the probabilities. This role is necessary to catalyze expansion and movement beyond the current status quo. Others will be available to focus on the process of getting there; the leader's role is continually to describe "there" and catalyze commitment and enthusiasm for "there."

*Premise III: It Is Cost-Effective to Focus Attention on Empowering the Workforce.* Once the vision is enthusiastically shared, the leader needs to focus on removing constraints to inspired performance from the organization's structure, systems, and culture. Remembering that it is normal for people to be reactive, leaders need to be continually on the look out for structures and patterns in the organization that protect the status quo and prevent movement.

As one obvious example, the reward systems of most organizations truly reward only the high potential performers — usually 10-15 percent of the workforce. An additional 10 percent who continue to aspire to high performance may also feel rewarded by the system. The remaining 75 percent of average and below-average performers almost always feel disempowered by the reward systems. It may be that the people judged to have "high potential" are those who have learned to emulate their management most effectively, and that a great deal of leadership potential is lost to the organization in the remaining population.

Performance psychologists consistently find that there are certain underlying conditions that need to be present to stimulate individuals and groups to inspired levels of performance. Among these conditions are the following:

- clear purpose and direction
- encouragement and opportunities for innovation
- seeing the individual's potential and gently demanding excellence
- establishing and gaining commitment to high but attainable standards
- creating challenging and meaningful assignments
- acknowledging and celebrating success
- setting an example of excellence
- holding to agreements
- holding positive beliefs about human nature and developing systems, practices, and policies that embody these beliefs
- capitalizing on individual differences
- allowing wide latitude for self-expression
- making educational opportunities available as needed

10

For the most part, these conditions can be created at any time. They require only leader commitment, not corporate permission.

As a final aspect of empowerment, we want to expand on the condition of capitalizing on individual differences. A reactive style reinforces conformity and predictability, with the frequent result that organizational members are tacitly expected to hold homogeneous views about priorities, processes, and styles of operating and relating to others. The truth is that people develop quite a variety of orientations and styles and will most willingly make excellent contributions if their individual gifts are sought out and recognized. Some people are action- and task-focused; some are more inclined to ideas, inspiration, and perspective; others are good at creating structure and providing logic; and still others prefer to focus on relationships and teamwork. All of these qualities are needed in the long run for excellence. If the manager of a group strongly exhibits one of these qualities and has a tendency to overlook the others, it is likely that he or she also will reinforce and favor those group members who reflect the same ones. Eventually those in the group who favor the other qualities will submerge their most natural "gifts" — or leave the group.

*Premise IV: A Systems Perspective Is Necessary to Avoid Emphasis on Alleviating Symptoms.* As has been stated, reactive operating premises tend to emphasize quick solutions to problems and a corrective response to situations as they unfold. As a result, the underlying causal factors are often overlooked. As one example, highways are often built in urban areas to relieve congestion and improve access to the city. Within a few years, developers take advantage of the new highways, creating office and apartment towers near the interchanges, with the result that congestion is worse than ever. Physicians often treat high blood pressure arising from stress by prescribing medication only. The result is that the blood pressure goes down — but the stressors and the individual coping responses stay the same. Eventually, something else in the body shows the effects of continued stress, and medication is given to alleviate those symptoms. Then something else begins to give out. In organizations, managers are often provided with training in new ways to manage, but back on the job, they continue to be rewarded for previous practices and receive little or no encouragement to use the knowledge and skills derived from the training.

Each functional part of an organization has its own parochial perspective on or interpretation of what should be done. We have discovered cases where the marketing function has had primary responsibility for "strategic planning" and has failed to request input from other functions (e.g., human resources, technical operations, and manufacturing). As a result, problems arise with levels of available manpower, skill requirements, excess inventory, and insufficient production capacity when plans are implemented. Much energy is expended within each unit as it attempts to solve these problems, but the core issue remains unaddressed because no one sees the whole picture. Various functions compete for resources and top management attention, and only temporary relief is achieved. What is needed is coordination of all functions through a systems perspective and a shared vision of the "whole" organization.

*Premise V: Attention to Needed Support Systems Is Essential to Achieving the Vision.* On the structural level, it is essential that the leader be aware of how adequately various support mechanisms are facilitating the desired outcomes. It is not at all unusual to find that the system defeats itself because the procedures needed to get a task accomplished are not in place. As an example, one of the most frequent reasons why strategic planning doesn't succeed is that as time passes the accountabilities for implementing the key actions become ambiguous, and everyone waits for someone else to initiate action. Another example is when a coordinative body, such as a task force, spends a great deal of time and effort developing a plan, only to find it rejected because it failed to gain the commitment of the constituent bodies.

On a more informal level, established work units are often too overloaded or improperly configured to respond adequately to unexpected complex demands. It is often appropriate for informal networks or temporary task forces to be formed and energized. This is infrequently done because of the fear of losing control (a major concern for those who are predominantly reactive) over such forms of organizing.

Support groups are often formed in major training efforts, and they are encouraged to continue meeting after the training has been completed to reinforce the training and facilitate implementation of the training learning objectives. Unfortunately, these groups seldom meet for very long, because they've been given no way to feed back their discoveries to the organization, or they've been given nothing tangible to accomplish. One thing that has worked very well in many organizations is to have top management work with these groups to identify real organizational problems, holding the group accountable for a set of recommendations. This allows the group to continue the learnings of their training and provides direct applications and influence into the ongoing life of the organization.

If organizations and individuals are to create powerful and positive results then it is necessary to adopt a Strategic Leadership Perspective. We must ensure that the environments in which we work encourage everyone to achieve quality outcomes, foster integrity, and support a creative style of thinking. It is only by consciously choosing the future we want that we will realize the potential we each have to make a difference with our lives.

## THE STRUCTURE OF THE BOOK

*Transforming Leadership* is divided into four sections. The first section describes some of the fundamental challenges facing leaders in organizations today. Section II, Changing Viewpoints, describes some of the mindsets of outstanding leaders—and ideas that can be adopted as experimental premises by anyone who chooses to operate from the creative, or leader, mindset. Section III, Leadership in Action, describes activities and behavior that leaders can undertake to help them realize a quantum leap or two in the results they are getting. Finally, Section IV contains some case descriptions of the results some leaders have actually achieved by using the principles described in this collection.

Each chapter is preceded by a brief abstract of its contents. The addresses of each author at the time of publication are provided on pages 14-16 so that readers can raise questions or share their own experiences with the authors.

*John D. Adams*
*Sabina A. Spencer*
Arlington, VA
April 1986

# Acknowledgments

I want to thank all of those readers of *Transforming Work* who provided feedback and suggestions and who are carrying the spirit of Organizational Transformation forward. The present volume has been created as a result of the energies and interests of thousands of people around the globe who are creating new ways of being in organizations and who are eager to share their ideas with others.

It seems almost inevitable that the creation of an edited collection of readings involves dealing with unexpected situations and moving through unforeseen delays. I want to thank each of the contributors to this volume for their efforts to meet our deadlines and for their patience when we didn't meet them ourselves.

# Contributing Authors

**Linda S. Ackerman** is a consultant in Oakland, CA, specializing in the management of complex change in large private and public sector organizations. She has worked extensively to develop leaders who understand and are skilled at guiding their organizations through change.

*Linda S. Ackerman, Inc., 6121 Castle Drive, Oakland, CA 94611*

**John D. Adams, Ph.D.,** is director and cofounder of Eartheart Enterprises, an international training and consulting firm with clients throughout North America and Europe. He has specialized in developing health, stress, and transition programs, and is currently focused on leadership development and performance enhancement work.

*Eartheart Enterprises, Inc., Route 5, Box 602, Winchester, VA 22601*

**Juanita Brown** is a trainer and consultant in Mill Valley, CA, working with a wide variety of clients throughout the United States and Latin America. She specializes in management and organization development and in the development of visionary executives.

*497 Loring Avenue, Mill Valley, CA 94941*

**Karen Wilhelm Buckley** is a consultant with Communicore in the San Francisco area. She has worked with a wide variety of organizations on transition management, meeting effectiveness, decision making, and vision clarification.

*763 Hillcrest Way, Redwood City, CA 94062*

**David R. Clair** was president of Essochem Europe prior to assuming his present position as a president of Exxon Research and Engineering Co., in New Jersey. He has long believed in the importance of the individual and of a supportive work environment in achieving important goals.

*Exxon Research and Engineering Co., P.O. Box 101, Florham Park, NJ 07932*

**Cathy DeForest, Ph.D.,** is an organization and management development consultant in Oakland, CA. She specializes in vision building, collaborative problem solving, creativity, large system change, and the art of organization celebration.

*2275 Mastlands Drive, Oakland, CA 94611*

**Sarah Engel** managed organization development and training for Essochem Europe in Brussels for five years. Her mission was to facilitate the creation, communication, boundary testing, sign-on, and celebration for Essochem's Long-Term Vision. She is now an independent consultant.

*1099 22nd Street, NW, Washington, DC 20037*

**Robert Fritz** is an author and lecturer and is the founder of DMA, Inc., in Salem, MA. He specializes in the development of programs that enable individuals to create what they want to create in their lives.

*DMA, Inc., 27 Congress Street, Salem, MA 01970*

**Willis Harman, Ph.D.,** is executive director of the Institute of Noetic Sciences in Sausalito, CA. He has for several years been active in promoting research on the human potential and on human consciousness, and has written and lectured widely on these topics.

*Institute of Noetic Sciences, 475 Gate Five Road, Suite 300, Sausalito, CA 94965*

**Dennis T. Jaffe, Ph.D.,** is a professor at Jaybrook Institute and a management consultant and writer in San Francisco. He specializes in organizational performance and health problems.

*764 Ashbury Street, San Francisco, CA 94117*

**William B. Joiner, Ed.D.,** is a founding partner of Action Management Associates of Concord, MA. He consults on large system change efforts (work redesign, automation etc.), facilitates the development of high-performance teams, and conducts leadership training seminars.

*883 Barretts Mill Road, Concord, MA 01742*

**Charles F. Kiefer** is founder and president of Innovation Associates of Framingham, MA. His work on coupling organizational effectiveness and personal satisfaction has led to the development of highly regarded courses in visionary leadership for senior executives and high performing teams.

*Innovation Associates, P.O. Box 2008, Framingham, MA 01701*

**Francis Kinsman** is a free-lance futurist in England and is the founder or director of a number of leading edge business networks. He specializes in exploring the impact of social trends on management and on enhancing the human dimension in business.

*4 Sion Hill Place, Bath, England BA1 5SJ*

**Ronnie Lessem, Ph.D.,** is director of the business development masters program at the City University Business School in London, England. He is an active author and consultant, specializing in "metapreneur" and enterprise development.

*The City University Business School, Business Development Programme, Frobisher Crescent, Barbican Centre, London, England EC2Y 8HB*

**Christopher Meyer, Ph.D.,** is a consultant in Los Altos, CA specializing in strategic organizational planning and development. His specialty is increasing an organization's capacity to succeed through organizational design, team development and leadership.

*844 Madonna Way, Los Altos, CA 94022*

**David R. Nicoll, Ph.D.,** is a consultant in the Los Angeles area, and is president of Merlin-Nicoll, Inc. His firm offers services in business strategy, organizational design, executive leadership, and paradigm reframing.

*10588 Cushdon Avenue, Los Angeles, CA 90064*

**Esther M. Orioli, M.S.,** is founder and president of ESSI Systems, Inc., a San Francisco firm which offers training materials dealing with stress management and optimal performance programs. She is also the co-author and publisher of self-assessment tools and products.

*ESSI Systems, 764A Ashbury Street, San Francisco, CA 94117*

**Harrison Owen** is president of H.H. Owen and Co., of Potomac, MD, which specializes in institutional and community development processes. He is exploring the uses of myth and ritual to facilitate transformations in organizations.

*7808 River Falls Drive, Potomac, MD 20854*

**Dick Richards** is a consultant in Philadelphia with an international practice. He is most interested in developing visions, after the vision strategies, leadership, close to the customer organizational cultures, and self responsibility.

*P.O. Box 150, Albrightsville, PA 18210*

**James A. Ritscher** is an author, lecturer, and organizational/management consultant in the Brookline, MA, area. He is founder of Organization Transformation Network and has a particular interest in the pragmatic application of personal/spiritual values toward the creation of high-performance organizations.

*1060 Beacon Street, Brookline, MA 02146*

**Cynthia D. Scott, Ph.D., M.P.H.,** is an active author and management consultant in San Francisco. She specializes in transition management, health promotion, and burnout prevention.

*764 Ashbury Street, San Francisco, CA 94117*

**Peter M. Senge** is director of the Program in Systems Thinking and the New Management Style at Sloan School of Management at MIT, and a partner in Innovation Associates in Framingham, MA. His explorations include the dynamics of social systems, organizational innovation, and holistic education.

*Systems Dynamics Group, Sloan School of Management, Massachusetts Institute of Technology, 50 Cambridge Drive, Cambridge, MA 02139*

**Michael Shandler, Ed.D.,** is an author and consultant working in the United States, Canada, and Europe. He specializes in applying human systems theory in the context of visionary planning and organization-wide culture change processes.

*227 Heatherstone Road, Amherst, MA 01002*

**David Sibbet** is a San Francisco based organizational consultant working on strategic management, organizational integration, and program design throughout the United States and Canada. He specializes in using graphics for group facilitation and was a Senior Fellow at the San Francisco Foundation in 1985.

*762 16th Avenue, San Francisco, CA 94118*

**Sabina Spencer** is director and co-founder of Eartheart Enterprises, an international training and consulting firm with clients throughout North America and Europe. She specializes in leadership development, creativity, and the management of differences.

*Eartheart Enterprises, Inc., Route 5, Box 602, Winchester, VA 22601*

**Joan Steffy** is president of Omega Point Productions, a San Francisco Bay area firm that produces leading edge executive video tapes for business leaders around the world. In her consulting practice she specializes in creative management and human resource development.

*P.O. Box 2055, Mill Valley, CA 94941*

**Thomas N. Thiss** is a management consultant and trainer who divides his time between London and Minnesota. He focuses on style, stress, influence, power, and negotiations issues in a broad variety of client systems.

*6110 Ridge Road, Excelsior, MN 55331; 28 Pilgrims Lane, Hampstead, London NW3, England*

# I.

# THE CHALLENGES
# OF LEADERSHIP

# CHAPTER 1

# Leadership from Alongside

by

**FRANCIS KINSMAN**

*With the advent of new organizational systems technologies and changing social demands and values of employees, organizations are changing their structures in the direction of more autonomous, smaller units. This shift calls for a new type of leadership which emphasizes democratic processes, individual improvement, entrepreneurship, and the legitimization of intuitive processes.*

*Change and decay in all around I see*

Embattled business leaders may be excused perhaps for muttering this line of a famous hymn while surveying the effects of today's political, economic, social, and technological trends on their organizations. But today is a joyride compared with what tomorrow is likely to hold in store. Politics and economics have always had clearly visible, short-term, cyclical influences, but it is the social and technological trends that are just now beginning to bite as never before.

## CHANGING STRUCTURES, CHANGING PEOPLE, CHANGING LEADERSHIP

Because of these technological and social trends, organizations are beginning to change their structures. There is the move toward "convergence" in information technology, whereby tomorrow's office is not so much a place as a system. Interconnected, integrated work stations in the future may be located anywhere—more specifically at the convenience of individuals, so that they no longer have to endure the inevitable daily trek to the concrete inner-city monolith. Moreover, people are voicing new social demands: to have a higher quality of working life; to be treated with dignity as human beings; to have their opinions, attitudes, and beliefs duly respected; and to do work that is fulfilling, nourishing, and rewarding in every sense.

These two trends combined are beginning to shoehorn organizations into structural change. There is now a distinct shift away from hierarchical systems to "heterarchies." Large enterprises are being broken down into a number of smaller, semiautonomous federal units. Here we no longer have an organization tree, but rather an organization sponge, whose units are supported by a central matrix that they nourish through their profitable activity in the marketplace.

The organization thus begins to feel more like a family or a series of linked families than it does a tribe or an army. So a new type of leadership is needed to deal with this change. The military style of management, at its worst aggressively domineering and at its best no more than patronizingly paternalistic, will gradually be seen as inappropriate to tomorrow's conditions. It will give way to a style that may be termed "materialistic," or, possibly better, "fraternalistic."

We hear a great deal nowadays about the crisis of leadership. In fact, the phenomenon is nothing of the sort. It is a crisis of "followership." Today's employees, and especially tomorrow's, will be neither manipulated nor cowed into obedience by old-style bluster and table thumping. They want to be at the forefront of their own, albeit smaller, parades. Tomorrow's leader must therefore be regarded as first among equals, rather than hooked on power and the smack of firm management. As far as power goes, this leader's major attribute will be to empower colleagues to be their own leaders.

This is similar to what is happening in the world of medicine, where the magic of the genius in the white coat with every astounding high-tech medical aid at his or her disposal is beginning to wear off. Patients now demand a return to the recognition that they are more than mere cases with number tags. They are human beings with not only physical but associated emotional, mental, and spiritual problems, too. This holistic attitude to medicine is catching on, and as we shall see, its underlying principles are also being stated loudly and clearly at the leading edge of business.

In the new network of matrix organization, everybody wins and all shall have prizes. The ever-changing future will demand diferent kinds of skills under different conditions and at different periods. Whatever the organization chart looks like, more and more management will be practiced by ad hoc groups that form, dissolve, and re-form into different shapes according to the task at hand. Thus, for one project $A$ may be leader over $B$ and $C$, while for another $B$ directs $C$ and $A$, and for a third, $C$ manages the other two. Sir Kennith Corfield, lately chairman of Standard Telephones and Cables (the British subsidiary of ITT), has described the new leadership as making demands similar to those placed on the skipper of an ocean racing yacht. In 12-meter ocean racing the skipper is likely to call on one helmsman in light variable winds and on another when a gale is blowing. The same principle already applies, and will increasingly apply, to business.

Sometimes a conservatively steady hand will be required, while at other times an entrepreneurial one will be more appropriate. Some people unused to such a concept find it a hard lesson to learn. They fail to realize that if things are going slowly for them it simply may be because the time is not right for their particular flair. This is a most important aspect of the effective deployment of management talent. Executives have to learn to accept objectively that when times change, the management team as an entity must exhibit those skills most relevant to the pertaining conditions. This does not mean that any particular individual's talents are good or bad or average, but merely that they are appropriate or inappropriate to the conditions.

The deployment of different kinds of talent to suit conditions as they develop, in not only a tactful but a motivating manner, is one of the most difficult arts required of the new-style leader. To soothe ruffled self-esteem in such cases, other means of recognition must be found besides mere position in the pyramid; this requires imaginative personal leadership at the top. For example, salary scales will need to be far less rigidly tied to status, and promotion should no longer be seen as the only mark of success within an organization. A whole range of experiments is already being tried out by managers attempting to solve the difficulty: fancy titles, declared salaries, job swaps, sabbaticals, detached social service, management buyouts, consultancy, and "elder statesmen" appointments. Most of these experiments depend on the leader's flair with people.

## UNEMPLOYMENT AND EMPLOYEE AGREEMENT

If we indeed experience the employment/unemployment scenario that is now forecast by many commentators, particularly Handy (*The Future for Work*, 1984), this will be only the beginning of the problem. In *The Collapse of Work* by Jenkins and Sherman (1979), unavoidable unemployment levels of between 20 and 25 percent are projected for the United Kingdom by the end of the century. Merritt (*World Out of Work*, 1982), anticipated unemployment as "One of the most widely shared conditions outside the usual human experiences of birth, hunger, sex, and death." The leaders of organizations will create this unemployment as they improve productivity, but they will also have to react to it by adapting their relationship to employees.

Handy postulates three types of employee in tomorrow's organization: a small professional/managerial support core, highly rewarded but working in extremely demanding and concentrated circumstances; a contractual fringe of self-employed "outworkers," many of whom are perhaps ex-employees, functioning individually or in cooperatives on a jobbing basis; and an outer ring of part-timers and temporary workers, a flexible labor force without careers as such, but simply receiving money in return for their work. In its purest form, the pattern may remain relatively uncommon for some time, but elements of it will soon become visible enough throughout the developed world.

What, then, are the implications for business leaders? In a personal interview, the Chairman of Imperial Chemical Industries, Sir John Harvey-Jones, made three statements that combine to create no small paradox:

- "I am going to subject ICI to as much change as I think either of us can stand . . . ."

- "I have 66,000 employees in the U.K. — by the year 2010, I expect to have about 3,000 full-timers and a hell of a lot of part-timers . . . ."

- "We must love our employees more . . . ."

All this turns much conventional wisdom on its head. What is a small company? What is a large one? How does one classify an automated steel mill employing a mere 17 technocrats? Even more relevant, what effect will it have on them and their relationship to the organization?

What Harvey-Jones is saying, is that employees must face the chilling realities of absolute change; therefore, to remain effective they need to be far more deeply and sympathetically understood by those who lead them. Traditionalists lament the old days when authority was more readily accepted. However, new values in society require that employees' agreement be sought rather than their obedience enforced. This removes the dead hand of centralized bureaucracy but also introduces a sense of shared endeavor in the face of future uncertainty.

Both the technological imperatives and the emphasis on management by consent require small units operating with as much autonomy as possible. Consequently, few businesses now envisage plants employing more than a few hundred people, as opposed to the mammoth industrial-relations death traps of the past. In the future, progress within agreed parameters will be monitored at the electronic center, with much more of the detail left to the discretion of the peripheral branches themselves. This involves a degree of self-confidence and creative success that is quite unlike anything that has been required to date.

The concept of employee agreement can be carried further toward a more formal participation, or co-ownership. Workers now see themselves and their labors not as costs but as assets. Like villagers, employees regard the organization for which they work as belonging to them rather than themselves as belonging to it. However attractive the nostalgic memories of benevolent dictatorship may be, genuine democracy is an inherent attribute of the working organization of the future. It is a prerequisite for the co-creation of its success by all those involved in it.

Organizations will be forced to accept that they are now villages, not only from the more obvious aspect of decentralization and small unit size, but also in regard to the right of tenure of the occupants, who perceive that the village belongs to them. "It is senior management's job to find something which we can do and they can sell," as one workforce recently voiced it. Contracting out work will muffle the effects of this attitudinal shift, but there will always be a core of village residents whose claims need to be considered. For this reason, the pure Handy model may be considerably modified in practice.

## ENTREPRENEURSHIP AND CROSS-UTILIZATION

The new fraternalism needed in the sponge organization of tomorrow will have as its salient characteristic the concern for a sibling's development rather than the traditional imposition of parental will upon it. In particular, the entrepreneurial flair to run any unit, whether small or large, will be of far greater importance than any organizational and administrative talent, since so much of the administration and organization will be carried out by electronic methods. Business leaders must therefore foster the entrepreneurial spirit in their managers, by brotherly encouragement. But how? Are entrepreneurs born or made? The question prompts the story of the army staff college candidate whose assessment read, "Major Jones is not quite a born leader yet, but his troops will follow him anywhere — if only out of curiosity."

As far as many large successful organizations are concerned, entrepreneurs are discovered by testing their mettle in the field. Shell U.K. Ltd., for example, is a group that has already tried various techniques to bring out the entrepreneurship of its young tigers. As John Raisman, its chairman and chief executive put it:

> We have taken over some smaller companies, peripheral to our main business, but fitting into the concept of our program of step-outs into related fields. We retain the management but put in one or two of our own brighter people, giving them an opportunity to stretch their wings on a less protected basis than in the main stream. We look for these sorts of acquisitional opportunities — as long as the business decision is sound, the career-broadening aspect is a bonus.

On the same conceptual basis, the group as a whole continually seeks potential startup situations, both subsidiaries and joint ventures, in which to put their promising younger men and women. Furthermore, they second people into organizations where a lot of intelligence needs to be applied quickly — usually in an early stage of development. These are mostly local enterprise agencies supporting small businesses in depressed areas, or firms being helped by them.

Young employees are being trained in entrepreneurial skills and given the opportunity to win their spurs, so that they will be able to take on the larger problems that will confront them higher up the organizational ladder. It is, in other words, a way of giving promising younger people a foretaste of life at the top.

Meanwhile, in a totally dissimilar organization, current leaders are given an aftertaste of life at the bottom. This is a technique practiced by the highly untraditional airline, PeoplExpress, and is known as "cross-utilization of jobs." It is easier for them to accomplish, perhaps, because the company is fiercely customer-oriented and needs to deal personally with the individual passenger in a highly competitive consumer services market. Nevertheless, the essence of the philosophy has universal application: "Everyone has to know what it is like to push a broom, and frequently to be reminded of the fact." Every single manager (the word being synonymous with "employee" in that company) regularly experiences someone else's job, from the chairman downward. Thus it is quite a familiar occurrence to find the chief executive acting as a steward on a Boeing 747 or to have the corporate treasurer help you with your baggage at the check-in desk.

This is tantamount to what chairman Mao Tse-tung tried and failed to do in China's Red Revolution, but interestingly, Chairman Mao did not espouse the doctrine himself; and it only really works when the leader of the organization also participates. The true leadership of the future will therefore have a fundamental understanding of the fact that people matter most to any enterprise — as consumers, employees, shareholders, creditors, suppliers, or as the public at large. The new leadership must not represent a means of manipulation (not least because being better educated and better informed nowadays, people will smell that a mile off and react violently against it) but rather have an ability to work alongside and with people demonstrating respect for their talents, their values, and their crises. Both the

Shell and the PeoplExpress examples reveal the creative effect of experiencing how other people feel at different levels in an organization, once the individual is moved out of his or her normal context.

## THE NEW ORGANIZATION — A MASCULINE/FEMININE BALANCE

Technology is hurtling us toward the state where electronic capacity is taking over many of the traditionally masculine attributes that have in the past been work's most important features—first muscle, now number-crunching and logical analysis, and ultimately much decision-making too, given the awesome advances in artificial intelligence today. The end result may well be that the computer will in effect come to represent much of the left-brain or rational aspect of the organization, leaving its people to play the part of the right-hand side of the brain. This is the more feminine side of a man or a woman's nature, which scores characteristically in the intuitive, creative, and generally supportive roles.

The traditionalist who snorts at the idea of anything feminine coming anywhere near his idea of leadership may prefer another analogy, namely the essential difference between the president's job and the chief executive's. The main duties and responsibilities of the chief executive have a general flavor of action and direct leadership, with the primarily assertive aim of ensuring that that organization is performing as effectively as possible from day to day.

The company president provides an equally vital contribution that is, however, subtly different: more detached, contemplative, even remote, more characteristic of the wise and experienced ambassador of the organization to the outside world. This is a father figure to his business, whom a psychologist might pigeon-hole as the archetypal elder statesman or high priest, as compared to the warrior archetype embodied in his managing director.

The point is that both archetypes are essentially masculine in character, so nobody needs to feel threatened. Both this and the masculine/feminine analogy hold well. The transformed leader of tomorrow—at all levels and in all sizes of organizations—must exhibit a better balance, showing more of the president's right-brain characteristics and correspondingly less of the chief executive's, as this role is mostly played today. Macho posturings will be out of fashion, and these other deeper elements will be more influential.

We have already seen how tomorrow's in-house entrepreneurs [or "intrapreneurs" as Norman Macrae (1976) terms them], besides being electronically monitored, will be aided by electronics in their decision-making processes. This means that the entrepreneurial characteristics that are going to be most valued for their scarcity will be the intuitive ones. The intuitive side of assessing situations, and then the harnessing of this inner answering system to provide a creative resolution, represents the epitome of tomorrow's management skill. But in addition to channeling intuitive resources into creative problem-solving, tomorrow's leadership must also induce a contagious effect whereby the leader enhances these qualities in colleagues and subordinates by supporting them. The leader must educate them in the true sense of the word and thus bring out the best of their own intuitive, creative, and supportive faculties.

# LEADERSHIP BY CONTAGION — THE FINDHORN FACTOR

To see this in practice in an altogether unlikely business setting, one needs to travel to Findhorn, a community in northeast Scotland. If you can imagine the most incongruous place in the world to come across an advanced mutant of one of the very latest management techniques, it could be this trailer lot on what used to be a rubbish dump near Inverness. Interestingly, the technique is similar to one adapted from the Japanese by far-sighted managements. It has been labeled "Theory Z" by Ouchi (1981), who has analyzed how many leading American and Japanese companies have used it to build successful consultative relationships between every level of management and the shop floor—in other words, an ambience where confrontation and threat are replaced by consultation and trust.

The trailer lot is the home of the Findhorn community, an organic farm and spiritual center of learning, where people live an "alternative" life style that might be thought by many executives to be from a completely different planet. However, when inspected more closely, it is evident that something else is going on that is in fact highly relevant to tomorrow's business. The active principle is based not so much on worker participation as on the co-creation of success, with the whole workforce being actively engaged toward this aim. Findhorn's results are based on spiritual principles but with a sound measure of practical impact. These people do not go around smiling at each other all the time and letting the milk boil over—they work hard and purposefully and they quite frequently win. "Trust in God *and* tether your camel" as an old Arabic proverb puts it.

Findhorn is a decentralized and democratic organization. Its different departments, whether educational, artistic, or maintenance, are based on a communal consensus. Each group and department has to stand on its own feet, though additional support is always available from the center, a small core group of ten, an executive of four members. Core-group decisions have to be backed by a representative body of the whole community, which determines and monitors the common will.

This combination of hierarchy and democracy that pervades the management of the whole enterprise is based on the interaction of two principles: focus and attunement. A group, however small, whether the horticultural college, the kitchen, the publishing department, or guest administration, is run by a "focalizer," a leader who takes the nondirigiste responsibility for sensitive leadership among the others. The focalizers are in effect the managers of something like 40 working departments who focus, rather than dictate, the energies of the people in their given areas "like water through a funnel," as one of them put it.

Focalizers help to make the decisions for the group, but on the basis of the second concept, attunement, in which everybody is allowed to state their views. Some person in the group takes the initiative and becomes the point of entry of an idea into it. Then the members of the group hold hands in a ring, close their eyes, and

**25**

concentrate on reaching a consensus through individual self-awareness. This is followed by a discussion on the basis of the communal purpose and what is ultimately conceived as the highest good. Returning yet again to this need for greater balance in leadership, the technique combines the best in the embodiment of both the masculine and the feminine principles of the psyche—or the yin and the yang of the Tao:

- *the right vision*—which incurs intuitively through the combination of focalizing and attunement, followed by

- *the right communication*—which involves vital emotional enthusiasm and support to all and from all, and finally

- *the right action*—which must then be effectively carried out from the intellect.

## LEADERSHIP AND THE INTUITIVE PROCESS

Learning from this, both actual and potential leaders need to do two things. First, they need to develop this balance of attributes within their organization, toward a more profound sense of its intuitive, creative, and supportive aspects. Then they themselves need to become more familiar with the practical applications of the intuitive process. Though varying in extent and manifestation in each individual, the conjuring up of this facility involves a sequence of six steps:

- *stop*—switch off your mind and shut out the surface buzz; or as one highly intuitive chief executive described it, "unscrew your head and leave it outside the door."

- *listen*—actually allow the intuition to canter round the field: this can be enhanced through meditative and self-development techniques, and the gentle psychoneurological exercise of the right brain and other areas responsible for the intuitive function—"brainjogging," in other words.

- *focus*—bring these wider-than-usual cavortings of the mind down to earth again, grounding them so that lateral and imaginative thinking can then be transformed into a plan of action.

- *act*—if this is right it will "feel right" in your bones, so turn it into reality by accomplishing the plan; trust the process, however outlandish the message might appear.

- *watch*—monitor the results of your actions and evaluate their impact; not only in the immediate, but also in the longer term in the light of events as they unfold.

- *acknowledge*—the psyche, or the unconscious mind (which we are dealing with here) likes to be appreciated; when the action taken turns out to be effective, the best way of ensuring that the process works next time is simply to thank one's subconscious for communicating a useful message.

# THE LEADER'S
# OWN SELF-DEVELOPMENT

Much has been made here of the new-style leader's personal support, the royal jelly that keeps the hive going by bringing out the best of the intuitive and creative in others. Tomorrow's leader must not be so self-interested as to be primarily concerned with personal success. The most important part of the function is equated with sympathy and compassion for others in the root sense of those words (the first Greek and the second Latin), each of them meaning the act of "feeling alongside with." Furthermore, a transformed leadership implies one where this feeling for others derives from a deeper-than-usual knowledge of oneself. Sir John Harvey-Jones, our previously quoted and exceedingly successful exponent of this art, says about the ideal president: "He should not be entirely dependent on the company for his livelihood. His vision can become stultified if preoccupation with his fortunes inhibits a dispassionate view."

These words originally related to financial dependency, but they further relate to the overall human qualities of the ideal chairman, and indeed to those of the ideal leader at any level of business in the future. It is a fundamental mistake for leaders to devote all their time and energy to the company's interests. They must take the time to develop themselves into whole and rounded human beings.

This doesn't just mean taking up tennis. Tomorrow's leader must learn to obey the dictum carved in stone above the entrance to one of the oldest and formerly most prestigious of futures consultancies, the Temple of the Oracle in Delphi: "Know thyself." Leadership entails self-development in the total and truest sense — intellectually, bodily, emotionally, and spiritually. Reflect on the success of Japanese business and consider whether it may well have a great deal to do with the Zen Buddhist and Confucianist elements implicit in the Japanese style of management. The Tao, or the One Way to enlightenment, consists of two aspects, the yin and the yang, roughly corresponding to the feminine and the masculine sides of the personality, which are in constant flow and constant balance. Balance and wholeness are the touchstones of this culture.

In a Western context, Jungian psychology shows similarly that every individual, whether masculine or feminine, contains the seed of his or her own "contra-sexual element"; termed *anima* in the case of women and *animus* in the case of men. Psychological enlightenment is only to be obtained by performing what a Jungian analyst should call the "inner marriage," by reconciling these two active principles. So although in business, as in anything else, it would be quite mistaken to go overboard for the feminine principle to the exclusion of the masculine, nevertheless in an area that has been so historically dominated by male principles, a reassertion of the feminine to create a new and balanced form is necessary now and henceforth. This being so, a change so colossal is only possible by direction from the top, originating within the psyche of the leader.

There are no more big daddies to make everything all right, and instinctively we know this. Maybe there never were, but in any event leaders must recognize it too. The first step is therefore "physician, heal thyself," and the second is "patient, heal thyself." Tomorrow's leadership will thus see as its prime duty the empowerment of others, and to this end the most vital requirements for a leader will be those of self-knowledge and inner balance. The most effective leadership will come not only from alongside but also from within—a transformed leadership that itself transforms everyone it touches.

# CHAPTER 2

# Leadership and Followership: Fresh Views on an Old Subject

by

## DAVID NICOLL

*We are at a difficult stage in our history. We can "see" the emergence of a new way of operating and describing reality while our education, socialization, and culture limit us to the "old" ways of thinking about and describing what lies ahead. This chapter introduces some of the concepts and modes of thought with which we must become conversant in order for us to truly understand the implications of a new leadership paradigm.*

Michael McCloskey (1983), a cognitive psychologist at Johns Hopkins University, demonstrates in his current research that many people are burdened with striking misconceptions about the movements of physical objects in apparently simple circumstances. McCloskey's tests illustrate that, although Newton's laws of physics are well known, many people believe that ordinary physical objects behave according to a theory of mechanics that was widely held by philosophers who were born three centuries before Newton. It seems that we explain the way a ball or a rock moves as if Daffy Duck — not Newton — had written the laws of motion! Naturally, these beliefs are inconsistent with "modern" principles of physics. Yet, for many of us, they are still alive in the last two decades of this century, more than 50 years after Planck, Bohr, and Einstein rewrote Newton.

McCloskey's observations mirror my own views on our current approaches to leadership. Although in many instances a number of us are talking about new ideas, most of us are, in critical ways, nonetheless prisoners of vastly outdated precepts. We harbor (mis)conceptions about leadership that are more in keeping with the "mechanistic" beliefs generated by Newton than with the "probablistic" attitudes spawned by Einstein. In *The Sleepwalkers*, Arthur Koestler (1959) asserts that Galileo, Copernicus, and Newton, while dancing in a new world, nonetheless managed to retain some remarkably outdated beliefs. These tenets, he suggests, limited these scientists' ability to settle completely into the new society that they, themselves, were founding. We are limiting ourselves in precisely the same way, even though the realities round about us are pushing us into a universe of new precepts, behaviors, and feelings.

# THE CRITIQUE

My basic concern is that we are ignoring the guts of our new paradigm. Our newest and best approaches to leadership—for example, those provided by James McGregor-Burns (1979), Warren Bennis (1985), and Abraham Zaleznick (1977)—are still rooted in Newton's hierarchic, linear, and dualistic thinking, so much so that they do not provide us with completely satisfactory models for the world we face. To our detriment, we still see a leader as one person, sitting at the top of a hierarchy, determining, for a group of loyal followers, the direction, pace, and outcome of everyone's efforts.

The problematic part of our grounding in the hierarchic, linear, and dualistic aspects of Newtonian mechanics is the way these beliefs bind our leaders implicitly to a picture of themselves as saviors. For them, and all of us as well, hierarchy reigns supreme. We consequently rely on, and consistently return to, our belief in *a* leader who will, from the top, do it all for us. Every four years, for example, we elect "the most powerful man on earth." We are fascinated by generals and CEOs, by quarterbacks, centers, and pitchers. We idolize John Wayne. Robert Johnson (1974), in his book *He*, says it well: "The notion that the welfare of a kingdom depends on the virility or power of its ruler has been a common one." Most of us, it seems, believe—with unquestioned faith—a very old myth.

This savior complex prompts a basic mistake: we equate leadership with progress. Taking the community to the promised land is, for us, the sine qua non of leadership. Even Burns, a Pulitzer Prize-winning author in this field, sees leaders as all-powerful. He portrays DeGaulle, for instance, in his last term of office, and Kennedy, in his only term, as presidents who were not "true" leaders because they did not "transform the flesh and fabric of [their] people's lives." They merely "stabilized" their regime (DeGaulle) or provided new meaning and consciousness for their society (Kennedy).

The problem with this view is not that transforming the "flesh and fabric of people's lives" is not one of a president's or a corporate executive's important tasks. It is. The difficulty is that this is only one of a leader's many tasks, and perhaps not even the most significant one. In today's Einsteinian world, an executive's accomplishments do not have to be purposefully directional for him or her to be a leader. DeGaulle, in stabilizing his country, and Kennedy, in providing a new meaning for his, contributed precisely what their nations needed from them at that moment in history.

Beyond this, it seems to me that persons who evoke the will of a people to stand up for their values and beliefs are leaders, even transformational ones. Martin Luther King and Gandhi are cases in point. Although their progressive institutional gains are being questioned today, there is no doubt that the strength and stance of their respective peoples will never be so limited as they were in the early part of this century. Neither King nor Gandhi succeeded in "saving" anyone or in taking them to the "promised land." But their presence and participation have transformed black, brown, and white persons alike, shifting our interaction and our issues to new planes of consciousness. Our savior complex leads most of us to miss, or at least to underestimate, this kind of contribution, especially when all we can see or talk about are "transformative" leaders.

Finally, our emphasis on the savior aspects of leadership is troublesome because it burdens our leaders unfairly, and undermines the confidence of the rest of us. In a recent "60 Minutes" interview, Richard Nixon asserted that leaders were different from followers. He said that he believed that followers thought this way too: "They [followers] *want* their leaders to be different." What he was implying—but not saying—was that we want our leaders to be higher, stronger, and better than we ourselves are: our saviors. This is probably true; many of us do want someone to save us.

This view places unmanageable burdens upon our leaders. We heap task after task, challenge upon challenge on today's politicians and CEOs; in the face of them all it is a wonder that any one of them survives, let alone succeeds. CEOs, for example, have always been expected to balance their budgets and make profits. Superb quality, excellent conditions of employment, and plant survival have, in the last two decades, become part of their package. We now are adding high performance and the transformation of our own lives to the list. These challenges are at least Herculean if not Sisyphean.

On the other side of the equation, our powerful-savior notion is troublesome because it connotes, to most of us, a passive followership. As Marie-Louise Von Franz (1981) points out, ". . .Christ is the Shepherd and we are the sheep. This is a paramount. . .image in our religious tradition and one which has created something very destructive: namely, that because Christ is the shepherd and we the sheep, we have [learned]. . .that we should not think or have our own opinions, but just [follow]." This notion of acquiescence is precisely what is not working. For those of us who are not on top, this image steals our power and drains us of responsibility. It lays us at the footstool of exploiters. Witness Hitler, Mussolini, or Nixon. Passive followership, although perhaps a traditional perspective, is neither functional nor preordained for today's probablistic world.

Our mechanistic blinders also impede our openness to the innovative changes coming at us from our new paradigm. For instance, the holographic aspects of our leader-follower relationships. Specifically, the holographic metaphor (each part contains the whole) suggests that there are/must be hundreds of significant people playing in our leadership game, not just one. For example, the "echo" standing behind Martin Luther King at the Lincoln Memorial, emphasizing, punctuating, and extending his "I have a dream" message. Or the "gardeners" in the field working the crowd before that speech, planting the "seeds" of King's principal tenets, giving the audience a context in which to explore the message he was to deliver. Or the Jackson Brownes of the same rally, singing chorus to the play being acted out, accentuating, through their words and rhythms, the drama of King's message. We have given short shrift to these people, vastly underestimating their contributions. If we were to rewrite the New Testament for the 1980s, we would have to give equal billing to the 12 Disciples.

Our emphasis on hierarchic leaders causes us, as well, to understate and miscast the interactive aspects of our leader-follower relations. This is more than adequately demonstrated by the new work of Zaleznick, Bennis, and Burns. Without a doubt, each of these authors has a clear feel for a new model of leadership. Despite their innovations, however, basically they talk only about the leadership side of the leader-follower equation. Their emphasis—if only by neglect—ignores followers and, by implication, imputes passivity to followership. They hide, thereby, many of the more important interactive aspects of this subject. For instance, when we are preoccupied with leaders, we overemphasize their role in transmitting their message, their delivered wisdom, to us. We create someone who is representative of, but not a *part* of, our needs and interests. The interactive paradigm we are building offers a different view. It suggests that wisdom and meaning come from the interplay between the led and the leader. Neither wisdom nor meaning is created by leaders and given to followers. Direction, for example, is not dreamed up and delivered to us by a leader. Nor are our goals. Both are new messages created within and through our interaction with a leader.

Finally, the interactive view suggests another point that is little recognized in almost all conversations on leadership: there is an element of belonging that is active in all good leadership. Presidents act on behalf of their nation; chief executive officers act for their stockholders *and* the people working in their businesses. This is not mere rhetoric. From the interactive point of view, it has to be the truth. If you read the Bible or the teachings of Gandhi on the one hand, or *Moby Dick* or *Mutiny on the Bounty* on the other, you will find confirmation that good leaders belong with their followers. They, unlike Ahab and Bligh, are part of the group. They, like Jesus and Gandhi, see themselves as members. Belonging does not eviscerate a leader's personal strength. On the contrary, to be a spokesperson, to be a catalyst, to lead from within, a leader must have a sense of self that is not submerged in the collective. But he or she also must have a quality-of-being that emanates from the group. "Speaking-for" and "acting-on-behalf-of" demands union. What is required is being separate and a-part-of at the same time. Leadership, first of all, bespeaks membership.

Most leadership thinking to date has consistently missed these points. Currently, we—like Galileo, Copernicus, and Newton before us—have a "blind-eye" for our new paradigm's fresh realities; we are holding on to critical pieces of a terribly outdated model.

## NEW VISIONS

It should therefore be obvious that even our freshest concepts of leadership need readjustment. Leaders, if they are to be effective in a probablistic world, need to incorporate the perspectives of our new paradigm. They need to begin thinking about their responsibilities and roles in startlingly new ways. I want to outline here some directions from which these new thought patterns and mind sets should come.

To start, leaders need to begin thinking about themselves as if they were part of an "action-dialogue" or a "shared-trusteeship." Action-dialogue is my term; shared-trusteeship belongs to Burns. The point in either case is that leaders must think of themselves, not as a solo act, but as part of a mutual, interactive process of creation. Their role, in our emergent society, is not that of solitary hero.

Either concept—action-dialogue or shared-trusteeship—if incorporated by our leaders into their feel for their jobs, would eliminate the polarized leader-follower equation inherent in our current approach. Either would eliminate the hierarchic bias built into the term leader, as well as the passive one rooted in our concept of follower. These biases, as suggested, split leaders and followers, and irretrievably, set the leaders on top. If our leaders could just strike these implicit prejudices from their thinking, we all would move a long way toward removing some of the disadvantages incurred as a result of our savior complex.

Beyond this, the notion of an action-dialogue accentuates both the holographic and the interactive nature of the leader-follower relationship. Like the "×" in the equation $2 \times 2 = 4$, the traffic light at a street corner, or the DNA in our cells, this concept connotes a real relationship, and patterns it. If leaders were to think and speak of their relations with their followers as an action-dialogue, they would jettison some of our outmoded pre-suppositions and assimilate some of the probablistic dynamics that are propelling our new paradigm.

If, for instance, leaders were to take the action-dialogue concept to heart, they would be relieved of the burden of single-handedly making others' lives meaningful. They would be drawn more naturally toward cooperative, synergistic relationships with their followers, for action-dialogues convey impressions of meaning-created-in-doing. This is actually what happens in the real world. Leaders and followers create meaning by doing things together. They start a new venture—together. They open up space—together. They combat racism—together. They launch a new product—together. All to the good, then, is a mind set that prompts this directly and unequivocally.

More than anything else, making this adjustment in thinking will require that leaders recast their views of followership.* This will be difficult because we all, without exception, as yet have failed to recognize one essential truth that our new paradigm is revealing: *there are no followers.* On the tail end of our leader-follower equation we typically see passivity where there is naught but control. We find reactiveness when there is only momentum. We assume a longing for deliverance where there is nothing but responsibility. This failure, and its consequences, are very understandable. Our historic thought patterns and language habits constrain us. They lead us to buy into (mistakenly) the idea that leaders alone may blaze a trail that others can only follow.

This old metaphoric view of the trailblazing leader comes, perhaps, from the days of hunting and gathering, when men did forage alone. Today, this perspective is too simplistic. Leaders no longer can presume simply that they are the people who step out first, who take initiative and the first risk, who come up with the new idea. They can no longer believe, unquestioningly, that they are the ones who express the new vision, who arouse the new awareness, who evoke the new excitement. Nor can they assume automatically that they are the ones who engage the new commitment, who build the new invention, who point us in the new direction.

---

*The ideas that follow stem from a conversation with Tony Rose, a friend and colleague, that occurred during the summer of 1981.*

Presumptions such as these, by their focus, obscure important action. They also place the burden of responsibility on the wrong shoulders. Davey Crockett and Daniel Boone provided our country a useful service. But so, too, did the wagon trains going west. Who was it, then, who provided the real, solitary act of leadership? Can we really tell? Was there only one hero? Should we even care? No. For now the best that can be said is that a pathfinder is seldom, if ever, immediately followed by other people. At best, he or she—on behalf of all of us—points the way, and we each then make our own way in the direction suggested, as best we can.

If, then, there are no followers, what is it that a leader does?

Our answer—if we ever are going to find one that is satisfactory—will require leaders to accept and believe that *followers use leaders to make a path*. This is fundamental. Our leaders must allow themselves—and us—to believe that followers are *not* passive, reactive tools of charismatic power figures. They are, instead, the creators of energy. They are the architects of the open moments into which some people must be the first to step. As followers, they are the agents who show their leaders where to walk. They are the ones who validate their leaders stepping out in a direction that has meaning for all of us.

We give nothing away in moving toward this kind of definition. Not wisdom. Not power. Not confidence. When leaders recognize that followers *allow* others to break a trail for them, we all will see that both acts—one of allowing and one of doing—are both necessary and reciprocal, an agreement to proceed into which all parties enter. That activity accomplished by those who are not blazing the trail is neither passive nor reactive. It provides the contextual foundation for effective, satisfying action.

At this point, none of us really believes this. We are too tied up in the passive-follower concept to accept the idea of active, meaningful roles for everyone. We also are too bound up in our savior complexes to permit any diminution of our leaders' solitary stature.

When, however, we do shed our old blinders, the creative, initiatory, and confirmational aspects of the follower dynamic are sure to emerge. Having once discarded these blinders, we will see, in an irreducible way, that leaders and followers each have their own responsibilities within an action-dialogue framework. Leaders assure movement. Followers proffer need and interest, suggest direction and purpose. When this is clear, our leaders will recognize that the approach our new paradigm is pushing them toward is one that requires us to believe that followers are not simply passive observers, but rather active and responsible *shapers*.

Our new paradigm is coming at us with these messages from all sides now. Planck, Bohr, and Einstein spawned them in the early part of this century. Others, such as Sheldrake, Prigogine, and Bohm, are now extending them. Television, the press, and movies, to name but a few of the more irresistible conduits, all incorporate and popularize these viewpoints. It is only a matter of time before this wave forces us to realize that viewing leadership as a solitary act of brilliant saviorship is outmoded. This image of our leaders as later-day Lancelots is just too narrow to encompass all that our world brings us. It is also too static a perspective—and too simplistic—to serve our present leaders well. Action-dialogue, or some similar set of concepts, must soon find their place in our world view.

Before we absorb this viewpoint and use it convincingly, we will have to expand and refine what we mean by an action-dialogue. Such a term must have depth if it is to survive. It must have scope, and flexibility. To be used successfully by any leader, it must have meaning in our daily lives.

Much will have to happen for this concept to take on such qualities. To be sure, I do not know everything that must take place. Of one thing, however, I am sure: leaders who want to be effective with this concept must tie together — in new ways — their own use of power with their peoples' everyday fears.

Both current research and our own everyday experience demonstrate that fear is a central dynamic in the exercise of power. It seems that we expect our leaders to move to control when we are afraid. If fearful enough, we want *them* to strike out. When our fear is connected to rage, we move them to destroy. When fear is persistently and trenchantly a part of our world, we become evil in our exercise of power. Axelrod's (1984) research shows that such behavior evokes in our counterparts reciprocal responses, creating potential runaway conflicts. If action-dialogues are to have any depth, our leaders need to find new ways to answer our fears, and the runaway power dynamics created by them.

A step in this direction for any interested leader is to admit that the members of his or her universe do have divergent interests, that every so often resources are scarce, and that, *in these circumstances*, we are blind to the long-term consequences of minimizing the value of our relationships. Until now, we have known these facts, but not appreciated them. Jerry Brown, the former governor of California, tried this approach, but he did not get too far. Recognizing divergent interests while still valuing our long-term relationships has not been legitimate. Consequently they have been a petri dish for our fears and have brought to us only acrimonious conflict.

Another crucial step leaders can take toward mastering our fears is acknowledging Irvin Yalom's point (1980) that each of us has certain "existential" anxieties, and that these are intimately connected with our day-to-day fears. Four of these anxieties — death, freedom, isolation, and meaninglessness — are inescapable parts of our existence, and therefore immutable parts of effective leadership. Death as a core concern comes alive in each of us as we confront the tension between the inevitability of our death and our wish to continue to be. Freedom refers to the absence of external structures, and suggests that each of us is the author of his or her own world. Isolation, the third existential concern, emerges from the tension between our awareness of our absolute separateness in this world and our wish for contact, our wish for protection, and our wish to be part of a larger whole. Meaninglessness is an overwhelming issue, because we are thrown into a universe that has no intrinsic meaning. These four concerns, all ultimate issues of life, are essential to our action-dialogues, because of the unconscious fears and angers that they spawn within every one of us.

Open discussion of these anxieties must become a central task for our leaders. Especially in organizational settings, leaders constantly face the realities that our denial of these anxieties produces. The apathetic, the alienated, and the anomic worker, for example, are all manifestations of these anxieties. We write reams upon reams about these people, explaining who they are and what they do or do not do. What we do not do is face our denial, call them what they are ("existential casualties"), and explore what responsibility they and our leaders have for creating their circumstances.

These anxieties spawn many of the interests and needs to which leaders must respond. Our usual reactions to the threat of death, freedom, isolation, or meaninglessness are frustration, fear, and rage. These feelings are like mirages in the desert. The water that shimmers so hotly in the sand exists; but it is not where it seems to be when we reach out for it. So, too, with these concerns: we do not easily—and never concretely—talk among ourselves about such emotions. They nonetheless are present. Our fear of them is deep, and it is painful. Too painful to touch, even to acknowledge. But this is precisely what our leaders must help us do. They must speak about them, the shape and form of them, the depth and breadth of them. Otherwise, the fear and anger that these anxieties breed will remain uncontrollable and will also remain breeding grounds for more misunderstanding and conflict.

If leaders are to channel the impact of these basic fears, they must harness their daemonic possibilities. I think this means incorporating balancing and healing influences into our leader-follower relations. The specific leverage for this healing and balancing lies, I believe, in leaders releasing both love and beginner's-mind into their action-dialogues.

This issue is beginning to be addressed. Harold Jampolsky (1979), for instance, in his book *Love Is Letting Go of Fear*, and Shunryu Suzuki (1976) in his book *Zen Mind Beginner's Mind* tell us that we create reality with our thoughts. The events we experience in the world are actually manifestations of our own thoughts, having no predetermined existences independent of our "believing them into being." Both men imply that, if we explicitly acknowledge our fears, call love by its proper name, and, at the same time, look with new-eyes for love in ourselves, in others, and in our interaction with others, we (perhaps) can assimilate our fears and affirm love's potency in our daily lives. We can allow action-dialogues into being. I think that these are concepts that leaders must explore.

Balancing and healing notions such as these cannot be too strange in the corporate world; similar ideas actually have been growing around the fringes of business for a long time. For example, we all know of Norman Vincent Peale and his power of positive thinking. We are beginning to learn of others—such as Sondra Ray, Michael Phillips, and Brugh Joy—who teach us to manifest good things. We are also hearing about the inspirational group efforts in such diverse companies as Toyota, IBM, Mary Kay Cosmetics, and Tupperware. Currently, most of us joke about such "pop" people and events. We laugh at their stories. However, their achievements should at least make us stop and think: these companies and their leaders *are* successful and, while we may not appreciate their methods, we certainly must respect their accomplishments. Perhaps, if we looked seriously, we would see that what is working for these leaders and their organizations are good examples of love and beginner's-mind at work within action-dialogue frameworks.

We are so used to looking at our leaders as people who *impose* their wills on passive followers, that leaders—and we—are likely to have a difficult time doing any of those things, which suggests that true leaders (those who articulate the needs and interests of their followers, those who take their constituencies somewhere) are in fact but simple instruments. This, however, is the probable truth, and one that must be accepted. True leaders are of-the-group, having found their own way to join. Metaphorically speaking, they have discovered a way of dying into their communities and yet retaining their own identities.

They know, it seems to me, how to *surrender*. Jesus established that this sort of release is necessary at the table of the Last Supper, saying ". . . he that is greatest among you, let him be as the younger; and he that is chief, as he that doth serve." Great leaders, such as King, Gandhi, and Lincoln, understood him. They practiced surrender well, releasing themselves to the will of their shapers at the same time that they themselves shaped their communities' thoughts. So much so that they could stand up in front of their shapers and speak their minds regarding common feelings, community meanings, and collective dreams. Surrender then—with love, beginners-mind, and recognition of the anxieties that our existential concerns produce—adds a depth and breadth to leadership that helps it come alive. All this is a state of mind our leaders desperately need.

## A CONCLUDING NOTE

Neither Galileo nor Copernicus nor Newton knew that they were opening up a new universe for the generations that would follow them. Each was simply working in his own world, trying to reconcile what he experienced in his work with what was, at the time, believed to be true. Copernicus for example, in placing the sun at the center of our solar system, was simply proposing a change that he thought would increase the accuracy of astronomical theory. More importantly, none of them knew that he, while dancing in a new world, was simultaneously holding onto some remarkably outdated beliefs. None of them had any idea that he could—and did—hold, at a profound level, presuppositions about what was real that were contradictory and dysfunctional.

We have no such disadvantage. We have absorbed the last 400 years of history. We have studied the mistakes made by men such as these. We know that there are fundamental precepts submerged in our unconsciouses, which guide our actions. We know that these precepts occasionally shift. Consequently, we understand that what we belive is true we make real.

This awareness, and our understanding that we ourselves are in the midst of such a shift now, enable us to reach out far beyond ourselves to create, for our own satisfaction and safety, the images that we need to continue living on this planet. We have the opportunity to stay abreast of ourselves, to help ourselves in startling ways to live and grow in our new organizations and communities. What we are doing with gene-splitting we can do in many other areas as well. One of these is leadership.

There is no doubt that we are on the threshold of profound changes in leadership. Already, we are altering our views on authority, control, and planning. This is evident everywhere; from the activities of Lee Iaccoca to the pages of Peters and Waterman's *In Pursuit of Excellence* (1982). We need, now, to extend our reach and to grasp the core of the changes that are coming at us. We must make, in our leadership beliefs, the alterations necessary for functional thinking and acting.

The first step, as I have outlined, is a new way of thinking. Recasting our views of leadership so that we see a leader-follower *equation* at the center is a must. Disciplined, bone-deep efforts are needed here. Only when we change the focus of our thoughts from solitary acts of leadership to mutual action-dialogues and the foundation of our beliefs from followers to shapers will we let ourselves, and our leaders, come to terms with the issues—such as fear, love, death, and surrender—which make this whole subject so desperately difficult for us. Once we have made this mind-shift, we will have in place a perspective that is more likely to guide us toward the wise action we obviously need. Having made this shift, we, and our leaders, will find that it is the Plancks, Bohrs, Einsteins, Sheldrakes, Prigogines, and Bohms of our world who are explaining and enlivening our organizational lives, and not Daffy Duck. This, for me, is a comforting thought.

*CHAPTER 3*

# Leadership
# for Organizational
# Learning[1]

by
## WILLIAM B. JOINER

*A fundamental challenge leaders face is how to translate their values and pur-*
*poses into practice while operating in a rapidly changing environment. This chap-*
*ter outlines a set of working principles leaders can use to develop organiza-*
*tions that are continually learning and adapting to change.*

You have values and purposes you care about very much. How do you put them
into practice in ways that lead to the desired results—especially when you're operating in a complex, changing environment? This personal and organizational question lives in the hearts of leaders everywhere.

This chapter presents a set of working principles that leaders can use to achieve
the results they need, even when the situations they face are complex and rapidly
changing. This perspective, which grows out of my experience as a management consultant, also draws on a synthesis of the latest research on exemplary organizations
and their leaders. My examples come primarily from the private sector, but the basic
principles are applicable to a wide range of organizations.

## LEADERSHIP CHALLENGES
## OF THE 1980s

In 1980 Robert Hayes and William Abernathy published a landmark article that
presented a bold analysis of the U.S. "productivity crisis." Entitled "Managing Our
Way to Economic Decline," the article pointed to "a broad management failure" in
America: "a failure of both vision and leadership that over time has eroded both the
inclination and the capacity of U.S. firms to innovate."

A surprising number of business leaders agreed that the productivity crisis was

---

[1]*I'm very grateful to Debra Whitestone for many helpful comments on earlier drafts of this*
*paper.*

symptomatic of a more serious long-term problem: the way in which U.S. firms were being led and managed. These executives were not the least bit naive about the powerful array of external forces that American corporations have to contend with. But they saw the need to evolve ways to manage these forces more effectively. They realized that traditional management methods weren't sufficient for adapting successfully to the rapid technological, economic, and social changes of the postwar era (Lawrence and Dyer 1983).

## The Challenge of Organizational Adaptation

The central concept behind this way of viewing America's productivity crisis is organizational adaptation. Beliefs, policies, structures, and practices that were adaptive at one point in time can become maladaptive when the environment changes. As significant external changes take place, organizations need to evolve new ways of operating; otherwise, they wind up like dinosaurs.

The organizational environment for American corporations has changed radically since the beginning of the postwar era. By the early 1980s, business leaders were struggling to adapt their organizations to a number of new environmental trends:

- globalization of the economy
- deregulation of key industries
- accelerated entrepreneurial activity
- rapid technological innovation
- changing, "demassified" markets
- a more diverse, well-educated workforce
- more complex networks of organizational stakeholders

These environmental forces continually interact like motorboats on a lake, zigzagging and crossing each other's paths, upsetting and amplifying each other's wakes. Together, these forces have created a complex, uncertain environment characterized by increasing diversity, heightened competition, growing interdependence, and rapid change.

## The Search for Postbureaucratic Leadership

What has kept the leaders of most American corporations from adapting more successfully to these complex, rapidly changing conditions is an overly bureaucratic approach to management. Their perspective has been too focused on short-range, quantitative goals: quarterly dividends, market share growth, short-term cost reduction. Insufficient attention has been given to broader objectives, like long-range risk-taking and innovation, quality, service, and employee involvement—areas where foreign competitors like the Japanese have been excelling (Pascale and Athos 1981, Lodge 1984).

Awareness of these limitations has opened the way for a renaissance in management practice. More leaders have acknowledged their need and desire to learn new approaches to leadership, new ways to reform and revitalize their organization. These executives have engaged in an active, experimental search for what Warren Bennis (1971) once called "postbureaucratic leadership."

In this search, executives are being inspired, in part, by new studies of consistently high-performing corporations (Ouchi 1981, Pascale and Athos 1981, Deal and Kennedy 1982, Peters and Waterman 1982, and Kanter 1983). Behind all these studies are the same basic questions: Which corporations have consistently excelled in adapting to complex rapidly changing conditions? What are the leadership and management practices that make these companies stand out above all the rest?

Many U.S. corporations were studied, but a few exceptional companies consistently came to the top: Dana, Digital Equipment, Hewlett-Packard, IBM, Johnson and Johnson, Procter and Gamble, and 3M.[2] These corporations have several things in common. Viewed over a period of 20 years, they've been consistently high financial performers and consistently successful innovators. They've occasionally had difficult periods, but they've responded to 20 years of change more rapidly and effectively than all other U.S. companies included in several major studies of long-range corporate adaptability (Joiner 1985b).

What is it that's made these corporations so much more adaptive than the majority of U.S. firms? In spite of some differences among these seven companies, they share an innovative approach to leadership. It's an approach that's shared by certain other leaders who've founded smaller companies or rejuvenated old ones: leaders like Kenneth Dayton of Dayton-Hudson, Bill Gore of W. L. Gore, Ken Iversen of Nucor, Mitch Kapor of Lotus Development, and Jim Treybig of Tandem Computer.

What does the emerging postbureaucratic leadership approach look like in practice? These leaders are creating sleeker, more responsive, customer-oriented corporations that stress values like quality, service, and reliability — "operations-driven" organizations that are flexible, decentralized, and have fewer management levels.

These innovative leaders have a strong people orientation that emphasizes informality, personal responsibility and recognition, lots of training, working hard and having fun. They exalt values like teamwork, initiative, creativity, and risk-taking — backed up by innovative policies and practices like guaranteed employment and semiautonomous work groups, and strong performance-oriented incentives like employee stock ownership and profit-sharing.

---

[2] *These conclusions are based on my own analysis of four major studies. The seven companies identified made at least three of four important lists: the 14 "most excellent" companies (Peters and Waterman 1982); the 18 "strong culture" companies (Deal and Kennedy 1982); the 33 companies considered the most innovative in management of people (Kanter 1983); and the 15 "best companies to work for in America" (Levering, et al. 1984). The Levering study was included as an indicator of effective adaptation to the changing American workforce.*

# THE ORGANIZATIONAL LEARNING
# PERSPECTIVE

It's clear that a new approach to leadership necessarily involves new skills and new ways of doing things.[3] But the latest management research finds that what makes the biggest difference isn't new skills and techniques, but rather a new perspective, a new management philosophy. However, the new perspective that's needed isn't fully captured in any of the new management books.

## Organizational Learning: The New Priority

In 1973, when I received my M.B.A. from Southern Methodist University, the dean of the business school was Jackson Grayson, a man who went on to become one of the nation's foremost experts on productivity. Grayson realized that much of what we learned for the then-current business environment would be virtually obsolete in ten years. He wanted to provide us, as the leaders of tomorrow, with something additional that would be more lasting.

Grayson's vision was that, first and foremost, his students would learn how to learn. He wanted his program to produce leaders who would be constant learners — not just in the sense of assimilating new knowledge, but by learning how to take effective action on the spot, whatever the circumstances.

This was a far-sighted vision of what the leaders of tomorrow would need. I'm very grateful to have benefitted from this unusual program. But today an even larger vision is needed. Leaders still need to develop the capacity to learn on-the-spot how to adapt to any circumstance. But now they also need to develop organizations that have the same capacity to adapt. Our corporations, government agencies, hospitals, and nonprofit organizations all need to learn how to learn.

At one time, change and turbulence marked a transition period between two relatively stable external environments. Managing organizational change, therefore, meant utilizing this transition period to unfreeze, change, and refreeze an organization's way of operating, so it was better adapted to the new environment. Some of these changes have been major ones, what some have called "organizational transformations."

Now, however, something entirely new has happened. Change itself has changed. Change and turbulence have become *constant* features of the external environment. As a result, contemporary organizations now face a challenge that's larger and more long term than any discrete change or transformation. They need to develop, first and foremost, the capacity to adapt continually to ever-changing conditions in ways consistent with their ultimate purposes. They need to learn how to learn, to develop a capacity for organizational learning. The great challenge for leaders is to develop learning organizations.[4]

---

[3]*For a discussion of some of the skills involved, see* The Collaboration Skills Training Manual *(Joiner 1985a).*

[4]*The concept of "organizational learning" comes from my work with Chris Argyris and Don Schon (1978) at Harvard and M.I.T.*

## A Model of Organizational Learning

The organizational learning perspective relates directly to the question posed at the beginning of this chapter: How can leaders take the values and purposes they care about most and translate them congruently into results, while operating in a complex, rapidly changing environment?

The perspective presumes that an organization needs feedback to translate its purposes into results. It needs to generate and attend to feedback on the incongruities between its central purposes, its current ways of operating, and the actual results it is achieving.

Achievement of these results in a complex, rapidly changing environment requires continuous adaptation. Continuous adaptation requires continuous feedback and scanning of the environment. Only through awareness of itself in relationship to its environment can an organization learn when and how it needs to change and adapt. Only through constant attention to feedback can an organization learn if the changes it has made are achieving the desired results. This process — whereby an organization takes action, pays attention to what happens, and takes new action to get more effective results — is organizational learning. Figure 1 presents a visual model that illustrates the organizational learning process.[5]

The circle in this model represents the boundaries that differentiate an organization from its surrounding environment. The horizontal arrows passing through these boundaries symbolize the organization as an open system, involved in constant exchange with other human systems (e.g., customers, suppliers, government agencies, etc.) that have their own purposes, perspectives, and priorities. The vertical arrows represent action and awareness. Together they symbolize the dual process of

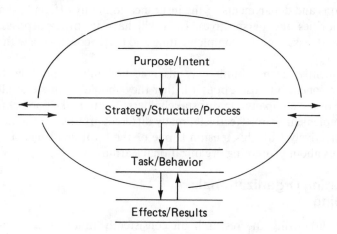

FIGURE 1.        The Organizational Learning Model

---

[5] *This model and the ideas directly associated with it were originally created by William R. Torbert (1972) as a generic model of "experiential learning" for human systems. Torbert was one of my teachers at SMU and is now dean of the M.B.A. program at Boston College.*

taking action and paying attention that is central to organizational learning. Proceeding through the model, a purpose or intent takes form via certain organizational strategies, structures, and human processes. These structures and processes are embodied in concrete tasks and behaviors that have visible effects on the outside world.

This, or course, is an idealized scenario. In practice, an organization's fundamental purpose can get muddled. Strategies, structures, and processes develop that aren't fully consistent with the purposes that do exist. At a more concrete level, people's day-to-day task-related behavior may be inconsistent with organizational purposes, strategies, and structures. Consequently, the organization isn't able to achieve the intended results.

These kinds of discrepancies can be corrected through an organizational learning process that attends to the relationship between an organization's central purposes, its ways of operating, and the actual results it's achieving. By generating and attending to this kind of feedback while scanning the larger environment, an organization can learn, over time, how to adapt to a changing world in ways that are consistent with its ultimate purposes.

This learning process can lead to changes in specific organizational tasks, in strategies and structures, or even in basic mission. For example, through awareness of its own performance in relation to its larger environment, an insurance company might decide to develop a new service. More fundamentally, it could decide to change its strategy. Rather than always following the lead of more innovative insurance companies, it could become one of the leading innovators in the business. Even more fundamentally, it could redefine its basic mission by becoming a full-fledged financial services company.

Organizational learning would be relatively uncomplicated if any given organization were "all of one mind." But no organization is. In the example just cited, even if the divisions and departments of the insurance company officially share the same ultimate priorities and perspectives, each will have its own purposes, strategies, structures, and tasks—partly complementing and partly conflicting with those of the other subunits.

Consequently, each subunit may disagree not only about how to make the changes mentioned, but also about whether they should be made at all. The same may be true of the company's major stakeholders. Yet to make good corporate decisions and implement them effectively, many different groups need to act in concert. Working effectively with this tension is one of the great challenges for any leader who is serious about promoting organizational learning.

### Activating Organizational Learning

After synthesizing the research on consistently innovative, high-performing corporations,[6] and integrating this synthesis with my own training and experience as a management consultant, I've come to two primary conclusions:

---

[6] *The corporate research studies I've synthesized include Ouchi (1981), Pascale and Athos (1981), Deal and Kennedy (1982), Peters and Waterman (1982), and Kanter (1983).*

First, to develop learning organizations, leaders need to practice three basic working principles. These working principles provide leaders with a way to meet each one of the three basic challenges of organizational learning:

1. *Shared purpose* helps to establish a strong sense of alignment between an organization's purposes, structures and processes, tasks and behavior, and the results it achieves.

2. *Active experimentation* helps to ensure effective adaptation to complex, rapidly changing environments by promoting creative, innovative action, flexibility, and rapid feedback.

3. *Open integrity* helps to integrate the action of different subgroups in a way that's consistent with the organization's purposes, yet respects the individuality and relative autonomy of each group.

Second, these working principles are most powerful when leaders find ways to apply them in all four domains of organizational life: organizational structure, organizational politics, organizational culture, and the management and development of human resources (Bolman and Deal 1984).

## THREE WORKING PRINCIPLES

### Shared Purpose

*Shared purpose* means that everyone in the organization has a clear understanding of their collective mission and a strong commitment to it. Shared purpose is not above question. It needs to be continually revisited and reclarified to test its relevance to new conditions. Nonetheless, a clear sense of shared purpose serves as the originating point for all effective organizational action, the reference point to which all feedback about organizational effectiveness returns.

*Explicit mission statements* help leaders of consistently high-performing corporations to establish a sense of shared purpose. These statements lay out the company's superordinate objectives, its philosophy of management, and its ethical standards. These mission statements usually give strong emphasis to at least the first three of the following superordinate objectives:[7]

- Strong financial performance
- Rapid, high-quality innovation and responsiveness to customer needs
- A high level of employee involvement that fosters a committed, highly motivated workforce

---

[7]*For examples of mission statements from five high-performing companies, see Ouchi (1981).*

- Acting in a socially responsible manner and serving the larger human community[8]

A mission statement alone, of course, can be nothing more than a "motherhood" statement, but it is a necessary condition for fostering a sense of shared purpose throughout the organization.

*Visionary leadership* is the key to establishing and maintaining a strong and lasting sense of shared purpose. Peters and Waterman (1982) found that almost all of their "excellent" companies have strong leaders whose central role is continually to clarify and reaffirm their organization's purpose. But how, specifically, can leaders foster a vivid sense of shared purpose?

Warren Bennis and Burt Nanus (1985) recently studied 90 innovative leaders in business, politics, and the arts. They discovered, first, that one of the outstanding characteristics of these exemplary leaders was their ability to foster organizational learning. Second, this ability was closely related to their ability to embody and communicate a personal sense of vision and purpose for the organization. Bennis and Nanus found that this had three aspects:

- *The management of attention through vision.* These innovative leaders all had a clear agenda, purpose, and focus on results. "Their range might be very narrow, and outside of that they might be very boring. But within their range, they were very intense. It was as if a bright filament was always burning." (Bennis 1983)

- *The management of meaning through communications.* To get people aligned with and committed to their purpose, these leaders found vivid, meaningful ways to communicate their visions. They often used concrete examples, symbols, and metaphors to paint a compelling picture of what they wanted to create. By combining this ability to communicate with a purposeful intensity, "They did not have to coerce people to pay attention; they were so intent on what they were doing that, like a child completely absorbed with creating a sand castle in a sandbox, they drew others in." (*Ibid.*)

- *Management of trust through constancy.* These exemplary leaders also exhibited a "courageous patience" by finding myriad ways to communicate their visions over and over. In doing so they demonstrated commitment and consistency that others could trust. "Of course, in our times if you stay the course too long, you can also keep going down a path that's the wrong path. But there is something profoundly important, I discovered, about making yourself known and making yourself clear. These are individuals who have clarity about their values, and that inevitably generates trust." (*Ibid.*)

---

[8]*To the three traditional business constituencies (stockholders, customers, and employees), the Business Roundtable's new 1981 statement on corporate responsibility adds a fourth: communities and society at large. "More than ever," it says, "managers of corporations are expected to serve the public interest as well as private profit."*

*Some corporations like Control Data, Dayton-Hudson, and Levi-Strauss already have strong commitments to social responsibility. By developing proactive strategies that go beyond reacting to external pressures and actually help solve social problems, they are leading the way.*

How can a leader's clarity about a personal vision make such a difference? What makes a difference is the extent to which a leader's vision is in tune with a deep, heartfelt sense of personal purpose. Evidence is growing that, when we can align ourselves with a unique sense of life purpose, we become animated by a creative intention that operates as a real, active force (Houston 1982, Ferrucci 1982, Progroff 1975). Peter Senge, a pioneer in applying insights about vision and purpose to organizational leadership, describes this dynamic as follows:

> A vision is powerful to the extent that it expresses one's underlying purpose. It is the vehicle for bringing purpose into the domain of acts and commitments. I believe the people who have done remarkable things in their lives have had a clear vision stemming from a deep and pervasive sense of purpose.
>
> Martin Luther King articulated a vision of equality of opportunity among different races. But that vision was an expression of a still deeper purpose . . . a fundamentally religious purpose dealing with God's presence in all people. This purpose so unified all people in his mind that his vision of racial equality was deeply compelling. (Gaffney 1984/85)

Tapping into a deeper sense of purpose is no quick-and-easy technique, however. Most of the time, we're not in touch with a unique sense of life purpose. Instead, our conditioning leads us to mistake a range of more tangible goals for a larger sense of purpose. Full alignment with this deeper level of experience is something we have to grow into through a process of inner questioning and exploration (Torbert 1972, Joiner 1984).

Alignment with a strong sense of purpose is something an organization has to grow into. In fact, it's best to regard the clarification of organizational purpose as a perpetually unfinished process that requires ongoing attention and feedback—a process Peter Vaill (1982) has called "purposing." One of the traps that CEOs most easily fall into is developing a rigid sense of mission that gets out of sync with a changing environment (Donaldson and Lorsch 1983).

Encouraging sustained attention to organizational purposing is important for another reason. Because the members and stakeholders of organizations are becoming increasingly diverse, shared purpose can't be simply imposed on them by the leadership. As Peter Senge has observed, it needs to emerge through a process of collaboration:

> As the process of individual visioning unfolds among a group committed to a common endeavor, the underlying purpose and vision of the group begins to emerge. Just as an individual's capacity to create draws from this alignment of his conscious objectives and his true nature and purpose, the same dynamic appears to operate for an organization. It is the organization's vision, not the individual's vision, that matters here. The group's vision is *not* the vision of the most articulate or dominant individual. It is a thing unto itself, just as the organization is an entity distinct unto itself. (Gaffney 1984/85)

## Active Experimentation

Shared purpose is concerned primarily with establishing an active movement from purpose to results, with everyone in the organization moving in the same direction. Active experimentation, the second working principle, is concerned with translating shared purpose into specific results under complex, rapidly changing conditions. It begins with the premise that achieving effective results under these conditions is like hitting a moving target. So what's needed, instead of predefining everything, are flexible arrangements that encourage experimentation toward results consistent with organizational purposes.

Active experimentation can be applied to a wide range of actions: developing new strategies, products, and services; implementing new policies, work practices, and training programs; experimenting with new behavior, and so on. In general, leaders who want to promote active experimentation need to establish three basic conditions in their organizations: small, semiautonomous units; rapid action/feedback cycles; and support for action learning.

*Small, semiautonomous units* allow decision-making to be decentralized to those points that are closest to the relevant information sources. As Peters and Waterman (1982) observed:

> Regardless of industry or apparent scale needs, virtually all of the [excellent companies] placed high value on pushing authority far down the line, and on preserving and maximizing practical autonomy for large numbers of people.

The combination of shared purpose and relatively decentralized decision-making makes it possible to set up a number of small, semiautonomous units that have the information, resources, and flexibility needed to respond rapidly and creatively to turbulent conditions. Utilizing small, semiautonomous units to promote active experimentation can take a variety of forms. For example:

- Task forces and temporary problem-solving groups
- "Intrapreneurial" new product development units
- Semiautonomous work teams that require workers to take on a wider range of skills and responsibilities
- "Small business units" at all levels of the corporation, down to the factory floor: operations-driven profit centers that run themselves like semiautonomous small businesses

*Rapid action/feedback cycles* convert inquiry into action in specific, concrete situations. Rather than the traditional emphasis on trying to analyze and design everything before taking action, active experimentation involves risk-taking: taking action that is innovative and creative and getting rapid feedback. For example, when Digital Equipment Corporation sets out to develop a new product:

> Instead of allowing 250 engineers and marketers to work on a new product

in isolation for fifteen months, they form bands of 5 to 25 to test ideas out on a customer, often with inexpensive prototypes, within a matter of weeks. (Peters and Waterman 1982)

This is what Peters and Waterman call the "do it, fix it, try it" approach: first take action, then learn from the action, then take further action, and so on, in relatively small, iterative steps. The initial results may be small. But doing something and testing the results makes it possible to learn quickly from your actions.

*Support for action learning* requires an atmosphere conducive to innovation, creativity, and risk-taking. This means fostering a whole new attitude toward success and failure. People need timely feedback to know whether they're producing results that are consistent with organizational purposes. What they don't need is a fear of failure, which saps their creative energy.

People bring to work their own mixed attitudes toward success and failure, but which of these attitudes prevails depends on the tone set by an organization's leaders. Leaders who act on the principle that people learn best when they're punished for their mistakes aren't likely to foster active experimentation. In high-performing organizations, the leader's role in promoting technical and managerial innovation is one of "nurturing good tries, allowing modest failures, labeling experiments after the fact as successes, leading the cheers, and quietly guiding the diffusion process." (Peters and Waterman 1982)

Bennis and Nanus (1985) found that leaders' attitudes toward their own success or failure are crucial to their ability to activate organizational learning. The innovative leaders studied had one thing in common besides their ability to communicate a compelling vision. Their positive self-esteem allowed them genuinely to view failure as something they could learn from. Rather than dwelling on the possibility of failure, they envisioned success. They emphasized their strengths instead of their weaknesses. "And more interesting, they bring out the strengths of others. . . . In addition to positive self-regard, these individuals had positive other-regard." (Bennis 1983)

## Open Integrity

Leaders sometimes express the concern that promoting increased antonomy will encourage subunits to develop parochial perspectives that are out of sync with each other and the interests of the larger organization. But parochial tendencies can be averted by changing the traditional ways that organizational subunits manage conflicts and differences.

When one part of the organization runs into conflicting objectives and perspectives from another part, the traditional reaction is what Torbert (1972) has called the "mystery-mastery" approach: each unit withholds information from the other (the mystery element), and each unit tries to influence the other, without letting the other influence them (the mastery element). This is essentially a win-lose approach for each party: either they overpower or outsmart the other, or they back off or give in.

Over the past two decades, as organizational subunits have become more and more interdependent, the traditional win-lose approach to managing differences has become increasingly dysfunctional. It's understandable that some leaders, seeing different parts of their organization falling into these dysfunctional patterns, would hesitate to promote increased autonomy. The result could be reduced efficiency and counterproductive conflict between subunits, as they push and pull in different directions.

This hesitation often reflects a legitimate concern about organizational integrity: the extent to which the different parts of the organization are integrated in a way that's consistent with its overall purposes. Without integrity, an organization can't reliably achieve its mission.

Given the traditional win-lose approach to managing differences, the traditional approach to ensuring organizational integrity has been to centralize authority and develop bureaucratic rules and procedures designed to mediate conflict among different groups. Excessive reliance on this approach, however, has tremendous costs. Because it creates conditions directly counter to active experimentation, it significantly reduces an organization's ability to respond to a rapidly changing environment. The cost of relying on this traditional approach is becoming more and more apparent as the environment becomes increasingly turbulent.

What's needed, then, is an alternative way to reconcile the need for organizational integrity with the need for respecting the relative autonomy of the various subunits. Put differently, what's needed is a way to reconcile the internal consistency of shared purpose with the rich diversity of active experimentation.

What's needed, in my view, is open integrity, the third working principle of organizational learning. Open integrity is based on the premise that, to achieve a high degree of internal integration in a complex, rapidly changing environment, organizations and their subunits need, paradoxically, a new kind of openness.

Open integrity is concerned primarily with the way in which an organization manages the conflicts and tensions that can arise from differences between an organization and its environment and between an organization's various subgroups. These conflicts and tensions aren't necessarily bad, nor is it possible or even desirable to try to do away with them altogether. Attended to appropriately, differences can be important sources of needed learning and change.

What's needed, then, are nonmanipulative ways to bring differences into contact with each other. Each party needs to remain clear about its own purpose and perspective while also understanding opposing viewpoints. This requires centered questioning and exploration, attending to conflicts and tensions without closing them off or being absorbed by them (Joiner 1984/85).

When open integrity becomes one of an organization's central governing principles, the result is what Michael Sales and I have called a "collaborative culture" (Joiner and Sales 1985): an essential condition for organizational learning. The difference that a collaborative culture can make is illustrated very well in *The Change Masters,* Rosabeth Kanter's study of the differences between highly innovative and noninnovative corporations (1983).

In the companies that had poor innovation records, Kanter found what she calls "segmentalist" management. The boundaries between organizational subgroups, both vertically and horizontally, were relatively rigid: there was little flow of information, people, or resources among groups. Conflicts and differences were managed in the traditional win-lose mode described earlier, leading to centralized mediation of conflict. Even problem-solving was approached with a segmentalist mentality:

Segmentalist approaches see problems as narrowly as possible, independently of their context, independently of their connections to any other problems. . . . Segmentalism assumes that problems can be solved when they are carved into pieces and the pieces assigned to specialists who work in isolation. Even innovation itself can become a specialty in segmentalist systems—something given to the R&D department to take care of so that no one else has to worry about it.

When she studied highly innovative companies, Kanter found a very different approach: integrative management. The boundaries between organizational subunits were clear, but they were much more permeable. Information, people, and resources flowed rather easily among groups; a lot of work was accomplished using temporary teams and task forces that brought people together from all parts of the organization. Conflicts and differences were managed more openly, directly, and creatively.

What Kanter found, in my view, were collaborative organizational cultures, open integrity in action:

Integrative thinking that actively embraces change is more likely in companies whose cultures and structures are also integrative, encouraging the treatment of problems as "wholes," considering the wider implications of actions. Such organizations reduce rancorous conflict and isolation between organizational units; create mechanisms for exchange of information and ideas across organizational boundaries; ensure that multiple perspectives all be taken into account in decisions; and provide coherence and direction to the whole organization. In these team-oriented cooperative environments, innovation flourishes. There may be differences recognized and even encouraged—an array of different specialists, a diversity of people—but the mechanisms exist for transcending differences and finding common ground.

The principle of open integrity can be applied to the management of differences not only among an organization's subunits, but also between an organization and its various stakeholder groups: stockholders, employees, customers, suppliers, government agencies, community groups, and so on. Getting "closer to the customer" by developing stronger marketing and service orientations; increasing the amount of time spent on political issues and public relations; implementing programs that increase the level of employee involvement—these are all examples of a movement toward managing companies more as open systems. But at the top levels, perhaps the most important dimension of this shift is in the amount of direct person-to-person contact some corporate leaders are initiating with people in various key stakeholder groups.

For example, consider this story, told by the president of a company that makes packaging and labeling products:

The focus of the [annual top-management retreat] was customers' concerns. We needed data, and decided to do something novel: Each attendee, at some point in the two weeks preceding the meeting, was to spend one full day with a customer, checking out his (the customer's) perception of us.

Half our people thought it would be a waste. Several were certain the customers would feel imposed upon. To the contrary, without exception the customers loved it! [We tried to ensure some objectivity] by dividing the pile of candidates into good customers, bad customers and average customers. The debate at the meeting was informed by live impressions, for the first time in memory. Just about all agreed that it was the best meeting we've had. And follow-up has been terrific—and concrete. (Peters and Austin 1985)

This is an example of a leader who's actively encouraging open integrity. These executives not only went out to meet an uncertain environment, ready to hear bad news as well as good; they also came back and tried to integrate their learnings around a central corporate purpose—responsiveness to their customers.

Again, the premise on which open integrity is based is that an organization in a turbulent, interdependent environment can achieve a more lasting, dynamic internal integration through open interaction with the environment than it can through manipulative interaction or by closing off. Applying this working principle in relationships with other stakeholder groups that have more serious differences with a company is definitely more of a challenge. But if issues like environmental protection, consumer product safety, and plant closings were approached more in this spirit, my belief is that the outcomes would be better for all concerned (Lodge 1984).

## A Dynamic Strategy

Together, shared purpose, active experimentation, and open integrity provide leaders with the basic working principles they need to promote organizational learning.

Shared purpose is based on the insight that purpose can be more than a goal in people's heads. It can be a much deeper, heartfelt sense of mission. Properly tapped, it can be a real, active force that comes from the whole person. Leaders who can align themselves with such a purpose can create a line of intent between purpose and results that's more powerful, more direct and more inspiring than goals alone can ever be.

Active experimentation is concerned with translating abstract purposes into concrete results that fit actual environmental conditions. By empowering small, semiautonomous units; building in rapid feedback; and supporting innovative action, leaders can greatly increase the probability of intelligent, timely response to changing circumstances.

Even when a clear shared purpose has established a strong, active force running from purpose to results, there are always opposing forces to contend with: obstacles, fears, resistance, conflicting priorities and perspectives. Open integrity comes out to meet opposing forces like these, transforming them into opportunities for organizational learning.

These three principles, working together, can be applied to action on almost any scale. Consistent in many ways with the working principles found in some Eastern martial arts, they provide leaders with a dynamic strategy for effective action in complex, changing circumstances.

1. *Shared purpose.* Be as clear as possible about your personal and professional purposes, what you value, what you stand for. Have a vision of the kind of results, consistent with your purpose, that you want to create.

2. *Active experimentation.* Move in the direction of your vision in incremental steps and build inquiry into your action, so you can test the results of your actions as you go along.

3. *Open integrity.* While maintaining a clear sense of your own purpose, remain open to other forces operating inside and outside the organization. Treat resistance and conflict as opportunities for learning.

## FOUR DOMAINS
## OF ORGANIZATIONAL LIFE

How and where leaders apply these three working principles depends to a great extent on the way they view their organization. Bolman and Deal (1984) have discovered that different managers look at the same organizational situations in fundamentally different ways, depending on the set of assumptions they hold about what organizations are like. Bolman and Deal call these basic assumptions "frames":

Frames are windows on the world. Frames filter out some things while allowing others to pass through easily. Frames help us to order the world and decide what action to take. Every manager uses a personal frame, or image, of organizations to gather information, make judgements and get things done.

Bolman and Deal have identified four basic frames that managers use when taking action in their organizations. Some primarily use one frame; others use two or more:

1. *Organizations are structures.* They exist to accomplish complex tasks. The central questions are: Given an organization's goals, technology, and environment, what strategies should the organization pursue? What is the best formal structure? How should roles be defined? What policies and procedures should be implemented? What information is needed, and what systems should be used to generate it?

2. *Organizations are political.* They are arenas where power and influence affect the allocation of limited resources among individuals and groups. The central questions are: Who has what kind of power and influence over whom in what kinds of situations? Through what processes of bargaining, compromise, or coercion are resources allocated and issues decided? Are the interests of different individuals and groups fairly represented?

3. *Organizations are people.* Organizations exist to serve human needs. The central questions are: How can the organization be tailored to meet its people's needs? What are the organization's human resources policies? Does

it provide a high quality of worklife? Is the organization sensitive to the unique needs of different kinds of individuals?

4. *Organizations are symbolic.* They are cultures, held together by shared values, norms, and beliefs that persist, in spite of ambiguity and uncertainty inside and outside the organization. They exist to enact historical dramas in which its members can participate. The central questions are: What are the myths, symbols, stories, and heroes that give the organization its sense of meaning? What rites and rituals are used to perpetuate and celebrate the meanings of the culture?

Each frame is valid in the sense that it illuminates one of the domains of organizational life. But each is also limited, because it doesn't provide the whole picture. In studying the latest research on highly adaptive corporations, I discovered that none of the new management books viewed its subject matter through all four frames. Taken together, however, they covered all four. By synthesizing the findings, the whole picture came into view: the leaders of the most highly adaptive corporations apply shared purpose, active experimentation, and open integrity in all four domains of organizational life.

The full range of the organizational learning perspective can be visualized by referring to Figure 2. The graphic symbolizes the fact that each working principle can be applied in all four domains of organizational life. Leaders get the most out of each principle when they find ways to bring it to life in all four domains. Put differently, an organization "learns" best when all four domains are involved at once.

## The Structural Domain

Clearly, different organizations require different structures. Yet more and more organizations need to cope with the same kinds of environmental conditions — heightened competition, rapid change, increasing diversity, and growing interdependence — conditions that require organizational learning. In the most general sense,

| | Shared Purpose | Active Experimentation | Open Integrity |
|---|---|---|---|
| Structural Domain | | | |
| Political Domain | | | |
| Human Resource Domain | | | |
| Symbolic Domain | | | |

FIGURE 2.    The Organizational Learning Perspective

54

what structural arrangements best support the three working principles of organizational learning?

Although Peters and Waterman (1982) don't use the organizational learning model, their research led them to recommend a generic structure for the eighties that simultaneously supports all three working principles. They describe this structure as resting on three "pillars," each dealing with one of the basic structural needs of large corporations in today's turbulent environment: stability, entrepreneurship, and structural flexibility.[9]

To promote stability, they recommend that the core structure be a simple, consistent form like the product-based division, with a lean corporate staff. This emphasis is consistent with the working principle of shared purpose.

To support autonomy and entrepreneurship, they recommend decentralization of authority and responsibility. This includes decentralizing staff groups into the divisions, so they can develop and utilize their own feedback and measurement systems. To facilitate rapid innovation, new or expanded activities are continually "hived off" to become new divisions. This entrepreneurial pillar provides structural support for the working principle of active experimentation.

To provide flexibility, Peters and Waterman recommend a third structural condition they call "breaking old habits." The basic form remains the same, but the organization restructures frequently "around the edges" to respond to specific needs: moving products or services among divisions, bringing top talent together on project teams, and so on. This condition is a structural application of the working principle of open integrity, requiring "a generic willingness to reorganize and reshuffle boxes (while maintaining the integrity of the basic, central form) as needs arise."

These structural applications of the three working principles can be applied to subunits as well as to whole organizations. But unless leaders utilize applications in the other domains, these structural conditions will provide only limited support for organizational learning.

## The Political Domain

The structural arrangements just described already set up certain organizational power dynamics, because of the way they distribute formal authority. But highly adaptive corporations do something more. For example, Rosabeth Kanter (1983) looked at how the leaders of these companies distribute and utilize "power tools" (information, resources, and support). She found that, compared to less innovative corporations, power in these companies "circulates" more, is more "accessible," and is more "focused" on results.

To ensure that the power necessary for successful innovation and adaptation is accessible to those who need it, these companies decentralize access to resources in two primary ways: (1) formal mechanisms for distributing funds outside the hierarchy (for example, 3M has innovation banks that make venture capital available in-

---

[9] *The structure I will describe here is primarily relevant to large corporations. Entrepreneurs and leaders of small or mid-sized growth companies may be interested in a set of ideas that say organizations need different structures at different stages in their development (Greiner 1976, Kimberly and Miles 1982, and Torbert 1976, 1985).*

ternally for development projects; and (2) decentralizing staff time via "slack" and local control, making it easier to utilize people temporarily without needing constant clearances from higher level managers. These strategies are political applications of the working principle of active experimentation.

Managing continual change and innovation requires cooperation among people in different subunits. Therefore, highly adaptive companies use two primary strategies to ensure that power circulates across subunit boundaries: (1) creating open communication systems by encouraging people to communicate informally across subunit boundaries, whenever ideas come up, and (2) fostering peer networks via mechanisms such as frequent job changes (often laterally rather than vertically), employment security (creating expectations of lasting relationships), and using teams and task forces (drawing members from a variety of areas). These strategies are political applications of open integrity.

To develop learning organizations, leaders also need to keep power focused on achieving results consistent with a shared purpose. Kanter found that the leaders of highly innovative companies focus power in the following ways:

- Top leaders set the overall strategic direction and retain control of large expenditures.

- Both top- and middle-level managers are involved in strategic planning, and their discussion serves to guide the choice of projects.

- A clear financial results-orientation limits requests for major projects. The ability to obtain essential resources is contingent upon a promise, usually implicit, to produce.

- Top managers don't abdicate leadership, in spite of the tremendous emphasis on delegation and teamwork.

## The Human Resource Domain

All the recent research supports the conclusion that the most consistently high-performing corporations are also the most progressive in their orientation toward people. These firms utilize the rich array of policies and practices you'd expect to find in companies known as human resource innovators:

- Strong financial incentives tied to performance: employee stock ownership plans (ESOPs), profit-sharing, gain-sharing, pay for performance

- An emphasis on job safety and employment security

- Progressive personnel policies designed to meet the needs of an increasingly diverse workforce: affirmative action, flexi-time, etc.

- A strong emphasis on developing people's skills and abilities: training and retraining

- Restructuring work to provide greater challenge and satisfaction: job enrichment, autonomous work groups, etc.

- An emphasis on employee involvement and communication: survey feedback programs, quality circles, participative management.

Behind these innovative policies and practices is a nontraditional management philosophy that's highly consistent with what Douglas McGregor (1966) once described as "Theory Y" management:

1. Management is responsible for organizing the elements of productive enterprise—money, materials, equipment, people—in the interest of economic ends.

2. People are *not* by nature passive or resistant to organizational needs. They have become so as a result of experience in organizations.

3. The motivation, the potential for development, the capacity for assuming responsibility, the readiness to direct behavior toward organizational goals are all present in people. Management does not put them there. It is a responsibility of management to make it possible for people to recognize and develop these human characteristics for themselves.

4. The essential task of management is to arrange organizational conditions and methods of operation so that people can achieve their own goals *best* by directing *their own* efforts toward organizational objectives.

   This is a process primarily of creating opportunities, releasing potential, removing obstacles, encouraging growth, providing guidance. . . . It does *not* involve the abdication of management, the absence of leadership, [or] the lowering of standards.

Theory Y management fits very well not only with the changing values and expectations of the American workforce, but also with the structural and political conditions needed to support sustained organizational learning. Why? In my view, it's because Theory Y is so congruent with the three working principles of organizational learning.

Theory Y leadership requires open integrity. It is open to people's needs and seeks their active involvement, yet it remains true to the basic mission of the organization. Theory Y is focused on achieving results consistent with an organization's shared purpose. But instead of trying to control *how* people achieve these results, it provides increased autonomy plus support and recognition for creative action. In this way, Theory Y encourages active experimentation toward results consistent with organizational purposes.

## The Symbolic Domain

The symbolic domain is the domain of organizational culture—shared values and beliefs shaped by symbolic actions. Developing an organizational culture that supports organizational learning is a real challenge, because it means that leaders need to act in ways that are consistent with the three working principles. I'm referring especially to symbolic actions that make an impression on large numbers of people.

I've already described some significant symbolic actions leaders can take to promote shared purpose, actions that Bennis and Nanus (1985) call the management of attention, meaning, and trust. Peters and Austin (1985) report two stories that illustrate how a leader's symbolic actions can promote (or fail to promote) active experimentation.

The first is about a chairman who wanted to establish entrepreneurship as a primary value in his company. The message wasn't getting through. He called in consultants to see if anything was wrong with his strategy, structures, or systems. There wasn't. Finally, the consultants did a detailed analysis of how he spent his time. Their discovery: he spent barely 3 percent of his time on his espoused objective. "His attention wasn't there. And his people knew it."

Contrast that story with this one:

> Bill Hewlett constantly wandered the engineering spaces at Hewlett-Packard, as did Barney Oliver, his head of R&D for forty years. Today, though neither is any longer on active duty, [a 24-year-old employee] can still say, "Believe me, each and every one of us [the 80,000 people on the payroll] thinks that Bill or Barney is likely to stop by our desk any minute and ask about the prototype we're working on."

To activate organizational learning, leaders need to take action that not only fosters shared purpose and active experimentation, but also generates open integrity. I'll conclude with a story that shows how all three can come together in the same situation:

Bill Torbert was on the faculty at SMU when Jackson Grayson was dean of the business school. Torbert (1978) describes an evening when he and several other faculty members were introducing 380 assembled students to an innovative course designed to help them "learn how to learn" from their own action. One faculty member was presenting statistics that showed how active, experimenting students had gotten more from this course the previous semester than had more passive students. But the students' attention began to wander. They started talking among themselves.

The faculty member pushed on, speaking faster and louder, until Torbert interrupted him—twice in succession—suggesting they stop and check out whether the students were still with him. After initially resisting the interruptions, Torbert's colleague stopped and checked out what was going on. He agreed that the information he was presenting could be discussed later in small groups.

Then a third faculty member intervened and suggested reviewing what had just happened, because he felt it was symbolic of what the course was all about. The first faculty member joined in a stimulating discussion that revealed his genuine openness to learning from what had happened. For most of the students, the total event generated tremendous respect for each of the faculty members involved. Torbert said he'd been able to act as he did, risking mutual embarrassment, because he and the other faculty member shared a strong commitment to action inquiry.

If it's hard to imagine the leaders of corporations, government agencies, hospitals, and universities acting in this way, it may be because leadership that actively promotes organizational learning is still very rare indeed.

# II.

# THE CHANGING
# VIEW OF LEADERS

# CHAPTER 4

# Spiritual Leadership

by
**JAMES A. RITSCHER**

*Spirit is the sense of vitality, energy, and vision which is at the heart of all organizations — with some organizations being more inspired than others in how they operate. One of the basic functions of leadership is to stimulate and focus the organization's spirit. This chapter explores ten characteristics of spiritual leadership that are essential in creating vital, effective, and profitable organizations.*

By spiritual leadership, I mean two things:

1. The leadership of spirit (in the sense of vitality or Esprit de Corps) in a business or other organization
2. Transformational leadership: leadership that draws on a spiritual force and hence cuts through to a deeper level and is more effective in creating a vital and effective business.

When I use the word spiritual, I am not referring to religion. A religion is an organization that professes to provide spiritual experience to groups of people. Spirituality, however, is more an individual matter; it does not rely on an external organization. Rather, spirituality is an experience of *depth* in life; it is living life with heart rather than superficiality. For some, spirituality involves the belief in a god. For others, it takes a different form. In any case, spirituality is the awareness that there is something more to life than just our narrow, ego-oriented view of it.

Spirituality pertains to *an experience of spirit,* and spirit is a matter of utmost concern to business. It comes in many forms. All athletes and performers exhibit spirit. Think of the energetic style of an olympic gymnast or a popular singer. There is a high correlation between spirit and results in the real world. It is often spirit rather than physical competence that determines the outcome of a sporting event. The same applies to any event or organization that involves people working together.

Businesses and other organizations assemble groups of people who must communicate with each other effectively to produce results. Businesses that are spirited tend to produce quicker, better, more effective results. For this reason, spiritual leadership—the leadership of spirit—is crucial to a business.

## THE CHALLENGE OF SPIRITUAL LEADERSHIP

The spirit of an organization is its heart, its vital nature. Spirit is a sense of vitality, energy, vision, and purpose. All organizations have spirit, but in some cases it is dull and tarnished.

The leadership and management of spirit in an enterprise requires specific skills much like, say, financial management. In my opinion, few understand the nature of this leadership process and are skillful at using it to their best advantage. If leaders do not meet the challenge of enspiriting the organization, it will be blown by the prevailing winds. Only an organization that is well grounded in its spiritual nature has the will and the strength to survive.

## TEN QUALITIES OF SPIRITUAL LEADERSHIP

When a manager is learning to master the leadership of spirit, the first questions that come to mind may well be, "How do I do it? What specific actions do I take?" These questions do not go deep enough, however. The real question is not "How to do it," but rather "How to be it." The qualities of leadership are inner, spiritual qualities. They do not involve "doing" as much as "being." If you have the "being" worked out, the "doing" will come naturally. The reverse is not true.

Management of spirit as described here requires an unusual set of leadership skills, which at best only superficially match the kinds of skills managers are taught at our business schools:

1. Inspired vision

2. Clarity of mind

3. Will, toughness, and intention

4. Low ego, high results

5. No separation

6. Trust and openness

7. Insight into human nature

8. Skill in creating people structures; groundedness

9. Integrity

10. A context of personal growth and fulfillment

## 1. Inspired Vision

At its core, leadership has to do with vision, which is fundamentally a spiritual phenomenon. Vision transcends, and this is precisely its value.

Every corporation requires cohesiveness and organization. Were it not for cohesiveness, chaos would ensue. Leadership through inspired vision provides cohesiveness through a common vision. The cohesive force is spiritual rather than mechanical. It functions inside the minds and hearts of the employees, and serves to draw them together. All are committed and drawn to the common vision. This is leadership in its true sense.

Leadership involves creating a vision that draws people forward toward a common desired reality. The corporate vision is focused on a goal, and this helps create a unified focus for everyone. Focus is one of the reasons why use of vision increases productivity.

A deep understanding of human nature is required to fully understand the spiritual or transcendent nature of vision. If people were only mechanical, vision would never work. The kind of thinking suggested here implies an appreciation of the profound power and range of individual human beings. All of us have within us the capacity for greatness. All of us want to love and be loved. All of us have a spiritual awareness, a connection with higher things in life. All of us are able to transcend our own personal boundaries to support and serve others.

Visionary leadership taps into this higher place in us. It is transcendent; it calls us to reach out and embrace something more expansive than ourselves. It is this quality of great leaders that draws us to them—we sense in their message a way to get in touch with a higher part of ourselves. Certainly the speeches of John F. Kennedy and Martin Luther King, Jr., exhibit this profound draw and uplift.

Fundamentally this is what leadership at its best is all about—it moves us to touch higher places in ourselves. It creates and manifests an inspired vision. The word "inspired" here is quite important. If a CEO says, "Next year we want to increase profits by 15 percent," that is a vision, but not a particularly inspiring vision. It does not create the kind of draw and uplift that I am talking about. To generate an inspired vision, rather, we must tap into an inspired place in ourselves. We must tap into our own greatness, our boldness, and our sense of purpose. Generally when we are getting close, there is a sense of tingling or energy in the body. An example of an inspired vision, one that caught the minds and hearts of Americans, was John Kennedy's statement, "We will put a man on the moon in 10 years, and return him safely to earth."

Sometimes inspired visions are created by groups, sometimes by individuals. It is more difficult for groups to create them, because they come out of the *consciousness* of the group as a whole; if any group member is not in the same inspired place, it will pull the entire group down. Although it's more difficult to create an inspired vision in a group, it's also an enormously valuable and powerful experience. And there is great value for an organization in having a group, rather than just one individual, hold the vision. When a group holds the vision, the job of communicating the vision is already partially accomplished.

Once an inspired vision for your organization has been developed, it still needs to be communicated. In order for true communication to take place, you must go back into that same inspired place in yourself you tapped while first creating the vision. What you say is less important than the quality of energy with which you say it. This is not, of course, to say that you should neglect the content.

You can learn alot about inspiration and energy from watching singers and other performers. When you communicate a vision, you are a performer. Although this is not a role all leaders take to naturally, it involves certain learnable skills. One final note—the communication I am referring to here has nothing to do with the kind of studied performance that is so common among business executives. It involves being yourself, and being *real* in front of alot of people.

### 2. Clarity of Mind

A close companion of inspired vision is clarity of mind. As executives and managers, most of us experience moments when we have a clear vision and sense of how things should be, but all too often this vision is clouded by the events of ordinary life. To retain clarity behind all the minor confusions and alarms that make up our work days requires special skill and discipline.

A good way of introducing clarity of mind is to look at creativity. When creative people describe what it's like to be in their most creative state of mind, they frequently report experiences that sound remarkably like mystical states. They say that time seems to disappear; that they have an expanded sense of self and a corresponding diminished sense of ego; and that they have a sense of gentleness and mental clarity. The creative ideas just come to them, and the process is almost effortless. We need to be able to tap into a similar place in ourselves of quiet and clarity. It is this clarity that permits the inspired vision just described, and it is this clarity that allows us to sustain the vision.

Now at this point some readers may ask:

1. Is this a quality of mind that the average, intelligent person can develop?

2. Assuming that it can be developed, what is its relevance to leadership?

The answers I would suggest are:

1. Clarity of mind *is* a quality that an average, intelligent person can develop.

2. To a great extent, clarity of mind is the core of leadership. It is the submerged portion of the iceberg, the solid foundation out of which the active portion of leadership springs.

A prerequisite for transformational leadership is personal imperturbability and clarity. Leadership involves having the clarity of mind to keep a balance amidst the vicissitudes of life. The following poem by the Sufi poet Rumi expresses this idea:

> The minute I'm disappointed, I feel encouraged.
> When I'm ruined, I'm healed.
> When I'm quiet and solid as the ground, then I talk
> The low tones of thunder for everyone.

The first two lines exhibit a kind of detachment toward life. They are similar to the idea "Work hard to achieve the result you want, but don't waste time with disappointment if you fail." The last two lines express the essence of leadership. Great leadership falls on the shoulders of people who have great solidity and clarity.

The power of quiet and solidity cannot be overemphasized. The single largest problem in organizations is a kind of anxiety and low-grade confusion. Leaders often make decisions based on anxiety, ego, insufficient experience, and the slightly crazy atmosphere that frequently accompanies group decision-making. Such decisions are no match for ones made by going to a quiet place, steeping oneself in the nature of the problem, and using clarity of mind to uncover the right solution.

As I think back to experiences in which I've observed managers, I can recall many times when decisions were made by reactive minds. In many cases the decision-maker was angry, or resentful, or disgusted, or out to settle a personal issue. I remember one manager whose style of gathering information was to ask questions for which the only acceptable answers were "yes" or "no"—with no explanations. And his pontifications were peppered with the question, "Do you agree with me?" Presumably the only correct answer was "yes." Needless to say, he made some destructive decisions.

This is not to say that managers with clarity of mind don't make mistakes; they do. But they make fewer mistakes, and they correct their mistakes faster. Their minds are more able to penetrate into the heart of a matter, to isolate the essentials, and to make decisions taking into account all of the parameters.

This kind of clarity requires a balanced mind. It requires both clear rational thinking and ready access to intuition and creativity. Of these two functions, it is the intuitive and creative aspects that frequently require the most development. Often business decisions are made from a purely rational, "content" basis; the intuitive aspect is frequently missing. Much better decisions are made when the intuitive aspect is allowed free play, when one pays attention to context as well as to content.

Clarity of mind implies focus, as opposed to scattering. Considering that the daily activities in a manager's life tend toward dispersion of energy, keeping mental focus requires discipline and skill. I know of one small company where all of the managers have a policy of not taking phone calls for the first two hours of the day. This is their way of keeping distractions to a minimum and allowing themselves time to develop their vision and focus.

How do you develop clarity of mind? The first step is to make it a priority. We tend to create those things we actively desire in our lives. Clarity of mind is so valuable, both from a business and a personal point of view, that we should make it our top priority. As a leader, your state of mind is your primary tool. It needs to be sharpened and polished. To accomplish this, you may wish to train yourself in any of a number of ways. First, it's important to spend some quiet time each day. The beginning of the day is a good time to think and reflect over your plans and goals. Spend some time reviewing your vision, where you are now, and how you can bridge the gap to where you want to be.

Planning some formal "non-doing" time is also wise. This might be a period of meditation (there are a number of techniques and teachers). For some, it's running or swimming—some activity in which there is a steady rhythm and time for the mind to relax and unwind. If you are a highly rational and task-oriented person, you might take specific steps to develop your creativity. Take up drawing. Write poetry. Compose a song. Take a pottery course. Do anything that involves a great deal of creative thought. It might also be advisable to develop your people skills. Enroll in personal growth workshops. Develop close friends. Spend time with friends who push you to be more real and authentic.

Overall, the process is one of calming the body and mind until intuitive wisdom comes through. Experience shows that the calmer we are, the more we have access to our creative and intuitive aspects. As we become calmer, we start to see dimensions of a problem we have never seen before. There is no standard formula for developing profound clarity of mind. Transformational leaders have a quality of depth, wisdom, clarity, and solidity; these are not qualities we obtain in a one-day seminar. But if we value these qualities, we can live our lives in a way that we gradually acquire them.

### 3. Will, Toughness, and Intention

Many people equate the spiritual with the "soft" side of life. Pursuing a spiritual path, however, requires dedication and courage, hardly soft qualities. The same is true for transformational leadership. Leadership is transcendental; it is a bold, existential act of courage and will. When you assume a position of leadership, you move away from the pack and all the support that the pack provides. This requires tremendous courage and will.

Leadership requires us to view life differently, to enter into an altered state of consciousness. For this reason, we find that it separates us from others. When we enter this state, we find we are looking at ourselves and the situation differently from other people. Suddenly we stand out in the group; we are perceived as being different.

I observed this recently during the founding of a new service organization. People came together for the purpose of discussing the possibility of forming such an organization. The discussion was typical of a shared-leadership group — each person in the group an equal, none particularly standing out as the leader. Then one woman, Linda, said, "I am really excited about this group, and I'd like to take on responsibility and leadership for it." Since no one else strongly desired the leadership and the work it entailed, the group graciously accepted her offer.

What happened in the next few minutes was interesting. It appeared that people were slightly in awe of this bold stroke of leadership. Before the group had exhibited shared leadership; now it exhibited shared followership. Linda became the center of attention. A fundamental realigning of energy took place. The group suddenly started treating Linda as someone quite different from themselves. She was isolated and in the spotlight. The act of taking on leadership alters both who one is and how one is perceived.

Leadership creates something from nothing; it is a bold step of charting a course and setting out. This boldness sometimes has strange effects on others. All too often, others are content to ride in our wake, to let us take all the hard knocks, and even to undermine our efforts in subtle and not-so-subtle ways. Thus, leadership has a strong tendency to create a "me vs. them" situation. When you stand up and say, "We should go this way," others try to pull you down and say, "No, we should go this way instead." This process is inherent in human nature. There are ways to reduce this tendency, but it is important to recognize it, or you will find yourself pulled down. As a result, transformational leaders must possess will and toughness. To lead people in the direction they are already going is not especially difficult, but to chart a new course and persuade people to align with a new vision is a challenge. It requires skill, toughness, and patience.

When I speak of toughness, I am talking about something different from what the word usually calls to mind. The conventional idea of toughness is of hardening yourself against strain so that you reduce your sensitivity. When I use the word toughness, I mean maintaining sensitivity, while strengthening the ability to accept and deal with situations as they are. In this sense, toughness means interacting with the situation in a grounded and nonreactive way. If people are shouting at you in a meeting, toughness might mean being aware they have strong feelings that they probably think you aren't hearing—otherwise they wouldn't have to shout. So the best strategy is not to get upset but to listen carefully. Toughness is not opposed to openness and sensitivity.

It takes courage and toughness to create a vision. But it takes even more courage and toughness to hold onto a vision and persevere when reality does not immediately reward our efforts. Vision comes from getting in touch with a sense of purpose; vision is intuitive. Consequently, vision often has the appearance of being opposed to the rational. This may not be a major problem when things are going your way; but when things are not going so well, to hold tight to a vision that appears to be irrational takes will, toughness, and intention.

Contrast intention and daydreaming. In daydreaming you say, "One of these days I'm going to strike out on my own and do something important with my life." With intention you say, "Next Monday I'm going to start my own business as an independent financial analyst." There might not be any concrete evidence that anything has happened, but in the case of real intention, it clearly is going to happen. Not so with a daydream.

Transformational leadership is fundamentally linked to intention. It is not enough to have a vision; you must have a sufficient level of intention to carry out the vision. Anyone can create a vision, but few have the guts and drive to move it out into the world of reality. Intention belongs to the world of action. You can have vision and not act on it. Intention, in its purest form, involves making a gut-level decision, at a deep level, to bring a vision into reality. It is a sheer act of will.

Making such a choice means, by its very nature, leaping into the unknown. It is an act of faith in oneself and in others. It involves a tremendous level of trust. It is an affirmation that life works, that life will respond to our will and direction. Because of this, it is a very attractive quality. A person with highly developed intention has charisma. (We are always drawn to and fascinated by people who draw on qualities that seem outside our range of experience.)

Transformational leadership is leadership by bonding and attracting rather than by coercion. The nature of this kind of vision and intention attracts people. Leaders tap into a deep place in people and cause them to want to join in the vision and work to make it happen. When the vision is attractive and fulfilling, and when the commitment to fulfilling the vision is sufficiently great people are drawn to participate.

Will, toughness and intention are qualities that are learned by doing. We need to continually work to develop them. We need the toughness to deal with the difficulties involved in leadership, and the will and intention to manifest our visions. To achieve these qualities, we need to reach into a deep place in ourselves; and this depth causes others to want to join with us and bring the vision to reality.

## 4. Low Ego, High Results

There is a popular misconception that "Great leaders produce big results, and to produce big results you must have a big ego." This view, which pervades the Western way of seeing things, is untrue and damages our ability to produce results. What makes it more insidious is that under certain circumstances, it seems to work. People with big egos sometimes do, in fact, get results. But these results stem from vision and intention, not from ego itself.

The fundamental concept here, which is often misunderstood, is that strength is different from ego. Strength is vital for a leader. Strength is essentially the same as the "will, toughness, and intention" just discussed. A leader must have strength to meet the various obstacles which present themselves and to push forward to achieve results. But because one has strength does not mean one has a large ego. By ego I mean overemphasis on self. Thus one manifestation of ego is a greedy attachment to personal self-aggrandizement and gain. Ego is, "I'll get mine, no matter what." Ego is a way of handling each situation so that I get more and others get less. The more here may be material or emotional. Ego is continually manipulating the events and people of the outside world so that they circle around "me" at the expense of you. Ego is me versus you.

The thrust of transformational leadership is to encourage people to give up petty, egotistical needs and work for the common good and the common vision. A leader must both encourage and exemplify a way of relating to others that keeps vision in the foreground and ego in the background. A leader who is clearly out to grease his or her own wheels will never get the dedication and respect of others. To take this reasoning one step further, ego is taking resources away from the organization and allocating them for personal gain. Non-ego says, "share fairly." Ego says, "I want it all."

Any time I use a situation to inflate myself at the expense of others, I destroy the cooperation necessary to produce results. If I criticize my secretary over trivial things, I decrease his or her willingness to work for the good of the organization. If I sabotage the project of someone I feel competitive with, I damage both the project and my relationship with that person. If I am miffed because someone did not invite me to a key meeting, my anger doesn't solve the problem; it just gets in the way and creates disharmony.

The antithesis of ego is caring, service, dedication, and excelling in one's work. When people see a leader *acting* in this way it causes a profound change in the atmosphere of the organization. Others are challenged to work at the same level of service and dedication. A mark of transformational leadership is *low ego, high results*. Another way of saying this is "service, cooperation, commitment, and dedication to results." "Low ego" and "high results" are bound together. If people are fixed on personal gain and ego gratification the organizational results will suffer. Conversely, if you see an organization with poor results people's egos probably are getting in the way.

This is not to put down the role of strong individuals and competition. Strong individuals are essential, and moderate amounts of competition are useful. But the thrust of transformational leadership must be to engage people's sense of cooperation and teamwork. This is the problem in most organizations: there is too much ego, too much energy running off in private directions that have little to do with the organizational vision. The problem is never that there is too much cooperation and communication.

The leader helps set the tone. A large portion of this tone is the leader's low degree of ego involvement. If the leader sets a personal example of low ego — of service, dedication, support and concern — others will take on this same challenge. The leader's role is one of service: his or her job is to create structures that allow each employee to produce the desired results.

## 5. No Separation

The idea of "no separation" is something of a paradox. As discussed earlier, leadership has within it the tendency to create separation. This is true both on an outward and an inward level. On an outward level, all the trappings of power tend to create separation: the leader has access to a level of power and control not available to others. On an inner level, the very act of moving into a state of leadership and responsibility creates an inner shift that causes a leader to act and experience reality differently from other people. Others, in turn, notice the shift and experience the leader as different or separate. This is sometimes expressed in phrases like, "I can't reach him," or "She never really seems to listen."

Perhaps because there is such a strong tendency to experience a leader as separate, transformational leaders have learned how to reduce this sense of separation. When you are with people like this, you feel that they are with you. The perceived paradox between these two aspects of separation — knowing that a leader is inherently separate from you, but experiencing a sense of intimacy and connection with the leader — is what creates a sense of charisma in transformational leaders. There is something appealing about these two aspects combined; either one alone is far less attractive. If a potential leader says, "I will lead you," but there is no emotional warmth, people tend to walk away. On the other hand, if a person is personally warm, but is not providing leadership, the person will be liked, but there is not the same power and charisma.

One way of understanding the power of "no separation" comes from the field of transpersonal psychology. According to transpersonal psychology, our normal experience of separation — the sense that you and I are made of such different stuff that we really can't understand or communicate with each other — is an illusion. True, we often have this experience, but the reality is that we have a very deep connection with each other. At the times when we feel the greatest sense of separation, such as at the death of a loved one or the breakup of a relationship, the grief or anger we feel is actually an expression of our connection to another. We do not become deeply angered at people we care nothing about.

This interconnection between people is the core of what makes transformational leadership work. It's what allows people to work as a team, experience a sense of community, and align behind a common vision. Creating a high-performance organization is like making soup: the idea is to merge a bunch of separate components into one, so that it produces a common result and a common taste.

Transformational leaders understand this basic connection with others not only intellectually, but directly and experientially. When you are with people like this, you don't feel distanced, but rather as if you are talking with someone you have known a long time. You have a sense that the person is really *there* with you, that they care for you personally. Note, however, that this sense of affection is not of the puppy-love variety. There are too many people *trying* to lead by gaining the affection of would-be followers. Rather, the affection I am talking about is the kind of love between you and a friend, that when you are doing something detrimental, your friend will confront you with it. In Eastern religions, this is known as "ruthless compassion."

Transformational leadership is leadership by inspiration, connection, and vision. It depends on the inherent interconnection of people. It is leadership that communicates "We are all in this thing together." It is leadership that believes "Each person is an honored and respected member of the team." "No separation" is the component that provides the cohesion necessary for an organization to be successful. Out of the cohesion provided by respect, affection, and equality comes the ability to produce the results to which the organization is dedicated.

## 6. Trust and Openness

Like "no separation," the qualities of trust and openness help create integration and cohesion in an organization. These qualities are crucial to transformational leadership. Trust is having faith in others and yourself. Trust is a predisposition to believe others will think and behave appropriately. By openness, I mean being unguarded, candid, truthful. In particular, openness means being willing to share the more personal sides of yourself, uncensored and unedited. Naturally, trust is a prerequisite for openness.

Trust is an attitude or viewpoint that a leader brings to a situation. I sometimes refer to this attitude as "tough-minded optimism." It is a grounded trust. It is relating to people from the point of view "I expect and look forward to seeing good things from you — but I will also help and support you if you have problems."

A peculiarity of trust and openness is that, from one point of view, they both represent irrational behavior. If one were to make a scientific study of the question "Are people consistently trustworthy?" I'm sure the answer would come back "No." Given this fact, it is obviously irrational to trust them. Leaders, probably more than anyone else, are acutely aware that people are not fully trustworthy. People agree to do something, and then it doesn't get done. People's commitment is less than total. In various ways, people sabotage both other people and the organization as a whole. Yet despite this, the transformational leader chooses to trust.

Most people generate trust (when they do) based on experience. A transformational leader generates trust as an act of faith. It is a predisposition to see people in a certain way because experience shows that this way of seeing works. A transformational leader works actively with this paradox: "I choose to trust and be open with people who are not always trustworthy." Although some transformational leaders appear to handle this paradox effortlessly, most experience it as a very active tension. It takes energy and effort to make it work. It is an act of will, a choice to trust when there is no objective evidence to trust.

This predisposition to trust creates a powerful energy field around a leader. People are drawn to this energy because they experience themselves as bigger people in the leader's presence. The leader's trust bolsters their confidence, and the leader's refusal to be conned creates a sense of stability and safety. The environment created is a safe and satisfying one. This kind of energy field always exists around transformational leaders. It is a big part of what creates the dedication of their followers. After all, if a person has a choice between feeling contracted or feeling expanded, which one will they choose?

Closely related to a leader's predisposition to trust is the leader's tendency to be open. When I talk about openness, I don't just mean about information. I am talking about openness at a personal level—being willing to really say what's going on personally, including one's emotional reactions to things. Transformational leaders exhibit a remarkable degree of openness—you find yourself being surprised at their easy candor. The reason openness is such a valuable trait for a leader is that the leader sets the tone and establishes the atmosphere. When a leader is open, everyone else has permission to be open. The atmosphere becomes more relaxed and candid. All of a sudden you find yourself dealing with the real causes of things rather than the reasons people give. While before a person would say about a project, "I'm not sure that's such a wise idea . . .", now they say "Well to tell you the truth, I think it's a pretty good idea, but I don't want to get involved, because the project involves working with Larry, and we don't get along very well."

You may recall times when you had something you needed to say to a manager or other person in authority, but you felt the person was not there for it. The minute you started to say something slightly threatening, the leader changed the subject and seemed unavailable. Many managers are afraid of openness and trust; when anything pertaining to emotions comes up, they tighten up.

Many managers want their direct reports to be open with them and even say things like, "If you have any problems, or anything at all you wish to discuss, please feel free to come talk to me." But this misses the point. No employee in their right mind is going to talk candidly with their boss unless the candor is being reciprocated. The leader needs to initiate the process. If the leader tells a story on herself or himself, the employee will often reciprocate. But the employee feels at higher risk; it is unrealistic to expect the employee to initiate the discussion.

Ultimately, this matter of trust and openness comes down to the type of organization you want to create. If you want to create a militaristic organization in which all you want from people is, "Yes, sir" or "No, sir" then perhaps it doesn't matter so much. If, however, you want to create an organization that prizes performance, relies on cooperation and communication, has a ready flow of information, and in which people are committeed to a vision and work hard to achieve it—all of these take trust and openness.

## 7. Insight into Human Nature

Leadership is basically a skill of human interaction. Working from a vision, a leader uses personal relationships to influence actions. Transformational leaders are characterized by an ability to read, interpret, and guide the actions of others. And this, in turn, requires a deep insight into human nature.

Transformational leadership is a connecting force that touches people at a very deep level. It is impossible to touch people at such a level, however, if you have not reached this level in yourself. You can only take people to the level of your own experience. Transformational leaders need access to kinds of experiences that are totally beyond the range talked about openly in most businesses and business schools.

Here are a few examples of the kind of life knowledge that leaders need to know. The discussion is far from complete, but can be supplemented by attending seminars, reading transformational books, working with individual teachers, and engaging in personal introspection.

*Polar Opposites.* It is inherent in human nature that people embrace an enormous number of polar opposites. The same person can beat his wife and be capable of enormous acts of goodwill and altruism. A person with a very strong sense of honesty can, at times, lie or steal. A woman can truthfully say to her husband, "I love you," while at the same time being angry and even hateful about some of his actions. As a leader, you can ask someone to do something, and they will be sincerely grateful that you asked them and at the same time be resentful about the perceived power differential in your relationship. Often these two emotions spring up at the same time: when you evoke "A," you automatically get "B."

I have stated these examples in the form of "positive-negative"; you could also state them as "negative-positive." For any negative action a person performs, there is a positive place in that person that is possible to access. One of the strongest examples of this phenomenon is when a group is angry. If the anger is faced and dealt with in an open and constructive way, you can watch a healing take place right before your eyes. People walk out feeling happy, enthusiastic, and proud. It's especially powerful when you remember how they were just a few hours back.

*Context.* Things only take on meaning in terms of a perceived context. The human being is a context-seeking animal: the effort is always to answer "What does this mean?" If a context is not quickly evident in a situation, people project it onto the situation. This is a simple and natural way that our mind functions to help us sift through information and to function in the world.

The most common context that people project is one of "for me" or "against me." Thus people see others as being on their side or on the opposite side; situations as for them or against them. Recently when a group of coworkers submitted a proposal to a woman, and the proposal contained some provisions that she found distasteful, her first question was, "Should I be worried about where you're coming from, or not?" It is generally to your advantage to help people supply the context for any events that surround you. Chances are you can provide a more positive context than the one which people will project.

*Expectation and Vision.* To carry the above discussion one step further, all of our actions and beliefs occur within a context. There is tremendous power and potential for good in helping people create high-level contexts for their lives. This is something that transformational leaders always do. If you have positive expectations for people, they generally rise to meet your expectations. If you have a vision that allows people to see their livelihood as service to others, they will link into that vision and work with great fervor. The power of helping people create context cannot be overemphasized.

*Capacity for Results.* People are not work machines; they are complex beings who, under the right conditons, can produce amazing results. Under the wrong conditions, they can produce stunning damage. In fact, people are such amazing beings that under suboptimal conditions, they can convey an appearance of acting in the interest of the organization while at the same time actively sabotaging the results of others. It is vital for a leader to know what conditions make people produce positive results, and what makes them produce negative results—and then create the right conditions.

*Safety, Security, and Community.* As part of the right conditions for positive results, people need a sense of safety, security, community, and emotional support. It is paradoxical that this fact is so obvious and so often violated. Think of how often in organizations we tell people we care about them and then do something that sabotages their sense of security and support. And then we wonder why people in organizations get cynical.

*The Bottom Line.* For many organizations, the "bottom line" (as the term is usually used) is financial. For people, the bottom line is almost always emotional. Despite what people say in order to cope in a world where rationality is king, the real reasons why people do things are always emotional. There is no problem in this, but it creates a problem if we believe the rational explanations people provide.

*Straight Communication.* Straight communication works. Telling people the truth, rather than what you think they want to hear, works. True, you can finesse a situation and slide by any direct confrontation, but at what long-term cost to your organization?

## 8. Skill in Creating People Structures; Groundedness

A transformational leader also needs to understand how people function in groups, how to structure those groups appropriately, and how to make the organization work in a grounded way. The following are examples of the things a transformational leader needs to know.

*Groups Have Lives of Their Own.* Most of us in organizations spend an enormous amount of time in groups. Though we may have developed some "street smarts," few of us have spent time actually understanding how groups work. What happens in groups is distinctly different from what happens in one-on-one conversations. So-called "group dynamics" is a real force in a group. There are typical issues that always get worked in groups, such as entry, inclusion, separation, safety, openness, power, and group norms. Through training and experience, one can learn to interact with and flow with a group in a skillful way.

All managers and leaders should undergo training in group dynamics. If you do not know groups inside and out, you are at a considerable disadvantage. Transformational leaders usually have exceptional skills in facilitating groups. They have learned timing, the kind of personal energy that works in groups, how to be honest and open in groups, how to maintain group focus, and how to facilitate others in exhibiting these same characteristics. When you learn to work skillfully with groups you can play a unique role in facilitating the kind of clarity, openness, and results orientation that will optimize the performance of your organization.

*Groups Are Trustworthy.* One result of the kind of training suggested above is that you start to realize that you can trust groups. Many managers are relatively comfortable and open in one-on-one exchanges, but in a group situation may tighten up and revert to grandstanding and other forms of manipulative and nonproductive behavior. This happens because at a deep level they don't trust the group process; they feel insecure in groups.

Since group activities influence the tone of an organization, it's vital to learn to trust the group processes. It's vital to create open, enjoyable, and productive meetings. By serving as a facilitator, you play an important role in establishing this kind of atmosphere. You reach the point where you can trust other people in meetings and trust groups to make effective and viable decisions.

*Organizations Have Lives of Their Own.* Organizations are structured collections of groups. Since groups have lives of their own, it is natural to assume that organizations have lives of their own. And they do. Think of how often someone in a medium-sized company will comment "Boy, it sure is different here. I can remember when I'd just shout down the hall to Ralph when I had something to say." Organizations have lives of their own; their own ages, their own spirits, their own stories, their own identifies. At least metaphorically, organizations have their own souls.

*Institutionalize the Human Side.* One way that you can attend to the organization's life is to institutionalize the human side. By this I mean actively create structures and symbols that remind people of your concern for the human side of the business. A few examples:

- Have a weekly social get-together
- Recognize and reward individuals and teams for accomplishments
- Make sure people know what each department in your company does
- Create an internal company slogan
- Have large-scale social get-togethers designed for fun
- Encourage mild competitiveness between groups

74

- Use the newsletter for heart-to-heart communication rather than just PR fluff
- Print a company T-shirt
- Put on skits in front of the whole organization
- Put up home-made posters with creative ideas about human relations
- On a rotating basis, put up photos of various people and groups

Though such things may seem frivolous, they are important — and the larger the organization, the more important. Touches such as these help to keep a human feel in an organization.

*Organization Work.* Many traditional managers are narrowly results-focused: "We want to produce a result, and if we have to step on a few toes and slit a few throats in the process, that's all part of the game." The organization is viewed as a results machine. The impression you get in some companies is that if the CEO could replace everyone with a robot, he or she would. People are treated as incidental to the process. They are usually not recognized at all, and when they are noticed, it's on an exception basis: "Sullivan's not producing. Is he having trouble with his wife or something?"

A transformational leader's relationship to the organization, on the other hand, is based on the idea that organizations work: not only can the organization produce the desired result, it can also be supportive and responsive to its people. And as a matter of fact, an organization that is not supportive and responsive to its people cannot fully produce the result.

An organization that works is one that scores well in a variety of areas, both in terms of performance and in terms of people:

- The organization is a top producer, and frequently outdistances the competition.
- The organization is highly profitable.
- Individuals do their jobs responsibly, effectively, and professionally.
- There is strong Esprit de Corps.
- People are committed to a common vision and purpose.
- There is effective communication, respect, and cooperation.
- There is a strong sense of community.
- There are effective methods for problem resolution.
- Employees feel happy and fulfilled.

In this list, some managers would key in on the first three items and think the remaining items were just fluff. The point is, it's all interrelated. You can get some level of performance from people by using tactics of fear and intimidation. But if you want superior performance, you must create a more humane and cooperative organization. Is it possible to have it all, or do we have to bend to a mechanistic, results-only organization that clearly kills the spirit of its employees? If one is a leader in an organization, does one have to stick to old feudal models, or can one structure the organization in a visionary but grounded way that supports both the desired results and the spirit of its people?

## 9. Integrity

The subject of integrity is something of a motherhood. One has the feeling that it's a matter of mouthing the right words and watching heads nod up and down, but knowing that the words bear no resemblance to what happens in actual practice.

Having integrity in an organization creates an experience of soundness, robustness and vigor. An organization without integrity is like a rotten log: when you hit it, it gives a dull thump and goes limp. It invites worms and parasites. An organization with integrity, however, is strong like a well-rooted tree. When an outside force attacks it, the organization can withstand the blows. It has springiness and resilience. Woodpeckers and parasites avoid it because there is no decay.

What specifically is organizational integrity? It is the sum total of the integrity of individuals in the organization. For each person, it is the tendency to do that which is praiseworthy, effective, and right and avoid that which is reprehensible, ineffective, and wrong. In an organization with integrity, everyone shoulders their responsibilities, conducts their business in an upright way, and expects everyone else to do the same.

Organizational integrity has a lot to do with group norms. In some organizations, if you do something to shortchange the customer, people just smile and treat it as a joke. In other organizations, this same action will be universally rejected and the doer censored.

Of course, this is easy to talk about. But how do you go about creating integrity in an organization? The person who has the most to do with establishing this quality is the leader. The leader must both talk about integrity and practice it. Stories about a leader's integrity — or for that matter, lack of it — spread rapidly through an organization. Leaders have to avoid any possibility of their actions being misinterpreted. Better to err on the side of integrity than on the side of expediency.

Ultimately, integrity comes down to a fundamental question: "Which is more important to me: my relationship with myself or my business success?" Frequently the person who chooses the former gets both, and the person who chooses the latter gets neither. But the choices don't always look this simple when you're in the thick of it.

It may appear that organizational integrity is an issue that can be left alone until a problem crops up, but if floors aren't swept, they collect dust. There needs to be constant housekeeping in an organization. To avoid this is to invite trouble. As a leader, part of your job is to create a culture that demands integrity. Integrity creates the foundation for any other work in the organization.

## 10. A Context of Personal Growth and Fulfillment

A transformational leader is a person who catalyzes a dedicated, spirited, close-knit organization that singlemindedly pursues a common vision and produces effective results in the real world. To a person from the outside, such an organization may look like a bunch of "crazies" who seem to have an unexplainable dedication and commitment to a cause. People in such an organization have a deep respect for themselves and for each other; they are bringing something personal of themselves to the work; the work is an outlet for their energy and dedication.

In these organizations, work is more than what you do to earn a paycheck; it involves personal commitment, personal satisfaction, and personal growth. Work flows from and is a natural outgrowth of a desire for challenge, stimulation, feedback, success, and association with others in meaningful activity.

*Work as Personal Fullfillment.* There is a widely held myth that "Personal is personal, and work is work, and never the twain shall meet." But in actuality, "personal" and "work" are always integrally combined. What we need as people, and what the organization needs, are surprisingly similar, as the following table illustrates:

| The Person Needs | The Organization Needs |
| --- | --- |
| A source of livelihood | Financial success and profit |
| A sense of personal effectiveness | Organizational effectiveness |
| Personal direction | Effective leadership |
| The experience of fulfillment | Success in attaining its vision |
| The experience of community and cooperation | Effective communication and cooperation |
| Happiness and "aliveness" | Spirit, Esprit de Corps |
| Emotional support | Employee dedication and commitment |
| Personal growth | Organization development and growth |
| Personal success | Organization success |

The needs of people and those of organizations consist of the same stuff: people are the building blocks of which organizations are made. A transformational leader knows that personal fulfillment and organizational goals are always strongly connected; the trick is to link the two so that each supports the other. To ignore the personal is to ignore a major source of energy that can be used toward organizational objectives.

Transformational leaders do not fall into the trap of treating people as cogs in the mechanism. They treat people as individuals who are seeking their own satisfaction and fulfillment. They assume people are actively working to improve themselves. They engage people on both a personal and a task-oriented level. They help people link their personal desires with the needs of the organization.

*Work as Personal Growth.* Personal growth is a vehicle that can link an individual's search for fulfillment with the needs of the organization. Organizations that support personal growth acknowledge the personal components of organizational life and actively encourage individuals to treat the organization as a place in which to engage in their development. This is the opposite of "leave your personal and emotional issues at the door." Rather, it is "Look, we're going to be interacting with each other in ways that will push personal buttons. Let's not pretend those situations don't exist; let's find ways we can actively work with them, and with our own personal issues, so we can enjoy interacting with each other and best fulfill organizational objectives." In short, it's meeting problems head-on rather than running from them. This involves a lot of trust, which is why trust has been emphasized throughout this chapter.

When an organization creates a context for personal growth, the result is a subtle but profound improvement in the atmosphere of the organization. This occurs for two reasons. First, such a context creates a mechanism by which organizational problems get resolved: there is a pre-existing, officially sanctioned channel for handling personal and emotional difficulties. People know that if they have problems with a coworker, the norms of the organization make it safe to go to the coworker and talk out the problem. This tends to relieve an enormous amount of organizational tension and stress.

Second, the emphasis on personal growth helps individuals wake up, take personal responsibility for their lives, and stay focused on personal and organizational goals. When individuals in an organization take this approach, the net result is an organization with a sense of vibrancy, action, and buoyancy. People feel "up" and ready to take on challenges. They are ready to devote their energy to help fulfill the vision.

Creating this kind of organization requires a new form of leadership. It is obviously not the kind of hierarchical, top-down leadership that says "From here on, everyone will be emotionally open in meetings." Rather, it is the kind of leadership that creates safety and support for people, leading by example. As a leader, the best way to create a context of personal growth is to engage in it yourself. It helps if you show a few of your rough edges. You can talk about the kinds of personal issues you are currently dealing with. You can talk about your feelings during meetings. You can talk about the process of personal growth in an organizational setting, and why it's valuable and important. You can make sure people feel safe; that they won't be shot down if they happen to mention an emotion.

When a transformational leader places organizational emphasis on personal growth in this way, it transmits several messages to people, including the following:

1. I am a real three-dimensional person. I have a life outside the organization, and I know you do, too.

2. I take my personal life seriously.

3. We care about you as a person.

4. This is an organization in which you can bring all of yourself, not just selected portions.

5. You are responsible for your own life, and we support you in handling that responsibility.

6. We care not only about our final product or service, but also about the process by which we create and deliver it.

7. We want communication, negotiation, and cooperation rather than back-room politics, backstabbing, sabotage, resentment, misdirected communications, and other forms of denial and manipulation that sap organization energy.

8. We are committed to having this organization work, both personally and professionally.

9. We want and expect from you an active approach to solving problems, communicating key information, cooperating with others, and in general making both the organization and your own life successful and effective.

10. We want to support you both in succeeding at your job and in being personally fulfilled.

11. We have trust and faith that working together in this way will not only be possible and effective, but will also increase our mutual respect and enjoyment.

Through placing emphasis on personal growth, a small change in the way you interact with yourself and with the organization can have an enormous influence on the atmosphere and effectiveness of the organization. The ten leadership qualities outlined in this chapter *all* have to do with personal growth.

## THE POWER OF SPIRITUAL LEADERSHIP

Each of the leadership qualities described here has a spiritual component—each is in some sense transcendent. They each have a quality that is different from and rises above everyday reality. For example, creating an inspired vision for your organization has quite a different feeling than mowing the lawn.

Transformational leaders draw on these ten qualities as they work to shape the spirit and performance of their organizations. To create and catalyze spirit, you cannot use the mechanical tools such as time-allocation forms and financial controls (valuable as such tools are). The mechanical does not contain spirit; you cannot squeeze water from a stone.

The ten qualities outlined here do contain spirit. By embodying them, the transformational leader creates organizations with great vitality and high-level performance. In a sense, the leader is tapping "human potential energy"—energy and talent that was always available but seldom put to use. Spiritual leadership provides a way to harness this energy and channel it into productive work.

Each of the ten qualities provides an important leadership component for the organization as a whole. *Inspired vision* and *clarity of mind* provide a sense of clear direction and purpose. *Low ego, high results* keeps the focus on the end result rather than on individual selfish needs. *No separation* and *openness and trust* create bonding and cooperation in the organization and help to establish mechanisms for solving problems. *Insight into human nature* and *skill in creating people structures, groundedness* constitute the underlying wisdom the transformational leader draws to work effectively with individuals and to structure the organization appropriately. *Will, toughness, and intention* provide the force necessary to create forward motion. *Integrity* provides a solid base on which to produce results. *A context of personal growth and fulfillment* is the attention to people's inner needs required to create the results.

# CHAPTER 5

# Becoming a Metapreneur

by
## RONNIE LESSEM

*In many ways, we continually look to our past experience for leadership models
to carry us into the future. This chapter introduces the concept of "metapreneur"
to describe the kind of leadership needed in the coming years. Seven archetypal
dimensions of leadership are developed and implications for developing these archetypes are reviewed.*

## WHAT LIES BEYOND MANAGEMENT?

The nineteenth century was the age of the entrepreneur. In the twentieth century, the manager took command. Business administration took over from business
entrepreneurship. The managed organization took over from the pioneering enterprise. The twenty-first century, as I view it, will see the rise of a "metapreneur."

In the 1980s we are witnessing a swing away from analytical management. As a
result, in both Great Britain and America, we have gone back to the entrepreneur
and to the business leader. Dissatisfied with the conventional managerial wisdom,
we have resurrected its predecessors. Over the long haul that can never work — the
Japanese will defeat us at every turn. The world has changed, and we in the West
need to change with it.

The transformed leader, the *metapreneur*, will be to the next century what the
manager has been to this one. The transformed organization, the *metaprise*, will be
to the future what the enterprise was to the past. We can all become metapreneurs,
and my intention here is to pave the way. For this new construction I have put together not only novel theory but also outstanding practice; what results is a genuine
metamorphosis.

## METAMORPHOSIS: A CHANGE OF FORM

Metamorphosis means, literally, change of form. In order to change one form
of leadership into another, you have to take it apart and put it together again differ-

ently. Leaders, as somewhat different from managers, are distinguished by their personal qualities. In fact it is the very impersonality of management that has led toward its growing unpopularity.

In America and Europe, our businesses, economies, and institutions have gone wrong because they have lost touch with our "human being." That human being is not the soft underbelly of an otherwise hard corporate machine. It is the totality of our individual and institutional thoughts, feelings, and actions. It includes aggression as well as cooperation, toughness as well as sensitivity. Metapreneurs and metaprises are simply combinations of thought, feeling, and action in particular contexts. They are the sum of our individuality, the true spirit of our personal and corporate being.

If the three building blocks of human being are put together as overlapping circles, we create a personality, or business spectrum (Figure 1). The personality spectrum provides us with metapreneurs, and the business spectrum with a metaprise.

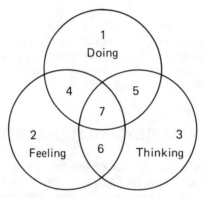

FIGURE 1.         Building Blocks of Human Being.

## IDENTIFYING METAPRENEURS

There are seven archetypal metapreneurs, which I shall present briefly both in theory and practice. The examples are taken from outstanding businessmen and women in the United Kingdom; certainly their equivalents exist in the United States and in continental Europe.

### Doers

Doers are action persons—they make things happen, get things done, travel through the physical unknown. This metapreneur is an *adventurer*. Anita Roddick is a good example. She started an enterprise called "Bodyshop" in the late 1970s and there are now over 100 franchised outlets in Europe and Canada. Anita has traveled the world, like the great explorers of old, not to discover new territory, but to uncover natural products. In creating Bodyshop she has combined a love of nature with a restless physical energy, emerging with a chain of natural hair and skin care outlets.

As she continues to travel to distant lands, picking up more natural ingredients, Anita's life and business merge into a relentless personal and business adventure.

### Feelers

These metapreneurs are as closely in touch with the corporate culture as with their own feelings. They are animated, enthusiastic, "people" people. I have borrowed the term *animateur* from the French to describe these natural motivators. Originally, the animateur was someone who brought life to the neighborhood or community. Nelli Eichner, in creating Interlingua 30 years ago, brought and kept together dozens of different nationalities under one small roof, just like one happy family. Today her company is the largest translating and interpreting company in the world.

Nelli developed her business in the 1950s, not only to profit financially, but also to apply her love of languages to a family enterprise. Virtually from the day they were born, her five children were able to apply their energy, enthusiasm, and, subsequently, knowledge and skill to the business. With husband Fred as the technological innovator, the business has advanced from a cottage industry to an electronic cottage, with networked linkages worldwide. But Interlingua's high-tech headquarters remain in a rural setting, surrounded by plants, animals, and numerous grandchildren. Nelli's love of people and languages has led not only to animated business transactions but also to shared happiness. She is reminiscent of Mary Kay in America.

### Thinkers

As knowledge advances, so the role of thinkers in business develops. These are people who are motivated by self-expression rather than traditional self-interest. They seek opportunity to apply knowledge, to channel ideas, and to learn faster than the rate of change. They are the free spirits, the truly flexible types who thrive in networks and who spurn hierarchies. As such a *change agent*, Stephanie (Steve) Shirley has created a business out of a social cause.

Steve has in fact freed women, including herself, from having to choose between home and career by providing them with the opportunity to pursue both. Freelance Programmers, which has since grown into F (for flexible) International currently involves 1000 women, the majority working from home or on the client's premises. Steve operates in Britain and in continental Europe. F International has developed the project-based, networked approach to programming and systems analysis to a fine art. As a refugee from Nazi Germany, and an idealist, Steve has turned the cause of personal freedom into a highly flexible business.

### Willpowers

Strong will, which is quite independent of thought, is expressed through a combination of feeling and action. This is the world of the traditional entrepreneur, who loves challenge, achievement, self-assertion, and risk.

The new breed of *intrapreneur* are willful individuals who choose to work within, or alongside, existing businesses. They are more like what Michael Maccoby (1978) has called the modern "gamesman" and less like the traditional "jungle fighter." The intrapreneur is more assertive than aggressive, motivated more by psychological than physical hunger.

Jack Dangoor, an Iraqui Jew who attended university in Great Britain, is a good case in point. His father is a traditional merchant, and Jack himself dropped out of his physics course, after two years, to pursue his own entrepreneurial path. After learning the business ropes within the electronic watch trade, taking many a financial risk along the way, he decided that there were more opportunities in the growing market for small business computers.

Unlike the entrepreneur of old, who struck out on his own, Jack has collaborated with three major business institutions, to create his company, Advance Technology. In less than two years by teaming up with the electronics manufacturers, Ferranti, with National Semi Conductors on the service side, and with W. H. Smith for retail distribution, Jack has built up a hardware business worth tens of millions. In the process, he needed not only the courage of his convictions but also the capacity to make deals by knowing how to collaborate with the establishment. There were many occasions in which his proposed deals were on the verge of breaking down, but in the end he broke through.

## Organizers

While the willful intrapreneur combines strong feeling with versatile action, the organized *executive* is more conceptual as well as practical. He is comfortable with planning and authority to a greater extent than any of his fellow metapreneurs. The executive thrives in a structured educational or corporate environment and, when at his or her best, is able to create such an environment rather than merely manage within one.

John Harvey-Jones, current chairman of Imperial Chemical Industries (ICI), is an outstanding chief executive. In a short time, he has played a leading role in turning his corporation around by infusing it with a new authority and purpose. Striving for all-around excellence, he has restructured his board so that it now functions as an integrated whole. Harvey-Jones' limitless capacity to provide direction, to reconceptualize and revitalize ICI's business, has paid handsome dividends. For the first time ever, in 1985, ICI made a billion pound profit.

## Intuiters

Where Harvey-Jones is authoritative and dynamic, Mary Quant is intuitive and magnetic. Intuiters, in fact, combine thought not with action but with feeling. They sniff things out, have a nose for the next fashion or trend, can sense potential, and can see the way the market is going. When they become like Uri Geller they can not only bend spoons but also find oil under the ground!

Many designers, in fashion, in automobiles, and in electronics, can recognize and enhance potential in products and markets. The person I have termed the *new designer* is also able to do this sort of thing with and through people. In the field of organization development, such a person is called an "enabler." Enablers design environments to enhance human potential. The new designer can enhance both the physical and the human variety.

**84**

Mary Quant, who has become a household name in fashion and cosmetics, has displayed remarkable design ability for over 30 years. She has recognized and harnessed the potential of materials and markets previously unexploited. Mary has intuitively sensed what women have wanted, and in association with numerous manufacturers and distributors all over the world, has come up with the right products at the right time.

In recent years Mary Quant has made a particularly strong impact in Japan, where her subtle colors and designs go over extremely well. Not surprisingly, her Japanese company runs as a joint venture, which suits the designer's associative frame of mind.

## Creators

The business creator is someone truly inspired, possessed with vision. Creators have the imagination and the energy to completely transform an industry. Henry Ford was such an example in America. He combined thought, feeling, and action in creating a production revolution. In the United Kingdom, Terence Conran is an example of a man who has revolutionized retailing.

The truly creative businessman is a genuine *innovator*. Unfortunately we have recently begun to confuse innovation, entrepreneurship, and change. The innovator, like Conran, creates a fundamentally new product and market. That is not usually the prerogative of the entrepreneur or change agent.

Conran started by making available his own new furniture designs. Ten years later he established a new business concept, at first in retail furnishing, through "Habitat." Today he has created a design-led retailing revolution that covers not only furniture but also kitchen accessories, clothing, toys, and books. His stores are now spread throughout Britain, Europe, and America, and each is uniquely identifiable. Through the Conran Foundation he has also had a major influence on the course of industrial design in this country.

## The Archetypes

If we want to develop a full spread of metapreneurs within our companies, we have to start by creating a new map of the managerial world. At present our mental maps are filled with managerial grades and functions. We see ourselves as production or marketing executives, for example, and as junior, middle, or senior managers. None of these has anything to do with our innate human being.

We may alternately view ourselves as participative or autocratic, bureaucratic or entrepreneurial, but these are still restrictive stereotypes. They bear no direct relation to the fully functioning individual or corporation.

The metapreneurial map of business is more varied, complex, and dynamic. Like the seven continents, it includes seven archetypes. Creative innovators, intuitive new designers, high-performing executives, willful intrapreneurs, flexible change agents, enthusiastic animateurs, and energetic adventurers all have their place in the map of corporate consciousness. Separate and picturesque portrayals of these archetypes gradually lead to a change of corporate awareness and orientation.

In order to identify with a favored metapreneur, individuals need these externalized reference points, but a degree of self-awareness enables them to internalize this new-found identity. A "spectral inventory" may be used to help individuals identify their natural orientation. In small work groups it is also useful to invite comment from others. Is the person in question seen as:

- physical energetic and adventurous?
- socially gregarious and animated?
- mentally alert and adaptable to change?
- emotionally committed and willing to take risks?
- well-organized, authoritative, and practical?
- sensitive, intuitive, and aware of potential?
- creative, imaginative, and possessed of vision?

# DEVELOPING METAPRENEURS

## Apprenticeship Revisited

People develop in life and in business because they are given the right support and challenge at the right time. While we start out in life with certain personal attributes, we have the opportunity of developing others along the way, most likely when we are ripe for them.

From 15 years' experience in management training and business development, I have come to the conclusion that real personal change and development is possible, but it does take years rather than days or months.

I find, as a result, that the traditional idea of "apprenticeship" is more helpful than our modern "training" perspective; the key to real development lies not only in prolonged endeavor but also in that blend of action and learning that results in emotional, mental, and physical change. I want to introduce, therefore, the terms *apprentice, journeyman,* and *master,* and at the same time to broaden their usage. The apprenticeship is the five-year period, or thereabouts, during which the individual acquires mastery of one particular mode of metapreneurship. 'In his mid-twenties, for example, he may be apprenticed to adventuring and in his early thirties to intrapreneuring.

As a journeyman he travels on a particular path through each phase, accompanied by a suitable mentor (setting examples) and coach (helping along the way), provided with a suitable learning environment, passing through particular landmarks or milestones, and attaining a special brand of mastery. Thereafter the journeyman completes his one phase of apprenticeship in business and life, and is ready to move onto the next.

## Archetypal development

This is how the individual can develop through each metapreneurial phase:

*Adventuring:*

- This involves constant movement. Adventurers are keen on traveling from place to place, seeking out physical challenging situations.

- Their mentors will have demonstrated mastery in getting through scrapes, being involved with the rough and tumble, recouping energy, and keeping physically on the go.

- Their coaches will help them store up energy, learn how to physically relax, and provide a physically stimulating environment to work in.

- Their passage will be marked by physical landmarks. For example, while the everyday manager will balk at the opportunity of working in Ethiopia or Lebanon, the adventurer will welcome the physical risk involved.

- Learning divorced from action makes no impact on the adventurer, so that hard knocks and physical duress become part and parcel of his development.

- Demonstrated mastery in physical transformation, as has been the case with Anita Roddick's Bodyshop, is a sign that the adventurer can move on.

*Animating:*

- This involves a social or cultural circle. The more engaging the animateur, as is the case with Nelli Eichner, the bigger the circle involved.

- Animateurs learn through progressive association with ever more broadly based communities, and through the example of respected others.

- Their mentors will already have created such a community and will be closely in touch with the corporate culture as a whole.

- Their coaches will create a supportive environment within which they can exercise their communicative skills, and they will be challenged to do so both externally and internally.

- Each community formed, whether family, locality, or culturally based, will represent an emotional landmark along the way.

- Once animateurs have created a culture with an identifiable and coherent history, mythology, and set of social activities, they are ready to move on.

*Enabling change:*

- Change agents naturally seek out a path of learning. They are the most likely to read management texts, take short courses, and seek out varied experiences.

- A course, a book, or a new project may serve as an intellectual landmark in their development. They love to be constantly on the move, but mentally rather than physically or emotionally.

- In fact, if their coaches do not give them opportunities to stretch their minds, they will turn in on themselves, and opt out of development.

- Their mentors, at the same time, should be persons of great intellectual caliber, able to cope with complexity as managers of change.

- Once they have demonstrated mastery in the design and implementation of a large-scale project then they will be ready to move on. In that way, Steve Shirley moved on from change agent to entrepreneur.

*Intrapreneurs:*

- Intrapreneurs naturally seek out an emotionally testing path and one that is circuitous rather than direct. They love to confront obstacles to be overcome, and to take risks that are emotionally thrilling.

- Theirs is a workstyle that is full of ups and downs and of mistakes from which to learn. The best of them treat failures as stepping stones rather than stumbling blocks. Action learning, whereby they are obliged to reflect on the consequences of their actions, is ideally suited to them.

- In fact, it is their coach's job to help them learn from failure, in initially small doses, for they are only able to learn from such emotionally laden experiences.

- Intrapreneurial mentors, like Jack's own father, provide an example of calculated risk-taking, willful assertion, and tactical negotiation at its best.

- In their work, intrapreneurs require progressively larger territories to conquer. It is the function of the intrapreneur's coach to see that such challenging opportunities are made available at the right time.

- Each battle won, each new piece of territory acquired, each acquisition secured is a landmark in the intrapreneur's dramatic journey.

- When they have conquered sufficient territory, and gained intrapreneurial mastery in the process, they are ready to move on. A natural step is from intrapreneur to executive.

*Managing:*

- Managers, and prospective executives, naturally pursue a linear path of development. They rise through the hierarchy in the same way as they accomplish a task, in a series of cumulative steps, usually within a particular function.

- They learn through a combination of practical experience and formal training, and welcome the opportunity to upgrade their expertise through formally accredited institutions and courses.

- Certified qualifications, as well as progressively more elevated positions and grades, are executive landmarks.

- Mentors are people who possess the personal authority and institutional status to command respect for their knowledge and accomplishments.

- Coaches are immediate supervisors who can provide clarity of structure and manageable targets within which to work, so that the manager can advance along a planned path.

- Once executives have succeeded in managing a function or division successfully, they are ready to move on to another metapreneurial path. For example, John Harvey Jones advanced from divisional and main board executive to corporate leader.

### Developing:

- The new designers follow a path that is neither linear nor bounded. It is lateral, diagonal, and associative, picking up threads along the way and weaving them into a gradually emerging pattern. Because of this nonlinear development they are obliged to move outside of the organization's formal boundaries in order to grow and develop.

- Their mentors, therefore, should be people who have developed themselves outside of the formal hierarchy and, in the process, profoundly enhanced the potential of products and people.

- Their coaches should be creating the sort of physical, social, and learning environment that will facilitate the individual's development.

- Given the time and space to think and feel deeply, the new designers will learn through their own insights, through prolonged observation, by watching and listening, and by connecting one idea or experience to another.

- They evolve rather than progress and interweave rather than conform to a set pattern of organization. Landmarks, for people like Mary Quant, are those significant ideas, experiences, objects, and people that deepen and broaden the quality of what they produce.

- When they have engineered, over an extended period of time, an integrated product or organization development, one that fulfills a higher business or social purpose than their own self-satisfaction, they are ready to move on.

### Innovating:

- Innovators, finally, naturally follow the transcending path of a spiral. Over time and space, their central idea(s) spirals downwards and upwards, inwards and outwards, becoming progressively transformed.

- Product/market breakthroughs, intermingled with flashes of inspiration, form the landmarks along the innovator's intrapreneurial journey.

- Innovators, like Conran, learn from imaginative leaps, backwards, from whence their art or science came, and forward, into the social or technical future. They require, therefore, the deep and firm foundations that only a far-reaching cultural and scientific tradition can give them.

- Their mentors are the innovators, through history, who like Gropius, the originator of industrial design, are the artistic and scientific trail blazers.

- Their coaches are the more accessible and humble teachers who, as both smaller scale innovators and enablers, are able and willing to dedicate themselves to the more gifted innovator's cause.

- When the innovators have made their technological or cultural breakthrough, like Conran, who turned from creative artist to business entrepreneur, they are ready to move on.

## Development Dynamics

There is no one metapreneurial path that should cover an individual's entire life or work span. All of the metapreneurs that I have cited, although archetypal of a particular way, have moved on in life. Metapreneurs are able to move on if three conditions prevail:

1. They are recognized for what they are, at the outset of their career, so that they start off on the right metapreneurial footing. Often youngsters are naturally adventurous or animateurial; in our thirties we become intrapreneurial and in our forties managerial; thereafter we become enablers (new designers), leaders, or innovators. But this is a very rough indication rather than an inevitable life path.

2. During their apprenticeship metapreneurs are provided or provide themselves, with the right environment to learn, with appropriate mentoring and coaching, with suitable landmarks for their journey, and with the right material to master. Remember, for each metapreneurial path, all of these features will be different.

3. The mentors or coaches, if not the individuals themselves, recognize new attributes and motives that merge during the metapreneurial journey. At a certain point there will be a shift in inner gear as the individual prepares for a transformation from, say, intrapreneur to executive. It is the failure to recognize this latent transformation that has prevented so many individuals and enterprises from adapting to change.

These conditions are unlikely to prevail within the ordinary business corporation. I have therefore sketched a design for a *metaprise* that will accommodate the transformed leadership outlined here.

# THE METAPRISE

## Complex Form

Peters and Waterman (1982) assure us that excellent corporations possess a "lean form." I remain unconvinced. If metapreneurs are to flourish, in all their guises, then a lean and skeletal form just won't do. A living organism is a complex one, and a living metaprise contains:

- a nucleus or corporate psyche, which is the "holding company" for the creative imagination
- an evolving organism that reflects the new designer's unfolding and intuitive awareness
- a formal structure that accommodates and channels the manager's ordered approach
- semi-autonomous profit centers through which intrapreneurs can willfully assert themselves

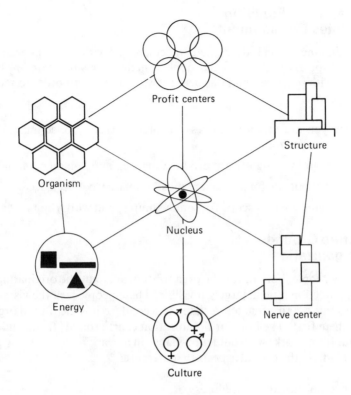

FIGURE 2.                    The Metaprise

- an interactive nerve center through which change agents can communicate and adapt
- a binding corporate culture that contains the myths and rituals, the social activities and ceremonies, that animateurs nourish
- the energy sources, both human and physical, with which business adventurers are associated

## The Nucleus Is the Originating Idea

The nucleus should contain the originator's vision, which so often gets lost in the cobwebs of history or entanglements of bureaucracy. In order to reclaim a lost vision you need to rediscover:

- your historic origins and corporate destiny
- the image you project to the world
- the fundamental values that you impart
- your underlying product or service
- the way you transform the environment

## The Harmonic Function
## Stimulates Development

The originating vision is developed and connected with emerging technological, economic, and social trends by the harmonic function. This function links past with future, actual with potential, and one activity with another. In order to recognize it, you need to discover:

- where you are in your business's evolution from pioneering enterprise to mature corporation,
- where your most significant product, market, and human potential lie,
- with what outside forces you are most intimately connected,
- where is the greatest scope for joint ventures, and with whom.

## Structure Grounds
## the Organization

For many people, both inside the organization and out, the originating idea and harmonizing function remain largely invisible. These people lack the vision and sensitivity to imagine the first and appreciate the second, so it is the formal organization that strikes them first. The familiar organization chart grounds them. Indeed, without a skeletal framework, we would all collapse in a heap, no matter how active our hearts and mind. So the formal aspects that arise are:

- formal policies and procedures
- explicit plans and strategies
- formal structure, including lines of authority and responsibility
- specialized business functions and divisions
- formal controls and lines of communication
- delineated responsibilities to stakeholders

## Intraprise Turns Product
## into Profit

By virtue of organization, the metaprise keeps itself in production. By virtue of intraprise, and through the acquisition of customers and resources, the company turns productivity into profitability. Intrapreneurial cells lie close to the customer and are powered by acquisitive, achieving individuals, who ask themselves:

- How do we get in the best people?
- How can we popularize the inventions of others?
- How can we put the best deal together?
- How much of a risk do we want to take?
- What financial incentive can we offer?
- How much profit will we make?

### Learning Must Be Greater than the Rate of Change

Intrapreneurial cut and thrust, fueled by strong emotional drive, must be accompanied by intelligent communications if the business is to continually adapt to change. In fact, if learning does not exceed the rate of change, the metaprise will eventually become extinct. If this is not to happen:

- plans must be accompanied by monitoring systems,
- there must be organizational flexibility,
- experimentation must be encouraged at all levels and in all functions,
- new forms of employment contract, such as networking, need to become the order of the day, and
- intelligent machines need to be installed, wherever possible, to speed up response time.

### A Binding Culture Compensates for Nonstop Change

Individual freedom and constant change can lead to fragmentation and chaos unless counterbalanced by a binding culture. In the absence of shared values the metaprise will eventually fall apart. In addressing the following questions, you will be developing a cohesive culture:

- How can you provide ongoing social contact between people within and outside the business?
- How did you uncover and reveal a rich tapestry of anecodote and myth?
- How do you establish supportive rites and rituals?
- How do you ingrain a cast of metapreneurial characters into the cultural fabric?
- How do you provide everyone with access to a wide range of group activity?
- How do you create a family atmosphere within and alongside the metaprise?

### Ultimately There Is Physical Energy

At the end of the day, however cohesive the culture, no matter how quickly people learn, however intraprising the product champions, no matter how well structured the organization, however well attuned the new designers are to human and physical potential, however revolutionary the originating idea, the metaprise will have produced nothing if there is no energy. You need to explore:

- What facilities you have to help your people keep in good physical shape.
- How nourishing is the food you provide.
- What facilities you offer for relaxation.
- Whether the work involves a good balance of physical, mental, and emotional activity.

## Metabeing, Metapreneur,
## and Metaprise

We have now covered the full personal, metapreneurial, and business spectrum. The fully functioning individual, manager of the future, or future business corporation can each be seen in the same "meta" light. Table 1 summarizes the position.

TABLE 1.          Metabeing, Metapreneur, Metaprise

| Individual | Future Manager | Business |
| --- | --- | --- |
| creator | innovator | nucleus |
| intuitor | new designer | harmonic function |
| organizer | executive | formal structure |
| willpower | intrapreneur | profit centers |
| thinker | change agent | adaptive systems |
| feeler | animateur | corporate culture |
| doer | adventurer | energy |

I mentioned at the beginning of this article that individuals and organizations function at different levels of development. Not every willful individual, for example, is a budding intrapreneur. Nor does every formal organization structure channel authority and responsibility effectively. The state of an organism's development is a function of both its differentiation and its integration.

In other words, the successful intrapreneur is the one who can align his or her achievement motive with, as in Jack Dangoor's case, organizational ability and physical momentum. Highly developed metapreneurs function on at least three, if not seven, different cylinders.

They have succeeded in not only developing different parts of themselves, during the course of their lives, but also in integrating them into their composite personalities. While there are seven basic paths to metapreneurial development, each one is enriched by the other—internally, within themselves, and externally, within a business. Metapreneurs are both strong individuals and also whole people.

# CHAPTER 6

# Visionary Leadership: Moving a Company from Burnout to Inspired Performance

by
**DENNIS T. JAFFE**
**CYNTHIA D. SCOTT**
**ESTHER M. ORIOLI**

*Preventing the burnout of key organizational members has become a widespread concern. A number of organizations have made important discoveries which not only have proved to be successful in preventing burnout but also inspire people to peak levels of performance. This chapter describes some of the key personal and organizational skills and attitudes that differentiate the burned out leaders from inspired performers. It is based on the* Heart Work *seminar that has helped leaders and managers renew their connection to their work.*

A company's most valuable resource—the energy, dedication and creativity of its employees—is often squandered by a climate that limits or frustrates the pool of talent and energy that is available. At the extreme, many workers experience "burnout," which is a chronic state of depleted energy, lack of commitment and involvement, continual frustration, often accompanied by physical symptoms, disability claims, and performance-related problems.

Burnout in milder forms has become a problem to leaders and managers at every level, in every type of work. The burned-out manager comes to work bringing a shell rather than a person. He or she experiences little satisfaction and feels uninvolved, detached, and uncommitted to work and coworkers. While one may be effective by external standards, one works far below one's own level of capability and productivity.

At the other extreme, companies have discovered the inspired performer. This manager is excited about work and sees the job as an opportunity to expand his or her capabilities. Their vision and energy is contagious, and they are a great natural resource to a company, as they inspire others and continually exceed expectations. The problems facing the leader—of the organization or the work group—is to create a climate that leads a critical mass of employees toward this performance state.

There is little evidence that people are temperamentally inclined to either burnout or inspired performance. A research study by Robert Golumbiewski (1983) found that if one member of a work group is burned out, then chances are high that the rest of the group is as well. Other researchers have found no personality characteristics that correlate with burnout; anyone seems susceptible under the right conditions. The evidence is growing that certain qualities and norms within work *environments* promote burnout or inspired performance.

For example, recent research on coping with stress finds that certain attitudes seem to promote health. Suzanne Kobasa (1979) compared groups of the healthiest and the unhealthiest managers in a high-stress work environment. The healthy group, who seemingly thrived under stress, differed from the unhealthy group in that they were more *involved* in their work, *welcomed change* as an opportunity to grow and learn, and felt a greater sense of *personal power*. Other studies of healthy personal styles add two factors to this list of qualities of stress-resistant people: drawing on other people for help and support and having a personal sense that what one is doing is important and meaningful. Perhaps an organization whose climate embodies these values might enable all its employees to thrive under stress.

Such research suggests that the same personal qualities that promote health seem also to promote productivity. Inspired performers combine high productivity, personal satisfaction, health and well-being. Burnout represents the opposite extreme. Burned-out managers experience all manners of stress-related ailments—physical and emotional—and their performance is impaired as well. While some people naturally adopt workstyles that lead to burnout or to inspired performance, an inspired performer can be put into a work setting that burns him or her out, and a person prone to burnout can be catalyzed to inspired performance. For this reason, more and more leaders are wondering how to create a climate for inspiring performance.

When leaders are asked to think back to a project or a situation where they felt they were an inspired performer, and then to define the key elements of this state of performance, their reports are surprisingly similar. They felt valued as individuals within their work group, were given a clear project or task that was *meaningful* to them, had the *autonomy* to pursue the project to its conclusion, had clear and open *communication* with other team members and with other parts of the organization, felt they were using their *creative resources* and *growing and learning* within the project, and received *rewards* appropriate to their success. Burned-out executives report that the meaning has gone out of their work, that they do not feel valued or supported in their job, that they can't get things done or don't know what is expected of them, and that they don't feel that they can use their skills in their work.

When the qualities and attitudes that foster an inspired performing system are specified, then a leader can begin to promote them. A research program at ESSI Systems has developed a model of five key skills and attitudes of inspired performance, which holds both for individuals seeking to enhance their effectiveness and for organizations creating climate of health, well-being, and productivity. What follows is a short description of these elements with examples of them as practiced.

The key to developing inspired performance and an inspired organization lies in cultivating resources that lie within the person—deep resources of internal creativity, energy, commitment, and work spirit. In promoting health and managing stress, people need to learn how to pay attention to their inner person. The visionary leader, as we call such a person, is a master not just of the external world, but of the skill of *inner visioning*, a process that involves focusing one's attention inward with the quiet expectancy that something important and relevant will emerge.

The skill of visioning underlies each of the key elements of creating inspired performance, because inspiration involves balancing attention to the external and internal worlds. In this way a leader calls on hidden resources of creativity, commitment, and ability that might have remained out of use. Inspired performers universally report that they regularly tune in to themselves.

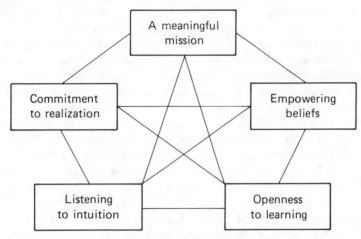

FIGURE 1.　　　　A Model of Inspired Performance:
Key Values and Attitudes

## A MEANINGFUL MISSION

A key function of leadership is to articulate the meaning and purpose of what an organization or group is doing. Many organizations have become so diffuse that they are unclear about their purpose or do not take the time to articulate their mission. Profits are not the mission of a company, just one of its objectives. The articulation of mission—the unique purpose and set of values that guides a company (or a work group)—takes place at two focal points in organizational life. First, when an organization makes a major shift or meets a major challenge, the mission must be redefined. The leader is often effective because he or she has such a powerful sense of meaning that he or she can inspire and carry others along with it.

But it is not enough for one person alone to define a mission. One new CEO, when appointed from outside, held meetings with small work groups. He outlined his vision of what the company was about, but then, instead of saying, "are you with me?," asked for other views. From his conversations, he then drafted a collective mission statement that incorporated many of the themes he had heard along with his input. The commitment level rose perceptively, as managers felt that their sense of what the company was had been recognized and affirmed. Mission-setting is a collective process, not the sole job of the leader.

It is not just an organization alone, but every work team and every individual, that need meaningful missions. When people start jobs, they need to learn about what the organization stands for and connect it with their own needs. When new employees enter an organization, they usually go through an orientation. In some places, they are shown their workspace, the book of procedures, and told to start. In a public utility company, people tell each other during orientation why they have come to work there, they draw pictures that represent how they view their work, and they hear about the company as a whole from their district leader, who talks to them under a large banner with the words "We light up the world." In which situation is the new employee likely to feel more connected and perform better?

People need to feel that what they are doing is meaningful and important and to connect that work with the overall work of the organization, and that what the company does matters to the world in some way. This is the mission of the company, and in order to promote inspired performance, the mission needs to be more than a vague statement of values in the annual report. It needs to be felt by each worker and to be a part of the fabric of the environment. People cannot be expected to perform difficult, stressful, demanding work unless they feel the work is "for" something. Inspired performers report that they feel what they are doing is important, and they identify and feel connected to their organization's goals and values; burned-out employees talk about how they work for their paycheck alone, and have no sense of value of what they do. Defining the organization's mission as a way to inspire employees to want to be part of it is more and more seen as the CEO's key task. Think of how much the inspirational ability of Lee Iacocca was able to mobilize a dispirited workforce when he moved in to Chrysler. Similarly, when any work team or division sees how their new project or task matters, they feel excited to call on more of their abilities and energy. Burned-out employees are quick to say that they feel their efforts don't make any difference.

In one training company, the management team spends a few minutes together each morning talking about their major tasks and goals for the day and relating them to their personal mission. Thus, each person finds a way to discover and create meaning and importance in his or her work.

People have a personal life mission as well, which inspires their careers and development. When it is missing, burnout can occur. For example, in working with a group of physicians, we found that their stress related to the realization that they had entered medicine with an exalted goal of becoming healers and making a difference to others. A key exercise for helping people discover and reconnect to their personal mission is for them to sit quietly and reflect on the early period in their lives when they first decided to enter the field, and recapture in the imagination that spark and excitement. Think of what they decided to stand for, then think of their work right now, and try to see within it the thread of their excitement and dedication. What does the work mean to them? How can they bring that spark into their work *right now*? Often this exercise helps trigger a process of rededication or renewal to managers who are feeling burned out.

## EMPOWERING BELIEFS

People have a set of beliefs and expectations about themselves, about the organization, and about the world. They have, for example, beliefs about their own limits and capabilities ("I'm not a people person"), about their company ("People who do things on their own aren't listened to here"), and about the world in general ("People just don't care"). These beliefs are neither true nor false; but they are the operating premises that guide our choices, our attention, and our efforts. The history of science is filled with examples of research that challenged cherished beliefs and was ignored because it contradicted established wisdom. Sets of beliefs form the culture of the organization.

Certain beliefs help create inspired performance; others can only lead to burnout. For example, in a very well-known activist organization, one belief was that if you were dedicated to the organization's ideals, you should be completely exhausted, overworked, and frustrated about your work. Thus, commitment was defined as burnout. Little wonder that turnover was so high!

Of all beliefs that lead to inspired performance, the most essential one is a sense of personal power, which is held by every person within the organization. The sense of personal power, the belief that one can make a difference, is one of the key elements in inspired performance, and in determining personal health. Power is not the capacity to make others do things, but rather an inner sense of capacity to act and receive reasonable responses from others. Empowered employees feel they have the capacity and support to do their best and to make a contribution.

Some people are so self-critical and have such high expectations that they never feel any sense of satisfaction or achievement. Other people feel so distrustful of others that they wouldn't dream of asking for help or expecting a colleague to come through. Such attitudes become prisons, keeping one continually frustrated and isolated.

Many managers think such attitudes are faithful reflections of the real world. They cite the school of experience, and say that of course their attitudes are "realistic." But in fact, the reality is that attitudes create experiences by fostering certain courses of action. One effective exercise to help managers increase their performance level is to take a job situation they think can't be changed, and brainstorm with a partner or colleague at least ten potential ways the situation could be modified. This generates amazing creativity. For example, one manager talked about how her boss would listen to her initiatives, not acceptingly, and then she would hear nothing further. In brainstorming, she saw how she always left the ball in her boss's court. If she assumed her own personal power, then she might approach him with a request to allow her take action—in her case to negotiate a contract with a client. Thus she would not be waiting for him to act. The response to her request, in fact, was that her boss was excited about the possibility and admitted that he hadn't had the time to act on her previous suggestions. She got a promotion and greater respect.

One theme comes up repeatedly when leaders recall inspired performances. Not only do they feel a sense of personal power, but everyone in the inspired work team feels power as well. This suggests a rule for inspired performance: power is not seen as something one person (the leader) has and others (employees) do not. Rather, in an inspired team everyone feels power. There is not a sense that if I have power you lose power, but rather a perception that as I gain power, so do we all. Inspired performers report that they feel personal power because they feel valued; that whatever contribution they choose to make will be accepted, and that they can take initiatives and be creative.

Some of the mythology about entrepreneurs as creative leaders has a dark side in the area of empowerment. Recently researchers like Manfred Kets and Danny Miller deVries (1984) have explored the phenomenon of "entrepreneur's disease." There seems to be a need for control so great that it will not allow others in the organization to feel a sense of power. The entrepreneur feels he or she is the only one who can be creative, and does not see other managers as having the same needs. Other organizations flourish because the founders are genuinely excited about working with other creative people and define each new role while taking the unique creative capacities and interests of the employee into account. They write a job description around the person, rather than fit a person into a slot!

Like an individual, an organization has attitudes and beliefs as well. These form the organization's climate and culture: the set of expectations, norms, values, and ways of seeing things that make it unique and special. The attitudes that foster inspired performance are those that expect the best from managers, expecting them to improve and come through, and that value people who work there. A good example of the shift in an organization toward empowering beliefs is represented in the current U.S. Army campaign asking recruits to "Be all that you can be," which contrasts with the concepts of warrior and automation, which has historically been connected with the soldier's image.

Empowering responses by leaders can inspire resources in many situations. One way to empower people in an organization is not to communicate decisions from on high, but rather to explore how to implement them with the people affected. In one place, there were two managers in line for a key division leadership position. Traditionally, the hierarchical structure of organizations makes the person who is passed over feel so disempowered that he or she soon leaves, depriving the organization of experience and dedication. Here, however, the CEO first met with the woman who was passed over. He told her the reasons for the decision and asked her to stay. Then, he offered her a month's sabbatical and asked her to think about her role and about how the organization was run. He recognized her deep feelings of loss and worked to help her discover a unique way to use her creativity. She defined a new staff role, did not accept the tempting offers from other organizations, and worked side by side with the new division chief.

## OPENNESS TO LEARNING

One of the greatest obstacles to inspired performance in an organization is when a person has a good idea or sees something that could be changed but feels the people above, or the organization as a whole, "doesn't want to hear." In an era when innovation is the norm (when, for example the whole mission and direction of the world's largest corporation, AT&T, has shifted in the space of a year), it is suicidal to not want to learn and explore new possibilities, to be chained to traditional ways. An organization, like an individual, must continually grow, change, adapt, and learn new things, or it decays and dies. Perhaps the most important factor that leads a person from normal to inspired performance is a special challenge or an exciting idea that really moves them. Then the innovator is willing to dedicate tremendous time and energy to see the project through, often above and beyond the organization's expectations. Unhappily, many organizations respond to such excitement the way the original employers of the founders of Apple Computer did when presented with the idea of the portable personal computer—"we're not interested."

Studies of values and lifestyles conducted by SRI International (Mitchell, 1983) note that a growing number of managers are motivated less by external rewards and status than by the inner sense of challenge and creativity of their work. They assume that they will be well paid and respected; but in addition they want to learn and grow in their work. High-tech companies are recruiting talent not by offering the highest salaries, but by offering the opportunity to work long and hard on difficult problems. In both studies, the challenge of work was high on the list of incentives, while pay and external perks were much further down.

A willingness to learn implies a willingness to make mistakes. Management theorist Warren Bennis, in his book *Leaders* (1985), notes that successful leaders are always willing to fail (although they never use that term), seeing risk and making mistakes as an inherent part of success. Every inspired performance involves some element of risk—trying something without any certainty of a successful outcome. The excitement of a sport, or learning a new skill, comes from pushing oneself slightly (but not too far) beyond the boundaries of what one is capable. This is inspired performance—the risk generates the excitement. A company needs to reward risk-takers, people who are willing to bend the rules for what they believe in, and who make mistakes that they learn from along the way.

What happens if an organization decides to promote risk and innovation? First, many employees at all levels become involved in problem-exploring, planning, and in change-oriented groups such as new product or problem task forces that span many levels. In one organization, there is a group of new project teams generating ideas, and any employee can serve on one or more of them. When an innovation such as quality circles or a stress-management program is to be instituted, another task force is created to put it into place.

A learning climate in an organization is one where any employee is valued because he or she might be the source of the next creative innovation. Open channels of communication, which many places preach, means that people at many levels and within many different areas and work groups have the opportunity to get together and exchange information. When there is a problem in an organization, it is not shunted to one person or one department, but several groups look at it from their disparate perspectives. The solution generated by many groups, which are open to learning from each other and not competing for who is best, is better than that of any creative individual.

Finally, a learning climate means a willingness to anticipate and listen to bad news, so that the final word does not come when the roof falls in. For example, in one company there was a CEO whose response to anyone questioning his rosy projections was to cross-examine that person mercilessly. The norm was soon established that bad news does not flow upwards. Such was the case in Nixon's White House during the Watergate crisis.

Many managers burn out because they see ways to innovate or things they want to do, but they assume they are blocked. An exercise helpful in liberating blocked energy is to think about what they want to have happen on their job, and then to define several risks they could take to make it happen. This often involves testing, or even challenging, an organizational norm, such as not airing a conflict in the open, or not suggesting a change in an established procedure. However, the usual discovery is that fear of risks is more internal than external, and many organizations are actually appreciative of a manager who takes chances. Risks are scary because the outcome can be negative; for example, one manager told a group about an innovative program she put into effect that had outstanding results with clients. Six months later she was fired. She later said that being fired was the best thing that ever happened to her, because she found a new position in a place that really valued her creativity and energy.

## LISTENING TO INTUITION

Many organizations see careful planning as a process of rational exploration of alternatives and deliberation within a fixed decision format. But, looking at inspired performances and creative problem-solving, the most powerful ideas and responses rarely were obvious or rational outgrowths of data. As the environment of an organization shifts, it becomes impossible to rely exclusively on rational planning. Inspired performers utilize another form of planning and decision-making. This is intuition, a way of knowing, which according to psychologist Frances Vaughan (1979) recognizes the possibilities in any situation. Many decisions involve what are labeled "hunches," meaning that they go beyond the information given about a problem, to see it in a new way, or see a new possibility. A study by management professor Weston Agor (1984) found that intituitive managers are more likely to be found at the top levels of the organization, suggesting that this skill is important for top performers.

Every person receives intuitive hunches about many things. Most people do not attend to them, or dismiss them as irrational. Inspired performers report that they immerse themselves in data and problems, and then they sleep on it, consult with a wide variety of other people, or just spend unstructured time letting things settle, until a new pattern or way of seeing it becomes clear. When the new way appears, there is a feeling sense, usually an energizing effect, that this way will work. The person who makes this intuitive leap is usually excited about it and willing to take responsibility and put excess energy into getting it done.

This skill is reported by most inspired performers, *and can be developed by anyone through practice.* One helpful technique is the use of guided imagination. Persons close their eyes and rest quietly, getting a whole sense of a problem or decision. They see themselves as observers, detached yet interested, and allow their minds to create a picture or image that relates to the issue in question. The resulting images often contain important information about unintended consequences, unexplored possibilities, hidden dangers, or questions that lurk just below awareness.

Tracy Kidder, in *The Soul of a New Machine* (1981), about the high-performing team that created a new computer in just over a year, reports how the project leader was feeling negative and uninvolved in the project until an image of how the internal storage system of the computer could work in a completely new way turned him on and mobilized him to dedicate himself to the new project. From this vision of a new way, he was able to inspire his similarly dispirited work team. His excitement about his innovation was communicated to others, who now felt they were working on a creative breakthrough rather than a humdrum rehash of a competitor's product.

It is important to see how intuition is an extension of rationality and empirical data, not a rejection of it. Intuitive leaps reportedly take place after a long period of reflection, when all the data have been deeply studied and explored. Then, as happened above, there comes a period of tiredness, when a wall appears, blocking the solution. The intuitive leader then switches gears. He or she takes time off, or changes pace. Often a walk in a garden, or a game of tennis, can lead to an intuitive leap much more quickly than another day at the computer!

Another way imagery can be used to generate intuition is to take a possible course of action and imagine, in as vivid detail as possible, how it will work out in practice. While other ways of thinking about decisions and planning are certainly important, inspired performers report that the utilization of such intuitive and inner imagery-based processes often provide the breakthrough that creates excitement and new direction.

## COMMITMENT TO REALIZATION

There is quite a difference between creative daydreaming and actually making a creative project come to fruition. Inspired performers aren't dreamers, they validate themselves through results. Similarly, some of the most burned-out managers are people who came to their jobs brimming with excitement, new ideas, and a sense of possibility. One difference between the two groups is that the inspired performers have explicitly committed themselves to making it happen and have recruited a group of people within their company with a similar orientation. This group then makes sure the organization commits to the project and does so with the resources — time, money, and energy — to make it go.

Commitment is saying that one will persist in making something happen despite adversity, unexpected obstacles, and a great energy investment. It involves a sense of inner certainty, which even extends, in many inspired performers, to actually seeing oneself achieving success. For example, in the absurdly competitive world of movie screenwriters, those who succeed all have stories of how many years they persisted in their labors before their big break. They do not see their break as lucky, but rather as the logical outgrowth of the immense, unfailing energy and belief in their project.

Inspired leaders are known for their single-mindedness of vision. They do not go it alone, but continually present their vision to others. In this process, the vision becomes expanded to fit other people's resources. A successful vision, in coming to reality, must pass through several sets of hands. When this coalition-building process is successful, the project gains the commitment of the whole organization.

Another aspect of commitment is the response to setbacks and frustrations. A burned-out leader takes a setback, such as a vote of no confidence, as cause to scrap the project, and to blame the person or situation that caused the difficulty. An inspired performer does not pull back or give up, but rethinks and continues to press or explore alternatives. This aspect of commitment, knowing obstacles will occur and seeing them as challenges to overcome, is a characteristic of inspired performers. Organizational folklore is overflowing with stories of how people forged approvals, convened groups in secret, or went around negative reports or nay-sayers, to finally achieve success. Gifford Pinchot's account of internal change agents, *Intrapreneuring* (1984), talks about the lengths to which creative managers have gone to bring their vision into reality. The theme of these stories is that creativity, risk, and, finally, persistence and commitment, lead to payoff.

The essential task of the commitment phase is the creation of a personal action plan. With a mission, personal power, openness to learning and intuitive planning, an inspired performer must now commit to a course of action. The creation of a personal action plan, to realize explicitly a set of goals flowing from one's mission, is as necessary for an individual manager as it is for a leader and an organization. When a person has a sense of direction, and criteria for success and achievement, then his energy can flow freely into a project.

Until a few years ago, managers tended to accept the assumption that an organization by definition has to frustrate individual excitement, creativity, and initiative in order to pursue its collective goals. Now, a new image is emerging. The negative consequences of organizations that frustrate and neglect the human tendency to be alive and creative, in even the most mundane types of work, include burnout, diminished personal performance, lack of motivation, poor morale, and poor organizational effectiveness. These hurt the organizations and create pain and difficulty for individuals. What is new is the possiblity that organizations can grow to utilize the potential of individuals to become inspired performers and that this new type of organization, which values people, is precisely the organization model best suited to adapt and thrive in the new business environment.

A visionary leader can create a climate in an organization that creates inspired performance and diminishes burnout. As an added consequence, the evidence is that the pursuit of inspired performance, as defined here, is also related to personal health and well-being of employees. While external structures and exciting projects are important aspects of effective organizations, our theme has been that the organization also reflects certain inner values, attitudes, and utilization of managers' inner resources. The visionary leader, we suggest, is one who is able to tap every employee's inner capacities, to liberate commitment, spirit, and creativity. Each of the five key areas we have presented can be valued and cultivated in management processes—as part of planning, organizational design, management development, conflict resolution, and evaluation. They are essential tools for the transformational leader.

# CHAPTER 7

# Transformed Leadership: Two Contrasting Concepts

by
**WILLIS W. HARMAN**

*Two of the characteristics frequently cited as being needed by modern leaders are participatory skills and creative/intuitive skills. These skills are rooted in quite different conceptual processes, and in order to fully develop both, an understanding of these different processes is needed. This chapter explores each skill area and list the implications of each for leadership behavior.*

Two current concepts of transformed leadership concur in the conviction that bureaucratic or hierarchical forms of management are due to be replaced by something better. One concept stresses participatory management; the other, intuitive leadership. These two concepts have different underlying assumptions about the nature of the human mind, about decision-making and about the nature of power. These contrasts have profound implications for management and for leadership education.

## PARTICIPATORY MANAGEMENT

Abraham Maslow (1954), as much as any single person, articulated the underlying dynamic of the familiar concept of "new" leadership. He elucidated the distinction between deficiency-motivation and being-motivation, or self-actualization. The deficiency-motivated person fits compliantly into bureaucratic management. As more people display self-actualizing tendencies, there is more chafing at the oppressiveness of hierarchies and demand for a more democratic form. Leadership becomes shared power, rather than the use of power to direct resources to achieve desired ends.

In the familiar concept of participatory management, decisions are made with the maximum feasible involvement of those whose lives are affected by the outcome. Efforts are made to foster humanistic values—trust, honesty, cooperation, caring, and personal responsibility—and to develop authentic personal relationships. Participatory management may appear to be inefficient initially, but in the end, it raises morale, increases the sense of involvement with meaningful activity, increases individual incentive, improves efficiency and productivity, and encourages a sense of social responsibility.

This concept of leadership is based on two conflicting premises. The first is that persons need, and rightfully demand, opportunities for learning, self-validation, and individual growth in all their social roles, especially as workers and concerned citizens. The second is that management must contribute to organizational goals such as efficiency, institutional growth, bureaucratic self-preservation, and productivity. Management must not seek to achieve the person-centered goal of meaningful, self-chosen, fulfilling, growth-promoting work in ways that threaten organizational goals. In general—and there are few exceptions—organizational goals take precedence over humanistic goals, and this evaluation is taken to be reasonable, practical, and inevitable.

The second concept of transformed leadership would have seemed so visionary as to be unworthy of serious attention until recently. Some background is required to discuss it.

## ACCESSING THE CREATIVE/
## INTUITIVE MIND

How leadership is viewed depends on the image of the leader and his or her ultimate motivations. There is a trans-Maslovian image emerging in the culture, and to some extent in science, which is associated with the second concept of leadership.

The form of science that evolved in Western industrial society has strongly influenced the prevailing images of ourselves and of our relationships to one another and to the universe. That form has been strongly positivistic and reductionistic; that is, what is real was assumed to be what is physically measurable (e.g., brainwaves are real in a sense that conscious awareness is not). Preferred explanations were in terms of elementary phenomena (e.g., color in terms of wavelengths; hate and love in terms of the chemical composition of glandular secretions). The bias was toward scientific knowledge that would be useful in creating technology—knowledge that would enable one to predict and control.

Nobel laureate neuroscientist Roger Sperry pointed out (1981) that overemphasis on this kind of science leads to neglect of the realm of human inner experience—that deep intuitive realm out of which individuals and societies obtain not only their most creative and noble impulses but also their sense of ultimate values and meanings.

The power of scientific persuasion was such that in the conflict between science and religion that characterized the earlier part of this century, it was widely assumed that materialistic science had won, hands down. The victory was so complete and the prestige of science so intimidating, that people either denied or concealed their sense of the authenticity of their own spiritual experience to avoid appearing naive.

A significant reassessment of the situation has been taking place over the past quarter-century. In the popular culture there is renewed interest in a wide range of religious spiritual, and psychic topics. Some of this activity seems to be a wholesome search for self-understanding; some of it smacks of escapism or neurotic grasping for certainty. It could be assumed that these interests are a passing fad, except for the related scientific developments relating to human consciousness and unconscious processes.

Central in these new developments is the recognition of the key role of the unconscious mind. Only the smallest fraction of our total mental activity is conscious; the greater part is unconscious, known only by inference and rarely glimpsed. This includes reflexes, habitual behavior, and psychological defense mechanisms (e.g., repression). It includes the unconscious conditioning and cultural "hypnosis" we have picked up from the "suggestions" of the surrounding milieu. It also includes that "supraconscious" activity implied by such terms as intuition, creative imagination, symbolic dreams, aesthetic sense, and spiritual insight.

Our perceptions, motivations, values, and behavior are powerfully affected by our unconscious conditioning — in a sense, our unconscious beliefs. The unconscious belief system limits us in pervasive and powerful ways. In our intellectual abilities, in our leadership capabilities, in effectiveness of communication, in our ability to heal our own illnesses, in our capacity for awareness of the joys and deeper meanings in life, we limit ourselves by our beliefs and expectations. Particularly limiting are unconscious beliefs in our own unworthiness or inferiority.

These limitations restrict access to the creative/intuitive mind. The annals of scientific discovery are replete with anecdotes describing how insight seems to come from some behind-the-scenes creative process, often after the conscious, rational mind has "tried everything," and often when the conscious mind is distracted from the problem, as during a nap or a walk. Business executives, architects, inventors, poets, artists, and composers have all experienced this creative process, yet we have been largely unwilling to draw its fuller implications.

There has been a recent proliferation of leadership development courses and seminars that use self-suggestion, affirmation, and inner imaging to access and use the creative/intuitive mind. Most startling has been the sudden popularity of the firewalking workshops in which thousands of business and professional persons have, in the past two years, dramatically demonstrated to themselves the power of their own minds to enable them, by a change of consciousness, to walk barefoot over burning coals without harming their feet.

Whereas in other, "prescientific," societies there may have been beliefs that one's mind could affect another at a distance, or one could clairvoyantly perceive distant strayed cattle or relatives, or one could walk barefoot on burning coals, those sorts of phenomena were not observed in the course of the usual scientific investigation, nor typically encountered by the sophisticated and well-educated. It comes as a shock to recognize the extent to which the internalized belief system, the cultural and subcultural "hypnosis," affects the apparent occurrence or nonoccurrence of such phenomena.

Thus it is by no means clear what limits exist for the creative/intuitive mind. The more this "other" part of the mind is trusted and used, the better it seems to perform. Many of the most successful leaders seem, by their own testimony, to have taken a next step. If this other mind is so much more knowledgeable and wise than one's conscious ego-mind, if it has access to all the knowledge available to consciousness and more, then why stop at submitting to it only the specific problems and questions that the ego-mind has classified as difficult? Why keep it for emergency use only? Why not turn to it with all decisions, including the most important, such as the question: What do I most want to do with my life?

This proposal arouses considerable inner resistance. We need not seek far for the reason. To choose to have one's life guided by the deep intuitive mind, the "true Self" or "divine Center," is to dethrone the ego-mind. It gives deep intuition precedence over plans and expectations, goals and ambitions, rational analyses, ethical and moral rules, and all the other ways in which the ego-mind seeks control — and which we were all taught were admirable ways to make decisions. The ego-mind typically throws up a flurry of reasons as to why this challenge to its authority is both foolish and dangerous.

Of course there are some legitimate cautions. Not everything that sounds like an inner voice turns out to be trustworthy. Just as you can be fooled by an optical illusion, it is possible to be deceived by what appears to be an inner vision. There are appropriate tests and safeguards.

Interestingly enough, both the basic proposal to relinquish choice to the deep mind, and the practical understanding of tests and safeguards, turn out to have been around for thousands of years. The world's spiritual traditions represent a universal human experience, however much the outward forms of the various religions may differ. In this esoteric "perennial wisdom," the central advice is precisely to discover this inner intuitive or spiritual guidance, and to turn life's choices over to it.

A host of sages, from Socrates to Ouspensky, have insisted that we are hypnotized from infancy by the culture we are born into, and that a central task of adult life is to "know thyself" — to become enlightened, or dehypnotized. In that enlightenment comes the realization that the mind is far vaster than the ego-mind, that individual minds are not as separate as we may have been taught, and that each individual mind has potential awareness of the whole.

During the heyday of positivistic, reductionistic, behavioristic science in the earlier part of this century, it was fashionable among the highly educated to assume that science had thoroughly debunked this and all other religious concepts of a transcendental, essentially nonmeasureable aspect to total human experience. In the 1980s we are on the whole far more humble with regard to claiming that the measurements of science preclude the existence of the unmeasureable, and also more optimistic that further scientific exploration of human consciousness will tend to support rather than debunk the basic premise of human spirituality.

A variety of techniques can be found in these various traditions for discovering these aspects of the mind, and for reprogramming the unconscious belief system to better serve us. One of the most potent of these is self-suggestion — repeated self-reminding of one's intention to refer all choices to the deep mind.

## CREATIVE/INTUITIVE LEADERSHIP

This changing perception of the human mind and spirit leads to a new concept of leadership, or, an old kind of leadership returning to favor. This is leadership in which the creative/intuitive mind is not merely relied on for solutions to problems and good business decisions, but in which problems are transformed and decisions are made in a much broader and deeper context.

Perry Pascarella (1984), executive editor of *Industry Week,* writes in his recent book *The New Achievers*:

> A quiet revolution is taking place . . . in the business corporation . . . The revolutionaries are not from the ranks of the downtrodden, but from upper management. They recognize that people can do more and be more than is generally expected of them in the workplace . . . Although we have been hearing more and more about corporate efforts in human resource development in recent years, we may miss the essential truth about what is happening: Individuals are awakening to the possibility of personal growth and finding opportunities to attain it. The team building we hear about is secondary to the development of the individual.

Kiefer and Senge (1984) observed a "new Management style," in (mainly small) organizations characterized by:

- a strong and deep sense of *purposefulness* and a *vision* of the future
- a high degree of *alignment* of members at all levels, involving commitment to the shared vision
- a *shared sense of ownership* and personal responsibility for performance
- *decentralized* and *flexible* organizational structures
- an environment that emphasizes growth and *empowerment* of the individual as the key to corporate success.

The role of power in this concept of management is distinctive. Whereas in traditional management power is used by the manager to utilize resources to achieve desired ends, and in participatory management power is to some extent shared with those being managed, in this "new leadership," power is given away. As Pascarella puts it:

> Management is heading toward a new state of mind — a new perception of its own role and that of the organization. It is slowly moving from seeking power to empowering others, from controlling people to enabling them to be creative. . . .

The function of the leader is to *empower* others to use their own creativity to accomplish goals that are emergent in the total situation.

Notice a key implication of what was stated earlier about the changing concept of mind. If minds are joined, as is suggested by these arguments and research findings, then the knowledge potentially available to assist in making wise decisions is not limited to one individual's education and experience. Moreover, the kind of solution to be expected is qualitatively different. If my mind were separated from others, my supraconscious mind might be expected to provide a solution that would be in *my* self-interest; if our minds are part of a "collective supraconscious mind," I can expect to be furnished a solution that will be best for *us*.

This suggestion that the deep intuition might be able to lead us to the best choices, individually and collectively, may sound at first like a dreamy religious concept long since supplanted by a more scientific approach. But this sort of decision-guiding, by collective referral to the deep intuition, is precisely that recommended by those eminently practical individuals known as the Founding Fathers of this nation. Almost all of them were strongly influenced by the Rosicrucian/Freemasonry tradition in which true choosing results when the person puts himself and his work in the service of "the Divine Architect." (Hall, 1923) To remind future generations of the kind of decision-guidance implicit in their concept of democracy, they selected (1782) for the reverse side of the Great Seal of the United States (now reproduced on the back of the dollar bill) an unfinished pyramid with the All-Seeing Eye in the capstone position symbolizing that the structure is not complete until the divine intuition is in the central guiding position.

Leadership is always oriented toward some goal. *If the goal is inadequate, the leadership cannot be good leadership*—no matter how efficiently the enterprise is managed. Superior leadership implies a deep intuitive sense of ethical values and human goals. That is to be distinguished from both adherence to some set of ethical rules and from overemphasis on external organizational goals.

We earlier noted an inherent conflict in the first-described concept of humanistic-participatory leadership, namely, the conflict between the humanistic goals of the leader and the assumed goals of the organization. In the second concept, which has many of the characteristics of the first but also an essential difference, the conflict is resolved in a way that may not be obvious. If my choosing is guided from the deep intuitive mind, which is in touch with all others, I would not expect that guidance to be in conflict with that intuited by my fellow human beings. I would not expect, for example, that it would be in conflict with the real best interests of an organization I am employed by, or those of the constituency that elected me.

The "perennial wisdom" has been around for thousands of years. It is found at the inner core of all the world's religions, Eastern and Western, ancient and modern. It is woven into institutionalized Christianity. Its Hermetic, Cabalistic, Sufistic, and Rosicrucian forms affected the history of the Middle East and of Europe. It is not ultimately in conflict with the spirit of modern scientific inquiry. As previously noted, its Freemasonry form played a critical role in the American democratic experiment.

A concept of leadership that has its roots in this ancient wisdom seems to have something going for it.

# CHAPTER 8

# Leadership
# by Indirection

by

**HARRISON OWEN**

*In situations characterized by turbulence, rapid communications, and intense economic pressures—so very common to many organizations today—the usual modes of leadership are not sufficient. Owen suggests that organizations may be viewed as flows of energy and spirit, and that the leader's task is to focus these flows toward desired outcomes. Several case studies are included which illustrate the use of myth and ritual to focus organizational energy and spirit.*

*Take Charge!* This, suggests the title of a recent book on leadership*, is the essence of leadership. The notion of "taking charge" connotes a powerful, controlling force, which, against all odds, molds and shapes an organization in the ways of high performance. The leader emerges as the dominant power, brooking no interference and directing the destiny of HIS (I use the masculine possessive pronoun intentionally) ship. Taking charge, assuming command, directing with authority, all are part of the ideation and vocabulary of organizational life. But is it adequate, and more specifically, is it adequate to the kind of world we inhabit?

We know without documentation, although documentation is readily at hand (Naisbitt 1983, Toffler 1981, Yankelovich 1981), that these are the days of Ready, Fire, Aim. The environment, and organizations within that environment, are changing so fast in themselves and in relationship to each other, that the days of quiet planning preceding action are numbered, if not over. Plans are overtaken by events, and the leader who would take charge, assume command, and direct the course of events may be excused if a sense of frustration, and even despair, creeps into consciousness.

Of course, there are methods and technologies available to deal with the potential mayhem—not the least of which is the rapid increase in the quality, capacity,

---

*Leaders: The Strategies of Taking Charge *(Bennis and Nanus, 1985). In all fairness to Bennis, he presents a rather different view of leadership than the connotations of his title would suggest. Perhaps he should have chosen a different title, but in any event the notion of powerful direction is deeply rooted, and the words he selected capture the idea.*

and speed of our ability to communicate with each other given us by the omnipresent computer. As the world speeds, so must we speed our capability to bring information from the site of decision-making to the point of action. Yet the computer, which seems to be our salvation, is also the problem, for as we are able to communicate more rapidly in one area, all other areas slow down proportionately. Einstein was right—when dealing in the world of high energy and speed, everything is relative. We have joined Alice *Through the Looking Glass*.

> Said Alice to the Red Queen, following a mad dash through the garden, "Why I do believe that we have been under this tree the whole time!" "Of course," said the Queen, "what would you have it?" "Well in our country," said Alice, still panting a little, "you generally get to somewhere else . . . if you ran for a long time, as we have been doing." "A slow sort of country!" said the Queen. "Now here it takes all the running you can do just to keep in the same place. If you want to get somewhere else, you must run twice as fast." (Carroll, 1891).

Running twice as fast, on the same old track, just does not seem to be in the cards—not unless we can make some major, and highly improbable, changes in human physiology and psychology. It appears that we are approaching, if indeed we have not passed, the point of burnout (witness the current proliferation of stress management workshops.) Perhaps it is now time to follow the advice of Peters and Waterman (1985), and go "back to basics." The basics I have in mind are not the "fundamentals of a business," but rather the elemental realities that underlie business—and in fact all of human life. The critical question is, is the "same old track" the *only track*, or is there a different way to go? And if there is a different track, is there a new way of running that is both appropriate to the circumstances and to our capacities? Put bluntly—is it possible to lead without killing yourself?

In what follows, I propose to explore precisely such a new track (which is, in fact, a very old one) along with a new way of leading, which has been practiced in one form or another since the dawn of recorded history. The new track exists at the level of energy and spirit, and I would call the new leadership, *leadership by indirection*.

When events and organizational structures come and go with the rapidity of trees viewed through the window of a speeding train, discreteness and form disappear in a blur. For those who seek to lead by controlling each structure and every event, the net effect is severe eyestrain and, ultimately despair. However, were it possible to make sense out of the blur and pass over or beyond the discrete entities of experience—the structures and events—what is presently a maddening and impossible situation might be converted to something of greater sanity and utility.

But how do you make sense out of a blur, which by definition is nonsensical? In physical terms (on the train) this may be accomplished by letting go of the effort to see each tree in its separateness and concentrate on the pattern or flow. But in the real world of organizations, such visual sleight-of-hand seems less than possible, unless of course there is "something" underlying the events and structures that might become sense-able, were we able to perceive it. Taking a bold step, with no effort to prove my statement, let me suggest that the "something" is energy—or more appropriately *spirit*. The forms and structures of our world would then become momentary expressions of that spirit as it moves on its way — trans*forms*, if you will.

Conversations about spirit have typically been reserved to the shadow world of religion and strictly avoided in the harsh realities of everyday business. It is true that occasionally leaders will slip and say something about the importance of spirit, as in the "spirit of this place" or "esprit de corps." But beyond that, the references are minimal and not generally enlightening. The truth of the matter is that we have forgotten how to talk about spirit, and thus, when called upon to do so, we have little to say. Our forgetfulness was not happenstantial, but rather a direct derivative from our Western scientific tradition which, upon occasion, seems to be saying "if you can't count it, it doesn't exist." Since nobody has ever counted or measured spirit, at least in terms of therms, ergs, or pounds, there has arisen a tacit (sometimes overt) assumption that it doesn't exist. Most of the rest of the world (numerically) is not afflicted with a similar impediment, but then most of the rest of the world has not been subject to the benefits *and liabilities* of Western scientific thought.

So we speak of spirit at some risk. But on the off chance that the rest of the world knows something we don't know, and that the lapses of our leaders, when they refer to spirit, are more than just words, I propose a project of thought. Let us suppose that spirit (literally "breath" or "wind") is that vital energy or force that underlies all physical reality. Our organizations then, including their structures and forms, are purely and simply manifestations of that spirit, which may exist in time and space only to pass away to be replaced by new forms. What endures is spirit. Thus, if we were to "get back to basics" — that which is truly primal — we would see our organizations as spirit and flow, and leadership would be understood as the capacity to focus the spirit and enhance its power.

## ORGANIZATION AS SPIRIT

Imagine that your organization is no longer a collection of bodies, buildings, and machines. Rather, it is a flow of energy and spirit directed toward the accomplishment of certain concrete tasks or objectives.

The essential task is to keep the spirit coherent and directed toward the job at hand. Under the circumstances, turbulence is to be avoided, if only because that represents a nonproductive dissipation of energy. By the same token, little side-eddies of spirit constitute a net drain on available power, for they are not focused on the task at hand. Ideally, the spirit will be focused with laser-like intention on the job. The quality and level of power will be sufficient for the task, but no more. Too much power, and the "deal will be blown;" not enough, and things will never lift off the ground.

But notice that there is not just one job in the immediate future, but a series of them. If we have learned anything about the nature of our present environment, it is that things are in constant change. Therefore, we may assume that whatever the new job may be, it will be different from the present one. That is the meaning of ready, fire, aim. In the "old days," we might expect the same old thing, time after time, but now, the same old thing comes almost as a surprise. Like AT&T, we wake up one

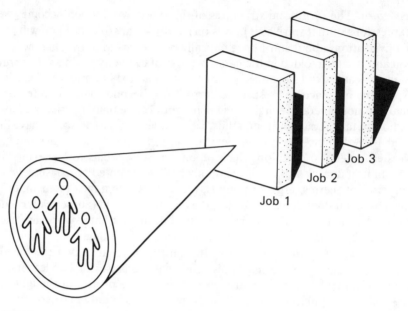

FIGURE 1.

morning and find that the whole world has changed. We used to be the phone company, but now it seems that our spirit is required to focus upon whole new occupations, quite unlike anything we have attempted before.

So the issue in front of us is not just doing the job, but perhaps even more importantly, redirecting and reconfiguring the energy and spirit to perform a whole new task—quite unrelated to what went before. The military has a phrase that neatly captures the idea: "redeploy the force." Indeed the military is a prime example of the issue at hand. Under the conditions of peace, there is a structure (configuration of spirit) that is appropriate to the circumstances. But under the conditions of war, something very different is required, and the peace time way of doing business will no longer work. The difference in circumstances may be obvious, but the time available for the change is infinitesimal; indeed, it may well be measured in nanoseconds. Traditional strategies for transition management are overwhelmed by the speed and magnitude of the change, and victory will go to the swift.

How do you focus spirit and, if required, cause its rapid redirection? Superficially the needed action may appear as a flurry of memos and orders, which all too often are lost or misunderstood. But what is the alternative.?

We would do well to remember that the object of our concern is spirit and energy. Whatever it is that we do should be appropriate and efficacious in that realm. At this point, we might borrow a leaf from the notebook of the high energy physicists who had an analogous if not similar problem. For them the question was, how do you focus energy so that a particular task might be accomplished—splitting an atom, for example. They discovered that sledgehammers were too gross, and chemical reactions did not reach the needed level of intensity. In short, the old ways of directing the elements of the environment were ineffective at the level of their concern.

**114**

To direct energy, the physicists had to use energy. This meant constructing cyclotrons and linear accelerators that could create high energy fields (magnetic fields) through which they might shape and direct the errant particles (or were they waves?) toward their intended destination. When the focus was clear, and the power great, the task was accomplished. The atom split.

The analogue, for our purposes, is the *culture* of the organization. Anthropologist Edward Hall (1977) says that "culture is man's medium," which we may understand as the nutrient milieu in which man, in all aspects, grows. Culture should not be limited to its artifacts—specific pieces of art, architecture or music. Each of these artifacts is expressive of culture, and important for the shaping of man (we really should say spirit), but culture is something more. *Culture is the dynamic field within which the spirit of man assumes its shape and gets the job done.*

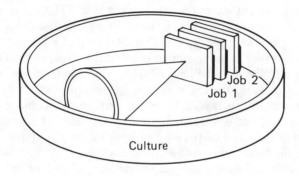

FIGURE 2.

In the powerful, well-formed cultures, the spirit is strong, and tasks are accomplished with dispatch. But when the culture (dynamic field) becomes weak, flaccid, and incoherent, the spirit loses its intention and direction. So if our intention is to ensure that the spirit of a particular organization is adequate to the task at hand, and to those tasks that may lie just over the horizon, our area of operation will be the culture of the organization.

But how can we effectively influence something as diaphanous as a "dynamic field?" A clue is provided by the word "culture" itself. You will notice that the first four letters of the word "culture" are *cult*. This suggests, at least in terms of the structure of the way we say things, that somewhere in the heart of every culture there is a cult. While this may be on the order of "chop linguistics," the derivation of "cult" and "culture" are interesting. Both come from the Latin *colere*, which means to nourish or grow. The word "cultivate" comes from the same root, as also "agri*culture.*" So what does the "culture" grow? People. Or more accurately, people in all their dimensions. On the assumption that words are more than an assemblage of letters, telling us something useful about who we are and how we got that way, we may be led to an interesting thought. If the object of our concern is spirit, the *medium* is culture, and the *mechanism* cult.

The use of the word "cult" may conjure up images of Jonestown and other strange phenomena, and certainly that is the way the word is most often used today.

To assume, however, that the definition of "cult" begins and ends with the Jonestowns of this world is to place unnecessary limits on a very powerful word. While it is quite true that aberrant forms of cult can be strange, even demonic, cult in itself points to a much deeper and more powerful reality. For the cult is that mechanism, internal to culture, which establishes values and behavioral patterns—in short, the way "things get done" or "should get done" in a particular culture.

The contemporary interest in organizational culture is a start, but to be more than a mere curiosity, this interest must move beyond superficialities and appearances to central mechanisms and what those mechanisms do. Cult is such a central mechanism. Whether it be a department store, AT&T, or the corner drugstore, there lies at the heart of each culture some "entity" whose job it is to care for how things get done. What is the proper mode of behavior worthy of reward, and concurrently, what is improper, worthy of censure? The operation of the cult may be quite informal, a vague but powerful sense of how things are here. Then again, the cult may become quite visible and structured, as in formal religions and other large organizations. But the task is always the same: the specification of right and wrong—values, which is really just a way of talking about the quality and capacity of spirit desired.

To operate effectively at the level of spirit, with the intention of focusing that spirit in meaningful ways, the key is the cult at the center of the culture. But how does the cult accomplish its task? The means may appear as black magic, or rigid authoritarian control, and it is true that some cults operate this way and thereby effectively constrain the spirit of people and limit its growth and development. But this need not be the case, and to stop with these answers is to miss the essential tools available to the cult. It is also to confuse *means* with *effects*, for the tools of the cult are neutral, albeit powerful. They may therefore be used in very destructive ways, but such destructiveness is not inherent to the tools themselves. It is value-added by the users.

The tools of the cult are essentially two: myth and ritual. In common parlance, myth refers to idle tales from another age with little truth and less utility. This is typically the best we can say about myth. Ordinarily, myth means lie or falsehood. Such an understanding is far removed from a classical definition, but more to the point, this usage limits or precludes our ability to perceive and utilize a very powerful aspect of our common life. Myth is not "just a story," rather, it is The Story—the narrative context in which our lives make sense. Myth is neither true nor false but rather *behind* truth, as that setting or paradigm (Kuhn 1962) through which we perceive the true to be true. Ritual is simply *acted myth*—The Story set to music and movement.

In simplest terms, myth is the story of how things are around here. When you know the story, everything makes sense. If you don't know the story, it's all one big mystery. Thus it is that the fortunate "new hire" in an organization is taken out and told the "real story." That is myth.

More formally, *myth is a likely story that arises out of the life of the group, through which they experience their past, present, and potential.* As a *likely story*, myth could have happened, but that need not be the case. As a matter of fact, some of the best myths never occurred historically, but they still do a marvelous job in communicating the spirit of a place. So myth is *not* history, but that does not make it any the less powerful.

116

Myth *arises from the life of a group*, which means that the terms of the story are indigenous to that organization and no other. Myth is literally Our Story. This means that it will probably sound quite strange to everybody else. Indeed, one of the clear signs to an outsider that he or she is hearing the myth of some particular group is when a story is told with awe and excitement and hardly seems to merit either. But this will always be true for the outsider, and in fact defines the outsider as just that. When you know The Story, and the story is yours, you are part of the group. If you don't know The Story, you just don't belong.

Lastly, myth is the means through which the group comes to *experience its past, present, and potential.* On the simplest level, myth recounts how everything got started, what seems to be happening at the present, and where it may all end up (otherwise known as hopes and dreams). But myth does not simply work at the level of "facts about," but rather it creates the circumstances under which the members of the group actually *experience* what went before, the significance of the moment, and the power of the dream for the future. In providing this experience, myth does not operate by black magic or mirrors, but in the manner of any good story.

Good stories—really good stories—don't just give you the facts; they make things so real that you are really there. We say of such stories, "they capture the imagination," and this is quite literally what happens. Really good stories create an open space in which the imagination grows. Details are important, but only as a way of defining the space in which the story takes place. In many ways, the critical thing is not what is said, but what remains unsaid. And think about where the story takes place—it clearly isn't on the printed page. It becomes internalized so that the story is you, and you are the story. The art of the storyteller not only captures the imagination, but more importantly, it captures the spirit.

Myth does no less. As the myth is told, those who participate not only hear the facts but are introduced to the spirit of the organization, not by way of fine anatomical description, but in a much more immediate and self-validating fashion. In the open space created by the myth-teller, the spirit of the organization appears as a holograph and captures the imagination and spirit of the hearer. To the extent that the hearer becomes enmeshed in the tale to the point that the spirit can be smelled, seen, touched, and tasted, the story or myth comes to define reality. Truth is true because it accords with The Story.

What myth really does is image the spirit, not with the kind of "objective" separation experienced in the art gallery where observer stands over against observed, but rather with an immediacy that excites, empowers, shapes, and enhances the spirits of all who participate. The one who tells the story defines reality and consequently, all the activities appropriate to that reality.

At this point we may return to the consideration of leadership. To the extent that leadership is concerned with focusing the spirit of an organization on the jobs at hand, the means is myth. How all of this might take place may become clearer with an example.

## THE JONATHAN CORPORATION

The Jonathan Corporation is a small shipyard located in Norfolk, Virginia. At the time I was working with them, they had a total of 500 employees, but they were doubling in size just about every year. A prime force behind their expansion was the fact that they were exceptionally good. Indeed they were the only shipyard in the United States that had always brought a ship in ahead of schedule *and* within budget. They were, in short, a truly high-performing system. The issue of the consultation was how to keep them that way. The president clearly recognized that as the number of people increased, so did the likelihood that the spirit and drive that marked the place might become diluted. Jonathan would not be the first organization that failed by succeeding.

My assignment was to analyze the culture in order to provide the president with a strategic view of what made them so good, and further, to suggest ways in which the focus and intensity of spirit might be maintained over time. The first step was to identify the operative myths. This was done through an extensive set of interviews covering all levels and sectors of the corporation. By the conclusion of the interview process, five central myths had been identified that set the tone or defined the spirit of the place. In no particular order they were:

*The International House of Pancakes.* In the early days of the corporation, before it really was a corporation, the president and his close associates would gather at the International House of Pancakes with a pocket full of dimes. Some of the dimes were used to buy the coffee, and the rest went to feed the pay phone, which did duty as the corporate switchboard. The value in this story was quite clear: "We don't worry about surroundings—just get the job done."

*The Phoenix.* Very shortly after the corporation started, a small group of senior members decided that the pastures were greener on the other side of the fence. More to the point, they wanted their own pastures. Consequently they left Jonathan and created Phoenix Marine. Immediately after the departure the president assembled those who remained and explained the situation. He indicated that he intended to compete "nose to nose," but that in spite of the pain and disruption caused by the schism, he acknowledged the right to such a choice and the basic competence of those who made it. A year later, the Phoenix had died, and Jonathan remained. The value communicated: even in moments of intense competition, people will be honored and respected for what they are.

*SS Speer.* The SS Speer was a naval ship that had an unfortunate encounter with an oil tanker. The Navy estimated the damage at $2 million and Jonathan bid $915,000 for the job. The nearest other bid was $2.5 million. Since this was Jonathan's first such bid, the Navy was understandably curious about the numbers and asked to see how they were generated. After looking, they had to admit that it all added up, but some skepticism remained. The Jonathan crew began work in the middle of winter under terrible conditions. They worked around the clock and refused to acknowledge fatigue. But victory was sweet. The ship was ready two days ahead of schedule for $913,000. The value communicated: "We can do it."

*Spirit Wagon.* In the early days, when Fridays rolled around, so did a pick-up truck loaded with beer. Work stopped in the yard, and all hands were invited to share a brew. Value communicated: "We celebrate our community."

*Norma's Apartment.* A secretary named Norma arrived home to discover that a fire had destroyed virtually everything she owned. Within 48 hours, without an official prod from anybody, money and material came in from all over the corporation, and Norma was back in business. Value communicated: "We care for each other."

These stories, with minor variations, appeared in virtually every corner of the organization, weaving a tapestry of meaning that defined and preserved the spirit of Jonathan. In understanding how this worked, it may be useful to think of Jonathan as a drum head with each story adding its peculiar flavor or tension. Thus no one story does the whole job. Rather it is the interaction of all the stories that produces the dynamic field (culture) within which the spirit of Jonathan grows.

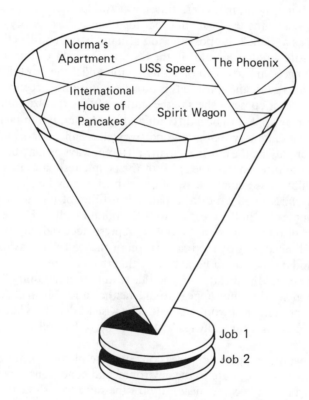

FIGURE 3.    If Figure 3 describes the field within which the spirit of Jonathan is defined and maintained, it also suggests the tools for what I have called "leadership by indirection."

## LEADERSHIP BY INDIRECTION

Leadership by indirection means leading at the level of spirit. The essential tools are offered by the myths of the organization, and the process may be understood as the manipulation of the mythic structure in order to tune the dynamic field and thereby focus the spirit on the task or tasks at hand.

I use the word "manipulation" with cautious intention, recognizing that for some people this is a "red flag" word, and well it might be. However, it should be remembered that "manipulation" has two primary definitions (Webster's Seventh). The first definition is "to manage or utilize skillfully," and it is in this sense that I use the word. The second definition, however, is a useful reminder of the dangers involved. That definition reads, "to control or play upon by artful, unfair or insidious means." If it is true that the realm of spirit is as elemental as I suggest—and its power so pervasive—then those who operate at this level must do so not only with care, but also with clear, life-enhancing values. The alternative will lead to the destruction of the human spirit. It is well to remember that perhaps the outstanding practitioner of what I am talking about, in modern times, was Adolph Hitler.

So how do you "tune the field" in order to enhance the capacity of spirit in addressing the tasks at hand? Suppose the job at hand is the construction of another ship. The requisite "tuning handle" is the SS Speer, which captures the kind and quality of spirit necessary to do an outstanding job under the most difficult circumstances. In order to guide the spirit in this direction, it is only necessary to bring this myth to a high level of consciousness in the culture of the organization.

Doing this may appear to be a difficult and arcane act, but in fact it may be accomplished in the same way that any good storyteller enhances his tale. The key is *orchestration*, or playing the tale in as many different ways as may be useful and appropriate in the culture, so that the spirit of the people resonates in a powerful and productive fashion. The actual means of orchestration may be as simple as passing out SS Speer T-shirts to all hands as a palpable artifact of the story. Or it may become more complex, as in the creation of a Corporate Hall of Heroes in which the faces and deeds of those who went before are represented. Indeed, the means of orchestration are limited only by the imagination of the leader, the available artforms of humanity, and the dictates of good taste within that culture.

The latter point, "the dictates of good taste in that community," is not a small one. Just as Wagner does not appeal to all, neither does Michael Jackson—some things will go, and some just won't make it. The wise leader has a keen sense of propriety, an awareness of what really resonates with his or her folks.

*A New Story.* It happens, on occasion, that the manner in which the spirit is shaped is no longer appropriate to the environmental conditions experienced by the group. At such a time it becomes necessary for the spirit to assume new form (transform), or alternatively, face the real possibility of extinction. Such is the case presently with AT&T, which used to be the phone company and now finds it essential to find a new focus for its spirit appropriate to a very new and different world. AT&T is by no means unique, and as our age progresses, it seems reasonable to assume that what may now appear aberrant will shortly become the norm.

Leadership under the conditions of transformation is a very different creature, and certainly a far cry from the old model that saw the leader tightly directing the forms and events of corporate life. In transformation, the forms tend to dissolve, and the events pass with such rapidity that they merge one into another as the spirit of the organization seeks a better way to be. Directing transformation by memo is rather like splitting atoms with a sledgehammer. It won't work.

But how do you lend new shape to spirit? The answer is, you tell a new story — or more accurately, create a new and more appropriate myth. Consider the situation of the nine cities and four counties that constitute the region in southeastern Virginia known as Hampton Roads, or Tidewater. For 300 years these several municipalities have spent the majority of their time in conflict or self-inflicted isolation. Over the 300-year period, this condition of warring fiefdoms made little real difference, for the cities had no real need for each other. However, at the end of World War II, the situation began to change quite radically. It all began in the city of Norfolk, where through local and federal efforts, a dismal place was physically renewed. With the success of that effort, the local leadership began to look beyond, to the region as a whole, and recognized that for the full potential of the area to be realized, it had to be treated as a unity. Each part was inextricably connected to all others — but nobody was very happy about the situation.

The thought of regional unity was anathema in most places, but the emergent leadership thought it worthwhile to give it a try. On the assumption they couldn't do it all at once, they began a step-by-step process. At one time it was the police, then fire or transportation. The effort was to secure cooperation in one area, which might then lay the groundwork for future union. But as this effort proceeded, it became clear that the results were not as intended. Typically, the leaders in some service area would gather with the best of intentions. On the first day, there would be "love and light." By the second day, the politics of 300 years would descend on the table, and by the third day, everybody went home feeling that the quest was in vain.

In 1980, I had occasion to do some work in the region, through which I came to know much of the local leadership and become familiar with their frustrated efforts. At one point, I proposed to the leadership that the tedious, one step at a time approach was doomed to failure, and that they would never succeed in their hopes for regional unity until they managed to fashion a dream that was large enough to include everybody — all 1,200,000 people situated in nine cities and four counties. They would have to abolish the turf battles by imagining a turf so large that nobody felt constrained. At the same time, this dream had to be *attractive* enough so that people would want to be involved. And it had to be *do-able*, in the sense that it was technically feasible and within the realm of possibility for that region. I could have said "myth" instead of "dream," but I felt that I had already approached the limits of credibility, and one more step, even in the interest of accuracy, would be too much.

The leadership was intrigued, but by no means convinced. They did, however, ask me for an example of such a dream. I replied that if I were living on the edges of the largest natural deep-water port in the nation (Hampton Roads), I might dream that this place should become the place in the world from which the oceans might be explored for the benefit of mankind. Clearly such a dream was large enough to involve virtually everybody. It was also attractive in that somebody was going to seriously address this task — and eventually that somebody would reap large rewards. And lastly, it was certainly within the realm of possibility, not only in general, but specifically in terms of this region, which already possessed major shipyards, was home port of the Atlantic Fleet, Jacque Cousteau, NASA, and NOAH.

Over the course of the next four years, this dream was orchestrated into reality. Beginning with a series of meetings involving all the leadership, in which they actively and intentionally envisioned what it might be like to live in a world described by this dream—on through endless small groups, community gatherings, symposia, and the like—the dream was fleshed out and made real. On one level, the effort appeared as a "standard community planning exercise"—but there was a difference. Although numbers were generated and reports written, the real activity took place at the level of ritual and myth. Each time the leadership gathered, the new story was told in color, form, shape, and sound. But the story was not so much about the sea and its bounty as it was about regional unity. And the telling of that *regional* story was accomplished not so much by words as by physical representation. The assembled leadership *was the story*, and even though their words might express hope for union "some day," the *fact* of their physical presence together spoke of union at that moment.

As of the moment, it seems that the new story has been born and is effectively channeling the spirit of the region in new directions. Whereas two years ago it was standard practice to presume a parochial viewpoint, from which one might argue for regional cooperation, it is now just the opposite. And there have been very tangible results, too. Perhaps the most remarkable is that the region jumped from being the 143rd market area in the United States to join the select few in the "Top 50" as number 33. This was not done by mirrors and black magic, but rather by the simple expedient of ending hostilities. It seems that up to the time of the project, the local hostility was such that it was impossible to get all the cities into the same statistical reporting area. Hence the largest aggregation ranked number 143. But when they all got together, they "miraculously appeared" in the charmed circle of the Top 50. That is not the only change. There is now a functioning regional sports authority that is hard at work with site plans for a regional stadium. The United Ways are now the United Way—and even the Chambers of Commerce are about to take the final leap.

But the real difference is a change in vision, a change in story, which has allowed the spirit of the region to gain expression in a new and more powerful way. The impetus for that change came from leadership operating by indirection. Not that there were any alternatives, for no common structure existed within which any one person (or several persons) held authority over anybody else. Leadership by memo, command, and direction was ruled out, as indeed it is in most situations where truly major changes of spirit are involved. Even in those circumstances where it may appear that the structures of authority are present, real and lasting change is rarely if ever affected by memo and command. Such change occurs when the spirit changes, in response to leadership by indirection.

# CHAPTER 9

# Leadership and the Art of Understanding Structure

by

**MICHAEL SHANDLER**

*The fundamental cause-and-effect relationships that are necessary for coordinating and channeling human efforts in organizations also interact in unintended ways to actually inhibit or thwart the attainment of the organization's goals. This chapter introduces basic principles of structural thinking and provides the information needed to work with organizational structures to ensure the fulfillment of goals and purpose.*

Miyamoto Musashi (1974), a master samurai of the fifteenth century, held a perspective on prevailing in combat that has profound implications for leadership today:

> When you have come to grips and you are striving together with the enemy and you realize that you cannot advance, you 'soak in' and become one with the enemy . . . you can often win decisively with the advantage of knowing how to 'soak' into the enemy, whereas, were you to draw apart, you would lose the chance to win.

Musashi's teaching kept in mind the samurai's ultimate purpose—to win. But he knew that to win, the warrior would have to deal truthfully and accurately with the enemy—the obstacle in the current situation. This leadership capacity is almost paradoxical, requiring both concentration on a future goal and absorption into present conditions.

This chapter has a similar intention. It is about keeping the purpose of an organization in mind while developing ways to understand the present "enemies" of that purpose. It follows that the vision of an effective leader has two complementary aspects—far-reaching vision of a desired future state, and penetrating vision into current functioning.

While the work of Kiefer and Senge (1984) and others has articulated eloquently the need for envisioning the future, the attempt here will be to enhance the leader's ability to see clearly into the sometimes murky and muddled day-to-day life of organizations. The key to developing this penetrating form of vision will be an understanding of the vital role that structures play in the accomplishment of organizational purpose.

# STRUCTURE

Structure is the difference between the molecules in a test tube full of carbon compounds and the molecules in an elephant. While the molecules in the test tube are simply blended together, those in the elephant are organized in a precise and complex way. Their respective structures account for the difference.

This use of the word "structure" reaches beyond its usual meaning in organizations. Here structure refers to the underlying interacting variables in a system that organize it in a particular and unique manner. This underlying structure consists of the prescribed organization (its stated goals, policies, procedures, and formal hierarchies), and the collective human attitudes (expectations, motivations, talents, and interpersonal relationships). It is the interaction between the prescribed and the human elements of structure that tend to drive organizations either toward or from their desired destination.

PURPOSE

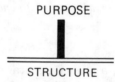

STRUCTURE

Prescribed structures ——— Human structures
(goals, policies, procedures, (attitudes, motivations,
formal hierarchies, etc.) relationships, etc.)

FIGURE 1.

## Principles of Structure

To understand the usefulness of a structural perspective, four principles of structure will be explained and illustrated. These key functional principles are:

1. Structures either accelerate or inhibit movement toward goals.

2. Unspoken rules take priority over spoken rules.

3. Symptoms point to structural weakness.

4. Every structure has its own payoff.

*Principle 1: Structures either accelerate or inhibit movement toward goals.* A trunk, while an entirely useful appendage for an elephant, would be inappropriate for a fish. Yet in organizations, structures are often found that do not effectively support a purpose. Too often, organizations have metaphorical trunks when they are in need of fins.

124

Transforming an inappropriate structure into an appropriate one can be illustrated by the case of an overnight freight business. Speed is the predominant goal in this industry. A few years ago, one major freight company, fighting to keep its market share, undertook an analysis of its package-sorting system. The analysis revealed that on any given night, regardless of the number of items to be sorted, the hourly paid staff took eight hours to process the packages. Therefore, no further movement of packages could occur until the shift was completed. Although this pattern was predictable, it meant that final delivery of packages had to be forced into the few remaining hours before the promised delivery times.

Company executives wondered why it always took the entire night to sort the packages. Was it that the workforce was poorly trained, simply inept, or ill-assigned? Most senior administrators believed the performance was typical of hourly paid employees. It was an expected and accepted result of employing unskilled personnel.

Two managers, however, did not agree with this judgment. They lobbied for an experiment, which was finally tried. Package handlers were told that when they were finished processing packages, they could go home. They would receive full pay for the entire shift regardless of when the work was completed. In short, their pay would remain the same whether they worked two hours or eight hours, as long as they got the job done.

The results of the new structure began to pay off immediately. Often an entire night's processing was completed with hours to spare, leaving more time for delivery of packages to their final destination. Efficiency moved to an altogether new level. In a short time, the experiment was adopted as formal operating policy.

This case highlights the impact that structures have on the actual behavior of a system. The second structure was more in keeping with the purposes of the organization than the original structure. The creation of a congruence between purpose and structure showed impressive results.

Although the principle that structures either accelerate or inhibit movement toward purpose may seem simple common sense, examples of its dysfunctional side abound in many of our prominent institutions. In Edward Luttwak's *The Pentagon and the Art of War* (1985), he vividly reveals how structural misunderstanding has infected the armed forces with a malignancy of inefficiency, overspending, complications, and ineptitude. He suggests that a structural decision made at the end of World War II is indirectly accountable for "a massive, muscle-bound, unresponsive bureaucracy, . . . increasingly complicated, expensive, and often unworkable weapons, not to mention those $10,000 coffee pots."

The culprit is identified as a decision to keep as many senior officers in active duty as possible despite the end of active hostilities. Fear of a new war characterized the consciousness of the military and the government in 1945. Relations with the Soviets were icy. A cold war might momentarily turn into a fiery one. Training senior military personnel is a time-consuming task. Therefore, in order to be ready for the next "big" war, a military establishment designed for rapid expansion required a large "stock," an impressive inventory of high-level personnel.

As a result, there are more generals, colonels, and admirals to lead 2 million soldiers today than there were senior officers to lead 12 million enlisted men during

World War II. With a massive, top-heavy bureaucracy entrenched, systematic over-complication in every aspect of defense is predictable. The structure impedes movement.

Just as in the military context, most leaders find themselves in situations where structures are blessings or curses inherited from the organization's history. Effective change seldom proceeds from imposing radical or obvious solutions on a system. Instead, a leader needs to "soak in" the system, to join with its purposes, and to enlist the help of seeming enemies to effect structural change.

***Principle 2: Unspoken rules take priority over spoken rules.*** Many organizations function with massive discrepancies between prescribed structures — the spoken rules — and what actually takes place — the unspoken rules. In some cases, these discrepancies merely reflect anachronistic policies that no one has bothered to alter to reflect new conditions. More often, however, such discrepancies are not a result of anachronisms, but rather are statements of the actual, day-to-day living conditions in the organization. In all cases, whether benign or subversive, the unspoken rules take priority over the spoken rules.

Where there is congruity between spoken and unspoken rules, the leader needs merely to ascertain whether these rules actually support the organization's goals and purposes. Where there is incongruity, the leader's role is more difficult, requiring strategic intervention.

The following examples illustrate how a leader might discern whether detrimental discrepancies exist between spoken and unspoken rules and might determine the always unique structural implications for a particular organization. These examples are drawn from three organizations: a $100 million consumer-products division of a traditional corporation; a manufacturing division of a Fortune 500 company; and a recently established, rapidly growing $50 million high-technology division of a multinational food and beverage corporation.

Organization 1 was undertaking a major cultural change effort involving every level of the organization. Near the beginning of the project, a structural analysis of spoken and unspoken rules was employed to determine whether these rules were congruous and in keeping with the organization's goals. Two interrelated rule discrepancies emerged.

- Spoken Rule 1:     Customer satisfaction is our highest priority.
- Unspoken Rule 1:   Customer satisfaction is the problem of the customer services department.
- Spoken Rule 2:     Quality is number one.
- Unspoken Rule 2:   Get it out the door.

Spoken Rule 1 and its subversive corollary will be considered first. The senior management team had become convinced that customer satisfaction should be the organization's highest priority. There was no argument in the company when the rule was mandated. The structure of the organization already provided for the edict; there was a department called "customer service." It was assumed on every level of this excessively compartmentalized organization that customer service would take care of customer satisfaction.

The customer service personnel found themselves representing a company that individually, departmentally, and collectively viewed customer satisfaction as someone else's problem. The result was that product quality was often below promised standards, and product delivery was regularly delayed. Because of the compartmental structure of the organization, the customer service people were left to handle the complaints but were given no power to change the quality of products or services. The isolation of one department from another was reinforced by this scenario. Those in customer service became more resentful of an unresponsive organization, and the organization became more disillusioned with customer service personnel's ability to satisfy the consumer. A vicious and destructive cycle had become entrenched.

While the disaster was palatable when considering the discrepancy between spoken and unspoken rule 1, it seemed unavoidable with the additional complications of spoken and unspoken rule 2. Executive decree had declared the supremacy of quality. "Quality is Number One" was to be the company motto. However, on the production floor, rewards were distributed for speed. Pride was taken in being "fast." The unspoken took priority over the spoken. Sacrificing quality was a daily routine.

These two examples were not the only discrepancies between the spoken and the unspoken. Taken together they formed an equation for interdepartmental frustration and institutionalized mediocrity. Creating congruity between unspoken and spoken rules by transforming structures has become the challenge for the company leadership.

Organization 2, a manufacturing division of a Fortune 500 Company, had direct orders from corporate headquarters. "Change and do it quickly" was the edict from on high. However, there was an unspoken rider on this seemingly uncomplicated command. Division executives had been informally advised that it was of utmost importance that everyone in the division, from union employees to office staff to managers, be aligned around the changes. These dual orders set the stage for the following contradiction between the spoken and unspoken rule:

- Spoken Rule:      Institute rapid change.
- Unspoken Rule:    Involve everybody and don't upset any group.

In this case, the unspoken rule quite obviously and successfully sabotaged the spoken rule. Although the proposed changes had merit, the change effort was doomed by the contradiction between the command to change quickly and the insistence on alignment. Indeed, this contradiction actually created greater divisiveness rather than greater alignment among groups within the division. All levels of the organization were able to blame other levels for the slow and ineffectual process of change.

Organization 3 also presents a common discrepancy between the spoken and the unspoken. Its problem is exemplary of generic structural issues encountered when traditional hierarchical organizations attempt participative management. This rapidly growing, high-technology company is unique within the larger organization environment of its parent corporation, a multinational food purveyor. Its leaders are attempting to capitalize on its uniqueness by divesting it of many traditional corporate philosophies incongruent with the needs of a successful and growing high-technology company. Participatory management has become formal policy of the division. However, informal policy revealed discrepancies between spoken and unspoken rules.

- Spoken Rule 1:    This is your business.
- Unspoken Rule 1:    Check with your superiors.
- Spoken Rule 2:    We're all equal.
- Unspoken Rule 2:    Some are more equal than others.

These rules revealed a confusion about decision-making power. On one hand, the company had the form of a nontraditional, nonhierarchical organization. On the other hand, traditional attitudes and procedures prevailed. In meetings, participation and quality in decision-making was loudly proclaimed, with people often being told "This is your business." However, time and again, decisions would mysteriously be made or unmade by a select few outside of those very meetings. When people who attended such meetings heard about these decisions, they would tend to be perplexed. Nevertheless, they continued to attend further meetings and to contribute vocally, only to learn time after time that decisions had been made behind their backs, behind closed doors. Two years after the original reorganization of the company, participative management had developed into a cynical joke: "We participate. They manage." The recognition of this hypocrisy enabled the company to understand the increasing frustration and the decreasing enthusiasm it was experiencing despite its phenomenal growth and success.

No attempt has been made here to provide solutions to the dilemmas of these three organizations. Solutions are partially and simplistically evident in the identification of the problem. The lessons generated by examining these cases can be generalized to all organizations. Congruity between spoken and unspoken rules is desirable. Therefore, vision into the here-and-now discrepancies between spoken and unspoken rules gives the leader powerful access to important dynamic structures inherent in organizations and can enable the leader to guide the organization toward structures that are keenly attuned to its purposes. However, depending on the size and complexity of the organization, structural change may not be amenable to a quick fix but may require system-wide, in-depth, long-term organizational change efforts.

***Principle 3: Symptoms point to structural weakness.*** An ancient Indian adage says, "There is no garbage, only manure for the tree." Wearing the lenses of the ageless sage, the leader can see symptoms of organizational malaise as clues to a structural cure that can strengthen the organization beyond the resolution of the immediate difficulty. From this perspective, problems are not bad. They should not be avoided, ignored, or denied, but acknowledged and carefully considered as valuable information. The messages they communicate can offer the secret for designing structures that support and accelerate the accomplishment of goals.

Two examples illustrate the value of symptomatic behavior. The first describes resistance to change in a high-technology company. The second portrays a personality conflict in a medium-sized manufacturing company.

*An example of resistance to change.* Toward the end of a strategic planning session with this author, the management group of a high-technology company began to fear that their plans would meet with resistance from the rest of the organization. The mood in the room became quite somber, and the managers began to confirm that in the past their programs and ideas had often met with just such resistance. They began talking to one another about how their well-laid plans had repeatedly been sabotaged by the skepticism of their employees.

They began seeking a cure for the rampantly negative attitudes of their subordinates. Resisting the temptation to offer medicine for the symptom, I showed them that such skepticism would make a positive contribution to the attainment of their goals.

They had become sincerely committed to creating an organization that would reflect their vision. They were well aware that this goal would require a great deal of work and behavioral change. In the past, programs instituted from the top had failed largely because executive behavior had remained incongruous with the professed policies. In honesty, the group had to admit that organization-wide cynicism was justified.

It was further suggested that the skepticism should be encouraged rather than discouraged—that management should *prescribe the symptom*. The cynicism and resistance were gifts—reminders that management's success would depend on its ability to "walk the talk," to match behavior with policies.

The acknowledged symptom had traditionally been the resistance of the workforce to change. Previously, managerial response had consisted of complaints about employee attitudes. This reaction was akin to concentrating on the proverbial pointing finger rather than looking at what it was pointing to. By using employee skepticism as a barometer of its own ability to act congruously, this management group has found a valuable instrument for staying on course.

*An example of a personality conflict.* During a year-long, intensive consultation for a manufacturing company, I observed a structural dynamic that severely handicapped the organization's effectiveness. To appreciate the dimensions of the difficulty, you need to understand the cast of characters, their professional goals and their relationships. The two main players were the director of sales and the director of marketing.

The director of marketing, call him "Tim," is a case in contrast. He is adored by none, detested by no one. There is only one exception. Jack, the director of sales, cannot tolerate Tim; nor does Tim harbor any hidden affection for Jack.

Jack's highest ambition, known to all his senior management peers, is to be director of sales *and* marketing. Tim's ambitions are less clear. He often complains about the lack of support for marketing in the company, and there is a suspicion that he plans to leave.

In the meantime, Jack and Tim maintain a relationship of public contact and private segregation. Following their leaders, the respective staffs of sales and marketing have as little to do with one another as possible.

The personality struggle between Jack and Tim has become a major focus of attention for the president and the senior vice-president. All difficulties between both departments are attributed to the personality conflict.

Taking the viewpoint that the symptom points to a structural weakness yields an entirely new perspective on the problem. The primary effort in analyzing the problem structurally is to put aside the particular personalities and personal relationships of Jack and Tim and look instead at the relationships between their positions and their departments.

Each director's department or territory can be considered in terms of the boundary between their respective domains. In this case, the following question can be posed, "If a fence could be erected between sales and marketing, what kind of fence would it be? Would it be a high wall, enabling each to keep their actions entirely secret from the other? Would it be a picket fence, so people on each side could speak freely with one another by mutual desire, but maintain their separation unless both wished to communicate? Or would there be no fence at all, enabling each to know what the other is doing nearly all the time?" It seems evident that in this case, sales and marketing need no fence at all. They serve interdependent functions.

Logic provides the next question: "Why are they separate territories?" If there's no need for a fence of any kind, there's only one yard. Sales and marketing should be integrated.

Simply consolidating, however, does not entirely clarify the relationship between the sales and marketing functions. Still another question is appropriate: "In this organization, does marketing serve sales or does sales serve marketing:" Given the nature of this particular company, the purpose of marketing is to promote sales — to increase sales effectiveness. Said differently, sales should direct marketing. Therefore, a structural hierarchy needs to be established that reflects the higher status of sales.

Structural analysis of the personality conflict does not concern itself with the personalities *or* their conflict; instead, it looks for an underlying structural cause, and proposes a structural cure. In this case, it would be suggested that marketing and sales be consolidated under the direction of a person who understands that sales is the company priority, and that marketing success will be measured by increasing sales.

Only after the structural analysis is completed are the personalities considered. The question becomes: "Who has the ability to best accommodate the structural needs of the organization?" While the intervention is now far removed from the original personality conflict, the institution of a new clearly defined structural arrangement (the appointment of a director of sales and marketing) will end the personality conflict and strengthen the organization as a whole.

Three possibilities exist for hiring a director of marketing and sales: Jack, Tim, or an outside person. It is time to consider the repercussions of each possibility. Hiring from outside is inappropriate because of an overriding need for continuity and because of the idiosyncratic nature of this business. The director of marketing, Tim, knows little to nothing about sales, he is inexperienced and passive, and his commitment to the company is questionable. By default, the obvious choice is the director of sales, Jack. While Jack will achieve his personal ambition, his ability to succeed in his new post is far from assured. Although his sales background is first rate, his marketing experience and abilities are suspect. To succeed in this job, he will need to acquire a new posture toward marketing. *He will need Tim.* He will need to ask questions and accept Tim's greater expertise. Their relationship must be transformed, or they will endure mutual failure. If Tim leaves, which is not unlikely, Jack will have to hire another marketing expert, but the relationship will be clear and therefore will not have detrimental ramifications throughout the organization.

*Principle 4: Every structure has its own payoffs.* "Why," you might ask, "do organizations maintain structures that plainly do not support their purposes?" The answer is simple: the structures have their own benefits.

Executives of a major division of a multinational consumer products company enthusiastically communicated their devotion to the organization's avowed goals. These goals were characterized by a commitment to maintain a competitive advantage in the marketplace, to excellence, and to growth. There was verbal agreement among the senior staff that the accomplishment of these goals would require diverse viewpoints, creative challenges, constructive criticism, and courageous risk-taking.

However, when the unspoken and prevalent attitudes within the company were examined, a structure antithetical to these purposes emerged. The culture was actually characterized by a generalized conformity, a lack of confrontation, and a safety orientation.

When simply asked "What's the payoff for behaving the way you currently do?" the answers were clear and honest. "This is a comfortable place to work. No one argues. Everyone gets their share of approval. There's a nice, cozy, safe feeling."

This kind of straightforward honesty deserves an equally honest response. The leader needs to ask with sincerity, "Are you really sure you want to give that up?" It's rare today, in the corporate world, that such a comfortable place can be found. Perhaps your ambitious goals are not worth the price?

This organization made a choice to institute its goals and purposes even though it would require considerable loss. For them, the envisioned future was more exciting and valued than the cozy current condition. Commitment to a vision is a prerequisite to transforming structures. For the leader to inspire structural change successfully, the promises of the future need to be more personally, professionally, and economically profitable than the payoffs in the present.

## SUMMARY

A vital function of the true leader is to possess dual vision — the ability to envision organizational purposes and the capacity to see current organizational structure clearly. In this chapter, the second aspect of vision has been the primary focus. Four structural principles have been stressed to enable a leader to guide an organization toward goals and purposes. These four principles are:

- Structures either accelerate or inhibit purpose.
- Unspoken rules take priority over spoken rules.

- Symptoms point to structural weakness.
- All structures have their own payoffs.

Like any art, the art of understanding structure is developmental in nature. It requires conscious effort and discipline to see organizations as dynamically interrelated structures. Sustained practice is needed to develop the wisdom necessary to guide these structures toward the fulfillment of organizational purpose. An artful eye enables such a leader to find equal fulfillment in the everyday efforts to attain results. From this perspective, leadership is as much about the here-and-now as about the future.

# CHAPTER 10

# Systems Principles for Leadership

by

**PETER M. SENGE**

*Our normal tendency often is to understand problems by isolating the symptoms and analyzing the system piece by piece. While providing short-term symptomatic relief, this normal tendency generates little control over the longer term dynamics of an organizational system. This chapter explores the fundamentals of system dynamics through developing a practical approach to systemic thinking.*

- In complex systems, obvious solutions often fail to produce intended results — in fact, they often exacerbate the very problems they are intended to resolve.

- In complex systems, cause and effect are generally *not* closely related in time and space. As managers, we typically assume they are.

- Complex systems tend to resist attempts to change their behavior. The most common cause of policy resistance is multiple "compensating feedback" relationships that attempt to maintain internal balances despite external interventions.

- Effective policy design requires understanding an organization and its environment as a unified system so as to shift management attention away from the large number of low-leverage policies to the relatively few high-leverage points.

- Such understanding requires an ongoing management education process. The objective of this education is to shift the style of thinking within an organization. In an organization intent on realizing its creative potential, fostering systems-thinking is a chief function of leadership.

A significant part of the managerial revolution sweeping the business world is a growing awareness that the competencies that underlie successful management and successful leadership are different. An extensive study of successful leaders in a wide range of fields led Warren Bennis (1985) to conclude that there are four distinct competencies for successful leadership: management of attention, management of meaning, management of trust, and management of self. Running through virtually all studies of leadership are common themes. Leaders are visionaries who see possibilities and orient themselves toward creating rather than maintaining. Leaders foster alignment and commitment. Leaders are teachers, facilitators, "growers" of human beings. In Chapter 11, Robert Fritz discusses the "leader as creator," a person whose fundamental orientation in life is "to bring into reality that which never existed before" and to instill this orientation in others.

For the past two years I have been coordinating a research program involving leaders of some of America's most innovative organizations. Many of these companies have been pioneers in advancing more decentralized organizational designs. In many cases, they have developed a sense of purposefulness and a commonality of values reaching deeply into the organization. These leaders are unanimously agreed that vision, alignment, empowerment, commitment, and inspiration are the marks of effective leadership in the types of organizations they seek to build. But we also feel there are subtler aspects of effective leadership concerned with organizational learning and predominant styles of thinking in the organization.

The subtler skills of leadership involve creating an environment where responsibility and wisdom advance together. It is to little avail to distribute decision-making responsibility broadly throughout an organization if individuals lack the insight to make effective strategic decisions. Vision and alignment will dissipate if people begin to blame one another as soon as problems arise. Empowerment will wither if success appears to depend on events and circumstances beyond the organization's control. Effective leaders in the more democratic organization of the future will not only encourage and inspire people to trust themselves, take risks, and innovate. They will also create a learning environment in which the lessons of experience can be distilled and transmitted far more efficiently than in the traditional authoritarian organization.

Bill O'Brien, president of the Hanover Insurance Companies, says that:

> As we move from the traditional authoritarian organization to the vision-oriented, value-driven organization, the skills required of effective leaders will change dramatically. Just as the "pilot's" skills were transformed in moving from the horse and buggy, to the automobile, to the jet airplane, so too must my skills evolve. The effective leader in a traditional work environment is above all else a strategist and decisionmaker. In the type of work environment we are creating at Hanover critical decisions are made throughout the organization. My job is more and more becoming that of a teacher and a coach rather than a decisionmaker.

In particular, we believe leaders in the future will be increasingly called upon to develop systemic thinking in organizations. Systemic thinking is integrative, synthesizing diverse viewpoints in order to understand the organization as a whole. It is structural thinking, focusing on the structure of interrelationships among marketing, manufacturing, R&D, and finance that determine organizational success.[1] Systemic thinking deals with "dynamics," showing how short- and long-term consequences of management actions may be different, even in the opposite direction. In short, systemic thinking is "general management" thinking. As organizations distribute general management responsibilities increasingly broadly, the process of developing systemic thinking must be made more orderly and efficient than in the traditional authoritarian organization.

But overcoming a lifetime of training in nonsystemic ways of thinking is not easy. Most of us have been taught since grammar school to understand problems by isolating symptoms and analyzing the pieces. Most of us were never taught how to integrate our understanding of different parts into a larger whole. The "Program in Systems Thinking and the New Management Style" is exploring how systemic thinking can be developed within the participating organizations (Senge 1984). This chapter shares some of the initial insights from this program. In particular, it emphasizes developing fluency in basic systems principles and ongoing exposure to "generic structures" as the foundation for management education in systems thinking.

## AN ILLUSTRATION INVOLVING MARKET GROWTH AND CAPACITY EXPANSION

The following example (based on Forrester 1968) deals with generic dynamics involved in the growth of virtually any type of enterprise. The simple model of growth dynamics serves to illustrate several important characteristics of systems:

- The nature of causality in complex systems
- Policy resistance: the tendency of complex systems to resist attempts to change their behavior through
  - compensating feedback,
  - better-before-worse behavior, and
  - shifting the burden to the intervenor
- Leverage points: the relatively small number of policy changes that can radiate desirable influences throughout a system.

Interactions of market growth and capacity expansion lie at the heart of many patterns of business growth and stagnation. In particular, the following simple model illustrates two management principles concerning market growth and capacity expansion—namely, that no firm can sell more than it produces over the long term (capacity-constrained growth) and that allowing performance standards to adjust in

---

[1] *The chapters by Fritz, Shandler, and Kiefer all directly emphasize the role of leadership to focus attention on underlying structures. Several other chapters do so indirectly. Systemic thinking represents the discipline that leads to understanding structure.*

times of crisis can undermine growth, even in the face of unlimited demand and unconstrained financial resources (eroding goals).

We begin by considering the self-reinforcing positive feedback relationship that links demand for a company's product or services with the company's resources to create further demand (feedback loop 1 in Figure 1).[2] Increases in demand create more revenues for the enterprise, provided there is adequate capacity to serve demand. Increased revenues, in turn, can be invested in resources to generate further demand. Demand-generating resources include marketing and sales personnel, advertising, and new product development. The reinforcing process of increased demand, higher revenues, and further investment in demand-generating resources is the basic engine of growth for many enterprises.

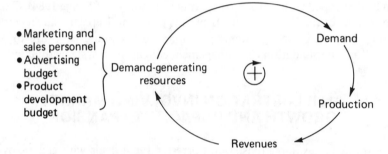

FIGURE 1.    A Self-Reinforcing Feedback in Market Expansion

However, if growing demand outstrips the enterprise's capacity to satisfy demand, adverse changes in competitive variables will limit growth. For example, in a manufacturing firm, demand in excess of production capacity can result in reduced product availability or lower product quality, or both. In a service firm, demand in excess of capacity to deliver the service lowers service quality. In a competitive market, lower availability or quality relative to competitors' performance will cause loss of demand.

The interaction of demand and capacity to satisfy demand is shown in Figure 2. The positive feedback loop, reinforcing growth of demand-generating resources, is coupled with a balancing feedback process (loop 2), showing how inadequate capacity to satisfy demand eventually limits growth. (Such balancing feedback processes are called *negative feedback loops*.) If capacity is fixed, rising demand will eventually outstrip capacity to satisfy demand. Capacity will become inadequate, and an erosion in competitive variables will eventually reduce marketing effectiveness and fu-

---

[2]*Positive and negative feedback loops are the basic structural building block processes in all dynamic systems. Positive loops amplify change through self-reinforcing pressures like those in loop 1 in Figure 1. Negative feedback loops are balancing, goal-seeking structures that respond to change by creating offsetting pressures that attempt to restore variables to their former values. Examples of negative feedback are temperature control systems in buildings, hiring policies that adjust workforce in a firm toward desired workforce, and the vast array of processes that maintain homeostasis in living organisms.*

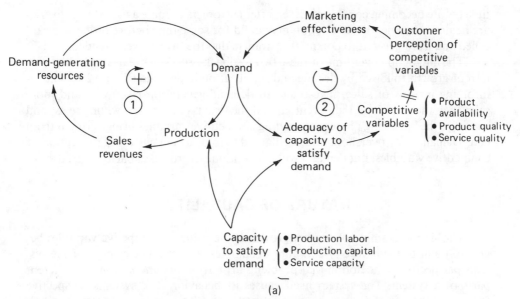

(a)

Feedback structure: Reinforcing growth of demand generating resources (loop 1) interacts with balancing pressures that limit demand through eroding competitive variables when capacity is inadequate (loop 2)

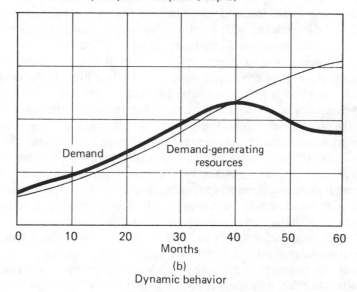

(b)
Dynamic behavior

FIGURE 2.    Market Growth Interacting with Fixed Capacity
Leads to Overshoot in Demand

ture demand. However, marketing effectiveness may not decline immediately in response to a decline in competitive variables, due to delays in market perception and reaction. For example, after ordering a piece of capital equipment expected to take several months to deliver, the customer typically waits until the promised delivery time before becoming concerned. Even after customers become aware that deliveries are behind schedule, dissatisfaction may build for some time before orders are cancelled and word gets out to potential customers that the firm is overextended.

The interaction over time of these two feedback processes creates a familiar pattern of growth followed by decline and stabilization in demand (Figure 2b). The reinforcing process of sales, investment in demand-generating resources, and more sales fuels the growth period. Eventually, if the firm is unable or unwilling to expand capacity, the balancing process of eroding competitive variables brings growth to an end. Demand may overshoot and oscillate, due to delays in customer perception of competitive variables, but demand will not continue to grow if capacity is fixed.[3]

## NATURE OF CAUSALITY

The simple example of market growth and erosion of competive variables begins to point to the nature of causality in complex systems. The essence of the systems perspective is the notion that problems arise from the *interactions* of different parts of a system. The system itself causes its behavior. The systems perspective focuses on the underlying *structure* of interrelationships among reinforcing and balancing processes that give each system its unique character.

In the example above, the *cause* of the firm's pattern of sales growth and eventual stagnation lies in the interactions of the two feedback processes shown in Figure 2. During the growth period, the reinforcing process (loop 1) of rising demand, revenues, investment in demand-generating resources, and further increase in demand creates continuing sales growth. During most of the growth period, the balancing process (loop 2) of eroding competitive variables limiting demand has little effect because demand is well below capacity, and competitive variables, and thus marketing effectiveness, are high and steady. The structure of the balancing process exists, but the process is dormant. But growth shifts the control in the system. When demand approaches capacity, competitive variables deteriorate and the balancing process (loop 2) becomes more active. Deteriorating competitive variables (such as rising delivery delays or falling quality) and declining marketing effectiveness eventually outweigh increased demand-generating resources and reduce demand. (If this were not true, demand could be increased indefinitely by continuing to increase demand-generating resources, even though capacity is fixed.)

The "system as cause" perspective shifts the way we think about problems. The conventional management perspective assumes that the causes of problems are related in fairly obvious ways to problem symptoms. If there are delays in developing new products, attention is directed toward R & D. Overruns in manufacturing costs focus attention on production scheduling and purchasing decisions within manufacturing. Falling sales lead to increased pressure on marketing and sales personnel. Lying behind such common managerial reactions is a perspective on causality—that

---

[3] *In Figure 2b, demand-generating resources continue to expand for some time after demand has stopped rising, due to delays in converting demand into sales revenues, in allocating revenues, and in acquiring demand-generating resources (such as sales personnel).*

cause and effect are closely related in time and space. When problems arise, we naturally assume that the causes lie in the same part of the system as the problem itself. Moreover, we assume that, once the appropriate local remedy is applied, the problem will be solved relatively quickly.

From a systemic perspective cause and effect generally are *not* closely related in time and space. The causes of a problem may lie in a completely different part of a system from the problem symptoms. In terms of the simple example above, the obvious symptoms of difficulty are falling demand and declining marketing effectiveness, which began to manifest around month 40. The underlying cause of the decline lies in a different part of the system: a fixed capacity to satisfy demand, which results in deteriorating competitive variables when growth outstrips capacity. Cause and effect are not closely related in space. Moreover, even if the cause of falling demand were recognized and capacity were increased, demand would not begin to grow immediately. It might take considerable time for the firm to reestablish a reputation for excellent quality and product availability and begin to attract new customers. (How long would depend on the damage suffered to the firm's reputation when capacity was inadequate and the other means, such as advertising, available to stimulate renewed demand.) Cause and effect are not closely related in time.

## POLICY RESISTANCE

One of the chief characteristics of complex systems is the tendency to resist attempts to change their behavior. Noted biologist Lewis Thomas (1979) has said:

> When you are confronted by any complex social system, such as an urban center or a hamster, with the things about it that you are dissatisfied with and anxious to fix, you cannot just step in and set about fixing with much hope of helping. This realization is one of the sore discouragements of our century.

Policy resistance leads to the frustratingly common managerial experience of seeing new policies accomplish short-term improvements only to find old problems recurring, of treating problem symptoms only to leave underlying causes unaffected, and of being drawn into a reinforcing spiral of intervention and dependency. One of the most persistent findings of systems research, as described by Donella Meadows (1982), is that problems in complex systems persist despite repeated efforts directed at their solution:

> The world is a complex, interconnected, finite, ecological-social-psychological-economic system. We treat it as if it were not, as if it were divisible, separable, simple, and infinite. . . .

> No one wants or works to generate hunger, poverty, pollution, or the elimination of species. Very few people favor arms races or terrorism or alcoholism or inflation. Yet those results are consistently produced by the system-as-a-whole, despite many policies and much effort directed against them.

In effect, this is the fundamental reason for a systems perspective—the ineffectiveness of policy changes based on nonsystemic understanding of problems.

The present illustration points to one of the most common causes of policy resistance—*compensating feedback*. Compensating feedback arises from unrecognized balancing mechanisms within a complex system. If problem symptoms are part of a balance a system is seeking to maintain, altering those symptoms simply causes the system to work harder to maintain the balance.

For example, around month 40 in the growth of the firm simulated in Figure 2, demand begins to decline, while marketing resources are still expanding. A crisis in marketing effectiveness develops. The average demand per marketing resource (for example, sales per salesperson) is low relative to the growth period. The morale of the sales force is on the decline. Sales commissions are down. Pressure on the marketing and sales group is intensifying. Under such conditions, there are a variety of standard responses of a marketing and sales department intent on boosting marketing effectiveness. These responses might include an increased advertising promotion, cutting price, increasing sales incentives, firing the less productive salespeople, or sales training to upgrade the average effectiveness of the sales force.

Each of these interventions would be intended to combat the problem of falling marketing effectiveness. By their nature, they do not consider the underlying systemic causes of the decline in sales effectiveness, but rather focus on the obvious symptom of low performance. There are many pressures leading to such "symptomatic" interventions. Even if the management of the marketing and sales group suspected that the source of the problem lay beyond the immediate symptoms, organizational pressures to "do something" about declining performance might still lead to efforts to boost sales effectiveness, even while managers might be inquiring further into the deeper causes of the problem.

The results of intervening to boost marketing effectiveness are shown in Figure 3. In this case, a sales promotion is implemented at month 46, six months after demand stopped growing. The promotion is highly successful—demand increases 15 percent over three months! However, over the longer term, demand begins to decline again, reaching its prior depressed level nine months after the promotion was initiated. The same outcome results from providing increased advertising, better sales training, and stronger sales incentives, or from firing less effective salespeople to boost the average effectiveness of the salesforce. The limitation of all such interventions is that they *focus on the symptom* of low marketing effectiveness rather than the cause of the symptom. The system *compensates* for the symptomatic intervention, eventually returning marketing effectiveness to its level before the intervention was undertaken.

Returning to the underlying structure causing the stagnation in growth, it is easy to see the source of the compensating feedback. The key structure leading to compensating feedback is the negative feedback loop, which interrelates demand and competitive variables like delivery delay and quality. As shown in Figure 4, if a sales promotion (1) increases marketing effectiveness (2), demand will increase (3). But, if demand is already near the firm's capacity to satisfy demand, increased demand will lower the adequacy of capacity (4), causing further erosion in competitive variables (5)—for example, lower quality or higher delivery delays. As customers

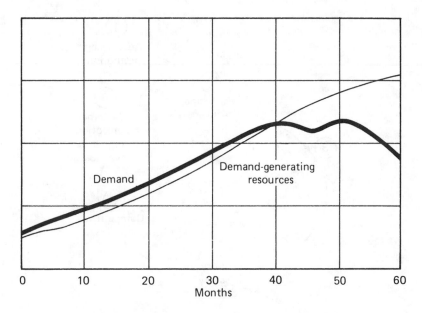

FIGURE 3.　　　A Sales Promotion boosting marketing
effectiveness through a promotion at month 46
leads to a short-term improvement followed by a
longer-term decline.

come to perceive this decline in quality or availability (6), marketing effectiveness will be pushed back down, offsetting the benefits of the initial intervention.

Compensating feedback arises because the negative feedback loop that controls marketing effectiveness seeks to maintain a balance between demand and capacity to satisfy demand. Over the long term, no firm can sell more than it can produce. However, in the short term, it is quite possible for sales to exceed capacity. But eventually, rising delivery delays, falling product quality, falling service quality, or some combination of the above send a clear signal to the marketplace. An intervention that succeeds in boosting marketing effectiveness when a firm is already near its capacity to satisfy demand can, at best, produce only temporary improvement.

Examples of compensating feedback abound in the failed interventions of many of the best intentioned social and organizational programs. If the problem is inadequate housing, as the urban problem was frequently viewed in the 1960s, we build more housing. If the problem is excessive costs of gasoline and heating oil to the consumer, we control gas prices, as we did throughout much of the 1970s. If the problem is inadequate national defense, we invest in further armaments, as we have done for the past 40 years. If the problem is growing government deficits, we raise taxes, as we will likely do in the mid-1980s. In each of these situations, a problem is defined in terms of its most obvious symptoms—poor housing, high costs of oil and gasoline, inadequate national defense, excessive deficits—and an action is taken to

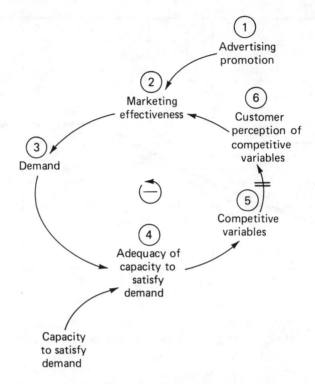

FIGURE 4.    Compensating Feedback. The feedback loop
linking demand, adequacy of capacity to satisfy
demand, and competitive variables compensates
for external changes in marketing effectiveness,
such as an advertising promotion.

correct the symptom. *The implicit assumption behind each of these actions is that a problem symptom can be controlled by a remedy closely related to the symptom.*

In each case, the underlying system generating the symptom also compensates for the intervention. In the 1960s, more people moved to the cities with the housing programs, defeating the intent to provide better housing for a city's low-income residents. In the mid-1970s, artificially low energy prices delayed the transition to energy sources other than oil and undercut incentives for conservation, thereby keeping energy prices high through limiting energy supply and maintaining high energy demand. Attempts to improve U.S. national security through increased arms build-ups have been defeated by increased defense spending by the Soviets. It is very likely that efforts to reduce government deficits through higher taxes will slow economic growth, thereby reducing the tax base and compensating for higher tax rates.

In each of the above examples, the intervention is "successful" if one looks only at its immediate effects. New housing *did* improve the living conditions of the urban poor *until* migration flows adjusted to create more people in need of housing. Energy price controls *did* reduce the burden on consumers *until* further price increases in imported oil occurred (in 1973, at the time of the first OPEC price increase, the U.S.

imported 20 percent of its oil; when the second wave of price increases came in 1979, the U.S. imported close to 40 percent of its oil). Building up defense stockpiles *does* increase perceived national security (and may bolster a nation's bargaining position in international negotiations) *until* the other side increases arms to offset the advantage. Raising taxes *will* lower deficit projections, giving national policy-makers the satisfaction of having "done something" about the problem, until the effects of higher taxes on economic growth are felt.

The delays in compensating feedback responses mean that many obvious interventions result in *better-before-worse behavior*. Just as the interventions to boost marketing effectiveness in the simple example above did raise demand in the short-term, so too are there inevitably many ways to ameliorate problem symptoms in the short term. Only over the longer term does the system respond. The multiplicity of short-term fixes is a great pitfall for political decision-making, both in the public sector and in corporations.

Because the connection between short- and long-term responses is often unrecognized, intervenors can get drawn into a *reinforcing spiral of intervention*. The longer the delay between short- and long-term response, the more likely is the repeated use of an ineffective intervention. Many developing nations have become completely dependent on foreign food aid because the delay between the short-term benefit, food aid and reduced mortality, and the long-term disbenefit, increased population growth and starvation, is 10 to 20 years. Similar dynamics underlie the increasing dependency of cities on federal support, the poor on welfare programs, nations on their military establishments, and of many corporations on their trusted "intervenors" (for example, the designers of sales promotions, the "motivators" of increased sales effort, or increasingly lucrative sales incentives). The longer an inappropriate intervention is continued, the harder it can be to break the vicious cycle of dependency. In complex systems, where cause and effect are often not obviously related, there are subtle pressures to shift the burden for maintaining internal balances to the intervenor. What begins as a one-time response to ameliorate a problem symptom becomes an increasingly necessary ongoing activity.

## HIGH- VERSUS LOW-LEVERAGE POLICY CHANGES

The chief benefit of the systemic viewpoint lies in distinguishing high- from low-leverage policy changes. The vast majority of policy changes adopted within organizations or within larger social systems are low-leverage. However, understanding the systemic causes of problems also reveals policy changes that do have a long-term beneficial impact on a system. The only problem is that these "high-leverage points" are almost always "nonobvious"—that is, not closely related in time and space to the obvious symptoms of a problem.

### Expanding the Model

Expanding the simple model of organizational dynamics introduced above provides an illustration of a typical high-leverage policy change. In particular, we will extend the model by examining internal pressures to vary capacity to satisfy demand. Most corporations engage in long-term planning for the purpose of defining baseline rates of expansion of production capacity and service capacity. However, planned rates of capacity acquisition are adjusted depending on current conditions. For example, during periods of low profitability, when incoming demands are easily met, capacity expansion is often postponed. In many firms, the cost and risk involved with major expansions in capacity means that capacity expansion is not aggressive until there are clear indications of excess demand, such as rising order backlogs or growing delivery delays.

Figure 5 shows the feedback structure whereby capacity to satisfy demand can be adjusted in response to pressure from current competitive performance. If adequacy of capacity is stressed by demands growing in excess of current capacity to satisfy those demands, performance of competitive variables erodes (delivery delays rise, or product quality declines), increasing pressure to add capacity. As new capacity comes on line, the firm is more able to meet demand, thereby restoring competitive variables. The decision to adjust capacity, from this perspective, stems from attempts to control competitive variables relative to standards for competitive performance. (Because capacity adjustment is motivated by attempting to control key competitive variables, it is part of a negative-loop balancing feedback process.)

The feedback structure in Figure 5 also allows for competitive goals to adjust. For example, if a new firm began with a goal of shipping products in two months, but after two years of operation had never shipped a single product in less than two-

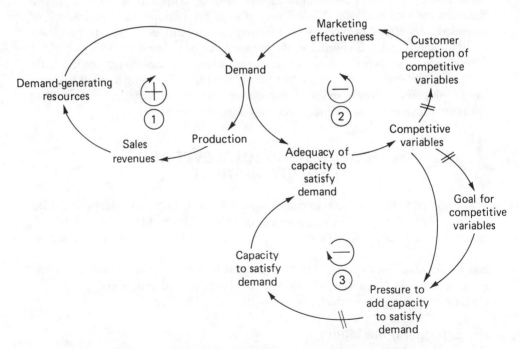

FIGURE 5.    Expanded Feedback Structure Involving Market
Growth and Capacity Adjustment.

144

and-a-half months, goals for delivery delay would tend to adjust. Organizations tend, as do individuals, to adjust goals in light of past performance. These adjustments are often rationalized as part of the learning process. They are strongly motivated by the psychological stress within an organization that is consistently failing to achieve desired goals. This goal-adjustment process is typically gradual, characterized by incremental shifts, many of which may not even be formally recognized. In Figure 5, goal adjustment is represented by a link from competitive variables to the goals for those variables. This causal link involves a substantial delay (indicated by hash marks), since goals are adjusted only gradually.

When the more complex structure involving simultaneous adjustments in resources to create demand and capacity to satisfy demand is simulated, the resulting behavior is surprising (Figure 6). We have used this generic model of organizational dynamics in training programs for literally thousands of managers. Invariably, most managers expect the structure to generate a pattern of growth interrupted by periodic downturns or plateaus. (People expect an unstable growth path because such growth is characteristic of most organizations, and because this structure has the capability of generating cycles, as evident in the preceding section.) Growth is almost always expected because a set of extremely favorable conditions conducive to growth have been assumed. There is no limit on the size of the market. There are no financial constraints on the ability to add capacity. But, even with an unlimited market and no financial constraints on expanding capacity, the firm does not grow. In fact, over the long term, there is a tendency for an initial period of growth to be followed by a gradual stagnation (Figure 6b).[4] Unlike the preceding case where growth stopped due to a physical limit of fixed capacity (Figure 2), growth is now stopping due to psychological and organizational limits to growth.

## Self-Limiting Growth

This generic structure of interactions between market growth and capacity expansion shows one of the many ways in which firms can self-limit their own growth. But, when an organization's growth fails to live up to expectations, there is a strong tendency to blame factors in the environment—for example, increased competition or inability to finance expansion. All too frequently, firms fail to recognize the leverage that may exist within their own policy structure to limit growth in demand. In particular, managers tend to assume demand as an external variable, particularly when there are demand shortfalls. In the absence of systemic understanding of how firm policies influence demand, managers consistently underestimate the long-term

---

[4]*In a computer simulation like that shown in Figure 6, numerous numerical assumptions are made regarding the specific length of time delays and the specific aggressiveness of different decisions. Within the structure of interrelationships shown in Figure 5, it is possible to vary these numerical assumptions substantially without altering the basic patterns of behavior shown in Figure 6. Variations in numerical assumptions can result in growth in demand followed by a plateau, or growth followed by decline, or even, if one picks numerical values very carefully, a very modest continued growth. But, given the present structure, there are no plausible sets of numerical values that will result in achieving the growth potential of the firm.*

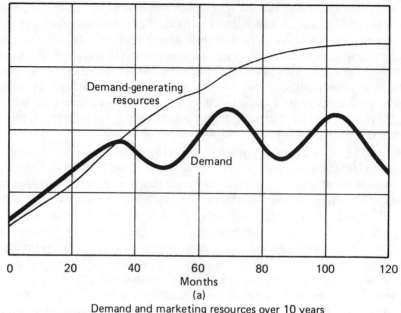

Demand and marketing resources over 10 years

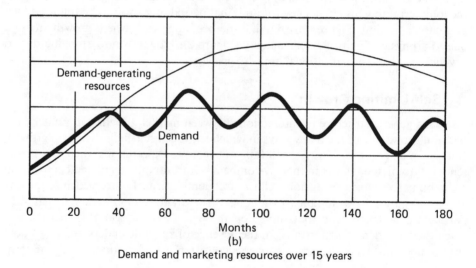

Demand and marketing resources over 15 years

FIGURE 6.    Simulated Behavior of Structure in Figure 5
Reveals Stagnating Growth

importance of policies within the firm. When things go wrong, we tend to blame the environment.

The periodic crisis of falling demand and marketing effectiveness shown in Figure 6 would tend to call forth the symptomatic interventions described in the preceding section. For example, note that the decline in demand beginning around month

**146**

36 presents the same symptoms of falling marketing effectiveness discussed previously. These symptoms would motivate interventions such as sales training or advertising promotions to boost marketing effectiveness, or might be seen as justifying the need for increased investment in marketing resources. However, none of the interventions aimed at the symptom of falling marketing effectiveness will beneficially alter long-term performance. Figure 7 shows the effects of an advertising promotion to boost marketing effectiveness (begun at month 46) and an increase in the marketing budget leading to more rapid expansion of all aspects of marketing resources (also at month 46). Clearly, neither of these policy changes has any long-term beneficial impact. In this structure, policies aimed at the symptoms of eroding marketing effectiveness are inherently low-leverage.

However, there are policy changes that *do* have the capability of achieving the growth potential of the firm. To recognize these high leverage policy changes requires understanding the dynamics that can cause growth to stagnate.

To understand the causes of stagnating growth in the present context, a manager must understand that, whenever the performance of key competitive variables is poor, two simultaneous adjustment processes are activated. Decline in competitive variables, such as rising delivery delays or falling product quality, sends signals within the firm to boost capacity. Decline in key competitive variables also sends signals to the marketplace. Customers learn that the firm is unable to deliver on schedule or is having difficulties meeting product- or service-quality promises. These two adjustment processes are represented by loops 2 and 3 in Figure 5.

Whether or not a firm succeeds in growing vigorously over the long term often depends on the relative strength of these two responses. In particular, if a firm is sluggish in adjusting its own capacity when its competitive performance deteriorates (i.e., loop 3 is weak), control shifts to the marketplace. Customers become dissatisfied with the poor product quality or availability, reduce demand, and thereby, in effect, correct the problem of the firm's inadequate capacity. Alternatively, if the firm responds aggressively to decline in its key competitive variables (i.e., loop 3 is strong), it adjusts capacity to control competitive variables before customers become dissatisfied. Regardless of whether the customers make the adjustment or the firm makes the adjustment, the condition of excess demand relative to capacity will be corrected, *because,* over the long term, no firm can sell more than it produces. The big difference, of course, is that if the firm's internal adjustment (loop 3) dominates, capacity rises to serve a higher level of demand. If the customers' adjustment process (loop 2) dominates, demand contracts to the limited capacity. In the first case, growth occurs. In the second, growth is limited.

One way to think of the dynamics of market growth and capacity expansion is that there are periodic crises in competitive variables that occur in the growth of almost all firms. These periodic crises represent "windows of opportunity." If a firm fails to aggressively adjust capacity during these times of crisis, the crisis will pass. That is, poor competitive variables will result in loss of customers and lower demand. The window of opportunity will have closed.

These periodic windows of opportunity are evident in the behavior of a typical competitive variable, delivery delay, relative to its goal. During the crisis of falling demand and marketing effectiveness centered around month 40 in Figure 6, delivery

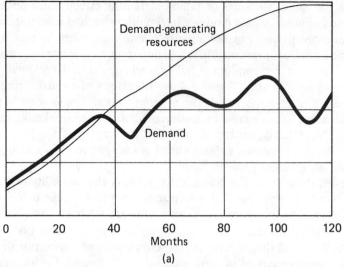

(a)
Advertising promotion starting at month 46

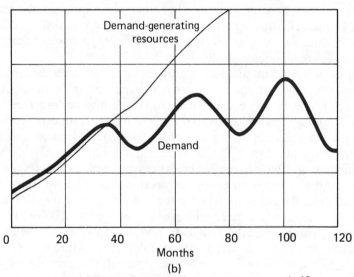

(b)
Increased budget for marketing resources at month 46

FIGURE 7.    Unsuccessful Attempts to Stimulate Growth
Through Responding to Declines in Marketing
Effectiveness

delay is high (see Figure 8). This creates a signal within the organization to expand capacity. But delivery delay does not stay high indefinitely. It begins to decline and has fallen back to its goal within about one year. By the end of this crisis period, the signals that might motivate further capacity expansion are no longer present, since delivery delay has fallen. The insidiousness of this dynamic lies in the fact that after

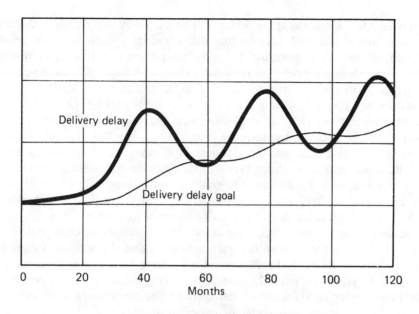

FIGURE 8.    The Dynamics of Eroding Goals. During each
crisis of high delivery delays — which occur
approximately every 3 to 3½ years — the firm's
goal for delivery delay adjusts upward.

a relatively brief period of time, "the problem goes away." Delivery delays have fallen, and the evidence that capacity is inadequate has disappeared.

The dynamics of interacting capacity expansion and demand adjustments explain a fundamental management principle: failure to serve the customer (through aggressively responding to declines in competitive variables) can undermine the long-term success of the enterprise. We can now see that, from a systemic perspective, this intuitive managerial principle is explained by the shifting dominance of the two generic responses to inadequate capacity. If the firm's internal response through capacity expansion is dominant, demand and supply will be balanced by growing capacity to serve a growing demand. If the external response through dissatisfied customers is dominant, demand and supply will be balanced by limited demand to meet limited capacity. *The critical point is that the relative strengths of the two feedback processes are influenced by the firm's own policies!*

## Leverage Points

In the present structure, there is one particular aspect of the firm's internal decision-making that is most critical for its ability to expand capacity aggressively. This concerns the way goals for competitive variables adjust to the past performance of those variables. Goal adjustment, which is common in many firms, can undermine the aggressiveness of capacity expansion by desensitizing management to poor competitive performance. The degree of goal erosion can be modest and yet the long-term effects significant. For example, Figure 8 shows that the delivery-delay goal has

**149**

risen from 2 to 2.6 months at the peak of the first delivery-delay crisis (about month 40). The goal is still well below actual delivery delay, which has risen to about 5 months at the peak of the crisis. From the perspective of managers striving to reduce a 5-month delivery delay, striving for a 2.6-month delivery delay as opposed to the original 2-month goal might seem like an insignificant difference. Indeed, the difference might be insignificant if the firm were not operating in a highly competitive environment where dissatisfied customers take their demand elsewhere. As shown above, in a competitive setting a firm is always in a "horse race." If it fails to adjust its capacity quickly enough, customers will make the adjustment by lowering demand. In a competitive setting, even a modest erosion of goals can be critical.

To demonstrate the sensitivity to goal erosion, Figure 9 shows the growth resulting from an explicit policy to not alter goals for competitive variables during times of crisis. This is the *only* change in structure or parameters relative to the preceding simulations in which goals for competitive variables were allowed to erode slightly during times of crisis. When goals are not eroded, the potential for growth is realized. After 10 years, the firm's demand is 8 times greater than in the eroding goal case; after 15 years demand is 23 times higher. This dramatic shift in performance highlights another highly intuitive managerial principle: *eroding goals can undermine the long-term growth potential of an organization.*

Observers often wonder how firms that were once highly successful fall from prominence. I believe that the dynamics of eroding goals often hold the explanation. The behavior over time of the delivery-delay goal in Figure 8 traces a subtle evolu-

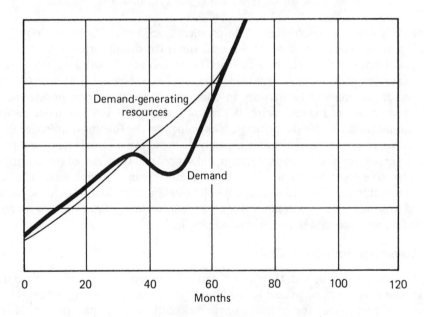

FIGURE 9.    Realizing the Firm's Potential Growth. When the goal for delivery delay is not allowed to erode during crises, demand and sales revenues (not shown) grow indefinitely.

tion in performance standards. During each delivery-delay crisis, the delivery-delay goal erodes slightly *relative to where it was at the beginning of the crisis*. As the crisis abates, the goal ceases to erode. When a new crisis develops, the goal erodes slightly further. The extent of erosion during each crisis is modest. But the *cumulative* erosion over a series of crises is significant — delivery-delay goals have risen over 100% after 10 years in Figure 8!

The danger of goal erosion stems from its gradualness. If a frog is placed in a pot of boiling water, it will quickly jump out. Its biological control mechanisms are well suited to responding to sudden threats to survival. But the same reliable control mechanisms can be fooled if the temperature is gradually increased in a pot of cool water. If the temperature is increased very gradually, the frog's internal temperature standard will rise to accommodate the stress and nullify the signal to jump to safety. As the temperature continues to gradually increase, the frog will become groggy, and if the experiment continues, the frog will boil. Analogously, many firms respond aggressively to sudden business crises, but fail to perceive gradual erosions in standards for quality, service, or reliability that occur over several years and perhaps through several generations of top management.

The effect of goal-setting on long-term growth illustrates the principle of *leverage points*. Repeated studies of organizational and social systems have shown that there are invariably a small number of policy changes that can have dramatic and enduring effects on performance. Not allowing standards for key competitive variables to erode in times of crisis is one such leverage point.

Perhaps the most intriguing feature of such high-level policy changes is that they are very frequently not apparent to the participants in the system. The inability to readily perceive leverage points stems from the nature of causality in a complex system: namely, cause and effect are not closely related in time and space. The tendency for all of us to focus on problem symptoms simultaneously leads our focus away from the very actions and policy changes that might have the most impact on these symptoms.

The principle of leverage points illuminates one of the most elusive qualities of great leadership: namely, the capability of great leaders to focus attention on a small number of critical success factors. For example, the eroding goals illustration suggests that one function of leadership is to identify appropriate standards for key competitive variables, such as quality and reliability, and to project these standards throughout an organization. To be effective, such standards must represent enduring values shared by the organization and its customers, and offset the tendency within the organization to gauge itself against recent performance. While most managers are drawn into a reinforcing struggle to battle crises, effective leaders must understand the critical dynamics for long-term success and distill this understanding into operational guidelines.

## IMPLEMENTING
## THE SYSTEMIC PERSPECTIVE

Developing systems thinking will be a primary objective for leaders in the more creative nonauthoritarian organization of the future. In the "Program in Systems

Thinking and the New Management Style," we are exploring ways that the substantial body of theory and tools for understanding complex systems, developed over the past 30 years, can help leaders in this task. To date our work has focused on developing shared understanding within an organization of (1) basic system principles universal to all systems and (2) the "generic structures" and management principles critical to each individual organization.

## System Principles

The first stage in assimilating the systems perspective is to distinguish between problem symptoms and problem causes. Managers continually find themselves drawn into reacting to symptoms. Frequently, problems are defined by their symptoms. In most organizations the pressures for immediate management intervention far outweigh the understanding to guide intervention wisely. While the willingness to tackle important problems is a necessary characteristic of effective leadership, the wise leader appreciates that efforts to manipulate problem symptoms are rarely successful in complex systems.

Our experience is that various physical exercises and games can be particularly effective in opening managers' eyes to the subtle nature of causality in complex systems. For many years, we have introduced managers to the systems viewpoint through a role-playing simulation of a production-distribution system reacting to an external customer demand. Producers, distributors, wholesalers, and retailers interact in such a way as to produce periodic inventory stock-outs and overordering. The participants invariably blame each other and the customers for the instabilities, since this explanation matches the symptoms of buildups and collapses in incoming orders received. It comes as a shock to most participants to discover, when the game is over, that the customer demand was constant and the true causes of instability lie in the very ordering policies that they themselves were following. This game-playing experience begins to build awareness that problem symptoms may be misleading indicators of underlying structural causes.[5]

Another physical exercise created by one of the organizations with which we have worked illuminates the difficulties of management control. The exercise starts with two roller skates connected by springs of different strengths. The "student" is given the relatively simple task of controlling one roller skate by manipulating the other. The task then gets progressively more challenging as additional roller skates are added to the chain, each connected with springs of varying strengths. By the time there are a half dozen roller skates, it becomes virtually impossible to control one end of the chain by manipulating the other end. It is then pointed out that this physical system is vastly simpler than the task facing a manager trying to control local actions through multiple tiers of a management hierarchy.

A gyroscope can make a splendid demonstration of actions producing nonobvious consequences. Because of the complex forces conserving angular momentum, if one side of the gyroscope is pushed upward, it actually moves sideways. If the same point is pushed sideways, it moves downward. Although the simple physical analogy lacks the complexity of the organizational system (in particular, it lacks the time

[5]*Information on this game can be obtained by contacting the author.*

delays that obscure the longer term unintended consequences of many managerial interventions), it makes a strong impression that unintended consequences are a common characteristic of complex systems.

Once people begin to appreciate the nature of cause and effect in complex systems, the next stage in understanding involves applying systems principles like compensating feedback. Compensating feedback arises from unrecognized balancing processes in complex systems. A useful question in discerning potential sources of compensating feedback is to *consider the basic balances necessary to the health of a particular organization.* For example, in a growing enterprise, important balances involve capacity to generate demand and capacity to satisfy demand, efforts to develop new products or services and abilities to develop new products or services, rates of labor expansion and capacity to assimilate new people into a coherent culture, and desired rates of capital investment and financial resources for investment. Imbalances in any of these areas produce stresses that will manifest in diverse problem symptoms. Attempting to ameliorate these symptoms will have much less leverage than correcting the underlying imbalance.

Unrecognized balancing processes that cause compensating feedback also include subtle balances involving *operating* (as opposed to espoused) *goals, habits, and implicit norms in organizations.* Often compensating feedback arises because an attempted organizational change contradicts an implicit norm or operating goal. For example, some "new age" companies that are very successful in promoting an image of health and well being for their customers have chronic burnout problems with their own employees. In one firm, the average tenure of managers was only one or two years because the pace was so frantic. The firm had great difficulty improving this situation despite a variety of corrective measures aimed at the problem. The first was a memo sent to all managers describing the company's commitment to the health and well being of its employees. The memo expressed concern over the long-term costs, both individually and for the company as a whole, of overwork. The memo had little effect. As the problem continued, a policy of discouraging after-hours work in the company's facilities was adopted. This too had little impact, as many ignored the new policy. The policy was given more teeth by closing company facilities at 7 P.M. Not surprisingly, people took their work home with them in the evening.

The failure of all of the company's efforts to reduce overwork and management burnout stemmed from an implicit norm in the organization's culture. The goal of employee health and well being was inconsistent with a norm that personal success stemmed from "breaking through perceived personal limitations." This norm in turn stemmed from the personal philosophy of the company's founder, which he had preached for many years. For employees, the philosophy of not being constrained by self-imposed limitations means a willingness to continually expand personal workload. So long as willingness to expand personal workload operated as an implicit norm for success, efforts to solve the problem of overwork and burnout were doomed to be ineffective.[6]

---

[6] *The norm of overwork as a key to success is an example of "implicit assumptions," the deepest layer of organizational culture. [See Schein (1985).]*

A similar example of conflict with established norms and operating goals occurred in an elaborate systems modeling project with a large capital goods manufacturer. At the end of a study lasting more than a year, and involving many of the senior managers in the corporation, it was concluded that the company's production and inventory policies had been responsible for eroding market share. It was determined that the company should maintain a steady production rate during the next business downturn, so as to build inventory and improve its product availability while competitors were cutting back. The policy change was a tremendous success. The company actually increased its market share during an ensuing business downturn and boosted profits substantially. Unfortunately, when the next major business downturn occurred four years later, production practices reverted to the traditional policy of sharp cutbacks and emphasis on controlling inventory costs. The firm lost more market share to foreign competitors.

The reason the successful policy had failed to take root was that it conflicted with an operating goal woven deeply into the company's traditions and culture. For many years, the president and later chairman of the board had preached the virtues of controlling inventory costs. In this particular business, the unit cost of inventory is very high and excess inventories can have a dramatic short-term impact on profitability. The fate of production managers who had failed to control inventories during business downturns was legend. For the individual production manager there was no greater fear than to be the person responsible for large inventory costs. Consequently, despite the *proven success* of the new policy of building inventories during a downturn, this policy conflicted with the traditional practice of successful production managers.

The above examples of thwarted organizational changes illustrate the "structural conflicts" that arise from multiple inconsistent goals (see Chapter 9 and 11). New policies involving new goals are often adopted with little recognition of the existence of alternative operating goals and implicit norms. Compensating feedback based on adherence to traditional goals and norms then defeats the new policies. Conversely, the importance of "aligning" local goals in an organization has become a predominant theme of the new management [for example Kiefer and Senge (1984) and Harrison (1984)]. The function of effective leadership to establish superordinate visions and values is now widely recognized. From a systemic viewpoint, an overarching vision and value system creates a field in which diverse local goals can be brought into greater harmony, thereby reducing the potential for goal conflict. Nonetheless, as illustrated above, compensating feedback can arise in subtle forms involving implicit goals and norms. It would be unwise to assume that simply establishing common vision and values is sufficient to automatically eliminate compensating feedback from conflicting local goals.

## Generic Structures and Management Principles

Assimilating basic system principles begins the process of systemic thinking within an organization. Continuing the process requires ongoing management education. This education should help managers clarify and test their mental models of strategy and operations and gradually develop a deeper understanding of the dynamics critical to the organization's success. If such an education process is to succeed, it must create a shared language for describing the organization and its environment as an integrated evolving system.

As we have progressed in our research program, we have had to re-examine some of our own initial premises regarding the nature of this education process. In particular, we have found it necessary to abandon our traditional style of consulting and teaching in favor of a more open-ended learning process. Proficiency with new thinking tools can be achieved only through application. That is, the managers themselves must use the tools! They must build and test their own system models to learn what systems thinking is all about.

This realization has led to creating a new process for catalyzing management systems thinking. We call the process a *strategic forum*. The strategic forum compares to traditional methods of consulting and model building much as the total immersion approach to learning a foreign language compares to traditional methods of teaching languages. A group of managers comes together to examine their strategy or a particular strategic issue. With the help of one or more systems thinking facilitators and dramatic new software called STELLA (and a personal computer with advanced graphics capabilities), the group of managers explores the assumptions about dynamics lying behind their own strategy.

The very process of explicating critical assumptions always proves useful and very often reveals startling inconsistencies. For example, in one recent instance, the CEO of a firm that had just spent two hours exploring the firm's strategy regarding growth in sales and sales personnel was compelled to stand up and ask if any member of the top management believed that their strategic plan was achievable. What he and the other top managers had discovered was that their own assumptions about relative productivity of new and experienced sales personnel, time to train new sales personnel, and turnover of experienced sales personnel were inconsistent with projected hiring rates—by a factor of 2! The top management had never thought through how projected rapid hiring rates would dilute the overall yield of the salesforce, force experienced sales personnel to divert more time to training junior personnel, and increase turnover in senior personnel. What had been lacking was a language for interrelating the insights of different members of the management team to examine salesforce growth systemically.[7]

As managers in an organization develop fluency in systems principles and conceptualization tools, a library of *generic structures* eventually develops. Generic structures are dynamic processes intrinsic to an organization's health and success. Understanding generic structures identifies the management principles that must guide successful leadership.

The model of interacting market growth and capacity expansion presented above is an example of a generic structure. Like all generic structures, it embodies important management principles by revealing the dynamics giving rise to the principles—for example, by showing how "eroding goals can undermine the long-term

---

[7] *The strategic forum concept is described in more depth in B. Richmond, P. Senge, and J. Kemeny, "Catalyzing Management Systems Thinking," a System Dynamics Group Working Paper obtainable from the author.*

growth of an enterprise." Our belief is that a relatively modest number (well less than 50) of generic structures will capture a significant portion of the dynamics of all organization growth and stability. For a given firm, the number of critical generic structures is undoubtedly much smaller.

The concept of generic structures clarifies what has always been one of the paramount tasks of organizational leadership—to understand an organization's critical dynamics. In the traditional authoritarian organization, a leader's understanding of critical dynamics could be purely intuitive. As unilateral strategist and decision-maker, the authoritarian leader needed only to be right in his judgment. He had only to tell people *what* to do, not *why*. What is changing in today's more locally controlled organization is that leaders must be able to conceptualize and explain what they had only to intuit formerly.

For example, in one of the participating companies in our program, the president has attempted to develop understanding in his organization of the differences between being a "growth-driven" and "quality-driven" company. A growth-driven company, in his terminology, is one pursuing sales growth as its primary objective. When business is going well, it aggressively expands its marketing and sales effort to capitalize on growth opportunities. On the other hand, a quality-driven company places service to the customer as its primary objective. When business conditions are good, the quality-driven organization invests aggressively in capacity, so as to expand business while maintaining quality.

This particular company president has been preaching the benefits of being a "quality-driven" organization for some time. He feels this message must be understood widely because local managers in his firm have considerable autonomy in pursuing their own policies for growing their parts of the business. Many of the managers in the company undoubtedly take the message to heart—because the president is a good preacher. But, for many, it remains more philosophy than operating practice. The instinct to seize opportunities for aggressive sales expansion, with little thought toward the longer term consequences, is deeply ingrained in most entrepreneurial managers.

We now understand the generic structure that distinguishes the quality-driven from the growth-driven company. It belongs to the family of market-growth and capacity-expansion structures presented above. Understanding the generic structure of interacting market growth and capacity expansion gives new depth of meaning to the principle of being quality driven. If the firm does not adhere to high quality standards that continually push it to build capacity as aggressively as it seeks new sales, inadequate capacity will eventually depress quality and erode market share. As managers are coming to understand these dynamics, they are discovering that being "quality-driven" is a principle for business success, not just a moral imperative.

The chief executive of another of the participating companies in the program, in a recent address at his stockholder's annual meeting, articulated a philosophy for coping with industry cycles. In particular, he argued that most companies react to short-term pressures on profits in a way that reduces long-term growth:

> Much has been said and written about American management's propensity to manage for short-term results. And indeed there is an unspoken virtue in

management's ability to produce smooth, continuously growing financial results. Investors understandably dislike the uncertainty implicit in wide swings in earnings, particularly when they have no other yardsticks by which to monitor performance.

But the only way to stabilize the output results of a business for unstable growth of demand is to destabilize the execution of long-term programs and the development of the organization. This may minimize short-term variations in earnings but only at the expense of long-term growth and profitability.

(Ray Stata, Analog Devices, Inc., 1985)

Stata believes strongly in this philosophy of gearing investment (in physical capital, R&D, and human capital) to long-term growth trends and not overreacting to short-term fluctuations. But he also knows that, in fact, these critical investment decisions are actually made by hundreds of managers throughout the firm. A gap between philosophy and practice will remain until there exists a learning process whereby managers throughout the firm can better understand the relationships between short-term fluctuations and long-term growth.

In an era when much of American business has drifted toward short-term profit maximization as the sole criterion of organizational success, organizations such as those participating in the Systems Thinking and New Management style program represent a much-needed counterforce. If we fail in developing a long-term systemic perspective guiding private enterprise, it is exceedingly unlikely that we shall succeed in doing so as regards public policy. Several years ago, the annual report of another of the participating organizations, the Kollmorgen Corporation, argued that American business had a special responsibility to nurture values of freedom and respect for the individual.

In a nation drifting slowly away from these concepts of freedom, and individual worth, and ultimate responsibility for one's own destiny, it is ironic that business may be the most free institution left in America. We believe that business must show the way by example to the rest of our institutions.[8]

Surely, a similar opportunity presents itself to business to demonstrate the practicality of systems thinking for effective leadership.

---

[8] *1979 Annual Report, available from Kollmorgen.*

# CHAPTER 11

# The Leader as Creator

by

**ROBERT FRITZ**

*Energy always moves where it is easiest to go, along the path of least resistance. Failure to acknowledge and work with this law of nature can quickly render the leader ineffective. The fundamental structures in most organizations channel energy naturally toward maintaining the status quo. To create lasting change, leaders must learn to create new structures which will redirect the system's energies toward the desired changes. This chapter presents a simple yet elegant way to accomplish this redirection.*

As we move toward the twenty-first century, great changes in the very nature of our civilization are taking place, with implications for every individual on the planet. With any turn of a century, it is common for new possibilities to emerge, new approaches to become common practice, new philosophies of living to become popular, new systems of organization to arise, new modes of thinking and feeling to appear and new qualities of leadership to help give birth to a new world.

We are already beginning to see signs of the twenty-first century arise as crocuses do in the spring, pushing their way through the hardened earth and up through layers upon layers of leaves. At first this growth seems small and insignificant compared to what appears to be a hostile and incompatible environment, and yet in a matter of weeks all of nature seems to have converted to the religion of growth, change and new life prophesied by the crocuses.

As we observe our times, radically new developments in support of that which is truly highest in the human spirit are beginning to sprout. At first they seemed insignificant in light of a hard, bitter, and indifferent world, entrenched in the ways of the past. And yet we can also observe the ground beginning to yield to the innate power and life-giving force of these new developments, which are both signs of the future and signs of the times.

For any lasting change to occur, it must be consistent with the fundamental nature of the universe. And yet too often, those of us who would be agents of change attempt to force our synthetic manipulations on a world that can only comply with natural law.

One of the principles of all of nature, including human nature, is that energy always moves where it is easiest to go—the route all energy takes is along the path of least resistance.

However, when we look to our institutions or organizations or to our own lives, this principle is often obscured by countless experiences of struggle, resistance, inertia, and seeming inability to change. Leaders who are designated or destined to be the premier agents of change often find that no matter what their technique or sincerity, they are rendered ineffective in a universe that appears unmoving, unyielding, and stubborn.

If energy moves along the path of least resistance, why is it so difficult to create change even in small matters, let alone large organizations or societies? It is because the fundamental structures in play do not lead toward change or growth, but rather toward reinforcing fixed patterns of behavior. When change is attempted within these structures, the structures compensate and actually seem to "resist" the change.

Despite all our experiences of disappointment, frustration, and powerlessness when we attempt to change the situations and circumstances in which we find ourselves, change in fact is possible. The agency of change must create structures that support change. This, alas, is highly unlikely for most people because they are unable to operate on the level of structure, simply because the realm itself is a foreign and unfamiliar territory to which they have not been initiated.

It is not that the realm of structure is unnatural, for human beings are structure-seeking and have an innate ability to create structure. Rather it is a lack of fluency in the language of structure itself, which is merely caused by being raised in a society that misunderstands the nature and power of creativity.

Even the word "creative" has degenerated to the point where it often describes merely a style or a manner in which to perform essentially uncreative acts. Most people have the erroneous image of a creator as primarily a rearranger of circumstances, a problem-solver, a generator of alternatives, or a freak of nature blessed or cursed with talents beyond those of most people.

In our traditional educational system, students are encouraged to learn the proper responses to societal pressures and respond "appropriately." The clear message is that circumstances hold the power, and people need to negotiate around or through them in order to fit into the fabric of society. A person is called "creative" simply on the basis of having an unusual, novel, or inventive style of responding to circumstances. The image of a creator in this context, then, is merely that of a manager of process subject to the whims and weather of changing circumstances. Within this premise, leadership is likewise relegated to being a manipulator of circumstances, managing tradeoffs among competing forces and assessing and fulfilling needs. Built into this life-view are limitations that confine true creativity, for the circumstances will always determine what should and will be created.

The true creator, on the other hand, lives in a quite different universe. Creators are not driven by the circumstances, and their creations are not simply responses to the circumstances. Creators can give birth to images beyond the circumstances, and beyond even rearrangements of or extrapolations from the circumstances. As the great twentieth-century composer Karlheinz Stockhausen once said, "We need to close our eyes for a while and listen. There is always something unheard of in the

160

air." In their imagination, creators can see what isn't there, and they can then bring into reality that which has never existed before.

Leadership in this universe of the creator includes enabling *other* people to bring into reality what at first does not exist. The leader within this premise must first and foremost have mastered the creative process personally. The leader as creator develops fluency in the realm of structure so that once a creation is envisioned, an underlying structure is established that makes the final fulfillment of the vision not only possible but actually probable. Bringing into reality what the leader wants to create, whether alone or in concert with others, becomes easier and easier. When a leader can envision a result to be created and can fulfill the vision by completely bringing into reality the full manifestation of the vision, leadership takes on a new meaning, a new scope, and a new power.

Furthermore, the leader as creator enables others to make a fundamental shift of orientation—a shift from reacting or responding to the circumstances in which individuals find themselves to an orientation in which they become the predominant creative force in their own lives.

Leadership in this new orientation is thus enabling strong individuals to join together in a collective creative act of bringing into the world what they all most deeply care about and want to see exist. This is not a utopian and impossible dream. There are countless examples of organizations that consist of strong individuals bringing into reality their vision. Certain sports teams, symphony orchestras, engineering groups, theater companies, rock groups, and management teams demonstrate that the universe of the creative not only can exist but does exist. Most people, however, do not live in that universe.

The structure in which most people find themselves does not lead them to creating what they want, no matter how they attempt to solve or manipulate circumstances.


## TENSION-RESOLUTION SYSTEMS

It is a principle found throughout nature that tension seeks resolution. From the spider web to the human body, from the formation of galaxies to the shifts of continents, from watch escapements to the movement of wind-up toys, we see tension-resolution systems. In nature and in our lives there are both simple and complex tension-resolution systems. The simplest tension-resolution system is a structure that contains a single tension. The structural tendency of this tension is to move toward resolution. A rubber band that has been stretched, for example, contains within the structure a tendency to relax or resolve the tension.

A simple tension-resolution system at play in your own life occurs when you are hungry. Hunger creates a tension. That tension is resolved once you eat. Similarly, thirst creates a tension. That tension is resolved when you drink.

A particular tension-resolution system is **structural conflict**. Structural conflict exists when a structure contains two or more tension-resolution systems with mutually exclusive points of resolution.

For example, as we have seen, when a person is hungry that hunger creates a tension and the tension is resolved by eating:

**Tension**

Hungry ⟶ **Resolution** Eat

On the other hand, when a person is overweight, this also creates a tension. The tension may be resolved through a diet (not eating):

**Tension**

Overweight ⟶ **Resolution** Don't eat

Together, these two simple tension-resolution systems are related to each other in such a way as to form a complex tension-resolution system:

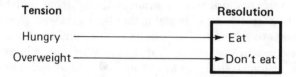

**Tension**

Hungry ⟶ **Resolution** Eat

Overweight ⟶ Don't eat

The two points of resolution cannot both exist at once—a person cannot simultaneously eat and not eat. Moreover, the tension also cannot be resolved sequentially, since the resolution of one tension increases the tension of the other system. When the person eats in an attempt to resolve the tension of being hungry, by eating he adds tension to the "overweight-don't-eat" system. When he does not eat in an attempt to resolve the tension of being overweight, hunger increases, adding tension to the "hungry-eat" system:

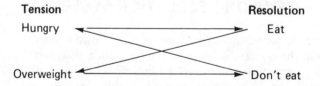

**Tension**

Hungry

Overweight

**Resolution**

Eat

Don't eat

This is an example of *structural conflict*. Since any attempt to resolve one of the constituent tension-resolution systems increases tension in the other, *one property of structural conflict is that it is not resolvable,* no matter what actions are taken.

Actions do, however, tend to be taken in an *attempt* to resolve structural conflict. In fact, a consistent, predictable pattern of behavior arises from the structure. The behavior is oscillation, as the structure compensates for each and every action. Within this structure, dieters lose weight and gain weight and lose weight and gain weight. Any action a dieter takes will ultimately lead to an opposite action, for within the system a continual shift of dominance occurs between the constituent tension-resolution systems.

Since energy moves along the path of least resistance, sometimes it is easier to eat and sometimes it is easier to diet. Within this structure, every action taken seems to be exactly what the immediate circumstance calls for. And it is. Structure has integrity, and this structure is perfectly balanced and sound. The only problem is, it is completely inadequate in enabling the dieter to maintain the weight he or she wants.

Structural conflict is an inadequate structure in which to create what you want to create. Unfortunately, this structure is the most prevalent found in most people's lives.

## STRUCTURAL CONFLICT

The structural conflict most common in everyone's life is formed by the component of desire on the one hand and an incompatible dominant belief in personal inability to fulfill one's desires on the other.

Most of what you learn in your formative years is about what you cannot do. Children are rightfully taught limitations essential to their survival. In one psychological study, children wore tape recorders for several days. When the tapes were analyzed, the psychologists conducting the study found that over 90 percent of what had been said to those children concerned either what they could not do, or how what they were doing was wrong. It is no wonder that an underlying impression of powerlessness lives on long after we know how to cross a street or light a match safely. A fundamental belief that all of us have is that we are somehow powerless to have what we want. Simultaneously we exist on a plane of reality that has as one of its governing principles structural tendencies. Within the sphere of the human being, these tendencies manifest themselves as desire. People both want to create what most deeply matters to them and simultaneously believe they cannot have what they want. This very human dilemma is actually a structural conflict. Desire creates a tension resolved by having what you want:

The belief creates a tension resolved by not having what you want:

Together, these two tension-resolution systems create structural conflict, since the two points of resolution are mutually exclusive:

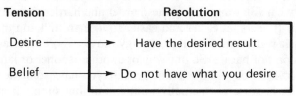

Once again, this structure is not resolvable. Here is an analogy of how the structure plays itself out over time. Imagine yourself in a room. Imagine yourself midway between the front and back walls of the room. Imagine further that the result you want is written on the wall in front of you so that movement toward that wall represents movement toward having what you want. Imagine the belief "You cannot have what you want" written on the wall behind you. And imagine that around your waist are two gigantic rubber bands. One rubber band, stretched from your waist to the wall in front, represents the tension-resolution system that would be resolved by creating the result you want. The other rubber band, stretched from your waist to the back wall, represents the tension-resolution system that would be resolved by not having the result you want.

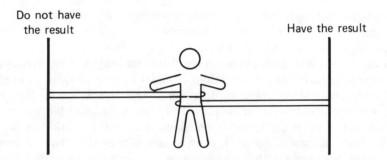

Now imagine what happens as you begin to move toward having what you want. As you approach the front wall, what happens to the rubber bands? The front one, of course, relaxes, and at the same time, the one behind you is stretched further. As you approach the front wall, where is it easiest for you to go? Where is the greater tension? Where does the path of least resistance lead?

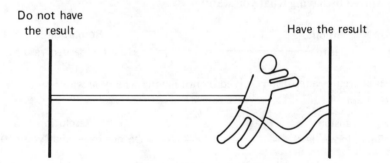

Clearly, the path of least resistance leads toward the back wall. As you move toward creating what you want, it becomes harder and harder to take the next steps toward having it. It becomes easier and easier to lose ground and move back toward not having what you want. In nature, energy moves where it is easiest for it to go. And you are a part of nature. So one way or another, sooner or later, you will move back the other way. You will do so not because you have some deep-seated self-destructive urge or because you actually want to fail, but simply because by doing so you are moving along the path of least resistance to which the underlying structure gives rise.

Now imagine what happens to the rubber bands as you move toward not having what you want and approach the back wall. Where is the greater tension now? Where is the path of least resistance? Where is it easiest for you to go?

Do not have
the result

Have the result

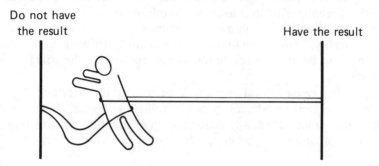

Obviously, the path of least resistance now leads back toward the front wall, toward the result you desire. Over time, you will tend to continue to move back and forth, back and forth, first toward one wall, then toward the other as the path of least resistance changes. These shifts may take minutes or years. Most often the oscillation occurs over a longer period of time, and the phenomenon can be difficult to observe at first.

Though the specific actions taken might differ, anyone in this structure would behave in fundamentally the same way, moving toward and then away from, toward and then away from what is desired. Moreover, the same pattern of behavioral oscillation would tend to arise no matter what result is desired.

### "Solving" Structural Conflict

At first sight, it would seem easy to "solve" structural conflict by breaking either of the two component tension-resolution systems. One "solution" is to change the dominant belief from "I can't have what I want" to "I can have what I want." There are many methods of attempting to change beliefs, but all of them fail in this structure. If you place the new positive belief *I can have what I want* (or some variation) on the front wall, *changing your belief* becomes your new desire. As you progressively adopt your new belief, the "Do not have what you desire" tension-resolu-

tion system becomes dominant. Ironically, it then becomes easier for you to believe you cannot have what you want than that you can have what you want, no matter how you may try to brainwash yourself.

The other "solution" to structural conflict is to give up your desires. This is inaccurately reported to be the way of Zen. If you attempt to relinquish all desire, relinquishing desire becomes your new desire, and the more closely you approach "no desire," the more the structural tendency to fail. Also implicit in "giving up desire" are spiritual goals such as enlightment or reaching "Nirvana" or being freed from the "illusion of reality." These function the same as any other goals in this structure: as desires opposing the tension-resolution system formed by the belief "I can't have what I want."

People often embark on attempting to circumvent the effects of structural conflict with great optimism, which is generally followed by great disillusionment. It is inherent in this structure that any actions taken as solutions actually only reinforce the experience of limitation, and hence the structure itself.

## Strategies

There are three major strategies designed to compensate for the fundamental unresolvability of structural conflict. They are: staying within an area of tolerable conflict, conflict manipulation, and willpower manipulation.

*Area of Tolerable Conflict.* A common strategy is to attempt to minimize the amplitude of the oscillation structural conflict produces. As one moves closer to either the front or back wall in our analogy, the structural phenomena often appear on the experiential level as increasingly uncomfortable feelings. The strategy of maintaining an area of tolerable conlfict is to minimize these uncomfortable feelings by remaining within an area in which the feelings generated can be easily tolerated. Within this area of tolerable conflict, the pattern of oscillation continues to occur, but with decreased amplitude. What determines the point at which a shift in direction will take place? For different people there are different points, because different people have different degrees of tolerance for discomfort. The point at which one shifts direction marks the outer limit of one's area of tolerance of conflict. Were one to take even a single step beyond this area, one would feel pronounced discomfort. Often, therefore, the shift actually occurs before the outer limit of tolerance is reached.

Since structural conflict consists of desire and a belief in one's powerlessness, the behaviors found in this strategy of remaining within an area of tolerable conflict

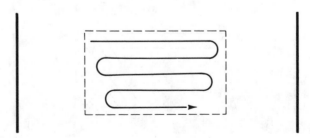

are to limit aspiration and to minimize loss. This is the strategy encouraged by most institutions and organizations, including public education, government bureaucracies, and corporate life. These organizations are not designed maliciously to thwart creativity and aspiration; they just do. The structural conflict begets the strategy of maintaining an area of tolerable conflict, which begets the behavior of reaching for only that which is "realistic" while minimizing risks. Predictability and certainty are highly valued, to the detriment of creativity. This strategy is found not only in organizations but also in the personal lives of vast numbers of people on our planet who have learned to minimize risk, limit their aspirations, and fit into a prevailing mediocrity society seems to reward.

*Conflict Manipulation.* Given the fundamental unresolvability of structural conflict, then, people often gravitate toward taking less and less action in favor of what they actually want. A common result is that people find they only take action when there is pressure on them. They then develop a strategy of mobilizing themselves into action by building up pressure. Often they apply this strategy to other people as well. In the strategy of conflict manipulation, one attempts to "motivate" oneself or someone else into taking action by presenting a vision of the negative consequences that will ensue if action is not taken.

Conflict manipulation always consists of the same two steps:

1. *Intensify the conflict* by presenting a "negative vision" of unwanted consequences of inaction or insufficient action, and

2. *Take action designed to resolve the conflict.*

*It is important to note that the action is not taken in favor of what one wants. Action is taken only in an attempt to reduce the synthetically manufactured conflict created by the vision of what one does* not *want.* A new program may be launched to avoid a potential loss in market share to a threatening competitor. An employee may show a burst of energy following a performance review at which his continued employment was called into question. A smoker may decide to give up cigarettes after hearing the latest statistics linking smoking and lung cancer. While this strategy can yield short-term results, over the longer term it actually makes matters worse.

Within the underlying structure, conflict manipulation produces movement first *toward* the vision of negative consequences and outside the area of tolerable conflict:

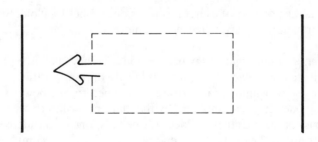

Movement in this direction continues, as the internal experience of conflict increases to a critical point. Then the structure compensates, catapulting the person in the opposite direction into action toward what is desired:

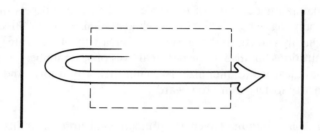

At this point the strategy of conflict manipulation seems to be working. Action is being taken in the desired direction and may even succeed in producing short-term results. The underlying structure, however, then compensates for the action taken.

Pressure was originally used to mobilize the person into action. Action was then taken to *reduce the pressure*. The more this action is successful, *the more the pressure is reduced*. The path of least resistance changes once again, as there is a shift of dominance from the "Desire-have the result" system back to the "Belief-do not have the result" system. The way it is easiest to go is then *away* from the desired result, so that becomes the dominant tendency. And, as the structure continues to compensate, the oscillation will continue:

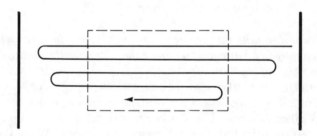

Generally, as shown, the oscillation will decrease in amplitude over time as the person gravitates back to an area of tolerable conflict.

As a long-term consequence of this structure playing itself out, the underlying experience of powerlessness will be strengthened in two ways. First, the strategy itself emphasizes the power of the circumstances one wishes to avoid. Second, despite one's best efforts, nothing lasting has been achieved.

*Willpower Manipulation.* Many people find that they take little or no action unless they motivate themselves through heightened volition, positive attitudes, or inspiration. The use of willpower is a strategy designed to overpower structural conflict by forcing oneself into compliance with what one wishes to see happen. If one succeeds, one is considered strong-willed. If one fails, one is considered weak-willed. Most people feel that they never have enough willpower to accomplish anything of significance, but they also believe that willpower or positive attitudes are the essential variable in whether or not they succeed. So their strategy is to fortify their willpower through positive thinking, exaggerated affirmations, motivational resolve, and inspirational fervor. These techniques are designed to overpower structural conflict by exaggerated determination. Movement takes the form, at first, of a drive directed toward what is desired and out of the area of tolerable conflict:

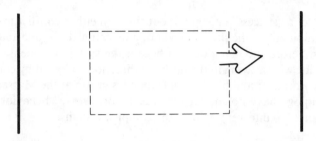

In the short run, a successful "breakthrough" may in fact be achieved. For willpower manipulation, like conflict manipulation, often does work in the short run, but with detrimental long-term consequences. For once again, even if the front wall is reached, the underlying structure is still in play. Keeping oneself at the front wall—"holding it together" and "getting oneself up" for each new event and each new day becomes exhausting. Eventually, the underlying structure compensates for the efforts and gives rise to movement in the opposite direction from what one wants. This movement away from the desired result is taken not because of a failure of "intention" and not as the expression of some hypothesized inner "resistance," but because the structural tendencies move along the path of *least* resistance as determined by this particular structure:

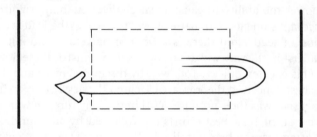

Over time, as the structure continues to compensate, the oscillation will continue, eventually gravitating once again towards an area of tolerable conflict:

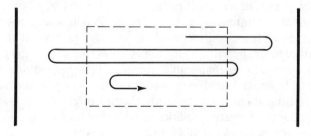

Like conflict manipulation, over the longer term willpower manipulation thus reinforces the impact of the underlying structure and the experience of powerlessness. It does so first through the message implicit in the very attempt to inspire and motivate: without such outside prodding, one's powerful inertia and "resistance" and negative thoughts would carry the day. Second, once again one has tried something and despite one's best efforts, it has not worked. No lasting change has occurred.

Often, after a "success" brought about through either conflict manipulation or willpower manipulation, the situation will first be better for a time and then actually be worse than before the manipulation began: the system compensates for a wide swing to one side with a swing in the opposite direction followed by continuing oscillation. As Jay Forrester and his System Dynamics group at the Massachusetts Institute of Technology have noted, such "better before worse" behavior characterizes "policy resistance" to intervention in many complex systems.

## THE LEADER'S DILEMMA

The structure in which most leaders find themselves does not support change, no matter what technique is tried and no matter what strategies are performed. Structural conflict compensates for any and all action taken.

Many leaders have discovered after years of experimenting on their own, learning and applying various approaches, developing leadership skills, attempting to attract the "right" people, reorganizing the configuration of their organizations, updating styles of management, implementing attractive incentive programs and so on, that not very much they do makes the kind of difference they want to see. Usually upon taking on the mantle of leadership individuals assume they will finally have within their power the ability to cause great changes enabling significant shifts of means and accomplishments. No matter how "prepared" the leader is, once assuming the position of leadership there is a built-in naiveté—a notion that from the position of leadership the way will at last be open to transform the destinies of those who are led. This is often quickly followed by discouragement and disillusionment as some of the best conceived theories are executed flawlessly only to fail to have the depth of impact that was their promise. Within the structures in which most leaders find themselves, all of their best efforts are followed by structural compensation. Their actions often seem to be neutralized. Within this structure, change does happen, accomplishments are produced, and some advancement can be made. However, the energy and effort expended are enormous and the total results limited.

After years of experiencing this phenomenon, leaders often conclude that their greatest aspirations are unreachable, their deepest longings cannot be fulfilled, and their true concerns with societal and world change are fantasy. If the leader in this situation is astute, he or she will develop approaches to enable some changes to happen within an essentially unchangeable universe, but this requires compromising what he or she truly wants. Usually those who seek positions of leadership are by nature uncompromising about what matters to them. Lowering aspiration, vision, and altruism diminishes their creative abilities while it simultaneously continues to fester as a point of sore discouragement and unspoken annoyance.

170

# THE LEADER
# AS AN AGENT OF CHANGE

Within the world of structural conflict, most of the organizations with which leaders work develop the strategy of remaining within an area of tolerable conflict. Whatever the leader does to overcome the basic inertia of the organization will tend to be a variation of either willpower manipulation or conflict manipulation, usually in the name of progress, vision, problem-solving, strategic planning, motivation, managing environments, analyzing the organizational culture or myths, etc.

In the approach based on conflict manipulation, for example, the leader may conduct a "problem census" or set up meetings at which executive staff, managers, supervisors, and line workers can discuss areas of possible improvement in their departments. At the level of appearance, these actions seem to make a great deal of sense: if one wishes to bring about positive changes, it certainly should help to have people throughout the organization engaged in identifying the most serious problem the organization currently faces. Structurally, however, the function of these actions is to cause change by taking the organization out of the area of tolerable conflict. The approach is to expose negative conditions, then emphasize the undesirability of these conditions, and finally, to whatever degree is necessary, exacerbate the conflict these negative conditions generate. If this effort is successful, the result will, in fact, be movement out of the area of tolerable conflict—first toward the "negative" and then, as the structure compensates, toward the "positive":

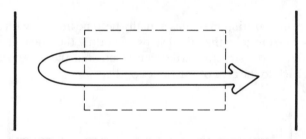

Thus the change effort may yield positive results in the short term. At best, many or all of the local problems will actually be solved. Over the longer term however, the structure will continue to compensate. Following the path of least resistance, the organization will gravitate back to the area of tolerable conflict. Within this range of tolerable conflict, aspiration will be limited, and reality will be interpreted as falling within a tolerable range. Aspects of reality beyond this range will be denied, reinterpreted, or ignored.

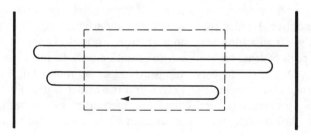

In the approach to change based on willpower manipulation, the leader may establish an altruistic mission statement, promote "peak performance," reinforce positive values such as high productivity and the pursuit of excellence, acknowledge outstanding members of the organization, encourage personal and organizational achievement, attempt to instill esprit de corps, or circulate articles about successful organizational change efforts.

Once again, at the level of appearance, these actions seem sensible. They seem likely to help people in the organization believe in themselves and inspire them to reach for more. Structurally, however, these actions are designed to cause change by moving the organization outside the area of tolerable conflict by presenting and supporting models of successful performance and new ways of thinking to overcome inertia and "resistance" to change. If the change effort is successful, there will initially be movement outside the area of tolerable conflict in a positive direction:

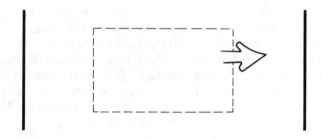

Members of the organization may thus actually become infused with a new sense of purpose and inspired to take the initial steps of putting their new goals into action. Over time, however, the structure will compensate and the organization will once again gravitate back to the area of tolerable conflict:

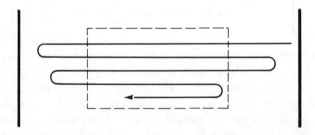

If the leader is skillful, then, the conflict manipulation or willpower manipulation will often work temporarily, and it will appear that the situation will actually change for the better. Ironically, however, the underlying structure, which is dominant, is usually left unaddressed. Since there is no real change in the underlying structure, the path of least resistance is to gravitate back to preexisting patterns, as outlined above. Often, on the way, things do in fact get much worse than they were before the change effort was undertaken—and the leader is usually blamed. In any case, the whole process has been extremely uncomfortable, usually divisive, and seems to have shown once again the wisdom of accepting one's limitations. The

172

people in the organization are left disillusioned and more entrenched than ever in the strategy of remaining within the area of tolerable conflict.

# A CHANGE OF STRUCTURE

Change is possible, but as we have seen, most attempts at change are strategies within structural conflict. Since structural conflict is not solvable or resolvable, actions taken within that structure can lead only to compensation and oscillation. When this structure is dominant, most human energy is wasted, and efforts to change patterns of behavior are unlikely to succeed.

To change the underlying structure there must be another structure in play, and this structure must be *senior* to the old structure. Since a senior structure will take precedence over a lower structure, change then is not only possible but probable. New structural tendencies arise. The path of least resistance changes, and energy most easily moves along that new path.

The structure that is senior to structural conflict has the following properties: it incorporates structural conflict into itself, and it transposes a complex structure into a simple structure.

I call this senior structure **structural tension**.

## Structural Tension

Structural tension has two components: vision and reality. From these components, a natural force is generated by the structure:

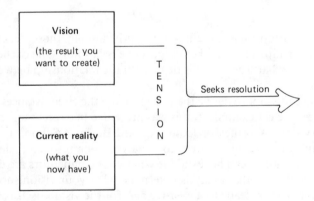

Structural Tension

The vision is a result you want to create. "Current reality" is a current and accurate awareness of what already exists that is relevant to the vision. In the beginning of the creative process, there will always be a discrepancy between what you want and what you have, because creators bring into reality what does not already exist.

The discrepancy between reality and the vision of the creator forms a simple tension-resolution system. This tension-resolution system is a higher order structure than structural conflict because it *includes* structural conflict as part of relevant current reality.

Once structural tension is established, the tension can be resolved in one of two ways. Either current reality can move to the vision or the vision can move to current reality.

If vision is changed to comply with current reality, the vision is no longer truly the result that is wanted. When this happens, structural tension is lost because one of the major elements is no longer in play in the structure.

Resolving structural tension by lowering or changing the vision to anything less than what is truly wanted destroys this structure as a dominant and senior force. Structural conflict will then become the dominant force.

When the vision is held and reality is clearly observed, the tendency will be for reality to move to the vision. As reality moves toward the vision, energy is released, enabling actions taken to directly bring the vision into reality.

The structural tendency, the probability, the path of least resistance, the direction in which energy will most easily flow is toward the full manifestation of the vision.

Structural tension is a powerful structure and yet deceptively simple. After years of being steeped in strategies designed to compensate for structural conflict, people often find it extremely difficult at first to establish a clear vision of what they truly want and a clear view of what they currently have.

This takes practice. It is easy to assume you have these elements in place and yet not have them in place.

## Vision

The word "vision" has caught on recently among those seeking fresh approaches to leadership. The actual concept thus far has not. One of the greatest misunderstandings of what true vision is deals with the relationship between vision and circumstances.

Most people attempt to derive their vision from the circumstances in which they find themselves. A clear example of this was presented in a recent management series on public television. A professor from Harvard Business School, commenting on strategic planning, urged his viewers to "analyze your resources, determine what your capital expenditures can be, examine what your competitors are doing, analyze market trends and from that analysis determine what your vision should be." "Derived end vision" seldom leads to a creative act, for the vision itself is limited by the analysis of current circumstances, limited by the biases inherent in the analysis, and subject to the influence of past aspirations and theories.

In order to generate real vision, the vision itself must be conceived independent of the circumstances. The vision must also be conceived without reference to the apparent possibility or impossibility of its accomplishment. Since most people have been trained to think in terms of responding appropriately to circumstances, the unfortunate policy of limiting what one wants to what seems realistic and possible forms a common counter-creative habit. It is actually astonishing to discover how little ability most people have simply to describe what they want to create. And yet, the premier creative act is to conceive of what one wants to create.

Real vision is the conceptual crystallization of a result a creator wants to bring into reality. If this vision does not come from an assessment of needs, a definition of the prevailing problems, or an analysis of market trends, from where does it come? Some people approach vision as if it were a deeply hidden treasure to be discovered and revealed. However, conceiving what you want to create is also not a revelatory process. Other people generate "brainstorms," which are designed to blitzkrieg through preconceived "mind sets" with fanciful free associations. But free association consistently misses the heart of the matter, which is the answer to the very simple question, "What do I want to create?"

How one conceives of what one wants is deceptively simple and profoundly sophisticated. It is perhaps the true secret of the creative process — a secret both directly pragmatic and philosophically astute. To those who have been raised to believe that circumstances are the driving force in one's life, this secret will seem to be either drivel or heresy. And yet every professional creator either consciously or intuitively thoroughly understands the principle of how a creator conceives of a vision. *The creator simply makes up the vision.*

Please do not miss the point. This is truly a remarkable insight into the deeper nature of the creative process. For creators make up the results they want to create and then bring them to full manifestation. Years ago I consulted with an engineering group in a high-tech organization. When I mentioned to the engineers this insight about the creative process, at first they looked at each other with knowing grins. Then one engineer after another said, "That's exactly what we do. We make up what we create." One of them added, "But then we have to write technical articles explaining how we made it up in such a way that it doesn't seem made up." While creative people know that they make up what they create, there is a strange prejudice in society against this notion. One reason is that the act of making up what you want does not rely on rationale and justification, and therefore seems unconnected to the circumstances to which everyone is supposed to respond.

## Vision Is Not Process

Rather than "make up" visions of desired results, most people have been trained to focus on process — methods of acting, steps to be taken, and forms to be followed. The *process* answers the question, "How do I bring what I want into reality?" This is a good question once you know what you want, but a useless question until you do. Most education, however, attempts to train students to consider process before any consideration of what the students actually want to create in their own lives. A typical approach to guidance counseling is to assess what a student has aptitude for and then to help the student design careers in which these aptitudes would be likely to lead to success. The circumstances of the student's aptitudes are presented as the major factors that should determine an entire life direction. Many students succumb to this advice and pursue careers consistent with their aptitudes only to discover 20 or 30 or 40 years later that they never much cared for a career they have spent a lifetime building. All of this emanated from the circumstance of aptitudes they happened to possess at age 15. The question "What do you want?" was never asked. Instead, the question "What do you want to do among the alternatives available?" was substituted.

When most people begin to consider the question, "What do I want to create?" they substitute the question, "What, among the available alternatives, do I want to do?" Vision degenerates into process. Process then is elevated to a position of time-honored formulas and conventions or even further elevated to a position of metaphysical truth. Cults of process celebrating this methodology or that methodology convert people into believers and beliefs into cherished dogmas, and the "vision" becomes the perfect performance of the process. The concept of the end result recedes as the reign of process intensifies.

While certainly this is an exaggeration, more subtle and therefore more insidious variations abound in reality. Upon conceiving a vision, process must not initially be considered. Vision is best conceived independent of process, for upon conception, how you might create the results you want is best left an unknown factor.

Those who would celebrate process inadvertently predetermine the results that can be created. Believers in process are seeking convention. Convention seeks to formalize the responses to circumstances. This mechanistic approach thwarts the true development of creativity, for in the house of the creator it is not convention but invention that is the most direct path to desired results.

The leader as creator understands that the spirit of convention will be prevalent in most organizations. Certainly common practice approaches to financial management, inventory control, secretarial support, distribution mechanisms, and so on are extremely desirable. They enable the leader to engineer systems that effectively and predictably maintain resources, strengthen organizational abilities, and heighten organizational readiness to help manifest the vision. But the mentality of convention too often fossilizes archaic processes to the detriment of needed invention. The leader as creator sometimes entirely reorganizes the forms and configurations of organizational design, and is only able to do so when the vision is independent of process.

## The Power of Vision

Vision is not the crystallization of a process, but rather the crystallization of the result the creator makes up. If the vision is truly what the creator wants, it will have great power. A creator brings into reality results that the creator wants to see exist and the power of the original vision emanates from the sheer desire to manifest the vision. The human spirit permeates the vision when the creator loves the vision enough to see it realized.

Vision also has power because in vision you can easily reach beyond the ordinary to the extraordinary. The inner eye of vision can see what is not yet there, can reach beyond the present circumstances and beyond any known processes and see what up to that point has never been there. It is truly an incredible human faculty that is able to see beyond the present and the past and from the unknown conceive of something not hitherto in existence.

The leader as creator is fluent in the vision, not because it is memorized or written in stone, but rather because the leader freshly asks and answers the question,

"What result do I want to create?" frequently. Sometimes the vision changes, but most often it does not. And as the leader crystallizes the vision with greater additive clarity, more and more people can see it, support it, align with it, contribute to it, add to it and join in its final creation.

The leader could never do this with an unclear vision or a vision based on a compromise. When the vision is established, the first component of structural tension is in place. Once it is clear where you want to go, the next question that establishes current reality — the other component of structural tension — is, "Where are you now?"

## Current Reality

Current reality includes a clear and accurate description of where you now are in relation to the fulfillment of the vision. Current reality includes the tendencies of structural conflict and incorporates structural conflict into itself as a relevant structure in play. Conflict manipulation, willpower manipulation, and maintaining an area of tolerable conflict — the three strategies generated by structural conflict — each require a misrepresentation of current reality.

Conflict manipulation portrays reality as worse than it actually is or exaggerates the negative implications of events that have taken place or may take place. Aspects of current reality that contradict the negative vision must be ignored or minimized in order to develop increased conflict.

Willpower manipulation portrays reality as better than it actually is or exaggerates the positive implications of events. Aspects of current reality which contradict the positive vision must be ignored or minimized in order to overcome the innate structural tendencies.

Maintaining an area of tolerable conflict misrepresents current reality by excluding or minimizing aspects of reality outside of the area of tolerable conflict. Reality may be portrayed as either better or worse than it actually is, whatever is needed to avoid leaving the area of tolerable conflict.

In willpower manipulation, it is "See no evil." In conflict manipulation it is "See nothing but evil." In the area of tolerable conflict, it is "See neither good nor evil."

Current reality often includes disappointments, frustrations, pain, injustice, unkindness, and circumstances that seem hopeless. Most people would rather avoid suffering the discomfort that can come from recognizing that such aspects of current reality exist. The leader as creator understands, however, the power of current reality — good, bad, or indifferent, for structural tension is impossible without a clear view of where you now are. The leader as creator realizes that at first most people would rather leave certain aspects of current reality unrecognized. But the leader helps others to view current reality objectively, accurately, and fully. For only through such awareness can necessary adjustments be made. If you are painting a painting, the ongoing changes on the canvas need to be recognized in order to move to the next steps of the painting process. In a similar way, the leader as creator must maintain a fluency in knowing current reality as it changes subtly or obviously. The leader must also be able to discriminate which aspects of reality are relevant to the vision and which aspects are not. Clarity of vision helps enable the leader to determine instinctively and intuitively what is relevant from the sea of over-information available in today's "information society."

177

To the leader as creator, current reality is the foundation upon which the creative process takes place. Rather than misrepresent current reality, the leader is able to launch the creative act from solid ground.

## The Leader's Alchemy

Alchemy was the act of transmuting "lead" into "gold." To the alchemists, lead represented innate potential. Gold represented the realization and fulfillment of this potential. In this sense, the leader as creator is an alchemist, transmuting the natural potential inherent in current reality into the "gold" of fulfilled vision.

The leader as creator understands and respects the play of forces, including structural conflict and structural tension. The leader establishes the senior force of structural tension by clarity of vision and clarity of current reality. Once structural tension is established, the leader functions as both visionary and realist for others, enabling them also to establish structural tension. The leader does not impose his or her vision on others, but the leader's clarity of vision can encourage and inspire others to conceive of their own vision. Furthermore, the leader as creator helps enable others to master their own creative process.

The leader is best supported by others who are the predominant creative force in their own lives. Those whose visions are aligned or compatible with the leader's vision can easily join as a concerted force to invent processes that directly lead to the fulfillment of all of their visions. Those whose visions are not aligned and incompatible may have to create a better vehicle for the manifestation of their vision than membership in the leader's organization. To the leader as creator, this is not a problem because the leader truly supports individuals creating what they each want to create. And beyond understanding, the leader as creator has the wisdom to allow the organic, natural processes of formation and disintegration to take place. It is all right for people whose vision is incompatible with the vision shared by those who are aligned to leave in support of both the organizational vision and their own. It is also all right to encourage all members of an organization to be true to themselves even if, for some, that means departure from the organization. Those who choose to support the vision join together in a powerful collective creative act, bringing into existence what they all truly care about.

There are those who may not share in the organizational vision and yet whose vision is not incompatible with that vision. This group of people may very well play an important role in the full realization of the organizational vision.

There are often four roles in this type of organization. Two of them require alignment and compatibility of vision. Two of them do not require alignment, but do require compatibility.

# ROLES

## Collaborators

Collaborators contribute unique dimensions of vision along with common aspects. Each collaborator increases the scope of the vision so that the total vision is greater than the sum of its parts. Collaboration may be either consensual or hierarchical. It is currently in vogue to glorify consensual forms and disparage hierarchical forms. This is unfortunate, because hierarchial collaboration is a powerful and effective means of co-creating. The Walt Disney Studios, Jim Hensen's muppets, most film and record projects, Thomas Edison's Menlo Park Laboratory, and the United States Space Program are all examples of hierarchical collaboration.

Consensual collaboration may also be useful as demonstrated by Lerner and Lowe, George and Ira Gershwin, the Julliard String Quartet, and certain improvisational music and theater groups. Consensual collaboration is actually somewhat more difficult in the creative process, and the somewhat strange, often romanticized notion of rigidly seeking consensus seems to come more from philosophy than from the pragmatics of manifesting a vision in reality.

To the leader as creator, hierarchy or consensus is not an aesthetic decision based on humanistic or other philosophical preference, but rather a choice based on which approach will do the most good when.

## Amplifiers

Amplifiers are those people who can take the common vision and add to its power while not expanding the scope of the vision itself. This role is very much appreciated by those people who have joined together to manifest the vision and very often misunderstood by onlookers. Those who serve in the role of amplifiers help the collaborators bring the vision into reality more effectively. They may, for example, have played no part in conceiving the vision, and yet they may use their skills and talents and alignments to bring a part of the vision into reality in ways that are true to the vision as a whole. The studios of Michelangelo, Raphael, and Leonardo da Vinci created some of the greatest art known to civilization through the relationship between the collaborators (master artists and patrons) and amplifiers (other member artists and apprentices). While collaborators expand the scope of the vision, amplifiers expand its magnitude. Some people are by nature collaborators and others by nature are amplifiers, and some by nature are both.

## Technicians

Another role that is often important is the role of technician. This role is separate from collaborators and amplifiers because technicians need not directly share in the vision. They do, however, play a valuable role in the final realization of the vision through the professional services they provide. Their spiritual connection to the vision is not as demanding as it is for collaborators and amplifiers and yet they are also fully appreciated as members of the organization. Alignment to the vision is not precluded by the role of technician, it is just not required.

## Supporters

Supporters are similar to technicians except that their role is less technically based. This may be a shipping department, a receptionist, office workers, building maintenance workers, administrative assistants, or even volunteers who play a valuable role in bringing the vision into reality by virtue of the support they provide. Again, alignment to the vision is not precluded by the role of supporter, but neither is it required.

# HOW TO GET THERE FROM HERE

Once the leader establishes structural tension by forming a clear vision and a clear view of current reality, what processes are used to move from here to there?

## Gathering Strength

Over the years many approaches to "motivating" people have been tried, from providing better pay and working conditions to giving people more participation in the decision-making process and more recognition and acknowledgment and greater personal challenge, to treating people in a more "loving" way and creating supportive "environments" in which their true altruism is more likely to flourish. In an age in which the focus has been on responding to circumstances, each of these approaches has seemed to produce limited results for a time. Yet all have failed to work as promised over the longer term. The leader as creator realizes that *any* attempt to motivate people constitutes a manipulation. Over time, manipulation destroys relationships, resentment builds up, and results become more difficult to achieve. The leader as creator does not seek to motivate people, but rather joins freely with those whose motivation arises naturally from the fact that there is a vision each wants to bring into reality.

When two or more people share structural tension within even an organization in which structural conflict is prevalent and the status quo is entrenched, change can happen. The leader as creator is not necessarily the person in a formal position of organizational leadership although often he or she is. What enables leadership to emerge is not the right environment or the right conditions, but rather precisely the creative process, in which vision and reality are paramount, no matter what the circumstances. The leader as creator does not look for converts, but rather for co-creators whose visions are authentic and whose views of current reality are unobstructed and clear. Over time, the natural appeal of this mode of being attracts those who deeply desire to be part of such an active and vital force. Success and effectiveness speak for themselves, and leaders are able to gain strength by additive successes, increased momentum, and expanded capabilities through the creative process.

## Making Primary and Secondary Choices

The leader as creator understands the relationship between choices that are primary (results) and choices that are secondary (strategic choices that support a primary choice). Creators designate hierarchy of values and functions. Often results may be of equal value, but the leader will need to designate one as more important than the others. Once one knows what choices are primary, it will always be clear how to make secondary choices. They are made so as to support the primary choice. A simple example of a primary choice might be the choice to develop a certain product. Secondary choices may include engaging in various types of research and development, making managerial time available, committing financial resources, and so on.

## Changing the Underlying Structures

The leader as creator will not attempt to overcome or compensate for structural conflict, but rather absorb those structures into the senior structure of structural tension. As more and more people in the organization make an essential shift from reacting or responding to circumstances to becoming the predominant creative force in their own lives, the depth of the influence of structural tension increases. It then becomes easier for the organization as a whole to move along this new path of least resistance in bringing into reality the organization vision.

## Experimenting

If the creative process is anything, it is a learning process. As the co-creators invent processes along the way, they are actually conducting experiments that add to the foundation they are building, specifically by increasing their ability to create the vision upon which they are presently focused, and generally by expanding their capacity to bring into reality whatever they choose to create. Some experiments succeed, and some experiments fail. Certainly, a cavalier approach is both foolhardy (it may put you out of business) and ineffective as a real basis of learning. The leader as creator maximizes the ability to learn by conducting experiments on a small scale at first, with limited investment. Greater experiments can then be built on lesser experiments, and the foundation for the entire creative process expands often geometrically.

## Creating and Adjusting

The leader as creator understands that the creative process is filled with adjustments in course and action once structural tension has been established. In order to know what adjustments to make, the leader continually seeks feedback. This feedback comes from changes or lack of changes in current reality. A critical mistake many people make is to make inaccurate assumptions about current reality. The leader as creator actively pursues knowing current reality and is aware of those times that the view of current reality is unclear.

### Keeping Vision Current

The leader as creator does not simply remember the vision, but rather is in current contact with it by regenerating a current perspective of the vision. The leader knows when he or she is in touch with the vision and knows when he or she is not. This is important information in the creative process, for if you lose touch with what you are creating, structural tension is lost, and actions become arbitrary and eventually degenerate into strategies of structural conflict. It is easy to assume the vision is in place when it is not. The leader as creator understands that a major part of that role is to generate and regenerate the vision. This can work only if the vision is real, authentic, and what the creator actually wants to create. Occasionally the leader as creator can assume this is going on but actually be using vision as a form of willpower manipulation. But if the vision is real, it will easily emerge when the leader answers freshly and truthfully the question, *"Now* what do I want to create?"

### Reaching for the Highest

Not all vision is equal. The vision with the most power is the vision that most deeply matters to the leader, what the leader holds dear, what the leader aspires to reach for. Most people do not actually know what they most deeply care about because they have not looked, explored, or considered this dimension of themselves. The leaders discussed here have genuinely "soul-searched." They know where they stand. They know what their values are. Furthermore, their commitment is to be true to themselves and true to their vision. This is not fanaticism or an overblown megalomania. It is rather the great power of dedicating one's life to fulfilling what is most profoundly deep and meaningful while simultaneously reaching for that which is highest. Furthermore, the creative act is the embodiment of two of life's most powerful forces—love and truth. The leader as creator loves the vision enough to be dedicated to its fulfillment. The leader loves the vision enough to see to it personally that this vision will exist. The leader also rests the creative process on the sure foundation of the truth of current reality—the power of objectively observing what does exist. Prejudices, biases, exaggerations, minimizations, distortions, misrepresentations, and omissions have no place. At first, people often do not take comfort in seeing what they may have hidden for years. But comfort is not at issue. And the great power of the creative act transcends all immediate circumstances in favor of that which is highest and deepest in the leader's vision. It may take years or an entire lifetime to bring the vision into reality, or perhaps even to bring the vision only the first step of the way. But to the leader, this is a life well spent.

# A WAVE OF THE FUTURE

As we move toward the twenty-first century, it is becoming apparent that people can only be self-motivated to build the new civilization and that their destinies rest in their own hands. The implications of this insight are important, vast, and profound. As they learn to master their own creative process, all individuals have the potential for being the predominant creative force in their own lives. As they become fluent in creating and put that fluency to use in the service of what they most deeply want and love, we see a new breed of leaders emerging, leaders as creators, transforming the meaning of the relationship of the individual to all of human endeavor and building a civilization unlike any before.

The impact of literacy on civilization was enormous. In a similar way, fluency in the creative process can easily bring new structures into play, change the path of least resistance, and forge a world of new possibilities for all of humanity. The leader as creator is helping to give birth to the new century, and signs of spring are all around us.

# III.

# LEADERSHIP
# IN ACTION

# CHAPTER 12

# Leadership in Metanoic Organizations

by
**CHARLES KIEFER**

*A revolutionary shift of orientation is occurring today in organizations, in which people are learning to collectively create the results they want, consistent with individuals' personal life purposes. The leadership required in such circumstances has some special qualities which are developed in this chapter.*

There is occurring today a significant shift of world view in certain parts of our society. At a personal level, people are realizing that they are a force of nature and essentially free to create their lives however they want them to be. Certain organizations are beginning to extrapolate this point of view to realize the extraordinary power of a group of people who, securely rooted in their individual creative power, bond together to collectively bring into being a vision that none could accomplish alone.

We have termed such an organization "metanoic."[1] A metanoic organization is one that has undergone a fundamental shift of orientation from the individual and collective belief that people must cope with life and, in the extreme, are helpless and powerless, to the conviction that they are individually and collectively empowered to create their future and shape their destiny. In a metanoic organization people help to create the collective vision, not merely to make money but because it is consistent with their own life's purpose. Consequently, the vision held in a metanoic organization is worthy of each member's highest personal ideals and commitment.

The leadership required to bring a metanoic organization into existence is of a special quality.

All great leaders stand for something. They have defined some value, issue or purpose to be of overriding importance to them. For Martin Luther King, Jr., it was freedom and civil rights. For John F. Kennedy, it was democracy and America's destiny. For Gandhi, it was freedom in India. For Lee Iacocca, it is the survival and prosperity of Chrysler and perhaps the U.S. auto industry as a whole. Each of these men embodied a strong commitment to his vision. His life spirit was involved in it.

---

[1] *Metanoia* is a Greek word meaning fundamental change in the way one thinks about life.

Because of their commitment, others were willing to commit themselves under the leadership of these men.

In a metanoic organization, the essence of leadership stems from the leader's soul rather than from his or her behavior. There are some managers in whose presence people grow and flourish, and others in whose presence people seem to wither and die. We have all seen examples of both kinds of managers, yet some of both kinds behave like autocrats, while others of both kinds are permissive and participative. Great leadership is not primarily a function of behavior and technique. It is the commitment of leaders that inspires others, and no amount of behavioral technique will substitute for the genuine commitment of leaders to their vision.

## AREAS OF METANOIC LEADERSHIP

The ability to *co-create* a collectively chosen vision is perhaps the weakest link in even our very best organizations. Our organizations are populated at senior levels by leaders who can be very masterful personally; that is, when the realization of their vision is dependent *solely on themselves*, they easily create what they want. However, when the vision involves mobilizing the committed union of numerous other people, this mastery declines dramatically.

For example, most executives would have no doubt about their ability to do an excellent job creating a report for which they possess all the necessary information. But if that report involved the coordinated efforts of the several people on their immediate staff, their level of confidence might wane a bit. And if the task involved the implementation of a five-year strategic plan that required the coordinated efforts of 10,000 people, they may have little or no certainty as to the outcome. A metanoic organization calls for leaders who have developed themselves beyond personal mastery to organizational mastery; that is, they have the ability to sustain a collective vision and work in union with others to bring it about.

Leadership in a metanoic organization functions principally in three areas. First, the leader is the *custodian or steward of the organizational vision*. The leader sees to it that the organization has a collective vision and that the members share that vision and are committed to it.

Second, the leader *empowers and coaches others* **to create what they want**; that is, to be true to themselves and to expend their life-energy creating results worthy of their human spirit. Third, the leader is a *creator of structure*. The leader maintains and shapes structures that channel the creative energy of everyone toward producing the results to which they are all committed.

These three leadership functions, while critical in a metanoic organization, have been much less important and obvious to leaders in the past. Only recently are leaders beginning to focus on creating a truly collective vision to which everyone can wholeheartedly commit themselves, and putting a priority on empowering members to create the results that *they* as individuals want to create. Very few executives have experience working with the often unnoticed elements of structure, such as beliefs and values, which are central in focussing and unifying human energy.

# CUSTODIAN OF THE
# ORGANIZATIONAL VISION

Unlike an individual vision, an organizational vision[2] effectively involves every member. Instead of answering the individual question, "What do I want?" It answers the organizational question, "What do *we* want?" A compelling organizational vision is vital to a metanoic organization.

The organizational creative process, however, usually begins with a number of individuals, perhaps at different levels in the organization, having personal visions of results they want to accomplish in their personal lives and in their jobs. One major challenge of the metanoic leader is to help weave the many threads of individual vision into a collective fabric which is satisfying to everyone's personal vision.

The process can begin by eliciting personal visions, welcoming any individual's attempt to formulate a vision for themselves, no matter how unclear or superficial. With encouragement, individuals can quickly reach deeper and more significant levels of vision. As this process continues, members' images of their ideal organizational life will begin to emerge. At first, they may see this only in terms of their own personal workspace and output. But if organizational imaging is encouraged, people naturally begin to create pictures of what they would like to see manifested in the whole organization. As they listen to each other's individual visions for the organization, members get their first sense of an organizational vision, and everyone becomes aware of the kind of vision they ought collectively to develop. By continuing to refine, clarify and enrich these individual visions a full and complete organizational vision will begin to emerge.

People often expect their leaders to define the organizational vision for them. And, in fact, it was historically conceived to be the job of the leader to establish the organization's vision unilaterally, obtain the commitment of the members to it, and courageously hold themselves and others to that vision, no matter what. This practice may be better than the all too prevalent coping-with-current-problems orientation, but it still falls short of what is possible. It also has some inherent weaknesses.

First, when the leader is the sole creator of the organizational vision, the members' own ability to envision the future atrophies, and they grow ever more dependent on that leader. When the leader departs, the organization is usually left with key players who lack the ability to create new visions of the future.

Imagine an organization whose helm has been dominated by the founder for 20 years—an extreme visionary and innovator. During those years, the

---

[2]An organizational vision, as the term is used in a metanoic organization, refers to a mental image of desired tangible results. Ideally, the vision is held by all members of the organization. For most organizations, their vision will be multi-faceted and may include business goals, but usually will go beyond them to embody noble and lofty qualities, such as a work environment where people flourish, products of superior quality, outstanding financial results, customers who are grateful and thrilled at the company's product, and so on. Each of these elements of the vision represents a definable state that could be achieved; and if it were achieved, you would know it.

organization tended to attract people who could implement his visions, but who weren't visionary in their own right. In fact, they tended to be the conservative stabilizing balance to his visionary thrust. Because he was so dominant, there really wasn't room for other visionaries. When the founder retired, the organization was populated at the senior level by people whose habitual mode was pulling back on the reins of his bursting entrepreneurialism. As a result, no one at the senior level was fluent with being a truly creative organizational force.

Second, to the extent that the vision established by a single leader is fixed and immovable, it effectively eliminates any significant degree of choice, ownership, or initiative on the part of the individual members. Given the differences among us as individuals, it is unlikely that we will ever find our vision completely embodied in another's. Accepting another's vision as if it were our own compromises what *we* truly want and results in a shallow commitment compared to what it is possible to obtain. Faced with an immovable organizational vision, members can either adopt the vision as presented (sacrificing a part of their own vision), live in compromise, or leave. In no case does the leader gain full commitment from the members. In fact, a more likely occurrence is that people will feel manipulated by the power of the leader's vision and may even, at an unconscious or conscious level, spontaneously resist it.

Regarding organizational visions, a new alternative has emerged for metanoic leaders. Their function is not to establish the vision, but to catalyze visioning among members of the organization. Recognizing that clarity and power of vision can come from the creative output of any individual, it becomes the leader's responsibility to *ensure that everybody in the organization is envisioning their personal future as well as that of the organization.*

A metanoic organization is managed in a way that fosters rather than suppresses the creative arguments that may surface.

> The executives of a small manufacturing and service company were in the process of establishing their mission. One item of their business strategy involved coming to grips with the issue of honesty. Having quickly established that they wanted to be honest with each other, the question arose as to whether this policy of honesty would be applied in dealing with their customers. The issue was particularly important since, in their industry, the standard mode of operating was routinely to commit to unachievable delivery times, in order to acquire the order. The vast majority of participants discussing the question were of the opinion that inasmuch as this practice was a characteristic of the industry, it should be continued. But to one individual in the group, this position amounted to a breach of integrity. And he said so.

> Over the next few hours of heated discussion, all of the remaining participants, one by one, adopted this vision of honesty for the organization. It was to be an honesty that transcended their internal dealings with each other and would include their customers and suppliers. They opted for honesty across the board, recognizing that it might very well cause them to lose business or even go out of business. Instead, in the following two years, not

necessarily as a consequence of this act only, the company grew faster than any of its competitors to acquire the largest share in its market.

At first glance, this might sound like a case of someone, perhaps even the leader, compromising his or her own vision in favor of another. But it is important to remember that metanoic organizations seek a vision to which everyone in the organization can wholeheartedly subscribe. In the quest for an organizational vision, a leader's own vision may indeed evolve and change during the group process. In this, the leader becomes a model for others in allowing the input of others to modify and enrich the collective visioning process. The new vision that emerges from this process will remain one to which the leader *and* the other members can be fully committed.

In a metanoic organization, each person's vision for the organization can be as vital as any other's, because it is in the differences of these visions as well as their similarities that the underlying purpose of the organization is clarified. Since each person's contribution is vital to that clarity, each person participates in the leadership of the organization, whether or not they occupy formal leadership roles. In this process they can experience a level of responsibility and ownership in the organization as deep as any of the formal leaders.

This honesty story provides an example of true consensus. During the hours of discussion about the organization's policy of honesty to their suppliers and customers, the members saw that the direction being taken in the organization was a result not of their compromising or giving up something important to them, but rather of their struggling to align themselves with each other. As a result of any creative disagreement they may have experienced, a more accurate picture of what was important to them had emerged. The desired state of alignment is one in which people can freely commit their life energy to a certain collectively desired result (an organizational vision). It is a state in which individuals realize that the actions they desire to take will allow them to be true to themselves as well as to their organization.

In a metanoic organization, then, the leader is primarily a catalyst of the collective vision. The leader acts as a channel for the expression of that vision. It is as if the organizational vision flows through the leadership rather than originates from it. Thus, the leader's custodial role is, first, to see that a genuine organizational vision emerges and, second, to make sure it remains alive and well.

As a leader, it is essential for you to verify whether or not you are committed to the organization's purpose and vision. If you are, then you will naturally be a channel for the expression of that vision. If you aren't fully, you won't be a channel for it. And, to the extent that you pretend to be, you will be manipulating yourself and others. Moreover, you will be unable to enroll others in it.

## EMPOWERING AND ENROLLING PEOPLE

The second major function of leadership in a metanoic organization is to enable others to come into the full presence of their own creative power. The essence of personal power is to be able to see clearly what you want to create and then habitually mobilize your resources to manifest that vision. When empowering others, the leader's task is to help them determine what is truly important for *them* and the results they will commit themselves to bring into being. This amounts to enrolling them in their own personal vision — not "selling" them, but simply allowing them to "place their own name on a roll" in favor of themselves and their vision. This state of enrollment evokes a far greater sense of personal responsibility for and commitment to a result than merely being "sold" a vision.

Most people in organizations find themselves in the position of complying with the wishes of others, particularly their superiors. Compliance does produce results; it is a proven and effective management strategy. Yet it pales in potency compared to the commitment accompanying true enrollment. There is a profound difference between doing something because *you* want to and doing something to fulfill the expectations of another. With the former, you bring an entirely different energy to the activity, a true creative energy.

In most organizations the best you hope for, and often the only thing that can exist, is compliance. In metanoic organizations this is known to be inadequate. Even so, the achievement of enrollment is made difficult by people's habit of complying, a habit acquired through years of practice as we grew up. Often compliance appears so sincere that we allow it to pass for genuine enrollment. But we really do know the difference in ourselves and others.

At the collective level, it is the function of leadership to evoke members' enrollment in the organization's vision, and thus elicit from them far greater commitment and personal responsibility to and ownership of the organizational vision than could be attained by any form of "selling."

In essence, enrolling people merely involves painting a vivid mental picture of the vision for yourself and for them. You thereby make your vision available to them and allow them to sign up for it. This stance requires that you have a relationship of trust and truthfulness with them, that you are on the level with them, and are willing to let the chips fall where they may. If the vision captures their spirit, they will enroll themselves. If not, they won't.

As an example, imagine having a bright new idea, perhaps having to do with a new product or procedure. In the past, you might have gone around the company attempting to convince others that they should adopt it. In essence, you would have been trying to gain their compliance through the force of your arguments.

This is quite different from enrollment, where others can consider whether your vision is one they may wish to share. Then, if they begin thinking and talking about the new idea, they are doing so because they want to, because it is in service of something they want. In this way, they are bringing true commitment to your vision — which is, in fact, no longer yours alone as it has been claimed by them as theirs as well.

A group of company executives, very successful in the past, were lapsing into a period of resting on their laurels, enjoying the security of a dominant market share and a good reputation. The CEO recognized the danger of that resting state and personally formulated a new vision for the organization that would require a substantial increase in commitment and energy. Instead of saying to the other executives "This vision of mine would be good for the organization for these reasons . . . It would be good for you too for these other reasons . . . Consequently, you should commit yourself to its achievement," he simply related to them his picture of the possibilities he saw for the organization. He gently encouraged them to find whatever part of it they agreed with and felt would be in their own best interests. The wholehearted commitment of everyone on his staff quickly emerged. They had signed themselves up, as opposed to his selling them. Moreover, the CEO learned a great deal about his organization in the process, and even ended up modifying his own vision as a result of the involvement of others.

Evoking creative potential from people and calling them to personal mastery involves continually and gently coaching them to clarify the results they truly want and encouraging them to mobilize their resources to pursue those results. This metanoic approach is in contrast to other approaches to staff development. A common presupposition of other methods is that subordinates lack certain qualities (such as responsibility, commitment, dedication, determination, motivation, and perseverance), and that leaders must do or add something to them to make these qualities grow. Such activity often involves manipulation, which diminishes a person's power, no matter how well-intentioned the activity may be. Coaching people to create what *they* truly desire is inherently non-manipulative because, at any moment in time, the power remains in the hands of the individual being coached.

One of the most revolutionary aspects of metanoic leadership is to encourage individuals to have their own personal visions, to enroll them in these visions, and to coach them in creating what they really want. The suggestions offered earlier for leaders to help catalyze visioning also work well in fostering enrollment.

In many companies it can be presupposed that the members are unaligned and that they do not share the same common interests. Thus, the metanoic approach would be potentially destructive of orderly organization functioning. The belief is that, left to their own devices — or creativity — people would pursue irreconcilably different goals. Everyone would have their own idea of what the organization ought to be doing. Under such conditions, leaders usually see manipulation and coercion as unfortunate, but necessary to keep people focussed on a common objective.

In metanoic organizations leaders create an environment for alignment[3] by evoking from the members a collective vision to which they can all be committed. In service to that vision, alignment among the members naturally occurs. Alignment is a natural by-product of a group of people striving together to achieve a lofty vision. It happens when people are focussed on a common objective that they also see as in some way fulfilling their own personal visions. In an aligned organization, any attempt to use manipulation or coercion would be resisted, because people are already focussed on a collective goal that includes their own best personal interest.

---

[3]The state of organizational alignment is one in which members operate as a whole, knowing that the actions taken will allow each of them to be true to themselves as well as to the organization. They see that the purpose and vision of the organization is worthy of the commitment of their life-spirit. And they, in effect, expand their definition of self, to enjoy a sense of unity with every other person in the organization.

The fact is, no one can lead an unaligned organization. In such a case, power must be used to gain compliance. Inasmuch as the members do not share a common goal and, left on their own, would pursue divergent objectives, a leader must wield power and authority in an *attempt* to reconcile these conflicting desires. But alignment will not be coerced; nor can it be created directly. Many organizations attempt to create alignment by designing ways to get people to work together, in the hope that they will then be able to achieve corporate goals more effectively. This rarely, if ever, works because people cannot commit their energy to a compromise or, particularly, to something that falls short of allowing them to express their personal life-purpose.

## Creating Structure

The third principal role of a leader in a metanoic organization is to create structures conducive to creating desired results. The structure of an organization channels organizational energy in the same way that your body and mind channel your personal energy. For example, the structure of the human body predetermines the range of its possible movements. Thus, the lower leg can swing backward but not forward; the fingers can be folded toward the palm, but not away from it. So, although a person's exact physical movements may not be predictable in advance, the general character of the body's movements can. In a similar way, structure largely predetermines organizational behavior and performance and is, therefore, very important, since poorly designed organizational structure will tend to limit energy flow among members and thwart inspiration.

Unfortunately, well-designed structure will not *cause* a free flow of energy or inspired performance. The most perfectly designed structure can only foster these results. The cause of inspired performance is to be found in the domain of vision and purpose.

Aligned, personally masterful individuals not only create directly what they want, they also create personal structures that are conducive to creating these results. In other words, when individuals have a vision of something they want to create, they self-consciously channel their life-force toward accomplishing that result. Simultaneously, they *create structure* which also channels their life-force toward that vision and reinforces its momentum. Leaders, however, not only create as individuals by building structures that channel their personal energy toward their visions, they also create structures that channel the energy of *everyone* toward producing the results to which they are all committed.

Symbolically, structures are like the walls and corridors of a building that govern the flow of human movement through that building. From the perspective of energy flow, structures can be treated as stationary, since they either do not change or change much less rapidly than people's actions and behavior. There are numerous structural relationships at work in organizations, the most familiar of which are those that *control* human energy. Control structures usually originate from management's desire to see that members are doing their proper tasks to best carry out the assumed purpose of the organization.

Most prominent among these control-oriented structures is the organizational *hierarchy of reporting relationships*. In this structure, energy is channeled and controlled from superiors to subordinates. Most corporations operate in such a structure, with the seniors clearly responsible for what happens to the organization, and the rest of the members simply accountable to those who stand above them in the hierarchy.

But there are other control-oriented structures in organizations, which are at least as powerful, if not more so, than the hierarchy. The structure of *rewards and incentives*, such as compensation and performance-review systems, is one of these. People will work or channel their energy toward what they are rewarded for or paid to do. If we all agree to the value of a certain objective, yet get paid for accomplishing something else, we are most likely to produce the results that get rewarded. For example, suppose that management and sales staff alike all want customer satisfaction to be their most important objective, yet salespersons are commissioned according to the number of closed sales they make. The creative energy in this structure will flow so that there will be numerous closed sales, but perhaps not as many satisfied customers.

Besides hierarchy and rewards, there are numerous other structural elements. One such area, usually recognized as vitally important but not thought of as structural, is that of personal and organizational *goals*. Having a goal sets up a discrepancy between what we want (our vision, or goal) and what we now have (our current reality). This discrepancy generates a creative tension such that human energy is clearly channeled to move current reality toward our goal. Organizations (and individuals) usually have many major as well as subordinate goals toward which they are striving and expending energy. At times, these goals may even contradict one another and seemingly confuse and defeat energy flow. Ways for organizations to creatively utilize and profit from such apparent conflict will be suggested later.

Other powerful structures—less obvious than goals and frequently not capitalized upon by executives—also influence organizations to achieve what they want. The first of these is *belief structures*. Beliefs are those deeply held, often unconscious assumptions about the way life is or ought to be and they tend to have a dominant influence on how people channel their energies, since people tend to behave in ways consistent with their beliefs. Strong beliefs function much like self-fulfilling prophecies. For example, if I believed people were basically dishonest and out to cheat me whenever they could, I would probably, if unconsciously, act in ways that actually provoke those behaviors in others. Over time, I would be likely to collect evidence to support that belief and in this way, my beliefs, in a very real sense, would create the reality that I experienced on a daily basis. It is unlikely I would expend my creative energies in directions I believed to be untrue, wrong, bad, or impossible. On the other hand, beliefs consistent with what I want can be enormously helpful in channeling creative energies. A desirable belief might take the form, "People are basically capable, trustworthy, dependable, etc."

Other often overlooked powerful structures for channeling energy are *values*: the qualities of life we care most about, such as freedom, truth, health, happiness, and the like. Whether we inherit our values or choose them, we direct our energies, subconsciously even more than consciously to their expression and accomplishment. So values too, are paths along which an individual's creative energies naturally flow. In any organization, the values held collectively by the members tend to function in the same way, creating a path along which everyone's energies seem to flow.

*Habits* are another neglected set of structures. At the organizational level, habits are called *norms* ("how we do things around here"). People quickly become socialized to the norms and styles of acting common to the organizations of which they are a part. Norms often provide subtle yet powerful mechanisms that redirect deviant behavior and keep people in line. Suppose one of the norms in an organization is to keep conflict from surfacing; keep it submerged. If a new employee began to act rashly and aggressively, stirring up conflict, they would soon receive substantial—subtle and not so subtle—feedback from the organization that their way of behaving is not appropriate or acceptable. Gradually over time, perhaps entirely unconsciously, their creative energies would begin to manifest in behavior consistent with the organizational norms.

These last three structures, beliefs, values and habits or norms, are often addressed through the myths and rituals of an organization.

The availability and flow of *information* is another powerful organizational structure. Here, the crucial questions are: How do people obtain the information they need to get their jobs done?" "Do they have free access to all the information they need, or is some of it kept accessible only to certain powerful people in the organization?" Suppose that everyone recognizes the importance of open, honest interaction among employees, but some of the information individuals need to do their jobs is restricted and held in the hands of a designated few. Such a structure will foster the notion that information is equal to power. As a result, people's creative energies will be limited by the information they have available and there will be a tendency to breed information monopolies, no matter how committed people say they are to open dialog.

Finally, the *physical processes* that occur in an organization are structures that enormously influence how people channel their energies. In a paper manufacturing company, the structure and flow of a physical process might be traced in the many steps it takes to transform trees in the forest into rolls of tissue on supermarket shelves. Another physical process is the flow of written reports in an administrative system. It is the structure of an R&D department that governs the path of a new engineering project from idea, to preliminary design, to collecting the right design team, to the creation of detailed engineering layouts; or of an advertising department from a new promotional idea, to consumer research, to designing ads, filming them, purchasing air time, and delivering copies of recorded videocassettes to television stations. The accomplishment of these processes in the appropriate sequence and the movement of physical goods from step to step almost invariably imposes physical limitations on how the human beings in an organization use and channel the creative energies they possess.

Creative energy will flow consistent with the pressures or constraints of the control structures; with what people are rewarded for or paid to do; with personal and organizational goals, beliefs, values, long-standing habits, and norms; with the availability of information; and finally, in accordance with physical laws and the physical processes of the organization.

The power and beauty of these personal and organizational structures is that, once constructed, they operate almost automatically and require very little conscious attention. Because of this, we as individuals are able to devote the major part of our time and attention to the functions of formulating vision and consciously evolving the structures and processes to foster its manifestation.

# STRUCTURAL CONFLICTS

A real difficulty stems from the fact that there are many elements in each of the classes of structure mentioned above. Each of these elements interacts with others within its own group and with those of other groups. Often they contradict each other or are otherwise in conflict. For example, I can have goals which are inconsistent with what I am rewarded to do, with certain habits I or my organization may have, even with other personal goals. In an organization, certain desired habits may be inconsistent with what is rewarded, or what is rewarded may be in conflict with important values. The possibilities are endless. The result is one elaborate, interrelated system of structural elements which largely governs the performance of individuals and the organization. As individuals, we each live with many demands and yearnings pulling us this way and that. Symbolically, it is as if we had thousands of rubber bands around our waist connected to different structures in our lives — sets of beliefs, values, habits, norms, physical processes, rewards, incentives — each of which creates tension that constrains or otherwise influences our behavior. In combination, some sets of rubber bands act to hold us in healthy balance. Some move us toward what we want, while others are contradictory, diffuse our energy and pull us in different directions.

Likewise in an organization some of the structures that seem to be in conflict with others can actually be helping to maintain a healthy balance in support of the overall vision. For example, suppose there is a conflict between some goal we want right now and one of our basic values. Our inability to immediately reconcile the discrepancy may cause us to ask which of the two results is more important to us. Such a conflict keeps us on track by challenging us to reflect upon who we are and what we truly want to create.

Since some of these contradictory structures do, in fact, cause us to work at cross purposes and expend our creative energies getting nowhere, structural conflict in organizations is generally viewed as undesirable. And some of it obviously is. Just as frequently, however, having cross tension in organizations can be quite healthy.

For example, engineering's desire to build one elegant prototype with relative insensitivity to the cost it takes to do so can represent a structural conflict with manufacturing's desire to build large numbers of these items at low cost. (This structural conflict frequently gets acted out in what appears to be a personality conflict between the head of engineering and the head of manufacturing. In fact, it has been said that over 80 percent of apparent personality conflicts in organizations are, at their root, structural conflicts.) In terms of the overall organizational purpose of being both innovative and profitable, it would serve the organization very well to sustain both of these goals — and also to tolerate the structural tension involved — but only to the extent that the people in engineering and manufacturing identify with the larger goal of the entire organization. Lacking that identification, the unhealthy result would be a pitting of one department against the other.

The job of leadership in a metanoic organization is to keep the primary structures, such as goals and values, continually in the organizational focus, so that a conflict among subordinate structures is always viewed from the larger focus. Leaders will also want to augment present structures with additional ones that enhance the flow of creative energy in alignment with the organization's purpose. Finally, leaders should always be seeking to identify those structural conflicts that are, in fact, dysfunctional and should be dismantled.

## LEADER AS DESIGNER OF STRUCTURE

The most neglected aspect of leadership is that of design. Imagine that your organization is like an ocean liner, and that you are the leader of it. What analogous role would you occupy in relation to the ocean liner? The most common response is "captain." But the person who has the greatest actual influence on the ship's performance is not the captain. It is the naval architect who designed the ship. No captain can get great performance from a ship which, because of its design, tends to list in the water or can't turn. The way a ship—or an organization—is designed is vitally important.

Because structural design is a major influence of organizational performance, it is an exceedingly important leadership role. However, it has often remained unappreciated for one obvious reason: the consequence of a great design is the absence of problems. When a system is working without problems, its great design is more or less invisible; it usually goes unnoticed and unrewarded. In contrast, what does get noticed in organizations are *problems*, and what gets rewarded are the people who solve them. We tend to recognize, reward and read management books about the white knights who ride in on their white stallions to save the day, rather than those leaders who design great structure.

For years, one of our major objectives as managers has been to engineer the optimum organization, that is, to obtain the highest performance while maintaining stability and predictability. Our hope was to design a set of structures in which one only needed to replace any departing worker with another person of moderately equal talent and the organization would experience no loss in performance. To my knowledge, there has been no evidence that such a mechanistic orientation has ever led to inspired performance. Inspired performance is a function of inspired people operating with vision and purpose in well-conceived organizational structures, ones that are designed primarily to foster the creation of a collective vision and to channel the creative energies of everyone toward producing the results to which they are all committed.

## LEADERSHIP AND INTUITION

Often, leading a metanoic organization seems overwhelming in its complexity. And if you were to approach the task with solely rational capacities, it would be. Fortunately, we have been provided with the capacity for intuition, which we can use to help simplify the enormous complexity of life. Intuition is a tool used by all great leaders to formulate and validate their visions, establish empathy and rapport with their followers, and deal with the convoluted and systemic relationships among structural elements.

However, intuition alone is insufficient. Metanoic organizations cannot be led by fiat. So, no matter how accurate your intuitive insights are, they must be confirmable through rational analysis, in order to be seen as plausible by others in the organization. Moreover, when you lack a rational confirmation of what you sense to be right, it is all too easy to be swayed away from your vision by another's rational argument, even when you know intuitively they are wrong.

Great organizational leaders, like great scientists, use intuition and rationality to complement each other. They guide their analyses with their intuition, and they verify their intuitive insights with rational analysis. In this way, at the deepest levels, leaders in a metanoic organization will apprehend the organization as a whole entity rather than as a machine-like aggregation of autonomous parts. They will know how people can operate independently yet interconnectedly to bring about results consistent with their dreams.

To create and lead a metanoic organization requires that you create and integrate your own versions of the ideas presented in this article. It also likely requires that you continue to build upon many of the activities you have been doing all along. It may require also that in the future you implement numerous leadership abilities we have yet to discover.

It would be nice if creating and leading a metanoic organization only required one to have a vision for the organization. In my experience, although formulating an organizational vision is paramount, the other two leadership abilities — enrolling and empowering others and designing functional structures — are just as essential.

The development of these skills and abilities is likely to be a lifelong task. But the commitment to a vision of your organization's greatness is something immediately available to you, should you choose it. It arises from the deepest part of you from which your leadership naturally and nonmanipulatively emerges, and will provide a powerful wellspring of energy to inspire all your actions. Connected to your own sense of destiny and purpose, and supported by its unfailing wisdom, you and the people around you will be able to achieve results that transcend the ordinary and manifest the highest in human aspiration.

# CHAPTER 13

# After the Vision: Suggestions to Corporate Visionaries and Vision Champions

by

**DICK RICHARDS**
**SARAH ENGEL**

*Creating organizational visions and working in organizations from the stance of visionary leadership have become common phenomena over the past few years. After articulating and communicating "the vision," however, a great deal of work remains to be done in bringing it into reality. This chapter outlines several ideas which have been effective in achieving organizational visions.*

It was as if a great bell called to me, far away, a light like to the faraway lights in the marsh, saying, "follow" . . . and I know that the truth, the real truth, is there, there, just beyond my grasp, if only I can follow it and find it there and tear away that veil which shrouds it . . . it is there if only I can reach it. . . .

*Lancelot*

What organization does not want its people, like Lancelot, to reach for something great that lies just beyond their grasp, to seek the "faraway lights" (Bradley, 1984)? What organization does not wish to challenge its people to pursue the best in themselves and the best possible future?

Today, in some of our most successful companies, a few visionary leaders truly are looking to the future and defining new realities. These leaders have discovered a powerful tool for capturing the spirit and energy of their organizations: the vision statement.

A vision statement is a document describing the way things could be. It is a declaration of the organization's most desirable future; it describes the faraway lights, and invites the organization on a quest to reach them.

The trend toward writing vision statements has been ignited by a widespread rediscovery of the centrality of human values in the conduct of business, and has been fueled by the publication and popularity of many books, especially Peters and Waterman's *In Search of Excellence* (1982), which struck a chord in the hearts of many executives and managers by affirming the significance of vision and values to corporate success.

Creating a vision statement is the responsibility of the highest level of management in an organization. The most successful visions seem to be those that come from the visionary's heart. They come from executives who say things like, "I want to leave something here that I can be proud of," or, "I'd like this to be a place I'd be happy to have my kids work in," or, "I know this company could be great if we all put our energy in the same direction." It is no simple task, this writing of a corporate vision; it requires a deep understanding of the organization and of oneself, considered judgment about what will be best for the organization in the future, and an ability to articulate that understanding and judgment in a way that is energizing, uplifting, simple, and direct.

A vision statement is a document around which an organization can build its culture, as American culture is built around the Declaration of Independence and the Bill of Rights. Edgar Schein (1984) has written that an organization's culture can be understood at several different levels. The first level is visible artifacts, like technology, patterns of behavior and dress, or documents. The second level is values, which is what people say are the reasons for what they do. The third, and deepest, level is its basic paradigm or framework for looking at the world and its people; its underlying assumptions about human nature, relationships, the nature of business, or the relationship between man and his environment. If it is to serve as the stimulus and centerpiece of an organization's culture, a vision statement must address values and underlying assumptions.

One executive whom we helped to write a vision statement believed teamwork to be important to his company's future. Teamwork is an artifact, a pattern of behavior. When we asked him, "Why teamwork?" he replied that he thought teamwork stimulated creativity. Creativity is a value, one level deeper in his understanding of the kind of culture he hoped to build. When we asked, "Why creativity?" he replied that he believed that to create was in the nature of people, and that without creation, life was meaningless. For him, creating was a reason for being. This then is the level of underlying assumptions, the kind of belief around which cultures are organized and visions ought to be written.

Vision statements frequently contain abstract terms like trust, creativity, or freedom; and sometimes more concrete terms, like "lowest cost producer," or "100 percent on-time delivery." Sometimes they contain statements about artifacts, like teamwork or communication. Some vision statements are quite brief, describing only a set of ideals and values. Some are longer, including perhaps an historical perspective, a summary of where the organization is at present, statements about the marketplace or the world at large, and guidelines for how people in the organization ought to work and be valued. Almost always a vision statement will include two things: a description of the organization's most desirable future, and a declaration of what the organization needs to care about most in order to reach that future. Often there is an accompanying slogan or logo that captures the essence of the message and becomes an important reference: "We feel good when you feel good;" "The customer comes first;" "Technology is our business;" "Partners in making dreams come true."

Vision statements are best written by one person—the senior person in the organization, who should seek input from allies, from others who might be key players in implementing the vision, and from people outside the organization who might offer a fresh perspective. Involvement of allies and key players will increase their commitment to the vision and help in its initial implementation.

After the vision is written, a visionary must be prepared to spend considerable time, thought, and energy helping to make it happen. One corporate visionary told us, "When you are looking at a long-range vision, you can't really delegate it to a few people and expect it to happen. We are all in this together—the entire organization. The prime reason for me to be heavily involved is that there is a certain weight to my support that can't come from anyone else. If I don't keep the momentum going, who will?" Also, the role of the visionary may change dramatically after the vision. The same person also said, "I am spending considerably more time on creating the environment that will make people more productive, and will make the vision happen, and far less time managing issues and problems, and monitoring the specifics of the business as closely as I used to."

Our experience indicates at least three situations in which companies can benefit from a vision statement. First is the *emerging* company, which is growing so quickly that things sometimes seem to be out of control. Often the founder is struggling to define a new role; he or she is no longer able to maintain daily contact with all employees, is beginning to think about installing personnel systems, and is worrying about how to preserve the values that marked the company's beginnings.

Second is the *retrenched* company, which has successfully completed some kind of downsizing effort, has felt the pain of coming to grips with its limits, needs to recapture the energy inherent in moving toward a desirable future, and has restated its mission.

Third is the *refocusing* company, which, because of increased competition, mergers, varying customer demands, new opportunities, or a host of other reasons, needs to consider seriously and communicate clearly what the company is about and what it must do to remain successful. For example, following the publication of *In Search of Excellence,* which demonstrated the importance of customer service, many companies are refocusing on a "close to the customer" orientation.

These three kinds of companies have in common a need to articulate what they wish to become, to define their best possible future. And that is the function of a vision statement.

Many difficult questions arise after a vision statement is completed and the quest begins: How will the vision be communicated? Will people be energized and excited? How can others be included in the process of creating the future? Publishing a vision seems to be an excellent means for stimulating an organization, yet there is little information about how to create the environment most likely to support useful and innovative actions leading toward realizing the vision. Perhaps we all have too little experience of quests.

While facilitating visions in large companies, we uncovered four processes involved in gaining an organization's commitment to a vision—*communication, boundary testing, sign-on,* and *celebration.* Visionaries, and others who are helping to facilitate organizational commitment to a vision, will have to give considerable attention to these processes.

# COMMUNICATION

The first after-the-vision process is *communication*—the presentation of the vision to the organization by the creators or by people designated by them, whom we will call "champions of the vision."

Initial communication is most often accomplished by distributing printed copies of the vision, holding meetings to talk about the vision, showing videos of the vision-maker introducing the vision, and discussing the vision at training events or seminars. The following suggestions and ideas about communicating a vision are based on our experiences during this first phase.

## Education

The concept of "leadership by vision" may be new to the people hearing the vision, and education about the visionary leadership process can be helpful to gaining commitment. When people experience something new, they try to fit it into their past experience as a way of understanding it and figuring out how to deal with it. If their existing experience is full of "management by objectives," "directives from management," "short-term goals," and "stewardship reports," they will tend to see the vision as just another set of objectives, directives, or goals, and something that will require formal stewardship. This can easily result in the vision being trivialized, discounted, and dismissed. It is important to tell people who are experiencing a visionary approach to leadership for the first time that the approach is different from their past experience, and how it is different.

There are at least three ways in which visionary leadership differs from what many organizations are used to. First, it focuses on hopes for the future, rather than on the problems of the present. Second, it deals in human values and assumptions about the nature of people as well as strategies and business objectives. Third, it involves the entire organization in the process of creating the future, pushing responsibility and authority downward within the organization.

There are many mechanisms to help people understand visionary leadership, ranging from simple explanations to in-depth training in visionary leadership for key people in the organization. For many organizations the process is so far outside the boundaries of their experience that constant reminders are required. In these situations individuals must feel free to challenge one another when they spot activities that are inconsistent with the new process.

## Creating the Environment

After the vision is written, a visionary must be prepared to spend a considerable amount of time, thought, and energy helping to create the appropriate environment for the organization to progress steadily toward the vision. This begins during the communication phase, when as many people as possible should have the opportunity to interact with the visionary or a primary champion. People will want first of all to test the sincerity and commitment of the visionary. Sincerity and commitment are far more easily communicated in person, and a face-to-face interaction gives a more realistic picture of the visionary and the vision.

In large decentralized organizations, where face-to-face contact between the visionary and all members of the organization is not possible, videotaped messages from the visionary are useful. These messages should be presented by champions of the vision who can provide the essential two-way communication with the audience, demonstrate their own commitment to the vision, and testify to their experience of the leader's sincerity and commitment. Printed material used to stimulate discussion is also effective.

Face-to-face contact also helps mitigate against the inevitable process whereby an organization places its leaders under a microscope, expecting them to be superhuman. During the early stages of communicating a vision, this process is accelerated, and leaders are expected never to behave in any way that might be seen as inconsistent with the vision, and, furthermore, never to have behaved inconsistently in the past. We do tend to expect too much from our leaders.

During these face-to-face sessions, it is helpful for first-time visionary leaders to acknowledge that the process is new to them, that they expect to make some mistakes, and that they expect to be challenged when they do. Also, there are many times when actions that in the minds of organizational leaders are perfectly consistent with the vision also seem perfectly inconsistent to others. It is imperative that visionaries explain the link between such actions and the vision. In one instance, a large corporation sold one of its many plants. The sale was, for many reasons, an action that fostered attainment of the vision. However, it was not perceived as such by many members of the organization until after the leaders were challenged and explained the link between the sale and the vision.

### Producing Miracles

People will want a "sign." You know, like a burning bush, or an old man with a long white beard, wearing a robe and sandals, stalking the corporate corridors carrying stone tablets inscribed with the vision, or a flood that wipes out half the auditors. History tells us it's probably a good idea to give them one—and one that is credible. In organizations where people are cynical and distrusting about the effectiveness of managers and leaders, it is particularly important for leaders to show the force of their intent and commitment by challenging "sacred cows," by changing the things that people believe impede the vision and by doing away with those things the vision renders irrelevant. Sacred cows might include rigid norms for how meetings are held, how presentations are given, how performance is appraised, how people greet one another, how competitive or collaborative people are within the organization, how managers relate to subordinates, etc. Changing ingrained patterns that impede the vision is often experienced by the organization as a miracle, and witnessing a miracle can move people a long way toward supporting a vision.

### Ambiguity

It is useful to remember that a vision statement is a leading-edge document. If it weren't on the leading edge, it wouldn't be a vision, and because it is on the leading edge, it can't be totally and satisfactorally explained at the beginning. This will be a problem in organizations where ambiguity is not tolerated, and leaders and champions will have to continually assure people that not knowing all the answers is OK. There are many questions about how a vision will be translated into action that ought to be answered with "I don't know." And "I don't know" ought to be followed by "Let's find out."

## Consistency

The process of sharing the vision must be consistent with the content of the vision. If the vision talks about two-way communication, there had better be lots of two-way communication about the vision, or the visionary and champions will soon be packing up the handouts and video equipment and retiring to their offices to dream about what might have been. If the vision speaks about change, creating an environment to discuss the vision that is recognizably different from the organization's typical meeting environment will give a signal that change is accepted and, in fact, happening.

One divisional manager believed that the largest impediment to realizing his organization's vision was an excess of formality and an overly critical attitude in his group that destroyed energy, creativity, and dialogue. He held a three-day meeting to communicate the vision, to translate it into actions within his group, and to begin changing unproductive norms around formality and criticism. Ordinarily, these meetings were characterized by formal agendas with hour-by-hour schedules, ritualized presentations, vu-graph projectors, copious handouts, and a lengthy meeting evaluation form. He began this meeting by inviting his people to join him in a ceremony, held on a beachfront, during which they burned a pile of agendas, handouts, and evaluation forms. In this way he clearly demonstrated his willingness to try something new, and their meeting was said to be "The best we've ever had."

## Accepting Criticism

Visionary leaders and vision champions must be sensitive to how others react to the vision, and sensitive in how they deal with those reactions.

It seems important to encourage people to express their negative thoughts and feelings about the vision. A vision is not truth, but hope, and people have fears attached to hopes, fears that often need to be aired, recognized, and responded to.

It is much too easy for visionaries, excited and energized by their vision, to overlook the reactions and fears of others about the vision; too easy to discount them, shut them off, discourage people from airing them. These reactions are often inquisitive, sometimes doubtful or skeptical, and frequently emotional. Such comments as, "This is obvious and it's about time somebody said it"; or, "Sounds good, let's see if they can pull it off"; or, "Just another directive from management" are sometimes unpleasant or threatening for the visionary to hear, but without airing and discussing these reactions and fears, it is doubtful that any true commitment to a vision can be achieved.

Inevitably some people will remain silent, hoping the vision will suffer a quiet death. The best a visionary or champion can do is pay careful attention to those who are sincerely raising their concerns, encourage others to do the same, and get on with the job of implementing the vision in the hope that enough people will support it and breathe life into it.

A vision can be seen as a stimulus to creativity, where a creative response is expected from the system in which the vision exists. A vision is somewhat like a half-formed idea waiting to be filled in. While it is important to hear people's concerns and fears, the best way to stimulate creative responses to a half-formed idea seems to be to encourage people to say what they like about it as well as what they don't like about it.

In organizations that reward analytical and critical skills, it may be too much to hope that people will embrace a vision without a good deal of analysis and criticism. However, a vision is as much about stirring people's hearts as it is about challenging their minds; discussions of a vision ought to focus on both.

It is particularly important that people explore the meaning of values expressed in the vision. What is the meaning of "integrity," "trust," or "cooperation"? One effective technique for stimulating such an exploration is to ask groups of people to decide on the opposites of those values. Concepts can be defined by their opposites, and talking about the opposite of integrity forces us to clarify what we mean by integrity. For example, in one organization, a discussion of the opposite of trust, yielded "suspicion" (we did not allow mistrust as an answer), and stimulated a discussion of how and why people in the group were suspicious of one another, and what they need to do to become more trusting.

## Focus on the Future

Discussions about the vision should focus on the future, not on the present or the past. This is not to say that the past is unimportant and shouldn't be discussed, only that when talking about where we are going, it serves little purpose to talk about how bad things are or have been, or even about how good things are or have been. It is less helpful to look at what was wrong in the past and try to fix it, than to look forward to the future and see what is needed to achieve a desired result. Besides, people can get testy if they think they are being told they are ineffective, and visions are not about criticism; they are not a strategy for giving feedback to an organization about how bad it has been — at least they shouldn't be.

## Visions Create Problems

A vision statement describes a different reality, not necessarily one that people will view as better. People will tend to look at a vision expecting it to solve some problem they face on a day-to-day basis. The truth is that a vision will probably create as many problems as it solves. For example, one organization that included the words "the customer comes first" in its vision statement found it then had to change the way many decisions were made, change aspects of how performance was appraised, discourage internal competition that caused delays in processing customer orders and complaints, and solve a whole host of other problems. That vision moved the organization in a positive direction, yet created many new problems along the way.

### Networking

The most important communucation problem, after initial publication and discussion of a vision, is how to build the critical mass — how to advertise evidence of change and build networks to promote change. Networking can be a powerful tool for building the critical mass. Networking strategies might include newsletters dedicated to publicizing evidence of the vision in action, computer conferencing among champions of the vision, and meetings of those who are working toward the vision, with no other agenda except talking about how that effort is proceeding and celebrating one another's successes.

# BOUNDARY TESTING

If the visionary is serious about his or her commitment to the vision, and the vision doesn't just fade away, communication of the vision will be quickly followed by *boundary testing*, which essentially means asking, "How will things be different?" Many boundaries will be questioned: the boundaries of leadership in the organization, as well as the boundaries of individual jobs, roles, influence, relationships, etc.

There are elements of organizational life that appear to be opposites, such as visionary leadership and rational management, efficiency and creativity, individual effort and teamwork. For all of these pairs of organizational elements, the more you have of one, the less you have of the other. Boundary testing should result in the best balance among these contradictory elements. What is the best proportion of visionary leadership to rational management, of efficiency to creativity, of individual effort to teamwork? Boundary testing efforts will answer those questions.

Boundary testing is also a critical component of gaining organizational commitment to a vision, for people will want permission to step outside the existing boundaries, to break long-standing patterns of belief and behavior, to try new things, and they will be sensitive to the reactions of others, particularly those of the visionary and other people in authority.

Boundary testing is the second process visionaries must attend to after the vision. Here are some ideas and suggestions for facilitating boundary testing.

### Challenging Norms

Norms are the unwritten rules of an organization that govern how people are supposed to behave and what they are supposed to believe. These behaviors and beliefs come to be considered by the organization's people as "normal." Often the norms need to be challenged and changed or they will inhibit achieving a vision. However, because they are considered so "normal," people in the organization are frequently not aware of them; thus they have no sense of how they might inhibit the vision and little sense of how to change them.

It is often useful to involve an outsider who has skill in identifying norms and assessing their impact. We once consulted with an executive group whose vision included "utilizing the creative potential in all of us." Their meetings were held in a formal room, around a long table, with formal portraits of the company founder

206

peering over their shoulders. Each person entered the room without speaking to anyone else, sat at the table, and took a yellow lined pad from a stack provided. Each person spoke politely in turn, and everybody wrote down everything that was said. These were the norms for meetings in the company for as long as anybody could remember. They were surely not conducive to creativity.

## Encouraging Leadership

The publication of a vision raises questions about the nature of leadership in the organization, especially if the vision is the first for that organization. One question that often arises is, "What is the difference between leadership and management?" In our view, management is mostly concerned with control, allocating resources, and solving problems. Leadership is about articulating visions, embodying values, and creating the environment within which things can be accomplished. Leadership is spiritual and emotional, characterized by uncertainty and ambiguity. Management is more focused on today, leadership on tomorrow. An effective balance between the two is essential.

During the early phases of a vision, it seems important that more time be given to leadership activities. These include ensuring acceptance and acceptability of the vision, creating common values, creating value-related opportunities, developing an environment that supports innovation and productivity, defining a global perspective, postponing closure on new ideas, nurturing the good ones, looking for "win-win" opportunities rather than "win-lose," being visible, and creating celebrations.

## Flexibility

Recognize that the steps to implementing a vision cannot be planned in advance—but after people understand and sign on to the vision, initial steps are usually obvious. After initial steps are taken, the next steps should be equally obvious if they are truly guided by the vision. Occasional midcourse corrections are recommended, and if these yield a slight change in direction, that should be considered a successful outcome. There should be sufficient flexibility in achieving a vision to make room for the needs of the people charged with achieving it.

## Risk

Since the outcome of a vision statement is unpredictable, and a vision will require boundary testing, risk is an integral part of the vision-making process. This is further exacerbated if "taking more risks" is part of the vision. It is no easy undertaking to change an organization from a low-risk environment, where outcomes are fairly predictable, to one in which risk-taking is acceptable and outcomes are less predictable. Reward structures must be examined to discover how they discourage or encourage risk-taking, and managers who say they want their people to take more risks had best start examining their own risk-taking behavior and become aware of new options and limits. A clear understanding of what constitutes a risk—and the differences among personal risk, career risk, and business risk—and some clarity about the kinds of risks required to achieve the vision are essential.

Also, it can be very helpful for managers to ask themselves, just after having made some decision, "What is the next biggest risk I might take?" If managers begin to calibrate risks—perhaps on a scale that reads "safe-risky-riskier-riskiest"—it will help them understand their own risk-taking, be aware of the limits of their commitment to the vision, and perhaps produce more creative solutions.

## Momentum

Another important issue is how to keep the momentum going—how to publicize evidence of commitment to the vision and to encourage as much networking as possible. After the vision has been communicated and understood, the visionary must devote time and energy to keeping up the momentum while the concepts in the vision are being integrated and the critical mass is building. This might involve discussions with champions on how to make things happen, defining changes in roles, exploring system or structural changes to move systems toward consistency with the vision, monitoring progress in new and creative ways, and helping to set new boundaries and ease the transition. A prospective visionary who simply sets the vision in front of people, and expects them to carry it out without his or her very active participation, is doomed to fail.

## Training

One effective means for introducing people to the vision and exploring new boundaries utilizes training sessions in which people are encouraged to explore the vision and are supported in reacting to it, as well as in sorting out what it means or might mean for them. Such programs will reflect the organization's degree of commitment to the vision. Do not expect to hold a few one-hour meetings and have people believe that there is great commitment; rather be prepared to demonstrate commitment by allocating resources to helping people get on board.

## Meetings and Stories

Perhaps the most difficult tasks for champions who are anxious to have the vision concepts implemented in their part of the organization are preparing for a "vision meeting" and engaging in the follow-up needed to make the vision happen. In preparation for these steps the champion must develop a clear understanding of his or her limits for change and risk, must anticipate as far as possible the inevitable gap between what he or she intends and what actually results, must be comfortable with the behavior needed to support people and make things happen, and must be open to subordinates' feedback, reactions, and fears. Further, the champion must be willing to walk the fine line between being committed and being involved and providing support on the one hand, and destroying creativity and enthusiasm with excessive control and interference on the other.

During vision meetings it seems useful to recognize actions that are consistent with the vision. One plant manager held a meeting in which he talked about his vision; then he invited people to tell stories of recent happenings that were consistent with the vision. He sprinkled his response to the stories with a lot of, "That's exactly what I'm looking for." His "laying on" of the vision was extremely gentle, which seemed to give people a chance to understand and integrate it. His sincere "attaboys" were energizing; people discovered what was expected of them; the process of hero-making, story-telling and myth-making began; he encouraged breaking unproductive norms and setting new, productive ones; and new boundaries were established for "how we do things around here."

The telling and retelling of "stories" in support of the vision are essential. Alan Wilkins (1984), writing about organizational culture, says, "Stories are powerful vehicles for transmitting values because they give concrete context to abstract values. They also provide scripts about how to get things done and what to expect in organizations."

Champions who are interpreting the vision within their own part of the organization also need to redefine limits and direction in an open manner to their group. However, people are less likely to respond well to broad statements of openness than they are to clear statements about what the new rules are; a great deal of time can be saved if these rules are developed and articulated up front. About the worst thing a manager can do after a vision is published is to lead people to believe that they can have or do things that he or she fully believes to be out of the question and therefore will not be able to support.

## Experimentation

Experiments are good methods to test new ideas and new ways of doing things. Creating an opportunity for individuals and small groups with common interests to design an in-depth experiment with fixed parameters to try out something new is an excellent way to generate energy and test boundaries. The experiments should represent a departure from previous ways of doing things, be within the control of the experimenters, have some element of risk, and, most important, be exciting to the experimenters. There should be no taint of failure attached to experiments that don't work out as planned; these should be viewed as learning and testing experiences, and rewarded as "a good try." And remember that consistency with the vision is a key criterion for the success of an experiment.

## Task Groups

Task forces are an inevitable part of the culture of most organizations, and it is essential that task groups emerging after the vision are consistent in both content and process with that vision. If the vision speaks about cooperation and flexibility, then task forces must work cooperatively and have flexible boundaries and membership. Sufficient time and resources must be made available for task forces to get on with their tasks.

One creative use of task groups is using them to implement the vision concepts in the same way they are used to solving organizational problems. Here are some ideas for using task forces for vision follow-up:

1. Set up task forces around key concepts or values expressed in the vision: a task force on "participation," one on "cooperation," one on "reaching our individual potential."

2. Set up task forces to explore how the vision might affect different people,

roles, or organizational processes: a task force on "the supervisor or the future," one on "getting close to the customer," one on "how our performance appraisal system impedes and facilitates the vision."

3. Provide each task force leader with a process consultant, a peer of the leader, who is chosen by the leader but is not a task force member, and who is responsible for consulting with the task force about its consistency with the vision. The process consultant, who should be a champion of the vision, monitors the task force's process and product.

4. Have task force leaders meet to apply the test of consistency with the vision to the entire task force process, to how task forces make recommendations, to the limits of task force authority, etc.

5. Select members of functional task forces with the vision concepts and values as well as the task in mind. This would mean, for example, that if the vision included a "close to the customer" orientation, employees who work in personnel and auditing functions would be included on task forces dealing with customer problems. They might not have the technical expertise the problem seems to require, their functional specialties might at first glance seem irrelevant to the problem, but if the organization wants everybody to understand what "close to the customer" means, then everybody needs the opportunity to be "close to the customer."

### Initiative

In multilevel hierarchical organizations, people will normally look to the levels above themselves for initiatives in support of the vision. Unless the vision specifically calls for that to continue, it is important to help people at all levels find areas within their control wherein they can form their own initiatives, take self-responsible action, and test the boundaries of their upward influence.

Facilitating boundary testing might be the most significant leadership challenge after the vision. Writing and communicating a vision are in the realm of words and ideas; boundary testing is in the realm of actions, where we encounter resistance from long-established ways of doing things, where our commitment becomes concrete, and where we test whether our ideas are credible. It is in boundary testing where visionaries and champions discover the real meaning behind the ideas and words of their visions.

# SIGN-ON

The third process that must be considered in order to gain organizational commitment is a *sign-on* by members of the organization. By sign-on we mean an individual's commitment to the vision. The kind of commitment needed to truly enact a vision cannot be coerced; it is a self-responsible acceptance of the invitation to the party. In order to make such a choice, one must feel free to make the opposite choice — not to come to the party — or one is likely to have a terrible time, be a bore, and maybe ruin the party.

Sign-on happens within individual members of the organization, and there is little else that a visionary can do to produce it except communicate well, facilitate boundary testing, and provide celebrations for actions leading toward the vision. Here, however, are a few ideas, suggestions, and things to keep in mind while attempting to get committed sign-on

## Action

The best indicator that someone has signed on is some personal action to carry out the vision, or some kind of missionary activity: preaching or teaching the vision, spreading the word, telling stories, networking with others who support the vision, and promoting and supporting changes that facilitate the vision. Visionaries and champions can help this process by providing formats within which these personal actions can occur: meetings, training events, reward ceremonies, and networking processes like newsletters and computer conferencing.

## Visions and More Visions

A critical step to sign-on occurs when each subset of the organization establishes its own set of values within the framework of the vision. By each subset we mean each division, department, or group, and, especially important, each person.

After establishing their own set of values, the next question for each organizational subset to ask is, "How will we (or I) put these into practice?"

A useful question to ask of organizational subsets that are preparing their own visions is, "What do you want to be like in the future?" This question — as opposed to, "What do you want to be doing?" or, "How do you want to work?" — encourages thought and discussion of values, purposes, and organizational climate.

## Personal Visioning

An effective way of getting people to internalize the organization's vision, and indeed the concept of visioning, is to have them develop their own personal vision of where they might like to be in the future. This involves collecting personal data about successes, interests, career and life stages, values, etc., and creating a personal statement of "who I am" and "who I want to be in the future." The process of personal transformation or change is analogous to organizational change, and encouraging people to engage in their own personal vision process, while exploring how the organization's vision is linked to their own, goes a long way toward obtaining a committed sign-on.

Asking people to create their own personal visions can also raise significant issues around the company's vision. One plant manager, after publishing his vision and getting sign-on from his management committee, sponsored a five-day program for his key managers to examine the vision and their role in implementing it. During the program, as an aid to writing a personal vision, each person was asked to select from a long list of values those which he or she held as most important. None of the 12 participants listed "helpfulness to others" as among their most important values. Yet the company vision statement called for "helping each person maximize his or her potential." This important discrepancy led to much discussion about the meaning of the vision and re-examination of personal values. Each person came away with a stronger commitment to the vision and deeper understanding of his or her own role as a facilitator of the vision.

### Patience

Visionaries can too easily forget that preparing their vision required soul-searching, study, risk, and time. Because their vision seems so obvious and right to them, they can come to expect it will be equally obvious and right to others and that sign-on will be automatic. It won't be, at least for most people seeing or hearing about the vision for the first time. Visionaries and champions must allow others the same opportunity for soul-searching, study, risk, and time that produced the vision. And they should be skeptical of sign-on that comes too easily, because easy sign-on often reflects shallow understanding of the vision, or shallow motives for signing on, and produces shallow commitment. More than anything, perhaps, visionaries must practice patience.

### Symbols and Ceremonies

A personalized symbol that reflects an individual's commitment to the vision can be a powerful aid to sign-on. During one meeting, where a group of managers were digesting and interpreting their organization's vision statement, each manager was asked to decide on his or her own personal slogan, a short statement that reflected a personal commitment to the vision. An engraver was brought to the meeting to make desk nameplates for each person; their slogans were engraved on the backs of the name plates. During another meeting, managers were asked to visit a nearby shopping district to purchase their own personal vision sign-on symbol.

A formal sign-on process, involving some tangible recognition of having signed on might be useful—a kind of baptismal ceremony, or a talisman of some sort.

### Bringing It Home

In many organizations people look upward within the organization for solutions to problems. A sign-on process requires that people look to themselves, asking, "What can I do to make it happen?" One visionary told his people, "You have to be comfortable that the overview is right, that the vision is correct, then the specifics have to come from you."

## CELEBRATION

The fourth process that visionaries and champions of a vision will need to pay attention to after the vision has been written is *celebration* of actions that foster the vision. We prefer to talk about celebration rather than rewards because the latter is a narrower term, and because celebration connotes ceremony, acclaim, and festivity.

212

## Why Celebrate?

There are two reasons why celebration is important after the vision. First, to reward and enjoy success. This is especially important where organizational systems and norms, such as performance appraisal systems, might impede the vision because they do not reward actions that foster the vision. Second, celebrations send clear signals to the organization about the kind of actions that support the vision, and are, in that sense, an aspect of continuing to communicate the vision.

## Accentuate the Positive

Whenever a vision is published, part of the organization will sign on quickly, part will resist, and part will adopt a wait-and-see attitude. Wait-and-see is usually the largest category. In many organizations, especially those that view managers as problem solvers, a great deal of time and energy will be spent trying to get those who resist on board; they pose a problem to be solved. In the meantime, those who have signed on and those who wait and see can easily become disenchanted and cynical. Celebrations are effective ways to focus attention and energy on those who have signed on, rather than on those who resist, and give those who wait and see something positive to see.

## Variety

Celebration means commemorating an event with a ceremony. Celebrations can be large or small, planned or spontaneous. They can occur at formal or informal meetings, seminars, or training programs. Visionaries and champions must be certain that celebration ceremonies fit the tone and style of the vision. Ways to celebrate include ovations, letters from top executives, weekend trips, dinners out with a spouse, flowers, lunch with an executive, a cheese and wine party during a training session about the vision, awards ceremonies, plaques, balloons, and cash awards. Often a handshake, smile, and "atta-boy" are enough. Hoopla is not required, though it seems important to many people. Be creative.

During the initial stages of communicating the vision, it is very useful to celebrate the aspects of the vision that already exist. If the vision talks about teamwork, celebrate the outstanding teamwork that the organization has had in the recent past; if it talks about customer service, celebrate recent examples of good customer service.

## Positive Reinforcement

Celebration is positive reinforcement. In *In Search of Excellence,* Peters and Waterman wrote that the most important output of management is getting others to shift attention in desirable directions, and that positive reinforcement is a potent tool for doing that. Such reinforcements tend to have more impact when they happen on-the-spot, when they contain as much information about exactly what is being reinforced as possible, when they are not easily achievable, when they are unpredictable and intermittent, and when the substance of the reward is largely intangible.

Frequent sincere celebration of the vision will provide an upbeat atmosphere around the vision, and will also—let us not overlook this—provide visionaries and champions with much needed reasons to celebrate as well.

## A FEW FINAL WORDS

Eight months after the publication of a vision for his company, a corporate president told us that he had three pieces of advice for others who would take a visionary approach to change in their organizations. We think it is sound advice, and worth repeating. First, he said, "Go from the general to the specific, from values and broad statements, to actions, as quickly as possible without short-circuiting communication." When a visionary is sure that someone or some group in his organization is clear about the vision and ready to act, often a simple statement is enough to get things moving. The statement probably ought to be, "Do it," or, "Why are you asking me?" or, "What do you need from me?"

The second piece of advice our visionary gave is, "Focus not on the problems of the past or the present, but on what will be different in the future." This is not as easy as it sounds, particularly because people trained as managers often view themselves as problem-solvers and are happiest solving the immediate problem. It takes courage to hold fast to the long-range view and delegate the day-to-day issues—courage, and trust in subordinates.

Finally, our visionary said, "The whole organization must be involved in creating what we all want. The top of the organization should do the minimum to get results, focusing instead on publicizing the vision and creating the environment in which things will get done." It can be quite a jolt for first-time visionaries when they shift from focusing on results to focusing on the vision and the climate of the organization. Success takes no less than a redefinition of the role of the senior people in the organization; they become less "producers of results" and more "keepers of the vision and values."

In this chapter, we have given some suggestions and ideas to visionaries and champions of a vision who are seeking an organization's commitment about the processes we believe will claim a great deal of attention after a vision is written—communication, boundary testing, sign-on, and celebration—and we know what we have written is not enough. The after-the-vision process is fragile and complex. It involves a total organization and a total human response-thoughts, feelings, and actions. It involves visionaries who must be visible, consistent, courageous, and creative; champions who must be innovative in publicizing the vision, sensitive in responding to the reactions of others, thoughtful in setting new boundaries, and ingenious in navigating the labyrinth of change; and finally, it involves the people who make up the organization, who must be willing to take risks, able to make commitments, and ready to experiment with themselves.

At the beginning of this paper we referred to the after-the-vision process as a quest, a reaching for the "faraway lights." We like the metaphor because the notion of quest calls to mind adventure, achievement, creativity, challenge, and leadership—qualities that we believe to elicit the best in all of us. It is our hope that more and more of our organizations will call more and more of their people to such a quest.

# CHAPTER 14

# The Art of Conscious Celebration: A New Concept for Today's Leaders

by
**CATHY DeFOREST**

*This chapter describes processes and ideas for honoring individuals, groups, and "life" within organizations in a creative, festive, and conscious matter. The more today's leaders permit themselves to be creative, conscious celebrators, the more opportunity there is for them to assist in transforming their organizations.*

Preoccupied with producing and managing, he [man] has lost touch with vast reaches of reality. His being has been borrowed and depleted. Therefore festivity is not just a luxury of life. It provides the occasion for man to establish his proper relation to time, history, and eternity.

Harvey Cox
*Feast of Fools*

We have lost our souls. Like those who went in search of the Holy Grail, we of the modern world have gone to the far corners of the earth to bring back profit and treasure to the Court of the Corporate King, while searching for meaning in our personal and work lives. Like those seekers, it is unclear what is illusion and what is reality. Is the creation of new markets, products, and larger profits each year our Grail? Like the knights and women of King Arthur's court, the search has twisted our minds and imprisoned our souls. What is the meaning behind our pursuits? How will the quest end?

We are far from the end of our search. While experiencing a dawning of technological innovation, we are also creating an age of spiritual exploitation and emptiness. While moving closer and closer to understanding how the mind works, we are using our wisdom to build materials that unbalance the ecological systems of the world and nuclear products that make our hearts ache.

Yet along this twisted journey are examples of corporations and leaders who see beyond illusion to a new reality. Their vision sees profit in the context of service and the need to feed the spirit as well as the mind and body. In order to survive the battles of competition, these leaders know they must address the spirit of their modern warriors and kingdoms in order to gain the greatest return on investment.

One element in each of these evolving organizations is leaders who recognize that the art of celebrating provides a way to nourish the spirit of an organization as well as create a moment in time when a glimpse of a transformed organization can be seen and felt. These leaders understand that celebration often portrays a truer reality of their desired culture than the illusions of modern management that have hypnotized our minds.

Like King Arthur's sword, Excalibur, celebrations are founded in sacred energy and therefore have the power to accomplish things that seem impossible by ordinary management means. As we begin a new era, which calls for creativity and innovation, excellence and networking, intuition and change in corporate culture, the spirit of celebration beckons.

## WHAT IS CONSCIOUS CELEBRATION?

Organization celebration is the process of honoring individuals, groups, events, achievements, the common and the extraordinary life within an organization in a creative, meaningful, and often festive manner. Celebration brings with it a parade of rich elements—rituals, myths, heroes and heroines, festivity, fantasy, symbols, choreography, story telling—all of which are deeply needed by modern organizations and their leadership in order to balance the pressures of the sometimes uptight corporate world. Celebrations are cause to set aside common everyday menial and strategic tasks. They also encourage fantasy, which invites managers and employees to imagine the impossible and envision new ways to do difficult tasks.

Traditional organization celebrations include: banquets, "roasts," ribbon-cutting ceremonies, and sales award dinners and trips. The celebrations discussed in this chapter are examples of conscious celebrations—events that mark significant moments that raise the consciousness of the participants to a higher order of reality.

"Conscious" means "knowing oneself," being concerned with potential," and being aware of inward "psychological and spiritual facts." Conscious celebrations come from a place of self-knowledge and are used to assist people to reach their potential and increase their awareness of the connection between material and spiritual life. They are a modern-day link to the spiritual dimension of an organization. They are also a link to the past—to history and the wisdom of the ages—and a link to the future—visions and dreams. Through these links, organization transformation can take place.

*Transformation may occur when the individual and collective consciousnesses of an organization are expanded through celebrating consciously.* There is an old saying, "as we think in our hearts, so we become." In conscious celebration our hearts are opened, and we become greater than who we were before the celebration began.

Conscious celebrations can be called "festivals of the spirit," "high touch events for a high tech world," "woven rituals of the soul," and "opportunities to live the vision of an organization." In conscious celebration we create moments that illuminate the deeper meaning of our lives and guide our footsteps into the future.

Conscious celebrations are a chance for us to experience what Harvey Cox

(1969) calls the interplay of our specialness with our commonness. Jim Channon, a consultant who has taught the art of ritual to a wide variety of managers, including Army generals, believes that organizations are "run on the fuel of the human spirit and as such, celebrations are an excuse to kick the juice. They allow the organization to run on high octane" (1984, personal communication).

The recording of "We are the World" (1984) by the USA for Africa organization is an example of a conscious celebration, designed to expand consciousness through celebration and song. In April 1985, thousands of radio stations worldwide played the song at exactly the same moment—an unprecedented event, a true celebration *of* the human spirit *for* the human spirit. The result of raising millions of dollars for food, medicine, and self-help is living proof that celebrations can expand consciousness and inspire the human spirit and, through this inspiration, create transformation.

## DISTINGUISHING ELEMENTS OF CONSCIOUS CELEBRATION

Celebrations, especially extravagant events, are on the upswing. Coca-Cola Co. staged a Broadway musical at Radio City Music Hall for 5,000 guests in order to introduce Diet Coke to its distributors. Equitable Life Assurance Society spent over 1 million dollars and a year in planning their 125th anniversary extravaganza for 12,000 employees, which included 36 Radio City Rockettes and an orchestra. To ease the tension in the AT&T breakup, that company held a "Super Sports Olympic Day" to create a cohesive family atmosphere within the company (Sheridan 1985).

Are these "industrial theatre" events examples of conscious celebrations or merely modern hyped versions of gold watches for retiring salesman? On the surface they could be classified as the latter. To discern a conscious celebration from a traditional event, each occasion must be examined in depth. Conscious celebrations have five distinguishing characteristics:

1. a specific values base

2. the use of symbols

3. ritual

4. storytelling

5. a special role of leadership in the design and implementation of these celebrations

### Values

Conscious celebrations incorporate all or most of these values—authenticity, humor of the heart, play, personal empowerment, elegance and aesthetics, spontaneity, and creativity—and come from a place of love and integrity.

*Authenticity.* Smart executives know that parties can be seductive and that peo-

217

ple often let their defenses down as they relax and enjoy such an event. Some managers capitalize on these occasions in order to manipulate their employees and gain further allegiance to the company. They also patronize them by making people "beholden" to the company for lavish gifts and holiday packages. Conscious celebrations, on the other hand, are events based on genuine appreciation for what people have done as well as who they are as human beings. Leaders of conscious celebrations honestly feel their organization could not exist without the work and dedication of its employees, and they express that feeling sincerely.

Celebrants must also feel that there is desire for their behavior to be authentic. They must not feel forced to contribute to a festive occasion in ways that make them feel uncomfortable or fake. If participants feel forced to mouth insincere words or say things only to impress others, they will not appreciate or enjoy the celebration.

*Humor of the Heart.* Unlike roasts and hazings, which often are the focus of a celebration, conscious celebrations use humor of the heart. Instead of using sarcasm and caustic jokes, the humor warms the heart and heightens the person's self-esteem rather than tearing it down. The jesting may still poke fun at the person's weaknesses and strengths and people have a lot of fun, but the intention is clear — to honor, not harm.

A group of scientists and engineers from the Department of Energy created a "This is Your Tuff Life Roast" for a consultant whose work was completed after a 2½-year association. (Tuff is the substance of a mountain they were studying.) Each manager described his or her appreciation, learnings, and feelings through cartoons, poems, songs, and symbolic gifts such as a bottle of aspirin. The roast included teasing, with such statements as "Despite our worst intentions you have guided us over the troubled waters, if not on a direct course, at least on one where we usually remained in sight of the path." The farewell concluded with the presentation of an album of poems, letters, cards, and photographs, including a card from the director of the project. Next to the director's signature was a heart drawn with footsteps on it, symbolically acknowledging the footsteps that this consultant had left on his heart.

*Play.* Deal and Kennedy, authors of *Corporate Cultures,* (1982) note the place of play in releasing tension and encouraging innovation. They state, "despite the fact that it has no real purpose and no rules, play in its various forms (jokes, teasing, brainstorming, and strategizing) bonds people together, reduces conflict, and creates new visions and cultural values." Tandem, IBM, and DEC all provide opportunities for play on company time through workshops, beer busts, and retreats.

Harvey Cox (1969) reminded us that during our industrial era, we grew "more sober and industrious, less playful and imaginative." Often the more creative the frivolity and the more meaningful the play, the more welcome is the balance of the work world.

*Personal Empowerment.* In traditional, hyped events, money is often used to put on a big production and to stage an event in order to impress the egos of the attendees and sometimes to intentionally bribe them into company loyalty. The main intent of a conscious celebration is not money or expression of power. These events can be elaborate, expensive events or occasions requiring no budget at all. True power empowers others. Conscious celebrations share two of the three basic power commodities Kanter (1983) discusses: *information* (data, technical knowledge, political intelligence, expertise) and *support* (endorsement, backing, approval, legitimacy). When people are informed and legitimized in a celebration, they feel energized and uplifted—empowered. This results in a natural desire to put the best possible skill and expertise into the company, rather than feeling forced or intimidated. They feel grateful to be informed of a company's new direction, if that is the reason for the celebration; inspired and compelled to do their part to achieve the vision of the corporation; and are convinced that the tasks they perform are inherently worthwhile.

On August 6, 1985, the fortieth anniversary of the bombing of Hiroshima men, women, and children gathered in a spectacular celebration of peace through individual empowerment. Through the vision of one woman, Justine Merritt, individuals from all walks of life painted, appliqued and wove images of peace on large panels of cloth. Each panel was joined with other panels, first in small towns and then in the capitals of each state, and lastly it was woven for six miles around Washington, D.C. Since that time, the peace ribbon has hung in galleries around the world, continuing to empower those who see it.

*Elegance and Aesthetics.* Conscious celebrators use the qualities of elegance and aesthetics in the overall design of their celebrations. This charm can range from the casual elegance of an old-fashioned ice cream social, which Syntex Corporation used to mark the achievement of a sales goal, to commissioning an artist to design an art deco poster to mark an anniversary, as did Interaction Associates, a consulting firm.

Elegance can also be experienced in the moment. Most meetings have "strategic moments." Celebrations have moments of "elegance." These are the climactic moments or the magical moments, which, when noted, can move a celebration to the next higher level of meaning. Like an actor's timing or the crescendo of a symphony, these moments can be sensed at the time as well as anticipated in the design of the celebration.

*Spontaneity.* Harrison Owen (1983) advocates the concept of "open space" in celebration. He believes that "transformation occurs in the open space between what has been, and what shall become." If the open space is there, a transformation can take place in a conscious celebration. However, if every moment of a celebration is orchestrated like a beauty pageant, there will literally be no room for this to occur. The use of open space creates room for surprise, spontaneity, and the unrehearsed meaning of the moment. During a conscious celebration, we cease doing and experience being. People cannot "be" if they are filling every moment "doing." The leader's greatest challenge is to have the courage to create the quiet and allow the space to be open.

*Creativity.* Each conscious celebration is custom-designed to fit the occasion, organizational norms, and personalities of the participants. This focus calls for creativity. Often the more creative the design of the event, the more honored the persons experiencing the celebration will feel.

One of the most creative celebrations in recent years was conducted through computer terminals. Meta Network is an organization set up to network people around the world in a computer conferencing and electronic mail system. Members of the Meta Network linked together to honor the birthday of the network's founder, Frank Burns. They sent invitations, via the post office, to each member of the Network. When the invitation was opened, small pieces of multicolored confetti fell into the invitee's lap. The creativity continued with the invitation itself:

> Shhhhhhh. . . . . . .
> You are invited to a surprise birthday party on November 23 for Frank Burns.
>
> We hope as many people as possible will sign on to honor Frank. To get to the party — type "join Meta: secret" at any "Do Next?" prompt. . .

The uniqueness of the celebration began the moment the invitation was opened and didn't finish until the secret ended on November 23, when the party-goers gathered via telecommunication.

## Symbols

Recent brain research and the writings of such people as Carl Jung and Jean Houston have raised awareness of the world of symbols. Celebrations in the past have been rich in the use of symbols, from the Japanese Noa plays to the Greek Festivals of Dionysus. In today's world symbols can offer the culminating image that bonds the meaning of a ritual and enables the celebration to live beyond its temporary existence.

In 1974, Dee Hock, then president of Visa International, gave a symbolic gift to each member of the International Organizing Committee to heal differences that at the time seemed irreconcilable (Deal and Kennedy 1982). Hock designed a unique set of gold cuff links for the meeting knowing that this meeting would determine whether the conflicts within the organization could be resolved. One cuff link was designed as a relief map of half of the world and inscribed around it were the Latin words "Studium Ad, Prosperandum" or "The Will To Succeed." On the second was the other half of the world surrounded by the words, "Voluntas in Conveniendum," or "The Grace To Compromise." The die to the casting was stored in a vault, to be destroyed if the meeting was unsuccessful, or kept for future sets of cuff links if the directors reached agreements. The cuff links have become treasured possessions and the symbols, the motto of Visa International.

## Ritual

Our culture is built upon ritual. Ritual passed down wisdom through the ages and translated the mysteries of our material and spiritual world to the next generation even before the written word was created. In the Information Age, ritual is necessary in continuing the translation of known technology and the essence of our cultural ideals. According to Igelhart (1983) rituals work on two levels: the psychic level (seen and unseen forces affecting material reality) and the psychological level (affecting people's actions by affecting their minds). As a result, the energy of each ritual carries over into other areas of corporate life.

Rituals can be spontaneous or planned, personal or collective. Companies such as IBM, Dana, Mary Kay Cosmetics, NCR, Holiday Inns, and Procter and Gamble have made ritual a serious part of day-to-day operations, often initiating a ritual around such common habits as morning coffee updates.

Yet rituals can easily lose their original meaning, becoming institutionalized and used to enforce the status quo of stifled behavior rather than to raise consciousness and bring meaning to an organization. At that point, new rituals need to be created and old ones abandoned. Rituals showcase the culture of the organization. If they are meaningful, they dramatize and reinforce the values and beliefs of the organization. If they are stiff or outdated, they telegraph dysfunctional messages to employees.

Ron Green, internal consultant with Alcoa, uses a combination of ritual and symbolism with participants in the corporate training programs. He explains his philosophy behind these events.

> Our program uses symbols and rituals to celebrate the skill, awareness, and knowledge gained by each participant. We end our professional development seminars with a graduation dinner, a group class picture, a diploma and a closing ceremony. During the dinners, which are light, playful, fun filled occasions, we present symbols to each participant to help celebrate the most important awareness or skill that he or she gained during the program—giant ears for listening skills, a clown's nose for appreciating the less serious side of themselves, a heart to remind her or him that people are important to a manager. These rituals are often the highlight of the seminar. They serve to bond the group together, become part of the corporate culture and act as a reminder that each member has begun a journey toward greater effectiveness (1985, personal communication).

## Storytelling

Culture is built on myths and stories. When leaders tell stories in a celebration, they embody the beliefs and values of an organization in a tale that can be easily remembered and repeated. Stories spread like wildfire through an organization. When a story is first told in a celebration, its value becomes heightened, because celebrations are special events that gather people together for public recognition. People inside the organization admire the hero in the story and secretly wish to be that person and have those experiences. Stories inspire people and promote admiration for the storyteller. Storytellers are really modern-day information brokers, and as the world becomes more invested in the Information Age, the value of storytelling will increase.

## The Role of Leadership in the Art of Celebration

What does a leader do to create celebrations that help transform an organization? An example can shed light on this question (Pyle, personal communication, 1985).

A senior vice-president of a major housing company was given the task of turning around 2 of its 12 decentralized organizations, both of which were losing enormous sums of money; were very disorganized; and were experiencing extremely low morale. In spite of the fact that people were working hard, little was being accomplished. The senior vice-president knew the employees needed job skills training and organizational help, but he also knew that somehow the people had to become inspired, literally had to have life breathed into them, if they were going to make it. He believed that if he could create a spirit in these companies, they could be turned around and become profitable. He decided to begin a job training program, a management development program, and a series of celebrations.

The first effort, a party quickly and poorly organized by the SVP, was a complete failure. Knowing celebration was the right idea, but that the process of creating it had been all wrong, the SVP called in a consultant for help. They decided to create a contest between the organizations and to involve all of the employees in the planning process. The group designed a picnic as a kickoff event, which included blindfolded piggy-back races, T-shirts, banners, and team names: the "Grizzlies" and "Vultures." The whole event was videotaped and later shown to spouses and participants at the awards banquet at the end of the contest.

Although the vice-president was aware that somewhere down the road he wanted to create organizations with a higher purpose than competition, the first step worked toward easing tension, creating some fun, inducing informality, and making it more fun to come to work.

Celebration, in and of itself, became a part of the company philosophy. The values of the company were written into a values constitution and informally and openly discussed throughout the companies. One of the clearly stated values was around celebration:

> We value celebration and believe it enhances work:
>
> We publicly recognize achievements.
>
> We encourage spontaneous celebrations.
>
> We know that if we're having fun, we will work harder, smarter, and longer.
>
> We evaluate managers on their enthusiasm and ability to create an environment in which it is a pleasure to work.
>
> Employees who spread gloom will be asked to leave.

Employees started living these values on a day-to-day basis. People began to have fun and began congratulating each other for their accomplishments. Clothes and conversations became more informal.

Deciding that it could be risked, the SVP asked one of the groups to meet one evening, have a light meal together, and then spend a few moments saying what they appreciated about each other. He began by telling a story of what one of the members had done that had been especially helpful to him. The response that followed was beyond the leader's wildest dreams. Touching, caring stories were told, laughter filled the room, and there were occasional tears as one by one, every single person was recognized for who they were as well as what they had done.

The group would clearly never be the same again. They had allowed themselves to be vulnerable, to be celebrated and appreciated. Every individual was a valued member of the team. The work which began to be produced by both companies, but especially by the group that had dared to go the farthest in their celebration of each other, was phenomenal. The SVP actually had to issue a policy: "Every employee must take off one day per week and two days back to back, at least once per month." They were inspired. The turnaround had begun.

What did this senior vice-president do to create these celebrations? He did what any leader can do to foster the art of celebration; follow a set of principles:

1. Recognize that celebration is an effective tool for reaching the goals and vision of an organization. Know that conscious celebration really is a modern-day link to the spiritual dimension of an organization. Through this link, transformation can be seen and felt.

2. Know what to celebrate. Organizations, like any living system, go through a multitude of changes in their life cycles. Celebrations can be held to mark these moments for many reasons:

   - celebrating *stages of organizational change*: expansions, reorganizations, closings, mergers, the end of an old technology and the introduction of new one, moves to new locations
   - celebrating *success*: financial success, promotions, awards, expansions to new markets
   - celebrating *loss*: mourning to let go of old patterns and make room for new opportunities and new life, loss of old procedures, financial opportunities, contracts, a job, status; death of a colleague; an experiment that failed
   - celebrating *people:* teamwork, team successes; founding fathers; winners of sales contests; employee awards; individual birthdays, marriages, reunions
   - celebrating *events*: a company's anniversary, opening day, holidays, articulation of an organization's vision
   - celebrating the *unknown*: paradox, ambiguity of the marketplace.

3. Use an internal or external consultant if assistance is needed to design or implement a celebration.

4. Lead the first celebrations and model the desired behavior for celebrations. For instance, leaders who avoid sexist and racist language as well as sexual innuendoes in celebrations will set this standard for celebrations throughout the organization.

5. Legitimize celebration within the organization so that others not only know it is okay to celebrate, but that it is a desired part of corporate life. Participate fully in celebrations so others will be encouraged to do the same.

6. When times are hard, don't stop celebrating. Look for small wins. Try cele-

223

brations for "The Martyr of the Week" or "the Best Try" — the person who genuinely worked hard, but didn't get results.

7. Once celebrations get rolling, let others lead the way. Keep reinforcing the spirit of celebration, participate in celebration, create some original celebrations, but as the spirit of celebration builds a life of its own, let the spirit take over.

8. Mentor others in the art of celebration. Some people are natural storytellers, entertainers, and, literally, masters of ceremony. Create space in the organization for them to use their gifts.

9. Understand that celebration is part of a process for transformative change. When used, it needs to be done with awareness in the context of other tools and change processes.

In addition to following these principles, another way to conceptualize the role of a leader in celebration is to describe five different roles: *imagineer, artist, shaman, shadow detector,* and *evocator.* Not every role has to be carried out by every leader, nor will every leader feel capable of fulfilling each role. A leader who doesn't feel comfortable with a role or doesn't have the time, can either carefully delegate these roles or work closely with others to jointly fulfill them. However, each role adds to the richness of conscious celebrations.

*Imagineer.* An imagineer is a person who can imagine the possible and engineer reality to create it. As the saying goes, "If you can dream it, you can create it." Leaders need to envision the potential of a celebration and build those moments into the fabric of organizational life. This is truly the challenge of a transformational leader.

*Artist.* Artists are the original examples of leaders who transform elements from one state of being to another — clay to pottery, thread to tapestry, acrylic to portraits.

Celebrations are creations. Leaders are the artists behind the creation — the designers, playwrights, choreographers, producers — and have the opportunity to use these experiences to transform their organization into another dimension through their imagination and fantasy. Like any true work of art, however, a leader must follow his or her own creativity and individual personality. A leader who's art is storytelling and humor will create celebrations of that kind; leaders who are shy will use their abilities to empower others to celebrate; leaders who are charismatic and inspirational will themselves become symbols of celebration; and leaders who are dramatic and extravagant will ride an elephant or do the hula down Wall Street.

*Shamans.* Some leaders are called to be shamans. They are the "spiritual teachers," the elders of a tribe, the old wise ones (Noble 1983). A shaman works with spiritual powers but doesn't seek to have power over others. A shaman brings healing to an organization.

The energy of a celebration creates a positive force that in turn creates an ascending spiral of energy as more people and energy are put in it. Participants talk about

224

being "charged," leaving an event "filled with energy," which will get them over the next hurdle.

Leaders must be aware of the energy force potentially present in celebration and then be able to tap into the energy in an ethical way. Leaders who are drawn to this role need to fully understand the parts they play as shamans, modern-day priests and priestesses, in the dawning Age of Organization Transformation. However, unless an individual leader has done his or her homework through developing personally, there is little hope for them to carry out such a special role. This kind of leadership requires ethics, discipline, integrity, skill, and alignment with a higher purpose beyond the individual self. Conscious celebrations are a link to the spiritual dimension of an organization, but they are not religious events and should not be used to force religion on someone. They are occasions that allow people to experience their spirituality, which may or may not be connected to any religious philosophy.

*Shadow Detectors.* To balance their role as shamans, leaders must also be aware of their "shadow side," their dark side, the driver of their unconscious behavior. Leaders must be aware of their individual shadow side so that their unconscious behavior does not creep into a celebration. For instance, leaders who are prone to being the center of attention will probably play out that side of themselves in a celebration, centering more attention on themselves than on the event or people being honored. Leaders who are perfectionists and have high control needs will try to control and choreograph every detail of the celebration "perfectly" and consequently leave no room for spontaneity, surprise, or the natural spirit of the festivity. Leaders who are not in touch with their feelings and are so driven by the hyped part of corporate life will use celebrations as hard sell marketing events, focused on action rather than on occasions where people can relax, play, and appreciate who they are as well as what they do. Since most of the shadow-driven behavior is unconscious behavior, a leader may need to ask colleagues, family members, or consultants for feedback in order to clearly detect their individual shadows. Once discovered, creative ways can be used to control the shadow rather than the shadow running the show.

*Evocators.* Evocators are leaders who invite others to initiate celebrations on their own. Evoke literally means "to call forth a spirit." Evocators arouse the spirit and emotion of an organization when they use celebration, for celebration is one of the most powerful processes a leader has to breathe spirit into an organization. When an evocator invites others to spread this spirit, people feel pulled to respond as if they are drawn to a magnet, and the spirit of celebration quickly spreads through an organization.

## HOW TO CREATE A CONSCIOUS CELEBRATION

Celebration, like any intervention into a living system, can be done in many ways. The following six-step formula is one way to create a successful experience.

***Dare To Do It!*** Celebration is not exactly the norm in most organizations—not yet. Leaders need courage to initiate celebrative ideas and sometimes pure faith to implement them. A celebration can fail if it is done half-way or gingerly.

Crocker National Bank has a successful quality circle program called WIN. Courage was required to design and involve traditionally conservative bank managers and employees to participate in a skit called the "Wizard of Win," which celebrated the successes of the improvement program. Most of the employees in attendance had never been to a meeting with their mangers or had a chance to hear a division manger or vice-chairman speak. In a time of cutbacks and low morale, the audience experienced managers and employees dressed as a Scarecrow, a Tin Man, a Lion, a Wizard, the Wicked Witch of the Status Quo, the Good Witch of Creativity, and of course, Dorothy.

At one point the Lion sang,

> Oh I could listen to all the voices
> examine all the choices
> Make problems go away.
> I could sort through the confusion
> and recommend solutions
> *If I only had a way!*

The Tin Man said, "My problem is that I need a heart badly. You see, I don't feel much involved in my work anymore. I'm just collecting dust and getting rusty." The troupe traveled past Cardholder Corner, Revolving Credit, the Island of General Services, and the Forest of Wire Transfer until they finally reached their destination . . . the great Wizard of WIN.

From the example of conservative bankers the challenge is there: dare to do it! The wins are significant.

***Listen to the Spirit.*** The words "inspire," "intuition," and "insight" all have a common message for us—to listen within to the powers of our creative minds in order to find guidance for our actions. Current brain research is finally legitimizing for the scientific and rational world what intuitive people have known for ages. Harman and Rheingold (1984) give us instructions for letting inspiration out. "Your unconscious idea processor is awaiting your beck and call. All you have to do is assign it a problem, instruct it, and it will immediately go to work on a problem for you . . . the more *clearly, completely,* and *intently* you formulate a question and direct it to the unconscious, the more quickly and effectively the unconscious can come up with an answer to it."

The importance of inspiration cannot be underestimated. David Wolper's inspiration for the 1984 Summer Olympics in Los Angeles was that "at the end of the opening ceremony everyone will feel the same." His inspiration was so strong and so on target with a universal unconscious mind that the athletes broke into spontaneous dancing and celebrating, which carried with it an international feeling of unity extending beyond the patriotism of any given country. When he received the Academy Award almost a year later for the design of that special event, Wolper repeated the inspiration for his vision: "Reach out and touch somebody's hand, Make this world a better place if you can."

***Seek Alignment.*** Since conscious celebrations use and generate sacred energy, it is important for the designers, celebrators, and the celebration itself to be aligned with a superordinate goal and a higher purpose beyond individuals. Those purposes might be the vision of the future organization, the connection with the mission of the organization, or evolving the spiritual dimensions of the people gathered. To consider what this purpose is, the entire context for the celebration should be analyzed.

In addition to context and purpose, the energy of a celebration needs to be aligned. To do that, certain questions need to be answered. Examples of these questions are:

- Who should be included in the design of the celebration?
- How can the designers be empowered?
- Who should be included in the celebration?
- What space should be used? (new, old, neutral, inside, outside, etc.)
- How much time should be given to the celebration?
- How much time should be structured? Unstructured?
- What should be the rhythm and pace?
- Who should lead the celebration? In what style?

At St. Joseph Hospital in Kansas City, Missouri, a celebration took place that exemplifies this kind of alignment. The Task Force on Organizational Climate made a presentation to the chief executive officer of a values constitution they had written for the hospital. This constitution was based on the values and mission of the Sisters of St. Joseph and the implicit values of the hospital. Hundreds of employees from all levels of the hospital contributed to the values constitution along with board members and physicians. The designers chose to have each task force member sit in a semicircle with the CEO at the end. Each contributing member held the document and spoke spontaneously about what the constitution meant to him or her. The presentation had a dimension that went beyond handing a report to the CEO. Their work was aligned with a higher goal, a vision of passing on the spirit of a hospital to future employees—a spirit based on the values of "human dignity," "social justice," and "the sacredness of human life." The celebration was a manifestation of these values, and everyone experienced a transformative moment—it seemed as if their vision had already been reached.

***Create the Design.*** Celebrations can occur either spontaneously or with designed intention. Those requiring planning need to have a design with a beginning, a middle, and an end. Within the design, all kinds of materials can be used:

| Artwork | Guests | Performers |
|---|---|---|
| Murals, Paintings, | Celebrities, | Actors, Clowns, |

| Artwork | Guests | Performers |
| --- | --- | --- |
| Photography, Sculpture, Tapestry | Dignitaries Founding fathers, Retired employees, Speakers | Mimes |

| Color | Media | Presentations |
| --- | --- | --- |
| | Movies, Slides, Video | Awards Certificates, Diplomas, Plaques, Prizes, trophies |

| Costumes | Music | Ritual |
| --- | --- | --- |
| Hats, props | Bands, dancing, Minstrels, Singing | Applause, Candles, Prayers, Toasts |

| Decorations | Open space | Signs |
| --- | --- | --- |
| Balloons, Confetti, favors, Lanterns, scenery, Wall hangings | | Banners, flags, Slogans |

| Displays | Participation | Surprises |
| --- | --- | --- |
| Exhibits, floats, Parades | Auctions, games, Skits, storytelling Tours | |

| Food | Plants | Symbols |
| --- | --- | --- |
| | Flowers, Trees | Mascots, wands |

All of the senses need to be considered in the design phase. The more the senses are stimulated, the more impact the experience will have. The more creative the design, the more special the celebrants will feel.

Signetics, a manufacturer of computer parts and a subsidiary of U.S. Phillips Corporation, has a Zero Defects Program. They created a superb design for a "Zero Defects Day" using an array of these design ideas.

The Zero Defects Program has been so successful their customers are constantly reporting zero defects for the Signetics products—a significant fact coming from customers such as Honeywell, Hewlett Packard, DEC, Xerox, and Westinghouse! The celebration of this effort was just as impressive. A high school football field was transformed into a carnival when over 4,000 employees gathered to celebrate and re-commit to zero defects. Each divison was free to design their own event. The Micro-processor Division dressed up as defect busters to the tune of "Ghost Busters" and came swiftly to the rescue every time a pretend shipment was threatened. A costumed gypsy read the palms of employees and predicted all employees would strive to per-form error-free work in the year to come. The climax of the festivity occurred when each member of every division signed a pledge to recommit to zero defects. This cel-ebration, like their everyday work, was designed and performed with zero defects— a true tribute to their spirit, hard work, and the art of celebrating.

The design of a celebration can be easy and simplistic. At an annual meeting of the Walnut Creek Kaiser Medical Center, the internal organization development consultant asked the managers and medical chiefs of staff to reflect on the past year, remembering the times on the job when they appreciated themselves or others. They quickly brainstormed a list, actually refusing to stop because they enjoyed naming these favorite moments. The consultant later went around the medical center photo-graphing each of the people who had been named and posted their pictures and the comments from the meeting for all to see. An easy, quiet moment of celebration spread quickly throughout the Center.

*Implement from the Heart.* Many of today's organizations are fear driven—em-ployees fear embarrassment, punishment, and loss of job, status, and opportunity. When people are fearful they cannot give and receive love easily. Before a celebra-tion, leaders may want to ground themselves in a quiet moment of preparation: to relax, release any fears they may have about the celebration, and get in touch with their feelings and the intention of the celebration. At this time, leaders need to let go of any ulterior motives or specific expectations they may have for the celebration. The best results come only if there are no expectations. Leaders can then speak to employees from their hearts.

When meeting with the participants, leaders may need to legitimize fears and honor each person's choice about how much they want to participate in a given cele-bration. Once people feel safe and comfortable, the passage from the toxins of the work world to the sacred space of the celebration can begin. Then people can begin to open their hearts and minds. If they are tight and self-protective, the exchange of heartfelt recognition will not take place. When leaders model being open to giving and receiving love, they create the space for intimacy and bonding to occur. Then magic can truly happen.

*Let Go.* Some celebrations need to be planned or they wouldn't occur; but spontaneous celebrations wouldn't occur if they were planned. Consequently, leaders need to learn when to let go. In order to let the spirit of celebration move through an organization, a leader must pass the baton. Spirit, when released, will flourish by its own power. There is an order and power in the universe that is greater than any individual. Leaders must do their part, then get out of the way.

## BENEFITS AND RESULTS OF CONSCIOUS CELEBRATION

On the surface, hard-nosed businesspeople may think celebration is trivial, only appropriate if things are going well, or that its proper place is in the home. On the contrary, celebration is tied to the very fabric of corporate culture. The more celebration is woven into the workplace, the more its results can be measured in direct productivity, profit, and people. Celebrations can:

1. build individual self-esteem—people feel empowered and important;
2. enhance communication—celebrations foster an open, informal communication where people feel more at ease and consequently share better information;
3. promote teamwork because people feel bonded and that their contribution is important;
4. create energy—people feel renewed, their batteries recharged;
5. make work more fun—there is a balance between work and play; a climate of festivity instead of a climate of fear or drudgery;
6. help people through transitions and changes (e.g., reorganizations, plant closings, leadership changes, job changes);
7. create a positive outlook—more energy is put into work and less into self-protection;
8. spawn creativity and innovation;
9. reinforce and showcase desired norms of behavior;
10. inspire people and build their faith that their visions can become a reality.

In essence, there are connections between celebration and good business, the human spirit and the bottom line, the spiritual plane and the world of work which produce significant benefits to organizations and their cultures.

# SPIRITUAL DIMENSION
# OF CELEBRATION

Celebration in its highest form is a spiritual experience. Rather than just experiencing an event, individuals experience who they really are—imperfect yet holy beings. Like the snake shedding its skin, like the caterpillar becoming a butterfly, we see our beauty and become more beautiful, we feel our joy and become more joyous, we create our visions and become more visionary.

We experience a transcendance of ourselves, as well as a transcendance of time. We remember the past, experience the present, and live in the future. We are able for a moment to live as Cox says, as if all the things we are struggling for were already accomplished. We see that our visions for the transformation of our organization are already a reality.

This transcendance bonds us in a collective consciousness. We are connected with an energy force beyond ourselves. We realize there are no boundaries between who we are spiritually and our work in organizations. We become beings with purposes larger than material gain, finding meaning more inclusive than work and feeling rewards greater than profit. We allow the spiritual side of ourselves to move within and through our organizations. We experience the deeper meaning of our lives and are guided into the future.

The New Age is calling the festivals of the spirit into the business world. We who are ready to evoke the spiritual dimensions of our work will continue to experience profound shifts in our perception, which will open us to further and greater individual and organizational transcendance. When we experience transcendance once, we can experience it again and again, and then at some point we can begin to create the space in which it can happen for others.

The spirit of celebration cordially invites us to embark on a fantasy of our collective imagination. The place to which we are going is one that is very familiar and at the same time, quite strange. This place is suspended in time, both timeless and a kaleidoscope of all times. We have been there in our dreams and fantasies, and we have also never travelled there before. This invitation is to weave the art of conscious celebration into the fabric of our organizational lives. The journey promises to enable us to rediscover our souls.

# CHAPTER 15

# The Invisible Side of Leadership

by

## KAREN WILHELM BUCKLEY
## JOAN STEFFY

*The new challenges to leadership are enormous as organizations are faced with an increasingly complex external environment and changing internal values and systems. In order to be effective through the resulting transitions, future-oriented leaders must work with the invisible aspects of the organization (culture, values, vision, etc.) as well as the more tangible, visible aspects. Two aspects of leadership necessary for this work — intuition and alignment — are developed in detail in this chapter.*

Organizations today are involved in profound levels of change that are transforming fundamental values and assumptions. Leadership is being redefined as leaders are challenged to work within multiple dimensions of the organization in order to transform behavior, structures, and consciousness. As an organization moves from a past state to an emerging future state, the disintegration and re-formation that necessarily occur during transition require particular leadership skills. Throughout the world, concerned leaders are seeking to acquire and develop these skills.

The leaders most successful in guiding transformative changes in organizations work equally with the invisible, subtle, and energetic elements of organizational life (e.g., culture, values, climate, vision, morale) and the visible, quantifiable aspects (e.g., authority structure, productivity profit margins, product quality). Vast streams of intuitive, creative potential can be tapped in the leaders themselves and in others during the transition passage, and, if tapped, this potential empowers the organization to a state of inspired performance.

Innovative leaders working in the invisible realms act on their subjective perceptions of the organization or situation as well as their objective, measured conclusions. Such leaders work with the invisible, subconscious mind to foresee impending chaos, to sense impacting forces, and to anticipate opportunities. They are able to turn chaos into creativity and to support the unquantifiable shifts in thought that must transpire in order for a transformative change to occur.

An organizational change must include the invisible elements in order to be transformative. Minor changes (surface alterations), or major changes (modifications in behavior or structure), do not become transformative without an accompanying change in consciousness or attitude (Buckley and Perkins 1984). Allen and Kraft (1982) define this consciousness aspect as the "organizational unconscious":

> The organizational unconscious represents those patterns of social behavior and normative expectations that become characteristic of an organization's functioning . . . These norms determine much of what people in organizations do, and even when the patterns of behavior have outlived their usefulness, people act as if they were the only ones that could possibly exist under the circumstances. "It's just the way things are around here."

Allen and Kraft go on to outline what happens when the organizational consciousness is not understood and dealt with.

> When a program is imposed upon an organization without dealing with its "unconscious," at first the change may appear to succeed, but gradually unseen forces take over until finally the change is no longer visible.

A shift in consciousness then, whether in the leader or in employees, is brought about only by work in the less publicized, invisible, and often unconscious realms of organizational life.

In working with executives and their organizations, we have found that leadership which is successful in shifting consciousness is based on two principles: *Intuition guides actions* and *alignment focuses energy*. The leader who operates intuitively, following his or her "gut feelings," and aligns peers and subordinates in working together toward a common purpose is using these two principles—essential ingredients in the creation of today's harmonious, healthy, and successful organization.

Often when leaders start to work within these invisible realms, they become soft in their thinking and in their action plans. We propose that these realms are not vague realities but are critical to organizational success and require precise thinking, determined action, and specific technologies. From the combined experience of the authors, in our years of research and development of an interface between our work as international organizational consultants and our personal intuitive practices, we have tested and found successful the following tools for the invisible side of leadership. The tools presented here, as with any tools, can be easily overused, misused, or poorly used. Our hope is that this summary might strengthen those great leaders already using similar tools and stimulate other leaders to work more intentionally within the invisible realms so critical to success.

## INTUITION GUIDES ACTIONS

During the unpredictable state of transition, a sole dependence on the rational mind limits creative opportunities. Because of the difficulty in tracking and synthesizing the complexity of dynamics inherent in change, a linear mode of thinking tends not to see beyond the predictable and obvious. Without the use of the intuitive capacities, the complex dilemmas that leaders face are often reduced to simple problems, resulting in unanticipated consequences with far-reaching effects.

> The more severe the pressure and the more urgently a broader view is needed, the more dangerously their business executives' mental vision seems to narrow down. This is especially likely to be true of a businessman who is obsessed with the idea of winning and sees everything in terms of success or failure. Such an executive may be almost unable to perceive that there is any room for intelligent choice among various courses of action. (Olmae 1982)

In transition, therefore, successful leaders must rely on their intuitive capacity to develop strategy, to increase options, and to monitor the effects of decisions and actions on the workforce and external environment. Intuition also senses and directs the more subtle consciousness shifts needed for a completed change.

Simply stated, intuition is the behind-the-scenes processing of information and images that occurs incessantly, although we neglect to pay attention to it. Many leaders experience their intuition as a "hunch," insight, "feeling in my bones," or "gut feeling." We have all experienced those intuitive moments when we have forgotten a name or fact, and as soon as we stop trying to remember it consciously, the missing fact pops miraculously into our mind. This is an example of the intuitive, subconscious mind continuing to process information without engaging our thinking mind. Einstein claimed he had his best ideas while shaving.

> Albert Einstein attributed his theory of relativity to a flash of insight, not to the cold rationalism of the objective, data-oriented researcher in the laboratory. True, his mind had been prepared by much study and thought, but as he said later, "The really valuable factor is intuition." So, too, in business, decisions based on shrewd intuition are often superior to those based on careful analytical reasoning. (*The Wall Street Journal,* June 21, 1982)

In working within the invisible realms of organizations, we find the following tools particularly helpful to leaders in accessing their natural intuition.

## Nondesk Thinking

Because intuition is accessed through the elusive right hemisphere of our brain, it is critical to break step in our normal, linear, left brain thought. A walk through the office, an informal or personal conversation, a run, a high-speed shuss down a powdery slope, a breath of fresh air, gazing out a window, a nap, or a vacation will result in an intuitively heightened awareness. Following such a spell of nondesk thinking, leaders report more precise critical thinking, clearer vision, and a pronounced sense of smell. Such subtle and invisible signals announce to the individual that the left brain is activated. Fresh insights about a stubborn problem, a deeper understanding of a complex dilemma, or a far-reaching sense of potential consequences emerge from the stimulated intuitive capabilities.

### Make a Request

A format for accessing intuition is to "make a request" of the intuitive, subconscious mind. Such requests can be specific and are best formulated as a simple question. Make the request once the issues have been boiled down to the most basic issue, such as who to hire, promote, or manage a project, setting time priorities, developing strategy for a new product, or seeking resolution to a well-defined recurrent problem. Think about the question in a focused and conscious manner, then set it aside. Do some nondesk thinking and, like Einstein, your answer will soon rise to conscious awareness in an intuitive insight or a message from an unlikely source (e.g., billboards, books, colleagues). Such unlikely sources provide the subconscious mind and organizational unconscious a means for expression. Accomplished use of our intuitive capacity allows us to stay more open and in tune with such information, and allows inspiration to guide decision-making.

This is exemplified by the experience of a naval commander, who asked the following question of his subconscious mind: "What specific obstacles will arise when instituting the cultural change in the Public Works Center to a competitive contracting arrangement?" Two days later, as he awaited an appointment in a doctor's office, an article on client-doctor relationships highlighted the changing demands of the public. For him, this was the specific insight needed to ensure success of the desired change.

### Lucid Dreams

In a similar way, dreams can be an effective means to access intuition. As you fall asleep, ask your subconscious mind to solve a problem or answer a question while you sleep, and you will find your dreams revealing the answer or will awake with insights or answers. Again, state such problems simply and concisely, with few excess words. It is also effective, as we will consider later with affirmations, to state the question positively to your intuitive mind: "I will awaken knowing who to hire for . . .," or "I will wake knowing the first step in the . . . project."

### Subtle Signals

Intuitive insights may come in the form of sounds, images, or kinesthetic feelings such as cold or hot chills, the air smelling sweeter, a different sound in the office, a breeze rippling warmly on your skin, or "goose bumps." These physical manifestations often accompany intuitive insights and can be used as a guide to their validity. Naturally, intuitive information must be weighed alongside the rational, to prevent distortion or unwise action. Invariably, however, leaders are finding that the intuitive information gained is of a high quality and of benefit to the individual, the stakeholders, and the organization.

### Inner Listening

A key to the fullest use of intuition is the concept of inner listening. Our intuition does not shout over our internal dialogue or chatter, or our mental analyses, regardless of their essential qualities. It is vital to free the mind from the left/linear mode by *listening* to mental dialogue rather than orchestrating it. Such listening to ourselves rather than talking to ourselves becomes the fulcrum which balances left and right, intuition and logic, and leads to a deeper appreciation of the inner, intuitive self.

Often, organizational life, with its demands for constant attentiveness to detail and rapid-fire decision-making, is not conducive to open, reflective time. Hence, a number of managers have found that inner listening can be assisted with a framework within which intuition can flourish. We have found the following five-step framework to facilitate inner listening:

1. Release preconceived ideas, letting go of the answer you "think" is right.

2. Quiet internal chatter and mental dialogue — empty your mind.

3. Ask a simple and specific question.

4. Listen without evaluation, noticing the answers without judgment (repeat steps 1-4 for additional information and clarity).

5. Examine the information rationally and act.

To implement the five-step process, begin in situations of low pressure, and allow time to experiment, with minimal distractions. Some managers find closing their eyes helpful in shutting out conflicting demands for time. The bus, airplane, or subway can be an excellent laboratory outside the organization. As with any skill, proficiency and trust in your capabilities develop over time. After repeated application of the five steps to various problems and dilemmas, leaders find that the framework becomes easily and quickly used under any circumstances.

The five-step framework was developed from our actual practice with a number of leaders who used their intuition on a daily, moment-by-moment basis. This simple structure organizes their thoughts and directs their attention. The quality of their decisions, breadth of their vision, and grasp of complex issues become known and counted on throughout their organizations. An article in the national newspaper *USA Today, "Best Executives Know Intuition Supplements Logic" (August 22, 1984),* elaborates on this theme.

> They don't deal with problems or issues in isolation. Instead, "They have in their minds a very elaborate network that relates issues and opportunities and problems and people to each other."
>
> For example, a manager who has to deal with poor product quality may relate that to problems in production control, management development and interdepartmental coordination — and end up solving all four problems together.

In summary, our guidelines for the successful use of inner listening are:

- Prepare for intuitive insights with nondesk thinking, a moment of silence, or simply a few deep breaths;

- Ask a specific question — the more specific the question, the more specific the answer;

- Invite unexpected insights, perspectives, information;
- Beware of premature evaluation or editing;
- Check with your common sense before acting.

By using intuition, leaders can transcend societal conditioning and past decisions that shape perceptions of reality, to make choices based on their own current knowledge and perceptions, a skill essential to transformative change. Because the use of their natural intuition increases the database, as well as the number and quality of available choices, leaders have found their intuition essential in decision-making, problem-solving, strategic planning, assessment of the environment, and identification of trends impacting business, as well as in personal relationships.

## ALIGNMENT FOCUSES ENERGY

A leader's ability to build alignment throughout the organization is critical to the implementation of an organizational change. Alignment is defined as: "to come into a line; to be in or come into precise adjustment or correct relative adjustment." Like the conductor of a symphony, the leader provides the musical score, training, and direction to bring the diverse elements of the organization into a harmonic expression of the organizational vision. Webster defines energy as: "the capacity for action, or performing work." When the diverse elements of the organization are aligned, the energy is focused, and the capacity for concerted action improved. Priorities become clear, and the contributions of each employee are maximized. As leaders learn that creating the passion and commitment of aligned action *is* the "stuff" of management, the awesome power of many would-be champions and inspiring visionaries within the organization will be unleashed.

Alignment of vision and action opens the system to feedback and input of critical information. Too often in organizations, the invisible signals of internal or external distress are ignored or invalidated. The capacity to receive internal and external feedback and input and to respond in aligned actions becomes particularly important during times of profound change when what was known no longer is, and what is to be has not yet emerged.

Our contemporary world is based on the invisible signals of radio, television, and telephones. We rely on these signals and, with proper equipment, we are able to use them. So it is in organizational leadership. When we do not build the right equipment or set up the requisite conditions for a clear reception of these signals, opportunities are missed, information is ignored, and crises develop. Organizations and the individuals within it become sick — out of step with the marketplace or economic realities — and their capacity for alignment is severely diminished.

Without an inspiring and on-target vision, the aligned action so necessary for an integrated change will not occur. While most leaders recognize the importance of developing a common vision, often when the organization is assessed, there are different and conflicting priorities in terms of the quantifiable and qualitative, invisible aspects. For example, financial profits and production quotas may conflict with quality of worklife and opportunity assessments. Our work has demonstrated that when alignment is sought only in the visible and obvious memos and directives, deeper levels of congruence do not result.

While the potential for change is enchanced in time of transition with the usual grounding gone, the disorientation and turmoil are greater. Successful leaders use the unfixed nature of a transition state as a creative opportunity by working in subjective, fluid dimensions to develop a deep alignment within the organization. This creates a climate of trust, high-quality interaction, and open interpersonal communications.

During transitions, invisible dimensions such as values, visioning, trust, and love are particularly critical to the maintenance of high performance, motivation, and morale. When the organization operates only in the overt, quantifiable dimensions of balance sheets, quotas, and productivity measurements, it is easily out of balance, and potential energy slips away. Similar to the intuitive realm, there are specific tools with which the innovative leader can achieve alignment.

### Silence

Just as our intuition does not shout to us over our internal chatter, alignment does not easily occur in the helter-skelter life of a fast-paced organization. It is necessary for the intuitive leader to create moments of inner listening, at best for the entire organization, and at least for the critical decision-makers. In Japan and certain companies in the United States, meetings are routinely proceeded by silence and often do not begin until all participants are breathing together. One strategy transformational leaders use is to begin a meeting with a few moments of silence. Participants are asked to use a silent moment to reflect quietly on the purpose of the meeting and to think how they might personally contribute to the situation at hand. These quiet moments allow the mental and physical space in which the invisible focusing qualities of alignment can occur.

### Visualization

The ability to create an idea or mental picture is a natural power of the human imagination. Visualization is the additional process of refining and shaping the picture of the desired future state the organization intends to achieve, and then impelling that vision with aligned commitment. Proven successful in many organizations, visualizations involving key planners, influencers, and implementers serve to surface hidden resistance and develop a common vision out of disparate ideas.

A fast-growing church in northern California is an excellent example of the benefits of visualizations. An expansion of the rather small physical plant was in order. Certain members had pushed for the expansion for several years but the project never got underway even though no overt resistance was voiced. Finally, with the congregation standing in the back and overflowing out the doors, the need became critical. A committee was again formed to plan the expansion. One of the essential ingredients of *this* committee's success was the repeated use of visualizations to develop a common vision of the expanded facility and to identify potential benefits, costs, and anticipated consequences. Once the blueprints and models were drawn up, the committee led visualized "walk-throughs" in the proposed building for hundreds of church members to identify needed modifications prior to construction. The visualizations served three purposes:

1. to intensify and make explicit the fears of the clergy and old-time members so that they could be worked with;
2. to improve the church's ability to plan ahead;
3. to develop widespread commitment and magnetize needed funds.

Visualization serves to create alignment within a shared vision throughout the organization, and true commitment is then visible in the congruence between attitudes and actions. An alignment develops in support of the goals of the organization that is deeply experienced and long lasting. "The process of transformative change does not occur on superficial levels, through mere 'positive thinking.' It involves exploring, discovering, and changing our deepest, most basic attitudes toward life" (Gawain 1978). Without these profound levels of inner and outer change, the organization does not transform.

The steps to implement the visualization process are:

1. Create a clear, specific image and refine it yet again to a simple, understandable outcome.
2. Check the implications and ramifications of the vision: look ahead to see effects of the vision on alignment within the organization.
3. Create a "working vision" for the organization by enlisting other participants in modifying and enhancing the vision.
4. Focus on the image, with particular emphasis on the quality and tone of the image, including the emotional and kinesthetic dimensions—does it "feel right" or "ring true?"
5. Focus regularly and repeatedly on the vision to magnetize and attract needed support.

The visualization process has proven useful to leaders and managers in strategic planning, role clarification, scenario development, and vision alignment.

## Affirmation

Much has been written about affirmation as a tool to strengthen support for and maintain quality throughout an organizational change effort. In brief, an affirmation is a simple, positive statement that declares a future, desired objective as though the goal has already been achieved. As with visualization, an affirmation is stronger if it is shared among members of the organization. We have found that several affirmations tend to produce more clutter than success. Santa Clara County, a large and populous California county, is working with the following affirmation as a value statement to develop pride in the county and a better self-and public image.

240

We have:

The highest calibre employees, in
The best managed organization;
In order to provide:
Quality service and
Effective county-wide leadership.

The county executive and her top management group built identification with and commitment for the affirmation in a series of meetings involving hundreds of employees. The affirmation was presented in a poster format and found in elevators and above desks. It was used in training and introductory programs, was the basis for the reward and evaluation system, and provided guidelines for management decision-making.

The guidelines for implementation of a successful organizational affirmation are:

- Create a positive, short, simple statement
- State it in the present tense as though the desired outcome has already occurred
- Support the affirmations by writing them on plaques or posters, and placing them on desks, at work stations, or on the cover of the annual report.

As a final note, affirmations are best employed to create a new situation rather than to restructure an old or outmoded perception or system. In this way, the emotional weight associated with the previous situation can be left behind, and the full magnetic and attractive power of the emotional and subconscious domains can be utilized to free the organization from the old and impel it toward the new desired outcome.

## Empowerment

An essential tool for developing an aligned organization is for the transformational leader to release and delegate power to associates. Such leaders give power away on physical planes to acquire power on the invisible planes. This exchange of power and encouragement to realize the fullest potential of each employee can release fear, instill caring, enhance sharing, and create a loving environment within the organization.

In one successful company, we observed its transformational leader walking with a visitor through the plant, talking with the employees by name. Each employee was complimented on his or her work, including a positive statement of the *potential* contribution of the employee. In every case, the leader added a slightly enhanced vision of the individual's work while speaking in the positive tone of a compliment.

That the employees felt acknowledged and inspired to work harder is demonstrated in the overwhelming financial success of the company.

The following guidelines strengthen empowerment:

- Accept the individual's unique combination of personal priorities, talents, and skills.

- Offer affection and understanding.

- Create a means for positive involvement in problem-solving and decision-making.

- Create appropriate tasks that elicit creativity.

- Highlight each person's contribution to the overall organization success.

- Encourage self-responsibility.

## Celebration

Cathy DeForest (see chapter 14) points out that a vital tool for aligning organizational energy is the simple and joyous celebration. Celebration is an important form of acknowledgement as well as an expression of gratitude and appreciation. The transformational leader creates, allows, and encourages organizational awards, rituals, and parties. Smaller individual celebrations include a spontaneous affirmation of work well done or a day off for work successfully accomplished. Like the leader who has done nondesk thinking, the associate will return to the job with a heightened sense of awareness and a rejuvenated attraction to the work at hand.

## Alignment Assessment

In order to diagnose organizational health and alignment, the transformational leader can employ alignment assessment as a tool. In this process, the leader invites key managers to list the invisible dimensions of the organization (e.g., morale, self-image, support), and then to use a color code to assess these dimensions subjectively: Green indicates a healthy system; yellow that caution and care are required; red that a particular area needs attention. This tool is used over and over, even on a weekly basis, in fast-changing systems.

The alignment assessment does not measure objective productivity or output, but diagnoses the subjective, invisible dimensions of the multidimensional organization. This is particularly essential during the transition state to provide continuous feedback for strategy revision and to track the different rates of change throughout the organization.

Successful leaders know that focused organizational energy and aligned visions are magnetic and tend to attract support and move easily toward the desired end. In this sense, leaders find that what we fear or dream, what we think about strongly, expect, or imagine has a magnetic quality. This is validated repeatedly as leaders see their aligned vision and values magnetize and attract talent, resources, support, and customers.

# RESONANCE

Organizational resonance is the state of harmony, balance, and maximal performance, both individually and organizationally, evident when an organization is balanced in the invisible and visible realms. In contrast to a habitual state, which recreates the mistakes of the past, in a resonant state the entire organization moves through the different phases of transition toward a new future. Whereas habitual actions limit the creative potential to what has been done in the past, resonant actions create the future out of new opportunities and alternatives.* Using the intuitive mind, the tranformative leader moves toward resonant choices to inspire the fullest organizational potential and performance.

Realizing the magnetic nature of resonant actions, the transformational leader intuitively stays in tune to when she or he is "on beam" or "off beam." When we are on beam and making resonant choices, the creative juices flow, and circumstances seem to have a synchronous quality that assists the transition process. The next steps become suddenly apparent, and there is an ease of action and high level of workspirit.

Resonance includes the total organizational environment, and the successful, intuitive leader can listen to resonance in the voice tone of others. Often we hear an associate concur with an idea or agree to do a particular task, while the voice tone does not resonate. Instead, we intuitively hear the tone that underlies the words say, "This project is doomed," or "I don't feel this is a priority task." Transformational leaders listen for the tonal resonance as well as to the words in order to align the organization into an energized, cooperative, and fully participative whole.

In addition, the entire organization listens to the leader's articulation of organizational vision. To an often unnoticed degree, employees listen for the resonance of an idea, suggestion, or complaint, and may react accordingly. If the vision resonates, it captures the spirit of the organization and inspires and leads the structural, behavioral, and particularly critical consciousness changes of the organization during the transition phase.

We have found that the leaders who apply the tools we describe in order to operate strategically in the invisible realms of the organization prove most successful in developing and transitioning their organizations. Transformational leaders applying the two principles of intuition guides actions and alignment focuses energy create an energized, resonant organization through the capacity to work within the invisible side of leadership.

_____

*Credit is due Milenko Matanovich Lorian Association for his development of the concept of habitual and resonant choices.

# CHAPTER 16

# Flow State Leadership in Action: Managing Organization Energy

by

## LINDA S. ACKERMAN

*This chapter describes a nontraditional view of organizations as bundles of ener-gy-in-motion. In order to increase performance, leaders must be able to release energy that is blocked, to free untapped potential, and to organize in ways that facilitate rather than impede energy flow. The basics of Flow State leadership are developed and guidelines for operating in this way are provided.*

America's commitment to strengthen productivity offers great opportunity for a fresh look at organizations and leadership. The search for new ways to design and lead organizations is indeed a challenging one. Perhaps your organization, like many, struggles with complex change, unable to redirect itself on a new course, sty-mied with old systems that seem impossible to undo, or burdened by patterns of be-havior that do not support the future. However precarious it may feel, letting go of traditional managerial models opens up the possibilities for deeper exploration of more nontraditional methods of dealing with change.

The nontraditional view presented here is based on the notion that the key to change is mobilizing and directing the energy of the organization. Energy is defined as the *potential for action*. It is the fuel or life force of the organization. This as-sumes that organizations are dynamic systems of energy-in-motion. When their en-ergy is flowing, they are functioning productively. When it is stuck or scattered, they struggle and resist change. The task of the organization's leaders is to guide the flow of energy toward higher levels of performance. To mobilize change, leaders must understand and work with the energy and spirit of their organization.

This perspective gives shape to a new leadership style. This style, called Flow State leadership,* paves the way for smooth performance and unblocks whatever may stand in the path of desired change. If you see the organization as designed to

---

*Flow State leadership is more fully described in "Managing in the Flow State: A New View of Organizations and Leadership," in* Transforming Work, *John Adams, ed., Miles River Press, Alexandria, VA, 1984.*

accomplish your chosen outcomes, then the purpose of your leadership is to ensure that the organization is staffed, structured, and fueled, or *energized*, to do so.

Energy, by nature, follows a path of least resistance. It flows most smoothly through clear and direct pathways. The organization is a complex system of channels through which the leader guides and inspires energy to move—energy of both the total organization and its individual members. The people ideally are supported by the organization in ways that ensure their own energy to flow. Your leadership task, then, is twofold: (1) to formally design your organization and its workflow to accomplish your mission, and (2) to create the conditions in your organization that enhance the flow of people's energy.

The model offered here is still evolving. In some ways, your exploring these strategies will be an adventure into a new way of looking at your organization and planning for change. You do not need to believe in this approach to have it work for you. Assume that the strategies outlined in this chapter are tools to experiment with.

The approach is presented as a series of strategies and steps that can assist you to accomplish desired change. It begins with an overview of organizational energy, laying out how to identify the elements of energy in your situation. Strategies are suggested for changing and working with these dynamics, with special attention given to altering the patterns of behavior blocking the achievement of your goal.

With an emphasis on getting energy to move more efficiently toward your goal, we will then look at how you can create the conditions that enhance energy flow. These conditions support the flow of energy in both individuals and groups within your organization. We will conclude with three additional strategies that help create greater awareness about the dynamics of energy during times of intense change. These approaches will assist you to activate and guide energy for change. Let's begin with exploring the first task of Flow State leadership, understanding the elements of organizational energy.

## THE DYNAMICS OF ORGANIZATIONAL ENERGY

To make use of this approach to leadership, you must first appreciate the dynamics of energy and how it affects the organization's ability to function. Working effectively with organizational energy begins with the ability to identify it. Leaders must be able to do a quick reading of their current energy dynamics to know how to direct the energy to accomplish a desired aim. This reading is called an "energy scan." An energy scan must be done in the context of some outcome, since the energy needs to flow *toward* some end—your goal. Without a direction, energy will naturally follow whatever path is easiest, regardless of aim or outcome.

Clarifying your desired goal, in fact, sets the energy in motion. Your outcome may be on a grand scale, such as the fulfillment of the organization's purpose or the achievement of a new direction, product, or service. Or, your goal may be smaller in size but of no less importance to the energy flow dynamic. Setting the outcome in positive terms is essential, since it is easier to move toward a new goal than it is to move away from an old, negative condition. Directing energy begins with defining the forward-moving, desired path.

With your goal in mind then, the energy scan can proceed. An energy scan consists of identifying what is working to support the achievement of your goal (positive energy dynamics), and what else may need to be created to help facilitate it (creative energy dynamics). You would assess the current state of each of the elements that impact energy.

## Energy Sources

Who or what is affecting the energy for action? Where is the existing energy coming from? Positive energy sources fuel a task and give it life; negative ones drain life from it. Energy sources generate or unblock energy for action. Examples of sources include key people, events, announcements, stories, rewards, goals, political relationships, shared values and purpose. At any time, they may line up in support of your effort, or be a hindrance to it.

## Energy Channels

How clear and direct is the pathway through which energy must flow to reach your goal? A channel is like a pipeline or a tunnel through which energy flows. The direction of the energy is aimed toward the "light at the end of the tunnel" — your goal. Examples of channels in the organization are the structure of workflow, communication networks, decision-making processes and meetings, supply and distribution systems, planning and review mechanisms, a project management process, production lines and sales systems. To achieve your target, the energy must pass through these kinds of channels. If the pathways are clear and directly supportive of the goal, the channels are well designed. If they are involved or blocked, they will hinder the flow of energy. Or, if a channel is designed to accomplish something different than your goal, it does not serve your purpose. To support your end, your role as leader is to answer the following:

- What kinds of channels are necessary to achieve your aim? Picture your goal as the light at the end of a tunnel. What must strategically and practically happen before you can reach that light? Consider decisions to make, communications, production, sales, people involvement, and so on.

- What channels exist that may be *contrary* to your goal? Keep in mind that people's political motivations may have them misuse or block a channel to your goal. Which ones may need to be cleared or redirected?

- What channels may need to be designed or created to help you?

## Energy Fields

What climate or mood will most serve your purpose? Energy fields are the widespread impact created as a result of some action or information being given. Morale is an example of an energy field. It occurs because of some event or communication that either upsets or excites the workforce in general. Organizational culture is another example of a field in which everyone participates. Culture is the widely shared set of values, beliefs, and work practices shaped over time by management and influential people in the organization. There are many causes of energy fields, such as rumors, announcements, celebrations, and your leadership style. For instance, consider the different impacts felt in an organization with a more authoritarian leader vs. a more participative leader. The impact of your style is the field that is created, the result of the energy source.

It is important to understand that energy fields can be started easily, yet are very difficult to stop from spreading once people are energized by them, positively or negatively. They can be started with a formal announcement, a rumor fed into the grapevine, a decision, a celebration, or any leadership behavior perceived to be symbolic of something desired or feared by employees.

It is not easy to change an existing energy field. A field may be slow to change depending on how deeply entrenched it is, how aware people are of its effect on them or how skeptical or suspicious they are of your outcome or behavior. Once you have identified the field that has already been created, here are some strategies to consider for changing unwanted energy fields:

- Clarify people's existing perceptions or assumptions; describe what you see actually happening in the organization.
- Provide new or more accurate data that supports your goal.
- Make a symbolic gesture that models your intent
- Emphasize what you expect with tangible followup action.
- Be persistent over time and clarify your outcome repeatedly in terms your people can see, hear, and feel as true.

As the leader then, your responsibility is to read what the current fields are and assess whether or not they will help achieve your desired end. With this information, you would strategize to change them or create new ones. Aim to touch people's emotions and beliefs to influence their reactions most deeply. Emotion and beliefs are key sources of widespread energy fields.

### Environmental Forces

What external factors play a role in the achievement of your goal? Environmental forces are demands outside the boundaries of the organization that may have an impact on how the organization functions internally. Examples include economic trends, government regulations, unions, technological changes, competition, or marketplace needs. Because these forces are outside the organization, they may also be out of your direct control. Your strategy must still take them into consideration, however, because they impact the flow of energy toward your goal. Use them to your advantage where you can and minimize the potential for negative impact.

### Energy Patterns

What repeating behavior or events will help or hinder the flow of energy toward your outcome? Energy patterns are the observable ways you detect energy movement or blockage along the way to your goal. They are indicators of what is influencing the flow of energy, positively or negatively. They are created by the structures of the organization or by people's behavior. Patterns are often best described by analogies that illustrate them visually. Examples include getting stuck in a vicious cycle, creating a bottleneck, railroading a decision, and sending up test balloons. Our descriptions of patterns already speak the language of energy. Table 1 lists many more examples for your consideration. Once you have identified the existing energy patterns in your organization and assessed their positive or negative effect on your goal, you would select strategy to alter them if necessary.

These categories describe the elements of an energy scan. A sample scan is presented in Table 2. You may choose to write out your scan, as shown, or use the elements as a guideline for discussion when initially planning for your change. Flow State leaders review these dynamics in the organization on an ongoing basis as the energy continues to shift. Again, your goal is to align all areas of the organization — people, attitudes, structures, and systems — to support your change effort. One particularly important area for strategy is altering energy patterns that stand in the way of your goal. These strategies deserve special attention.

## STRATEGIES FOR CHANGING ENERGY PATTERNS

Energy patterns can make or break a successful change effort. Created by both organizational procedures and people's behavior, they underlie most activity, or lack thereof, in the organization. Once your have identified what positive and negative patterns exist in your organization, consider the following strategies for altering them as you see fit:

1. Ensure that the people participating in the pattern clearly see what they are doing. Once people recognize their pattern, they may be sufficiently motivated to alter it for the better. When you are pointing out the pattern to others, it is important to present it as a choice they have in which to participate or not. Be descriptive rather than punishing. If they've chosen this one, they can just as well choose another that more clearly supports your intended results. Sometimes recognition and choice can be very motivational for people who have been stuck in their own frustrating behavior.

2. Intensify the pattern. For instance, if two members of a team are at odds and constantly chafing at one another, you might consider giving them an important, shared task, so that to accomplish it they are forced to deal maturely with the friction or fail at the task.

3. Overload the pattern so that it must end. If someone is acting as a bottleneck, try increasing their workload dramatically so that they are forced to clear the path or rechannel the work somehow in more productive directions.

    The one difference between intensifying a pattern and overloading it is that intensity will bring people to the point of choosing a degree of partici-

**TABLE 1.**        Common Energy Pattern Analogies

| Negative Patterns | Neutral Patterns | Positive Patterns |
| --- | --- | --- |
| Bottleneck | Charge | Building critical mass |
| Battles, skirmishes | Rhythm | Test balloons |
| Fits and starts | Snowball | Rowing team |
| Scape-goating | Cascade | Flowing river |
| Vicious cycle | Searching | Gear up |
| Pressure cooker | Hanging out | Bolster |
| Roller coaster | Vortex | Soothe |
| Stuck | Freeze | Waiting it out |
| Sink | Inertia | Eddies — opportunities to rest |
| | | |
| Setting fires | Open space | On a roll |
| Dissipation | Magnetism | |
| Explosion | Getting hot | |
| Uphill climb | Take a stand | |
| Collision course | Flashes | |
| Friction | Burning issue | |
| White water | Sprinkle water | |
| Dampen | Drive | |
| Spinning wheels | Pushing through | |
| Armor | Buffer, shielding | |
| Retrograde | Spiral | |
| Myth of Sisyphus | Triangle | |
| Vacuum | Cooling out | |
| Tug of war | | |
| Repressing, stuffing down | | |

TABLE 2.      Sample Energy Scan: A Case in Point

| | |
|---|---|
| Goal: | To reorganize the delivery of customer service, thus enhancing customer satisfaction and market responsiveness |
| Energy sources | 1. VP operations — positive support |
| | 2. Rise in customer complaints — negative |
| | 3. Increase in competition — incentive |
| | 4. Reinstating our values and mission to ensure customer satisfaction and quality service — very positive |
| | 5. First-line supervisors in service delivery units — resistant to change |
| | 6. Union — concerned over job security and craft specialization |
| Energy Channels | 1. First- and second-line organization structure is cumbersome and segmented. Needs to be realigned for efficiency and shared responsibilities. |
| | 2. Customer sales and marketing departments are not linked closely, not supportive of one another. |
| | 3. Customer complaint system must be linked to performance and communications to ensure feedback to employees. Minimize red tape for greater efficiency of response. |
| Energy fields | 1. New employee involvement groups (QWL groups) value increasing quality and responsiveness — positive effect |
| | 2. Rumor mill must be guarded against fear of losing jobs and union resistance. |
| | 3. Publish all positive improvements during and as a result of reorganization to build faith and to champion the effort. |
| Environmental Forces | 1. Media coverage not supportive of past performance. Feed the news! |
| | 2. Union — must collaborate and quell fears. |
| | 3. Seasonal increase in product demand approaching. |

TABLE 2.                    Continued

Energy Patterns        1. Studies are like spinning wheels, with no action. Must be a decision.

2. QWL groups build positive momentum and can go far in achieving a critical mass of support.

3. Using our new values and mission statement, we can overcome inertia and take a stand for what we want to accomplish.

4. Avoid collision course with union and close media coverage.

5. Remove bottleneck in customer complaint system.

pation in the pattern. If it is negative, intensification may not stop it, but it will usually curtail it. Of course, intensifying a positive pattern will likely build its positive effect. Overloading a pattern does result in exploding or breaking it down.

4. Directly break up the pattern. You may see one member of a group as the source of a blockage. Remove that member and realign the group to work unencumbered. Or, you may see people searching endlessly for some ideal solution without ever focusing on action. Give them a final deadline or constraint to react to. Then stick with it.

5. Change the motivation for the behavior. Use your goal-setting, performance review, or reward system to give people a clear message for changing what they are doing. Rearrange priorities to meet the needs of your outcome. Putting a compelling goal out in front of people will likely alter their behavior.

6. Alter the conditions surrounding the pattern. For instance, if a team has been struggling with how to reorganize a function or field location, you might decide instead to sell it off, relocate it, or merge it elsewhere, thereby changing the team's task. Or, perhaps you observe a roller coaster or seesaw pattern between production and sales. You decide it has to even out. Create a situation where the production and sales heads must become more interdependent and be evaluated accordingly. Altering the conditions surrounding the pattern will put in into a larger or different frame of reference, and thereby change people's participation in it. Using your vision of a different future will directly help to alter the conditions around current state patterns.

No matter what strategy you use, be clear about what patterns exist and whether or not they are working for or against you. Begin to watch how patterns emerge.

Over time, you will naturally create the conditions to nip them in the bud or strengthen those that serve your goal more fully.

Creating the conditions that enhance energy flow is a powerful approach to achieving your aim. Let's look more closely at this strategy.

## CREATING THE CONDITIONS FOR THE FLOW TO OCCUR

For productive energy to be released in an individual, special conditions must be present to trigger this energized state. As you become aware of the possibilities for greater performance flow to occur for you personally and in your work life, you can better master both your internal readiness and the external circumstances enabling the trigger to happen. You will be most successful at this if you are clear and focused about creating a more positive field for performance. The call to you as a leader, then, is to create the positive conditions for the flow state to occur in yourself, in the people of your organization, and in the organization as a whole. To begin with, it is essential to first have a deep appreciation for the power of the personal flow state experience before you can master creating the environment for the group or organizational flow to occur.

You cannot force the flow state to happen nor can you automatically flow at will. So, attention turns to what you can *influence*: the supportive conditions that encourage and enable it. Like creating the environment that allows a laboratory culture to grow, you must seek out what triggers the flow in your people and provide it for them. In workshop settings, I have asked over 300 people what conditions were present for them when they had a flow state experience. Their responses included the presence of self-confidence, openness, trust, focus, freedom, and commitment. Many also reported a sense of detachment from the result, a lack of need for control and deep sense of faith or connectedness with others and their task.

Within the organizational setting, you have two goals in creating an environment that supports these qualities in your people: one is to encourage individuals to perform in this enhanced way; the other is to motivate groups of people to perform well collectively. The conditions that help individuals generally seem to help groups. However, there are several actions that uniquely support group performance. Let's start with the individual.

1. Individual work performance factors:
   - Begin with a clear and heartfelt sense of purpose and desired outcome.
   - Be willing to try something different, to acknowledge the risk and the opportunity. Set up a "Go For It!" climate.
   - Given a clear expectation for outcome, provide freedom for choosing the method. Encourage innovation.
   - Create a reasonable sense of urgency, short of crisis. Heighten the dramatic tension.
   - Demonstrate confidence and trust. Encourage learning.

- Act as if the outcome has already occurred, as if it is already a reality waiting for full expression.
- Provide the resources necessary to support the effort. Do something out of the ordinary to demonstrate support.
- Buffer formal organizational demands. Protect the effort from red tape.

2. Group performance factors (building on those above):
   - Be clear about why the members of the group were selected for this particular task.
   - Design the startup phase to build a close, trusting, deeply bonded team. Provide some out-of-the-ordinary experiences in which the group members can be both vulnerable and strong with each other. Consider a physical and emotional event to break out of the normal organizational energy field (e.g., outward bound, field trip, or special team-building).
   - Provide extraordinary freedom and ensure that the shared stakes are high.
   - Reinforce strengthening the group's own identity, perhaps by providing special office space, a logo, or symbol for their efforts.

Creating these conditions are core skills of the Flow State leader. Actions can no longer be taken without first considering, instinctively or intellectually, how they affect the flow of energy and how they impact people's personal performance. What conditions are you creating in your organization? Are they helping or hindering the flow state to occur, especially toward your desired goal? In the past, how willing and able were you in making needed changes? Beyond creating supportive conditions, there are a few other strategies to consider to enhance energy flow towards your goal.

## STRATEGIES FOR ENHANCING ENERGY FLOW

With an emphasis on times of critical change, we have been addressing the two special conditions you must create: raised awareness about the energy of the organization and clear plans to influence and direct that energy. We have touched on both with the strategies described above. There are three other approaches to consider that can have positive impact on getting the energy to flow and stay on course. The first two may be particularly helpful in getting you started after your energy scan. Consider combining any or all strategies discussed in this chapter to ensure a positive outcome.

### Using Organizational Purpose

Energy in the organization seems to dissipate when people are unclear about why they are doing something, or the original purpose has lost its motivational impact for them. In light of what you want people to do to serve your goal, how clearly are you communicating the underlying *purpose* served by this work? To have motivational power, the purpose must have meaning for the people who support it. Ask and communicate why it is important to them and what contribution they make to it. A statement of purpose can be very powerful when people identify with it personally. It can help to bond large numbers of people together when they understand that each person contributes to the purpose in a unique and valuable way, thus linking everyone with a shared goal or energy field.

Using purpose to mobilize energy is essential at the start of any major new effort. However, once is not sufficient. Because of the powerful effect purpose has on energy, it deserves and requires repeated attention. Openly renew your commitment to your purpose regularly. Do so especially if you sense a loss in people's direction, devotion, or performance. Be creative in the ways you communicate your purpose and how you model or symbolize your support for it. Find ways for your people to demonstrate their own commitment to the purpose.

## Introducing Change by Telling the Organization's Story

Story-telling is both an entertaining and enriching way to engage people's interest. Your project has a story. Somehow, it fits into the saga of the organization's life history. Describe to your people how this effort came to be, how it first got started, and what trials and tribulations it has encountered. Tell the story in the context of your goal, using real events and people to dramatize the story line. Perhaps your desired outcome will symbolize a major rite of passage, a breakthrough, or some transformational leap into the future. Consider the following dramatic elements to enhance the intrigue:

- Risks and vulnerabilities: What challenges must be overcome to ensure success?

- The need for courage: How courageous is this effort? What is required to serve it? How are you pioneering new territory?

- Conflicting subplots and leading characters: What is the story line and who are the heroes and (potential) antagonists?

Have fun with this approach. Humor and dramatic tension are great sources of energy.

## Strategies for Managing Ambiguity

It's not so much that we're afraid of change or so in love with the old paradigm, but it's that place in between we fear . . . It's like being in between trapezes. It's Linus when his blanket is in the dryer. There's nothing to hold on to.

(Marilyn Fergusen, *Acquarian Conspiracy*)

255

Times of change are fraught with ambiguity. In situations where you're clear about where you're going, very often your methods of achieving it or the timing may be unclear. And there is rarely a guarantee for the success of your effort. Ambiguity is even more intense when a future state is not well defined because you don't know quite how to direct the organization's energy.

The place in between the trapezes is not an easy one to handle. These uncertain periods are particularly precarious in keeping a positive handle on the energy dynamics. However, the Flow State leader must remain "in the flow" and functional. In very ambiguous times, most people need a lot of informationand reinforcement. Flow State leaders are aware of these tendencies and work to generate as much clarity and understanding as possible. It takes courage to proceed in the face of the unknown. The Flow State leader knows that further action will reveal more data than taking no action. Things will become clearer as a result of your taking some careful steps. Consider these strategies for managing during ambiguous times:

- Visualize and affirm a satisfying outcome. Use your well-intentioned purpose to build faith.

- Pursue as much information, clarity, and understanding as possible. Observe patterns, signals, and trends that will support your effort.

- Shape criteria to test your decisions.

- Create lead or slack time for more information to surface and to give people more time to adjust.

- Take slow or partial steps that do not risk the entire ballgame. Send out test balloons and watch for emerging trends or tendencies.

- Encourage people to air their concerns and frustrations with the unknown and reinforce the climate for learning.

- Clarify existing questions. Seek what can be learned from both the question and the lack of answers. What skill and attitude is required to hold the question open while an answer is in the making? What can be learned from those who resist you?

- Stay unattached to and nonjudgmental of the present circumstances and reactions to you and your effort. Understand that this is part of the process.

- Draw on your sense of humor.

## CONCLUSION

This chapter began with the challenge to set aside your traditional view of organizations to entertain some fresh ideas about leadership and performance. We cannot throw away our management foundations; we must build on them and integrate fresh notions. This attempt to define organizational energy and how to work with it is a beginning. There is much yet to be learned about how to enhance energy flow. Patience, perspective, and the fun of experimentation will help during your planning and decision-making. Seeing the bigger picture will assist you to do an energy scan. Taking action from the point of view of releasing and getting energy to flow more directly will undoubtedly enhance your personal and organization's performance. The energy is there, whether or not you choose to recognize or work with it to serve your goals.

Struggle as we may, "fixing" will never make sense out of change. The only way to make sense out of change is to plunge into it, move with it, and join the dance.

(A.W. Watts, *The Wisdom of Insecurity*)

# IV.

# CASE STUDIES:
# EVIDENCE OF
# TRANSFORMED
# LEADERSHIP

# CHAPTER 17

# Leadership Can't Be
# Taught — Only Learned

by

**CHRISTOPHER MEYER**

*The leader's basic tool is his or her self — complete with potentials and limitations. As a result, self knowledge and continual learning are necessary. This chapter presents a model for leader development and describes the results attained by it in two large organizations.*

Contemporary thinking about leadership has undergone significant change in the last ten years. Formerly a subject that was dismissed as too fuzzy to work with, leadership is now among the preeminent themes in management literature.

Part of what fuels this change is the dramatic acceptance of action based on vision and intuition. One need only scan the *Wall Street Journal* to see corporate leaders positioning themselves as visionaries capable of leading us into the future. For example, Lee Iaccoca tells us Chrysler won't be the biggest, just the best.

This trend goes beyond business. The "Great Communicator" leads the nation using vision. Long criticized as a poor detail man, Ronald Reagan's strength lies in his constant public vision of a proud and strong nation.

How is this leadership developed? The answer cannot be isolated to one event. What Reagan and Iaccoca demonstrate is that leadership is not just a discrete set of learned skills: it is *lifework*. Their leadership is a reflection of their life experience.

A leader uses only one tool: him or herself. Like any other tool, the more we know the tool's potential and limitations, the more effectively we can use it. Leadership is therefore dependent on self-knowledge and awareness.

This article will present a model, the Organization Effectiveness Committee (OEC), for developing leaders' self-knowledge within the daily worklife of their organizations. The OEC is an effective organization improvement mechanism that also serves as an excellent leadership development tool. It is currently in use at two world-scale chemical plants owned by a Fortune 100 company.

# A BRIEF WORD ABOUT LEADERSHIP

Within this volume there are several articles describing leadership in depth. Rather than construct another theory, let me share what appear to be common elements. I will use these elements to describe and assess the OEC.

1. Connector—Leaders selectively connect people with their own life purpose, spirituality, energy, society, organization resources, vision, etc.

2. Visionary courage—Leaders take risks based on the self-knowledge that mistakes are opportunities, not failures.

3. Letting go—Leaders have the ability to let go of concepts that block new ideas or learning.

4. Balance—Leaders balance action/inaction, praise/correction, change/stability, etc.

5. Competence—Leaders have sufficient expertise and competence to make good judgments and get things done.

The above list of traits is contemporary but not unique. Over the years, management experts have tried to reduce effective leader behavior to a set of skills or traits. Typically, these skills are then taught to potential leaders.

We see the worst example of this in two- or three-day training programs. The students hear leadership theory, participate in behavioral exercises, and leave pretty jazzed up about trying something new back at the job. Upon returning, they may achieve some short-term success. The usual disappointment comes anywhere from a week to a couple of months later when they return to old habits.

What is happening is that we're trying to reduce lifework traits that come from knowing oneself to short skill-development sessions. In doing so, we embrace an overly simplistic, mechanical approach. This approach does not factor in the time it takes to integrate leader skills into daily behavior. Nor does it take the actual work environment into account. In sum, our sense of urgency drives us to show results from training. The motivation is clear: we need more leaders than we ever seem to have. And we need them quickly. What can we do?

First, we must accept leadership development as a long-term proposition. This requires a significant change in our practice, if not our thinking. We cannot continue to seek organization transformation and still develop leaders as we've done for the past 25 years. We must acknowledge that developing new leaders is part and parcel of developing innovative organizations. We need long-term development models that work on the job. The Organization Effectiveness Committee is one such model.

# ORGANIZATION EFFECTIVENESS COMMITTEES

The initial purpose of the OEC was to monitor and improve organization effectiveness. Very quickly the OEC was also recognized as an excellent leadership development vehicle.

The OEC's dual focus has significant advantages. First, it helps the organization achieve it's goals. This provides an immediate outcome. In practice, as long as the organization is getting value in the short term, management doesn't pressure the long-term leadership development for instant results.

The OEC is not a quality circle. Quality circles have a distinct structure, working methodology, and quality focus; OECs are flexible in structure, process, and mission. This is a distinct advantage for leadership development in that the leader does not have an administrative process to fall back on. Furthermore, the range of issues encountered by an OEC is much broader than that found in a quality circle.

The most common OEC membership is a volunteer, diagonal organization slice. This usually includes a senior manager combined with employees from other levels (Plant A case). A predominantly horizontal slice also has been used (Plant B case). The committees also spawn subgroups to work on specific issues. The two key roles within the OEC are the convenor and organizational consultant. The convenor is the leader and the consultant serves to support him or her.

OEC meetings are open to anyone who cares to attend. Wage earners are paid for attending, including overtime if applicable. The committee identifies issues through its members and visitors.

OECs have evolved differently at each location. Plant A formed the first OEC and was followed two years later by Plant B.

## Plant A

The OEC concept was born during the construction and startup of Plant A. As a grass-roots project, plant management was committed to broad-based involvement in decision-making. As the project grew in complexity, key problems stuck in the traditional organization structure, sometimes never making it through the hierarchy to be aired. Sometimes it was their slowness in growing important enough to be heard. In any event, all were keenly aware that the organization was not getting the amount of involvement desired. This frustration gave birth to the OEC committee.

Plant A's first committee was established in manufacturing. It was composed of six technicians, two first- and one second-level supervisor, a senior management representative, and an organizational effectiveness consultant. The initial purpose was to provide a forum to resolve startup issues that were being ignored.

The breadth of acceptable issues was enormous. The first concerns were minor organizational irritants such as housekeeping problems. Later issues included safety, work design, and plant operability. Within two years, similar committees were established in maintenance, engineering, laboratory, and support services. These committees continue to this day and they are the prime vehicles for organizational improvement efforts.

Although established to help the organization, the OECs became excellent vehicles to develop leaders. The greatest development opportunities were provided by the committee convenor. The convenor was responsible for keeping the committee focused and effective—a tough chore in a diverse, volunteer group.

Convenors were chosen from second-level supervision for a term averaging 1 year. They were carefully selected based on demonstrated leadership potential. The convenors were between 25 and 35 years old with at least 5 years company service. In time, the OEC convenor became a highly visible and coveted plant leadership role. Their job was to develop an environment in which people felt safe enough to air and work out problems that for whatever reason were not being addressed by the organization. The convenor had to lead the group to either direct the problem to the appropriate resource to be worked out or solve it themselves. When the OEC took on an issue, it immediately became highly visible throughout the plant. This required delicate handling, since these were the issues that had been ignored by all others.

The consultant attended all the meetings. His prime role was to develop the group's effectiveness *through* the convenor. To do so, the two worked closely. The consultant helped him or her to learn techniques during and following the meetings. Between meetings he helped plan strategy and communicate progress to the rest of the organization.

This relationship was critical to the convenor's long-term development. The essence of the strategy was to have a line manager be the visible leader with ongoing support from an expert resource: a planned mentorship. The more successful the leader was, the less visible the consultant appeared.

In Plant A, the OEC's success as a leadership development model is clear. Every convenor has been promoted at least once since serving. In a survey conducted three years after the first OEC was formed, all senior managers listed it as the top development opportunity in the organization.

## Plant B

Plant B started up approximately two years after Plant A and was served by the same organization consultant. One year before startup, the first OEC committee was formed. Plant B's first committee began with a different composition and focus, concentrating more on leadership development. This was possible due to the strong support and participation of the plant manager on the committee.

Plant B had a highly innovative plant manager whose immediate staff was dominated by traditional managers. The plant manager found his staff not nearly as supportive of his ideas as the next level of management. His direct reports diluted his ideas so much that the second-level management was confused. With the intent of building greater support for innovation, the plant manager formed an OEC composed of five second-level managers, himself, and the organization consultant. Committee selections were based on which second-line managers showed interest in the plant manager's innovative ideas. This OEC's original purpose was to explore how to build an effective, flexible organization.

When the plant manager informed his immediate staff of the OEC's creation, their traditional respect for authority kept them from directly stating their anxiety. With one exception, all were upset at having their subordinates work directly with their boss. Over the years, this concern has diminished but is still present.

The first question the OEC members asked the plant manager was what was the group's purpose. His answer was, to help build an effective organization. As you can imagine, that broad response did little to relieve anxiety among those present. In the weeks that followed, people tested the truth behind that statement, and once convinced, tried to grapple with the challenge. At the same time, it became clear to the plant manager and the consultant that to facilitate success, the OEC's operating norms needed attention.

As at Plant A's OEC meetings, rank was removed on entering the meeting. Everyone attempted to treat each other equally, including the plant manager. A confidentiality norm developed: what was said in the room, stayed in the room. Another norm was that any issue was open for discussion. The most important agreement was that decisions would continue to be made through the plant organization. If the committee elected to pursue a project, it too would have to go through channels.

What evolved initially was a weekly study group—a group that spent most of its time looking at how the organization was responding to the challenges of plant design, construction, and startup. From the beginning, there was a great deal of tension about when they were going to stop talking and start doing something. Within two months, the first project was undertaken successfully.

An important difference from Plant A was the convenor role. At Plant B this role rotated among the members, and the convenor was much less critical. The actual membership experience for each second-level supervisor was more intense than for Plant A's OEC convenor. Plant B's OEC dealt with critical personal, interpersonal, and organizational issues from its first meeting.

The first five meetings revolved around the lack of support given to the plant manager's ideas by his direct staff. As these discussions developed, committee members were challenged by each other to examine their own positions on these issues. Remember, they were discussing their own bosses' lack of support for the plant manager!

The effort paid off quickly. Immediately, people began to develop increased respect for each other's perspectives. In their absence, the plant manager supported his staff as well-intentioned, experienced people. This helped all to see how to work out the problem rather than blame a particular group. In fact, during the second six months of the OEC, it was the second-level manager's peers who became viewed as most resistant to new ideas.

Plant B started over OECs shortly after startup. They were more like Plant A's model in that they used a diagonal slice to work organizational issues while fostering personal development.

## IMPACT ON LEADERSHIP CHARACTERISTICS

Purposeful development requires a target. For the purpose of this chapter, I will use the leadership traits identified earlier as targets: connector, visionary courage, letting go, balance, and competence.

*Connector.* At Plant A, the convenor frequently had to reconnect people with the fundamental organization improvement mission of the OEC. This was frequently lost when committee members or management felt deeply about an issue. This was best done by good listening skills and firm but subtle meeting direction.

The convenor also needed to have his or her antenna out in the organization for help. Frequently issues brought to the OEC belonged elsewhere. The convenor needed to shuttle these concerns to these areas so as not to duplicate work. The convenor was also responsible for keeping the plant informed about the OEC's actions. This required communicating to a broad audience using different techniques for different groups.

At Plant B people connected strongly with their personal values. The plant manager and organization consultant both worked to have the OEC members test personal beliefs against each idea and possible action. This connection was vital to their leadership development.

*Visionary Courage.* The original Plant A committee was dominated by manufacturing technicians. These well-educated people called a spade a spade. More often than not they said what every manager knew but was unwilling to state publically, often for political reasons. The convenor was frequently asked to carry these feelings to management and transmit its responses back to the OEC. For example, a continual sore spot was the allocation of developmental opportunities, often step-up assignments. Management's perspective was that these should be awarded to those whom management felt were most suited. Field personnel had different criteria. The technicians were more concerned with step-up opportunity equity than was management. The convenor was at the focal point of this controversy. Imagine the situation: how to represent the committee while still having management see you as part of *them.* The courage to stay with what was best for the entire organization was always being tapped.

At Plant B the plant manager provided an excellent role model. Long recognized throughout the company as an innovator, people were continually challenged by his vision of what was possible. At one point during the construction, a company-wide policy was issued regarding respiratory equipment requirements. When this came up for discussion within the OEC, the manager disclosed a position that was not strictly in line with the new policy. The group was shocked and enlightened as his position was revealed. During that discussion he personified visionary courage.

*Letting Go.* In both plants, convenor and members alike had to let go of preconceived notions about people's beliefs and skills. This was most critical when technicians were on the OEC. At both plants, an unusually high percentage of technicians held college degrees.

OEC members had to throw out traditional notions of what could be done. Both commttees were relatively free of plant precedent, hence they could create solutions. Frequently these solutions collided with people's past experience. At those times, all were challenged to drop past experience for a better approach.

It was most important for the convenor to be a facilitator here. If he or she shut down new ideas, it had a stifling effect on the entire group. Creative group problem-solving training paid off handsomely for both OECs.

*Balance.* At Plant A, balance was the survival mechanism for the convenor. In other words, the convenor had to help the group maintain perspective without dampening the discussion. Frequently a vocal minority would capture the group's energy for a short period. The convenor was responsible to ease the group back to balance. During such times the convenor also had to withstand pressure from management to get the group to "behave." The balance between group expression/creativity versus management expectations/wants was always precarious.

There were times when Plant A management would ask the committee to take on issues because the OEC was the top problem-solving unit in the entire plant! These "gifts" were actually time bombs: issues that no one had solved to date. Many were about how they could be handled. A few were turned back as problems that belonged to management and not the OEC. As the spokesperson, the convenor learned how far he or she could go before damage was done to the OEC or its rapport with management.

Within Plant A's OEC, the convenor had to help members with their personal, functional, and corporate hats as appropriate. For example, step-up assignments were coveted as opportunities to demonstrate supervisory talents. The convenor had to lead the group through a process that separated individual concerns from those of the entire technician population. As one might foresee, solutions best for the majority could impact one OEC member adversely.

At Plant B, the balance issue had a more personal tone. Committee members had to keep support of the plant manager's new ideas in balance with loyalty to their direct boss. This later extended to peer group relations.

As an effectively leaderless group, Plant B's OEC members had to balance their own participation. Frustrating at first, this approach helped people manage themselves and learn how to lead others to do the same.

*Competence.* As mentioned, the technicians were not stupid. The convenor's competence was critical to effective leadership. The organization consultant helped the convenor develop effective group leadership skills. On an annual basis the entire group participated in a group development workshop to learn effective meeting and problem-solving skills. During the three years I worked with the group I saw it almost die twice when a convenor could not develop group leadership and problem-solving skills.

At Plant B, competence took on a different meaning. There was a subtle, unspoken pressure to become a competent OEC member. Due to the presence of the plant manager, competence was defined as having the courage to speak and think through your ideas before you did so. People were very quick to speak during the early days. As time went on, people developed a much greater understanding for the complexities involved in any issue.

## KEY FACTORS IN THE OEC SUCCESS

As I look back on the entire experience the following stand out as reasons for the OEC's continued success:

1. Real-world orientation—The projects and discussions were not fabricated case studies. Every issue dealt with was connected directly to the members' work lives.

2. Continued perceived benefit by management—The committee provided value added in the short term through organizational improvement projects and in the long term through leadership development.
3. Ongoing mentorship—While many organizations use consultants for projects, the ongoing use of the consultant seemed extremely effective. It provided the convenor and OEC members with steady support for learning and problem-solving.
4. Participatory management—In both plants, management encouraged participation in plant decision-making. This allowed the OEC to grow.
5. Long-term focus—The nature of the issues forced all to think in the long term. Few issues could be described as short-term ones.

### How to Select OEC Convenors

Long-term development is an expensive proposition. I don't believe everyone wants to or can lead. Careful selection is critical to success. The following are some pragmatic, commonsense suggestions to identify potential leaders. The key is to be selective.

Follow the crowd. When you look for leaders, they will most easily be found by the trail of followers. These leaders may not be the formally anointed ones. They will be people who for one reason or another are currently leading.

Keep your eyes open for people who make decisions using a systems perspective. People who stay tightly within their defined area may provide technical or conceptual leadership, but it is not my experience that they do well leading organizations. Having a broad organizational vision is an essential trademark of leaders.

Look for the integrators. These are people who get a lot done by integrating energies already in motion. Much like good athletes, these people do this effortlessly. It's as though creating synergy comes naturally to them.

Last, find the learners. People who learn are constantly growing and changing. The real jewels are those who are also interested in learning about themselves.

One quick point about how not to find leaders. Avoid an overemphasis on breeding. All too frequently, tomorrow's leaders are chosen based on yesterday's academic or technical achievement. At the risk of stating the obvious, who has not heard of the top salesperson who bombs as sales manager? Is the prestigious MBA a guarantee of much besides academic achievement and diligence? Don't get your wishes and expectations confused with people's demonstrated talents.

## CONCLUSION

The OEC is a pragmatic tool for developing leaders. It requires ongoing organizational investment to make it work. With that support, the organization benefits with increased leadership capability and problem-solving capacity.

Obviously the OEC is one mechanism to achieve leadership development. It avoids the traditional "instant leader" pitfalls that most organizations slip into. Its impact can be leveraged by the use of educative, job placement, and rotation strategies. The technique itself is not nearly as unique as the trust management must be willing to put in all organization members to contribute. If that trust and commitment to participation is present, then the OEC fits well.

Possibly the true test of success is the accomplishments of some of the Plant A convenors and Plant B members.

One convenor took the job having good support from the technicians but a poor image within management. If anything, he was considered closer to the technicians in outlook than a manager. After two years as convenor he is now the key liaison between plant management and product line management headquarters. Furthermore, he has been used for the last year to lead problem-solving meetings in the plant and headquarters. A second convenor has been promoted to operations supervisor. His promotion was directly attributed to the skills he gained as convenor by top management. The rapport he developed on the OEC has served him well in his new role.

At Plant B, one of the original members has been promoted to a headquarters coordination assignment. The plant manager suggested him for his position after one year on the OEC. Another member was moved from a staff role to a key operations position based on his OEC work. That same individual will shortly move to a leadership position within the product line.

Aside from the career progression, the majority of OEC participants have provided daily leadership in their plants. They continually demonstrate an ability to create followership among their colleagues. In the end, is not leadership assessed by followership?

# CHAPTER 18

# Real Management: A Developed Alternative

by

**THOMAS N. THISS**

*This chapter is a case example of one of the world's fastest growing international banks which has a unique management philosophy. This very dynamic organization has demonstrated that concepts such as spontaneity, trust, initiative, intuition, feelings, and flexible structures do indeed go hand in hand with outstanding levels of corporate performance.*

The Bank of Credit and Commerce International (BCCI) is in its fourteenth year. It came into being in the Middle East in 1972 and has enjoyed remarkable growth. In 1983 *Euromoney* rated BCCI the second fastest growing bank in the world over the last three years. What makes it unique is its management philosophy. Its president and founder, Agha Hasan Abedi, is the creative inspiration for the bank and for its philosophy, which he calls "Real Management." This chapter highlights the principal concepts with some illustrations of how the system works. Real management models itself on the laws of nature. The author refers to its as a management ecosystem.

## THE OPEN PLAN

The first thing that strikes you when you walk into the fourth floor of the bank's office in London is its openness. There are no private offices, only private conference rooms. All desks are in the open. The president's desk is no exception. The whole floor has an atmosphere of what one visitor called "dynamic serenity." This is one of seven floors in what is known as CSO, Central Support Organization. It is not central headquarters. The bank does not believe in central control. Its function is to support the various regions, not to control them. The same is true for the regions in their relationships with the branches. BCCI believes in being a "local bank." Decisions are made where the banking takes place—at the local level.

The bank is managed by a group called the CMC, Central Management Committee. And in turn, the regions are managed by the Regional Management Committees, and the branches by the Branch Management Committees. In their highest form the committees are continuously active although not always in formal session.

In the West we talk disparagingly about committees. We say that a camel is a horse designed by a committee! But to an organization whose roots are in the Middle East, a camel is a thing of beauty—its beauty lies in its utility. And so it is with a committee. The utility of the system is in the continuous interaction of people. This ongoing dialogue *is* the system. Nature does not separate function from beauty. Therein lies the fundamental organizing principle of BCCI.

## ALIGNMENT WITH NATURE

BCCI aligns itself with the structure of nature. It is a misconception, however, to say it is a "go with the flow" organization, for it is much more than this. The bank is not opposed to structure, but because it values spontaneity, trust, initiative, tuition, and feelings, it minimizes structure to facilitate these qualities. There is very little formal planning, scheduling, and budgeting in the conventional sense. Plans evolve and schedules change with the continuous interaction of people. They call it "dynamic planning." Sometimes things just seem to happen. Meetings are often impromptu and, if scheduled, late. But managers seem to learn not to sit around and wait but to continue working until the moment has come. There are cues—a phone call, a personal visit, or a manager's movement—that dictate the appropriate moment. It is all very fluid, but it works well and effectively.

It is not natural to isolate ourselves in closed offices, or to build hierarchies of power that inhibit interaction, or to create rigid statements of policy that stand in the way of change. Nature is an open system, ecologically balanced. Like nature, BCCI has its own ecosystem.

## QUALITATIVE ENERGY

Nothing is more intrinsic to nature than energy. It might be said that nature *is* energy. The old distinction between matter and energy is dissolving as scientists probe more deeply into the nature of things. Real Management visualizes each person as a human energy system, qualitative as well as quantitative.

For example, in selecting college graduates, BCCI recruiters assess the quality of the candidate's energy; that is to say, they are less concerned with grades and with past performance than with the person's qualities such as compassion, joy, courage, humility, and a sensitivity to feelings. If these qualities are present, the bank will provide the appropriate ecology for their development. They believe the primary function of management is to enhance the quality of its human energy.

What makes human energy different from all other sources of energy is its qualitative or spiritual dimension. If they deal only with the quantitative or physical aspects they place human energy in the same class with barrels of oil or tons of coal. It then merely becomes a measurable matter of horsepower, thrust, and BTUs. Human energy has a qualitative aspect that is not measurable and therefore tends to be

272

neglected by management. Qualitative energy is like the lines of force in a magnetic field. They are unseen, but they govern the attracting power of magnetism. The stronger the lines of force, the stronger the pull. Managers tend to deal with the tangible effects of energy and often neglect the intangible causes. BCCI is concerned with the unseen force behind the effect—the spiritual lines of force, if you will. When two or more human energy systems merge, we have interfusion.

# INTERFUSION

Interfusion is the vital principle of Real Management. It is much more than an exchange of ideas. It is an exchange of energies, and the vehicle of this exchange is feelings. Feelings must be present to humanize and energize the process. Feelings are qualitative. As such they are the common qualities that bond this corporate culture of 87 nationalities. Feelings unite where ideas divide. Ideas are static whereas feelings are dynamic. Each human energy system has its own unique configuration of qualities. These commingle with others to form creative combinations. BCCI works unceasingly to enhance this process. Virtually everything in the bank is designed to encourage this. The open plan is one of the more visible means of supporting interfusion. In the entire time I have associated with BCCI I have never been turned away from another's desk by walking over unannounced and uninvited. The bank places such a high priority on interfusion that it tolerates willingly the inconveniences and dislocations of being so accessible.

The president openly states that he has no power except the power to influence through interfusion. The quality of his energy, however, is such that his capacity to influence is extraordinary. Because interfusion is a sharing of power and energy there tends to be little individual recognition for achievement. The satisfaction is felt but not always acknowledged. In BCCI there are frequent references to "we." The pronoun "I" tends to be seen as somewhat arrogant. Recently a senior manager said, "We believe in sharing credit. Let is be unknown who did it. That is immaterial. Everyone is a coauthor."

Recently, I needed to see the president about a matter of personal interest to me. He was scheduled to leave the office in 15 minutes and he would not be back for two weeks. As I approached his desk I asked for two minutes of his time. After politely offering me a seat, he replied softly, "Mr. Thiss, you may have as much time as you wish." The president was sincere and I knew it. I tend not to abuse the time of one who so generously grants it. Like any president the demands on his time far exceed his capacity to meet them. Yet in the three years I have known the man, I have never seen him hurried. His priority is people, and his feelings reflect the genuine love and admiration he feels for all. You don't hurry relationships.

In summary, interfusion is a synthesis of energies. BCCI calls this a "joint personality." This creative union is the committee in its highest form. In Real Management it performs the control function. When the joint personality is functioning, traditional forms of control, power, and authority are counterproductive. In short, when the ecosystem is working, it regulates itself.

# THE COMMITTEE SYSTEM

Earlier I mentioned the Central, Regional, and Branch Management Committees. There are more. Additional management committees have been formed to include all managers. The primary purpose of these is to promote interfusion. Each committee is a self-regulating ecosystem of its own. These joint personalities of 10-15 people meet regularly to discuss management concepts or timely issues. This process aids the growth of the bank through an increased exposure of its people to a range of concepts and issues.

BCCI has also formed marketing committees. Everyone is a member of a marketing committee because the bank expects everyone to market its services. Marketing is the external application of the Real Management process. The concepts that underpin the practice of management apply to marketing as well. It might be said that "eco-mittees" run the bank. A more conventional term would be *consensus*. All of this interaction would appear to be random and unfocused were it not for vision and purpose.

# VISION

Vision, as they use the term, is a perception of the evolutionary process. It is a glimpse of the dynamics of change. It is not a vision, however, unless it can translate itself into reality. The first time I met the president he spoke of seeing "a painting before me," a vision of the evolutionary process of change and the possibilities for the bank within this evolving flux. He expressed his profound hope that others could see this painting as clearly as he. The president understands the power of vision.

In 1972 a group of people with a joint vision came together. They had a vision of a multinational, multilingual, truly international bank with a philosophy that would accommodate all nationalities, all races, all creeds. A universal institution that belonged to no nation but to all nations. One that would link the industries of the North with the resources of the South, the mysticism of the East with the rationalism of the West in a network of trade and transactions. Now at the close of its fourteenth year, BCCI employs 13,000 people, and its network spans 72 countries. *Businessindia,* a leading financial publication, featured the bank in a March, 1984, cover story calling it "The Fastest Growing Bank in the World."

In BCCI they are encouraged to make their management capability equal to the opportunity. Just doing better than last year is a limiting strategy. Vision, on the other hand, is seeing the limitless possibilities of what "could be." Opportunities lie in change, and this bank has succeeded largely because it has been more sensitive to change. In BCCI they call a series of changes a "bridge." BCCI has been traveling on the bridge of change since its inception 14 years ago. To become something they must change, and thus through change they can bridge from the present to the possible.

274

# THE MAJOR PURPOSE

At the heart of Real Management is the bank's stated major purpose. It is more than a mission statement. I have never attended a management meeting where it was not addressed in depth. It is stated simply in four points:

1. Submission to God
2. Service to mankind
3. Success
4. Giving

The first three are relationships based on giving. The fourth is highlighted as the key to the other three. BCCI states that it happens to be a bank, but it could have been something else. What's important is purpose. The bank is merely a vehicle to serve that purpose.

In 1982 the president sent a letter to all employees saying the bank would give them a cash gift representing 2½ percent of their annual salary. This was to be given to whoever they wished. The idea was to let each person experience the joy of giving. The amount has increased to 3½ percent and is now an annual event. In his 1985 letter on "Giving," the president said, "Today, in a world so precariously balanced between conflict and cooperation, between prejudice and faith, between love and hate, I am sure you will all agree from the depth of your conviction that it is in the delicate balance of the quality of Giving that the quality of its order and existence will survive." The concept of giving permeates all aspects of Real Management. It is central to the concept that every person is given the responsibility of managing.

# EVERYONE A MANAGER

The absence of organization charts and titles reflect the bank's emphasis on equality, and its dedication to the process of interfusion. BCCI sees every member of the family (a term commonly used) as a manager. The president urges all to see themselves as "chief executives." Although some are designated as managers, all are expected to be managers. The obligation is a dual one — to manage and to be managed *equally*. There are no superior /subordinate relationships, no reporting chains. The process of interfusion is title-blind. Each person is expected to influence and to be influenced by all others. The end result of this is a joint personality. In a very real sense, the joint personality runs the bank.

In 1983 when I moved to London I asked my sponsor, "Whom do I report to?" He replied that they did not have reporting relationships as such but that I would be part of a joint personality of four persons. We have operated that way ever since.

Members of the bank have a great deal of freedom to manage their own affairs.

Responsibilities are less clearly defined to maximize entrepreneurial activity. Managers are expected to reach out and take responsibility as needed. As one manager put it, "you are running your own show but you must use our controls (e.g., interfusion). It's up to you, however, to determine when you want those controls off." In short, they are free with the obligation to interfuse as needed—unhampered by the press of authority, by the restraint of departmental walls, or the limitation of "proper" communication channels. This is the dynamic essence of Real Management. Recently I talked with a young man at one of the London branches. He mentioned another branch manager's name as having been very helpful to him. The young man was not getting the help he needed from his manager. When the other manager sensed this, he assumed a personal responsibility to help the young man informally with periodic phone contact. In BCCI they share the responsibility to develop the quality of everyone they meet.

## GETTING PEOPLE "DONE" THROUGH WORK

Traditional companies define management as "getting work done through people." This puts the emphasis on getting things done at the expense of those who do the work. In Real Management, two terms are transposed to change the emphasis. We say management is the process of "getting people done through work." The development of people is what its all about. I can hear the critics now saying, "What are you running, a rehabilitation center or a bank?" The answer could be either, neither, or both. For now they must remember the ecosystem. The system demands that people interfuse. Interfusion is the creative process of growth and development. The job provides the opportunity for them to do so, and as they develop so does the bank. Through interfusion the person powers the evolvement of the bank; they are inseparable. The vital principle of growth is the vital principle of management. Work *is* the developmental process. Management is the art of developing people through work.

Real Management believes in a philosophy of success, but success is not viewed in terms of winning. Winning is a nonevent. People don't talk about it. They don't even talk about win/win situations. The word doesn't seem to exist. Winning is irrelevant in the cooperative pursuit of purpose where the only competition is with oneself. Success is keyed to the evolution of the person; therefore, what they do hear a lot about is the evolvement of the self. Some people are referred to as being "very evolved." To be less so does not carry a stigma. On the contrary, it is accepted as a stage in the evolutionary process. The bud is no less than the flower; it is just a different stage in the process of evolution. The person will evolve in time. The bank is extraordinary in its commitment to helping people evolve. A regional general manager said to me recently, "We never give up. We keep trying."

## INITIATIVE AND PATIENCE

I have observed two traits that are essential to the Real Management system. These are initiative and patience accompanied by an appropriate sense of timing.

Together they form perseverance. The better practitioners seem to understand the significance of these two traits in the evolutionary process. They know that they cannot control time but that they can control the timing of their initiatives. This they do; they continually monitor the process, waiting for the appropriate moment to intervene. Shakespeare said it well in *Julius Caesar*: "There is a tide in the affairs of men which, taken at the flood, leads on to fortune." Some months ago I was with a senior bank executive in New York City. He was called away to the telephone, and when he returned he said, "That man is amazing. He's in London and he knows exactly what I'm thinking a continent apart!" The executive in NYC had been weighing a decision. The man in London sensed he might need his help and called. It was exactly what was needed. The caller was totally tuned to the process. He is a superb practitioner of the art of Real Management. He has extraordinary perception and an acute sense of timing. It comes from continuously monitoring the process.

A young and promising international officer posted in Africa saw an opportunity to open an agency office in a neighboring country. Sensing it was the right thing to do and the right time to do it, he took initiative and moved quickly. Regional management was informed after it was done. He was commended for his entrepreneurial efforts. Flushed with his success he pushed on to contract with the government for full banking status and the legal right to open a branch. As before, he informed management after the fact. This time they were not as pleased. He had gone too far, too fast—neither the bank nor the government were ready. He had forced the process of change with premature initiative. He had not interfused beforehand. Had he done so, he would have known that the timing was not right.

In Real Management, if they know what's best, they are expected to take initiative. If they have any doubt, they are expected to interfuse. The process done openly and caringly will suggest the appropriate direction. The man in Africa is more experienced now two years after the fact, and he readily tells the story with humility to illustrate what he learned.

## HUMILITY

Humility is the precondition that powers the practice of Real Management. It is the key that unlocks the vital principle of interfusion. It involves the recognition of our limitations and the need to use our energies in the service of a larger whole where each of us plays a relatively smaller part. Operationally it is the art of openness. Accepting the reality that they don't "know it all" makes it easier to want to know more. It also helps them to be less attached to a fixed position and more easily accepting of change.

Humility also conveys a deep respect for the individual. The president sets the tone for this with this unflagging commitment to nurturing the unique qualities of each person. Recently he called a meeting to talk about inadequacy. The message was that we are all inadequate and that life is a progression toward adequacy, yet it is our relative inadequacy that makes us unique and interdependent and mandates us to interfuse to become more adequate. Therefore we should accept our inadequacies and those of others with humility and love.

## UNITY OF THE MORAL AND MATERIAL

In BCCI we talk about the unseen, the unknown, and the intangible. This is the moral or spiritual realm that powers the seen, the known, and the tangible. In BCCI the moral and the material are inseparable. Making a profit is very important. But it cannot be separated from the moral dimension — the quality of energy that produced the profit and the impact that energy had on others. The president has said that if we give more than we receive then we make a "moral profit." One very successful manager told me, "The way I see it, we are all either mercenaries or missionaries. I've been a mercenary, but not I'm a missionary." He went on to exclaim with great zeal the impact his region was having on the GNP of the small Caribbean country.

## PAY FOR PROGRESSION

Perhaps the greatest challenge to the system of Real Management began about two years ago. It was called "delinking." It involved disassociating the annual increment from performance. The bank was moving away from pay for performance. With this de-linking process the last bastion of traditional management began to crumble. If Real Management was to be a viable system, pay for performance had to go. Pay for performance is focused *results*. Real Management, like excellence, is focused *process*. The bank wanted to link pay with the evolutionary process of development. The key was to link pay with progression, the qualitative growth of the individual. The assumption in Real Management is that developed, or more highly evolved, people enhance the quality of energy. This, in turn, powers performance. Putting it simply, the idea was to pay people to develop themselves. Not through random efforts but through all the means available in the Real Management ecosystem: autonomy, interfusion, joint personality, entrepreneurial initiative, patience, clear purpose, broadly defined responsibilities, etc. In short, they are self-employed in the context of BCCI. They have as much responsibility as they can assume given the natural checks and balances of the system. In effect, de-linking gave people the opportunity to pay themselves. If they are not happy with their pay, they can develop themselves more fully and assume greater responsibility. The initiative is theirs. If people can be relatively autonomous in setting personal goals, why then can they not be in rewarding themselves as well? It is a bold move. And it had to happen, or Real Management would never be real.

In his essay entitled "Circles" Emerson wrote, "The life of man is a self evolving circle, which, from a ring imperceptibly small, rushes on all sides outwards to new and larger circles, and that without end." The primary responsibility of management is to provide the right ecology for these "self evolving circles." I believe that the ecosystem of Real Management is a developed and viable alternative to do just that.

# CHAPTER 19

# The Long Term View

by

**DAVID R. CLAIR**

*This chapter is a chief executive's description of how he worked successfully to articulate his corporate vision and to bring it into reality in a large multinational company. The case description illustrates how a senior executive can apply the concepts described in this book in practical and straightforward ways to generate outstanding results.*

## BACKGROUND ON ESSOCHEM

Essochem Europe is one of four regions through which Exxon Chemical runs its worldwide chemical business. Essochem covers Europe, the Mid-East, and Africa with sales totaling about $2.5 billion a year. The company is organized into a product line and geographic matrix which has been functioning smoothly for a number of years. Of its eight product lines, five would broadly be classified as commodities and three as specialties. These product lines do business through eight affiliate organizations, but with close central coordination from Essochem headquarters in Brussels. Products are manufactured in 11 different locations across Europe. The company has about 6,000 employees which are really the subject of the activities I'm covering here.

With a petroleum company heritage, it's not surprising that Essochem's product slate is heavily weighted toward commodity petrochemicals. However, the specialty businesses are quite successful and contribute significantly to total profits. The company still tends to be manufacturing and supply oriented with a strong cost control culture. However, in the 20 years since its separation from the petroleum business, significant research and development, marketing, and product development capabilities have been added. It is considered to be a successful petrochemical company, but while profit and return on investment are satisfactory on average, they rise and fall with the business cycle.

# LTV ORIGINS

I took over as Essochem's president in mid-1981 during the most prolonged down cycle the worldwide petrochemical industry had ever seen. My first two years were spent dealing with manpower reductions, other cost-cutting steps, and control of capital expenditures. During this time we significantly improved our overall cost control approach and techniques. We installed systems that could predict the industry's fundamental margin erosion for each of our commodity chemicals. We could then relate our cost reduction programs and activities to these basic trends. This lifted cost control out of the arbitrary category (which often involved judging costs relative to last year) and shifted the emphasis from controlling manpower and fixed costs to controlling all the elements of total cost.

By mid-1983, the recovery was starting to take shape and Essochem profits were improving rapidly. With this change for the better, the organization was in a receptive and even an expectant mood regarding any change of direction that might lessen the impact of future business cycles. This also became one of my fundamental objectives.

But the seeds of change had been sown earlier. During 1982, we had started a Managing for High Performance program for middle managers in the company. Participants in this course were sending signals that they were unsure of the company's long-term direction and also that they felt frustrated in their attempts to apply the lessons of the high performance program in their daily work. They were also suggesting that a similar program for senior management might make them more sensitive and receptive.

Sarah Engel, our organization development advisor, read these signals and convinced me to do just that. A program for high performance management was designed for all our vice presidents and affiliate chief executives. In preparation for the program, participants interviewed a broad cross section of employees to understand how they perceived the company and their jobs. The participants also filled out questionnaires regarding their own management style and checked these against similar questionnaires filled out by their subordinates.

At this point, Sarah asked me to write down my thoughts about where the company should be heading long range. In response to that request, I spent considerable time on what was the first draft of the Long Term View (LTV) of Essochem. My overriding objective was to shift the company's focus from simply refining its strengths as a commodity petrochemical producer toward correcting its basic weaknesses, which were its dependency on commodity chemicals and the resulting cyclical performance. I wanted to recognize our success of the last 20 years, but set a more ambitious target for the next 20—one that we were unlikely to reach by simple evolution. I also wanted to highlight the opportunity to be somewhat unique; that is, to become a first-class chemical company by being successful in both commodity and specialty chemical markets.

When the Managing for High Performance program for executives was held in October 1983, the initial draft of the vision statement was included in the material given to participants at the start of the program. It generated considerable interest, and the group spent much of that week analyzing the input from the many interviews and criticizing and revising the LTV statement. After the program, the process of refining the LTV continued, and we eventually solicited input from the management of the worldwide chemical organization. By year's end we had a final version which we then wanted to communicate broadly within Essochem. (A summary of the LTV appears on page 282.)

## COMMUNICATION AND ALIGNMENT

The LTV was packaged in both videotape and booklet form, with the latter translated into several languages. Fortunately, the LTV in its final form was the joint product of about 25 or 30 senior managers. Most of them had made significant contributions to its content, and as we started our communications, all these managers became disciples within their respective organizations. Because they had interacted extensively with each other and with me during the preparation of the LTV, they were well prepared to answer the questions and confront the doubts of their people. These senior managers also became the focus for translating the general thrust of the LTV into specific actions throughout their organizations.

The strong people empowerment theme, or message, in the LTV was probably the key to its ready acceptance throughout the organization. I have long believed in the powerful effect of the combined contribution of many people working toward common goals. This is true even though individual contributions may appear modest. Often companies behave as though only the brilliant contributions of a relative few individuals are critical to success. I maintain that you will get that from those few individuals anyway. We need to concentrate on getting contributions from everyone — and that requires special effort.

As the organization started to digest the message of the LTV, it was extremely important that the president and executive vice president of the region be highly visible in their commitment. We regularly interacted with product line, affiliate, and functional groups throughout the region, and the LTV became a critical theme for many of these sessions during the following year. In addition, we were invited to many additional meetings that had an LTV focus, and we tried to attend as many of these as we could. It's absolutely critical that as many people as possible get a chance to test the beliefs of the CEO and other senior managers first hand.

The alignment phase also featured a number of support activities carried out at the regional level. We created a small change committee of three senior managers plus Sarah Engel to assess in general terms where the organization was now, compared to the ideal described in the LTV. This group identified key areas that required change and some of the constraints to such change. They also developed a change strategy that emphasized that the responsibility for change was shared by everyone in the organization.

The Marketing Council, which is composed of the marketing manager from each product line, also tackled some useful projects. Using the general marketing-oriented statements of the LTV as a foundation, the Council developed a statement of Essochem's marketing philosophy. The specific guidelines prepared by the Council formed the basis for marketing strategies and plans for the individual product lines. The Marketing Council also initiated a marketing resource development project. This involved assessing the quality of our marketing resources, reviewing the

# ESSOCHEM LONG TERM VIEW

**The Vision**
- A first-class chemical company.
- Successful in both commodity and specialty markets.

**The Goals**
- Be the lowest cost producer of commodity chemicals.
- Significantly increase the percentage of specialty products in the product mix.

**The Path**
- Continued emphasis on process and product technology.
- Superior cost control system for each commodity product.
- A broad-based emphasis on new product development and marketing.
- Fully exploit cross-product line opportunities.
- People empowerment. Gain commitment of total workforce.
- Success. The customer is our best barometer.

criteria for promotion, reassessing the need for senior marketing positions in several of our product lines, and assessing our approach to classifying marketing positions relative to our key competitors. An in-depth review of marketing training was conducted, resulting in a significant addition of formal training courses and a three-year commitment to put the appropriate people through the higher level courses that they required.

As a result of a great many comments from the organization, our system for appraising and counseling employees underwent a major overhaul. The detailed set of performance appraisal and counseling instructions for supervisors was completely revised and an extensive program launched to educate all supervisors in its use. A new brochure describing the system was also prepared and distributed to all professional employees.

After about a year, Sarah Engel conducted a workshop for the same group of senior managers that participated in preparing the LTV. This focused on the differences between leadership and management and the need for supervisors at all levels to devote attention to both elements of their job.

## COMMITMENT BUILT ON CREDIBILITY

An organization can run only so far on enthusiasm. To convert alignment to true commitment, we needed to develop a rationale and some broad strategies to support the goals of the LTV. The goals supplied *what* we needed to do, but the strategies were required to indicate in general *how* we might go about it.

To support the low cost producer goal, we could point to the total cost control system mentioned previously. It had been evolving over several years and was recognized as a definite improvement. It helped us avoid arbitrary cuts in narrow cost categories without regard to the total cost picture. For example, it is frequently prudent to increase a fixed cost, such as technical manpower, in order to reduce an important variable cost, such as energy consumption. The control system also had a product line orientation. We didn't need to ask some affiliate to cut its costs 5% across the board. We could look at each specific business, decide what our basic objectives were, and manage cost accordingly. This could mean establishing severe cost reduction goals in commodity chemicals in order to stay abreast of the industry margin erosion predicted by experience curves. At the same time it could mean adding resources and cost to a specialty product group which had future potential. In summary, our strategy for becoming the low cost producer was to use a total cost focus, make it product line specific, and make differentiated cost judgments among product lines.

Achieving a broader, higher value added product mix represented Essochem's most challenging goal. As a total organization, we needed to become more market/customer oriented and more entrepreneurial as we tried to improve our ability to find, nurture, and exploit new product and market opportunities. In this regard we adopted a strategy which we termed "incremental everywhere." We felt that a broad-based attack involving all product lines, functions, and affiliates held far more promise of success than did concentration on a few groups or major items. We wanted to encourage an incremental multi-directional approach in all business areas, building on current strengths. In the long run this approach will involve less risk. However, it is also the most difficult to implement because if you go incremental everywhere, you need to involve everyone. In order to involve everyone effectively, we needed to alter some widely held perceptions and attitudes about what our company was willing to try and support. Many of the LTV communication and follow-through activities described previously were directed at identifying and making the changes that would eventually improve our performance in the marketplace.

As the organization digested these fairly simple and perhaps obvious strategies, another requirement became apparent. It was clear that we needed to remain committed to important programs for many years or we would never achieve the goals of the LTV. Yet we were clearly in a cyclical business, and historically when the down cycles appeared, important priorities were rearranged and often programs of a long-term nature failed to receive appropriate resources. Before employees were prepared to invest effort and energy in support of the LTV, they needed some reassurance that continuous commitment would be a prevailing theme. To answer this need we did considerable work on understanding the business cycles in the petrochemical industry. We developed some analysis techniques that allowed us to look beneath the cyclical volume and margin effects and to understand the underlying strength of our total business. When this was done, it became clear that we had been improving our fundamental performance for the past several years. We were exceeding this underlying business performance in the good years, and were under it in the poor ones, but on average our region was fundamentally sound. Most of our individual businesses were in reasonable shape, or we had clear and specific plans to get them there. This helped reassure the organization that there was no justification for pulling back from our basic goals. In fact, it was both logical and essential that we persevere with important programs despite the profit swings.

In further support of the continuous commitment theme, we broadly communicated actions and activities that supported the LTV. About three times a year we put out a newspaper called *Progress* which contained many such examples. We also included such examples in our annual business review which is put on videotape and sent around the region. This gave us a chance to visually feature many people who were actively contributing.


## LEADERSHIP PERSPECTIVE

During this process the meaning of leadership became much clearer to me. It means listening to an organization both collectively and as individuals. It means thinking through in broad terms where the organization should be going and how it might get there. It means not assuming that such direction is obvious and, therefore, needs no documentation or publicity. It means filling in with logic why the basic goals are correct, important, and achievable, and defining some broad strategies that support the goals. It means assessing both the organization's cultural strengths and weaknesses relative to the long-term goals and its potential for and receptivity to change. It means launching and nurturing many activities and initiatives that will improve the organization's fundamental capacity to change and to achieve. It means being a consistent and visible missionary who is not just intellectually, but also emotionally committed to the cause.

But most importantly, it means empowering the work force, concentrating on the environment in which individuals work, and determining what can be done to help them do their best. I don't believe you get the best out of everybody by closely managing all that they do. With broad general direction they'll initiate and do things that not even the most brilliant manager could conceive. If managers leave more of the job of preparing and implementing strategies and plans to the organization, that job will still get done very well. But if a manager spends all his time doing that, there is no way for the leadership void to be filled. Large segments of management responsibility can be delegated; almost by definition, leadership responsibility cannot.

The major deterrents to achieving an LTV are impatience and the quick-fix mentality. As with most business problems, there is no quick fix. Basic weaknesses in an organization coexist with the culture and are generally overcome only by attacking and altering that culture. Massive change is so difficult that basic goals and strategies must be set consistent with achievable change. Even then, results will be slow to appear. The basic path must be so logical and so well supported and accepted by many people that the organization becomes willing to fight for the survival of the initiative. As one of our people said, "The greatest danger to the achievement of our goal is that it be killed not by opposition but by indifference." Even in a receptive organization, the fundamental inertia is enormous, and it's almost impossible to overestimate the difficulty of accomplishing a change.

The Essochem story is unfinished and always will be, but at least a chapter has been added by a large number of talented people who have decided to invest an extra measure of current effort in the company's long-term future.

# CHAPTER 20

# Leading as Learning: Developing a Community's Foundation

by
**DAVID SIBBET**
**JUANITA BROWN**

*This case study chronicles the tenacious efforts of a CEO to pursue what he felt was best for his organization during a period of extraordinary growth, change, and pressure. It is another example of how creativity, intuition, and holding onto one's vision can catalyze outstanding results.*

Martin Paley, executive director of The San Francisco Foundation, is an acknowledged innovator in an organizational milieu more often associated with conservativism—philanthropy. While foundations across the country support a full spectrum of projects in the charitable and nonprofit fields, as a whole foundations are not progressive organizationally. The inertia from their political insulation, sense of trust to donors, and relative security leads most foundations to operate in a comfortably traditional manner, even if their grants are ground-breaking.

This chapter is the story of one's man tenacity in pursuing the best for his organization through a period of extraordinary growth and change, and the lessons he has learned while probing past the comfortable path of least resistance. It is the story of a man who has dared to be wrong and suspects that questions are more powerful than answers, even though his mind craves clarity.

- How can we keep ourselves creative and risk-taking?
- Can we lead by listening to the wisdom of the community itself rather than our own great ideas?
- What is the responsibility of our extraordinary power and influence?
- Can we be as exemplary a learning community as we are a foundation?
- Can our behavior match our purpose and principles?

Martin asks these kinds of questions of his board, his staff, the leaders of the community who are his peers, and most of all himself. "I'm one of the few people in my community who is not at the mercy of specific forces and interests—it is my personal responsibility to lead creatively," he says.

Martin works hard to practice the leadership characteristics Warren Bennis (1985) identified in his recent four-year study—managing attention through vision, meaning through communications, trust through constancy, and self through positive regard for himself and others. Yet he remains shy of accepting credit and wary of any implication of singular influence. It was only at the insistence of Juanita Brown and David Sibbet, two consultants who worked with the foundation and Martin closely, that he agreed to share his experience, but only then if it was clear that the insights were from his point of view and surely not representative of the full picture.

David's Senior Fellowship at the Foundation provided the opportunities in 1985 for Martin to engage in several interviews and review his approach to leadership. The results are anecdoctal rather than analytic, but truly reflect the way he thinks about his job and the initiatives he has taken. True to his own principles, he began to see this reflection and sharing as important for his own learning, just as the program evaluations he expects from grantees will contribute to theirs.

Driving over the Bay Bridge toward San Francisco from his home in Berkeley, Martin Paley can see the tall towers of the financial district dropping off toward Jackson Square, and the human scale of Telegraph Hill's flats stepping up toward Coit Tower. The pyramid-shaped Transamerica Building marks the line where government planning policy says the skyscrapers must cease, to provide some harbor for the intimate urban neighborhoods that are so central to the city's historic aesthetic.

A block from the base of the Transamerica Pyramid is The San Francisco Foundation, on the top floor of a new, eight-story brick building. Like its location, it bridges the financial, community, and government sectors. It is the country's largest community foundation and among the largest of any foundation. Founded in 1946, its assets are now over $536 million dollars, with $37 million dollars in grants given annually to nonprofit organizations and worthy causes throughout the Bay Area.

Martin thought back to when he began as executive director in 1974. The staff numbered eight and one-half people. The Foundation gave away only $2.53 million dollars a year, and the offices were located in a small suite right in the heart of the financial district. Little did he know then that he would be leading this organization through one of the most extraordinary transformational experiences in the history of American philanthropy—the receipt of the Buck Trust. This single bequest, one of more than 100 that the Foundation now administers, would grow from $7 million dollars in 1975 when Mrs. Beryl Buck died and left the residue of her estate to the San Francisco Foundation, to over $260 million dollars in 1980 when The Foundation received the money, due to the unanticipated financial impact of the 1979 oil crisis on the estate's oil stocks. Mrs. Beryl Buck lived in Marin County, the wealthy cluster of bedroom communities just north of San Francisco across the Golden Gate Bridge. As conditions for her bequest, she specified in her will that the income must be totally spent the year after it is earned for "exclusively nonprofit, charitable, religious, or educational purposes in providing care for the needy in Marin County, California, and for other nonprofit, charitable, religious or educational purposes in that county." This income would amount to over $25 million dollars annually.

Thus, in three short years, the $5 million dollars available for annual grants in the Foundation's five-county service area would become $30 million, with the majority limited to Marin. The Foundation staff would grow from 8 to 45; it would move to new offices in San Francisco (the one in Jackson Square) and open another in Marin County; it would become a major influence in Marin County public affairs, and a focus of national attention within philanthropic circles. The bequest would directly challenge the Foundation's root value of being a Bay Area-wide community foundation. In addition, Martin would champion the importance of involving the community in the work of the Foundation and in planning policies for the Buck money, launching processes that would make large demands on staff time.

Paley would also insist on maintaining an integrity with the history of the Foundation while simultaneously asking fundamental questions and taking real risks in the interest of the institution's future. How Martin Paley met and is meeting these challenges is a story of the transformation of a leader and an institution. It is a story still unfolding, and its lessons deal with fundamental issues of principle. The dilemmas are still with Martin as he comes to work today, but a leadership philosophy is taking root, not only in The San Francisco Foundation, but within other organizations with whom it deals.

## INTRODUCING A NEW MANAGEMENT STYLE

Martin can vividly remember his first trip downtown for The San Francisco Foundation in 1973. He was the president of a successful health-consulting subsidiary of Arthur D. Little. His destination was a meeting with the seven members of the distribution committee, the top governing body of The San Francisco Foundation. His colleague John May, then the executive director, had come to know Martin as director of the San Francisco Health Council in the early 1960s and later in his role as director of a regional hospital planning program for the Bay Area. Impressed by his performance and leadership, John had invited Martin to talk to the committee to see if there was any match between his abilities and their needs. John was retiring and liked Martin's ideas.

"The distribution committee represented old-line leadership and very responsible oversight roles," Martin remembers. "It included William Orrick Jr., who became a federal judge; Mrs. Gene Kuhn; Daniel Koshland, Jr., Chairman of the Board of Levi Strauss & Company; Emmett Solomon, chairman of the board of Crocker Bank; Ira D. Hall, Jr., executive director of the Stanford Mid-Peninsula Urban Coalition; Clark Biese, who had formerly been president of the Bank of America; and Brooks Walker, Jr., chairman of the board of U.S. Leasing International, Inc. My agreeing to interview was a little audacious, because they had been fending off all kinds of folks and were down to one. Why was I there? I made it very clear I was not an applicant at that point, but I talked with them about the job and said I would only consider the position if they were certain I was the one they wanted."

"I remember Emmett Solomon called me back and asked me to take the job. They wanted a manager and someone who could take charge when John retired. I asked for time to think it over and talk with some people. I didn't know much about the way the place was organized or managed, and didn't have a real sense of the process. But I did have a sense that here was an opportunity to play an important role in the Bay Area community, and to use money to affect programs, ideas, people — critical issues."

The Foundation represented then, and now, one of the critical sources of venture capital for nonprofits in the Bay Area. Its distribution committee members were each appointed by different blue ribbon institutions in rotation, such as the judge of the federal court, president of the United Way, president of the San Francisco Chamber of Commerce, the League of Women Voters, the president of the University of California, the trustee banks, and president of Stanford University. Of the dozens of separate trust funds left to the foundation as bequests, a minority were restricted to special purposes. Most of the trusts were unrestricted and open to distribution within broad Foundation policies, allowing program staff and the distribution committee unparalleled amounts of freedom to engage in creative grant-making. Because they manage multiple trusts, community foundations nationally are also a source of organizational innovation within philanthropy, as they evolve forms that fit the special needs of their individual communities.

"I started out by having staff meetings once a week. That was a new experience. They had rarely come together in a meeting to talk or ask questions. We got a coffee maker and modern duplicating machine, and a new calculator — these were symbolic things. And we remodeled, moving the conference room up to the front of the office, making it physically a more open spot — making it the entry."

The conference room was more than symbolic. Martin brought people in to start talking to staff and exchange ideas. He sought to shift the role of the distribution committee more toward policy-level decisions and away from administrative decisions. One of its first decisions regarded Martin's request to determine staff salaries and assess individual staff performance.

"This was a touchy moment," Martin remembers, "because the traditionalists said, 'We've always done it the other way,' But I outlined why it was unacceptable. It was the first critical test, and shifted my role from staff to that of a true manager."

In this move Martin began working on one of his top priorities, which was to build the professional quality of the staff. He hired several new program executives to work with grants, including Bernice Brown, an educational innovator from Lone Mountain College; John Kreidler, initiator of the neighborhood arts program with CETA in the early 1970s; and Henry Izumizaki, a seasoned street worker and community organizer. He promoted Doris Sams to Assistant Director and began holding regular meetings with community people and consultants to feed in ideas. He sought to be more explicit about politics and procedures, initiating the first annual grants budgets, targets by program area. For the first time the Foundation began publishing explicit grant guidelines for the community, using its new newsletter as a vehicle for regular communications.

"The biggest challenge in this period was the work on specific grants," Martin remembers. "I would carry about one-third of the caseload, so there were a lot of particular projects that I got involved with. But I found it very satisfying to have a sense of building an organization that was clearer about its purpose. We initiated the first off-site meetings, first on a full-day basis, then overnight for the distribution committee around our most important issues. It was during this time that they established a 10-year tenure policy to begin bringing fresh insights into the board."

"My approach then was to be challenging but respectful of the distribution committee's role as decision-makers. It led to a more vigorous, dynamic interaction. I always felt that if they had a good process and debated vigorously by definition whatever decision they came to was the right decision."

Martin saw the staff and distribution committee in those days as a kind of extended family, and preserving the give-and-take of the group remained a strong internal value as the Foundation headed toward a complete transformation sparked by the Buck Trust.

## COPING WITH THE IMPACT
## OF THE BUCK TRUST

The true magnitude of the Buck bequest did not emerge immediately. The Foundation knew there was money coming, and that it was going to be large, but the amounts tended to increase nearly every time somebody described it—$10, $20, $30, $50, $70 million dollars. Those were staggering figures for the nonprofit world, but not even close to the $250 million dollars that were actually turned over to the Foundation in 1980 after Shell Oil Company purchased the Bellridge fields in which Mrs. Buck had stock. There is no precedent in the history of American philanthropy of an unanticipated bequest of this magnitude designated for use in one, relatively small county.

"My general tendency, in these kinds of situations, is to seek expert consultation," Martin said, thinking back on his first reactions. "I reach for the phone and call two or three resource people and arrange a time to sit down and chat with them. This time I talked to quite a few—from all over the country. We even had one foundation executive come spend six months with us. We built on the concept that ideas would come from a number of sources, and we would be able to filter them out and put them in some order. I would ruminate about a subject for days and weeks, and then, given the right setting and the right questions, the answers would just pop out."

Part of what allows Martin to be open to such give and take is the depth to which he respects and manages on the basis of principles and values. This never came out more clearly than during the meteoric growth precipitated by the Buck Trust. He would probe and ask questions, not let people off the hook, and test, while at the same time ultimately trusting people's professional competence. "In those days I tended, more than now, to be a tough questioner. It reached its height in some of the sessions with staff a couple of years ago around all-day grant sessions, when I was still heavily involved. I thought it was a great, exciting learning experience."

Martin's belief in dialogue extended to the community as well. In 1979 he arranged for a series of five meetings throughout Marin where the community would be facilitated in a full discussion of what they thought would be the best use of the Buck Trust money. Professional facilitators from Interaction Associates, David Straus and Michael Doyle, and graphic facilitator David Sibbet were called in to help design the meetings. Melinda Marble, at that time working for the San Francisco Study Center, conducted some research on the communities as a catalyst for discussion. Martin and the staff attended all the meetings, and, in the spirit of learning and discovery, served as listeners and observers. Everything was recorded on large visual displays.

The results of these meetings were fed back to the community and to the distribution committee. "I remember one of our meetings, when we met to synthesize the information from all these community gatherings," Martin said. "We had just broken for lunch and when we came back, at about 1:30, the themes came—bing-bing-bing—focus on the family, focus on projects that reduce dependency, focus on projects that sustain diversity, focus on the environment, focus on the promotion and strengthening of appreciation of arts and culture, focus on projects that promote problem-solving, focus on those unifying concepts which grew out of the material in those community sessions."

These themes became the preliminary guidelines for Martin and the Foundation in the first years of Buck. Two years later he went back to the community with another series of facilitated meetings to report on results.

"Part of what I knew least about at this stage of the game was what it means to have this kind of power and authority in a small community such as Marin, and them not knowing what rules or procedures to follow to work with us. This was a situation without precedent. We were building this machine while it was running down the road, and there was not enough communication even though we thought there was. Our process-oriented approach was a major departure for a foundation—it was a break with tradition and was still not enough because we were dealing with so many unknowns. In some respect we were a parallel government without the normal characteristics of government—where you have access to it, and can lobby. Few could fully appreciate the implications of giving away this amount of money in a community the size of Marin."

The first years were painful, Martin remembers vividly. "The concerns of the community and the concerns of my colleagues in the foundation world seemed to grow by the day. There was even a national dimension to put up with. I couldn't go outside the Bay Area or even in the Bay Area without people leaning on me—'how could you do such a horrible thing, spending all that money in wealthy Marin County?' I got it from every angle, shape, and form. Money is an incredibly powerful part of our culture. It does the worst things to people, yet I am convinced that in the hands of wise and skillful leaders it can do wonders."

"I had a sense that, at the heart of this situation, there was an important organization that was acquiring a major responsibility, and I was terribly concerned that the basic institution of The San Francisco Foundation not be seriously jeopardized as we took on this new job. The Foundation, in my mind then, and now, is a critical community institution, holding a Bay Area wide leadership role, and that's what I tried to keep in mind. We had a process that required the distribution committee to make final judgments, and I wanted to preserve that process. We had a sense of relationship and communication with the broader community; I wanted to preserve that. This latter was the most difficult feature to sustain. How do you maintain the quality and integrity of an institution while you are undertaking an enormous change?"

"We had enormous pressures to build up quickly and to go for the big shot. This violated our basic concept of bringing the community along. We could have plunked down institutes and programs and buildings in Marin that would have been quite inappropriate and unrelated. So I found that those values of mine — of raising questions with the community, of listening to what it has to say, of trying to synthesize this in terms of some grant-making guidelines, and then get back to people for reactions — were a reflection of my personality and professional career, which had been aimed at reaching agreements and satisfying most of the people I dealt with.

"But the Buck situation with its attendant publicity and multiple special interests was unique. The fact that there were then and still are today unsatisfied people was difficult and sometimes painful for me. It drove me hard and sometimes even added to the problem. But this is where the balance between knowing why you are doing something and then how you are doing it is so important. I found there were people I respected who had many different views of how we should proceed, but I was only one person, in the final analysis, and had to make my judgments as a critical leader in the process. Big projects, moving faster, building permanent advisory groups — they just didn't seem to me to be, in the long run, the best way to go about things for the Foundation. I didn't want to grow so fast it would be cancerous. In the absence of footsteps to follow, I stayed focused on core principles."

## LOOKING AT CORE VALUES

"Early in the 1980s I decided that we needed collectively to understand what we believed in," Martin recalls. "I think 'values' was the term that we used. My thought was that philosophers generally consider values. I knew two prominent philosophers locally, and I talked to them individually. They both seemed appropriate so I invited them to design a series of sessions whereby they could help us analyze what we were doing and what values underlie our work at the Foundation."

"For nearly a year in 1982 Jerry Needleman and Al Jonsen sat in on meetings, all-day sessions, and helped us become more aware. We discovered that we needed to deal with more substantive issues. Ultimately the values work was the focus of one of the off-sites, which by this time had become annual three-day retreats at a seaside conference center near Monterey.

While not everyone supported the work wholeheartedly at the beginning, by the end of the sessions staff and Distribution Committee members came to understand that a core value of the Foundation was supporting people and groups to be at once independent and self-sustaining, and also interdependent and responsive to the community. The difference between "intrinsic" or ends-related values and "instrumental" or means-related values became clear. "My inclination," Martin remembers of this experiment, "is if it seems worthwhile, try it and enjoy the adventure of it."

Jerry Needleman eventually wrote an article for philanthrophy's national publication, the *Foundation News,* providing an early-on introduction into the community foundation world of the concept of managing by values. Martin also found himself emphasizing the themes of ethics and values in his work with other foundation people in the Bay Area. "It was an exciting time," Martin remembers.

# INITIATING A PLANNING PROCESS

In early 1983, with a staff of over 40 and operational issues in the new offices smoothing, Martin began a formal long-range planning process.

"In the initial rush of the Buck Trust, we had not had the time for formal planning. I felt we required a better sense of ourselves and where we were going. So I scouted around for somebody to help us schedule an initial session and came up with Juanita Brown, a seasoned international organization consultant who had been the lead resource on an innovative community planning project in the Canal area of Marin."

"At our first meeting I said that I wanted to set up goals down to specific tasks of what we ought to be doing next week, and next month, and next year, and how we ought to be spending the money. Juanita would listen patiently. I was more linear then, and likely to deal solely at an intellectual level. Juanita is more organic in her style. I tend to communicate with just words. Juanita communicates with everything she's got."

The two styles proved complementary and sparked an intense year of planning in 1984. Everyone in the Foundation, including the community, became involved.

"The intent was to have an agreement and an instrument that would guide this organization into the future, and would help make decisions and would allow for a transfer of leadership should I get hit by a car. We started with a fairly classic notion of planning, but then, as we thought about the work we had done with the philosophers, and thought about what was appropriate for our kind of organization, we decided that we weren't going to go at it from A to Z. We'd start A *and* Z and work towards the middle. This is essentially what we have done. The A to N portion was the articulation of the purpose, philosophy, and principles of the Foundation. The other was concurrent work from the bottom up, paying attention to basic operating concerns and shorter term objectives."

"I became familiar with some of the more sophisticated trends of recent times, of focusing on the more timeless, more profound abstractions as a way of unifying an organization, rather than on product and market share and growth percentages. In our case, this effort became a matter of articulating and giving some concrete substance to an organization culture which had been evolving for a good many years," Martin reflects.

Juanita conducted in-depth interviews with all of the program executives and associate staff. She met regularly with Martin in personal sessions aimed at clarifying his own goals and future visions for the Foundation. Special TAQ Teams (Take Action Quickly) moved on operational problems needing immediate attention, such as scheduling. The professionalism of the Foundation's support staff was recognized, and that concept of associate staff emerged. Special all-staff retreats were planned by staff to explore the relation between the purpose, philosophy, and principles and shorter term concerns.

In the spring of 1984, six critical sessions were organized with members of the community and former Distribution Committee members at the Foundation, with the results published and distributed. The purpose of these sessions was for all key constituent groups to provide direct input to initial drafts of the Foundation's purpose, philosophy, and principles statement. The project was called "Commitment to the Community." A final version of the purpose, philosophy and principles ultimately came to the Distribution Committee for formal approval in late 1984.

"The planning process gave me a vehicle and an anchor during the continuing demands of the Buck transition," Martin recalls. "There was something constructive happening that I knew, if properly carried out, would begin to redress some of these concerns and would assure more balance and a more informed process of decision-making. That's what I hung on to, and it was essentially my sustaining force. It was a very troublesome period. The Distribution Committee was going through periods of enormous soul searching, with not a meeting going by for a year when the issue of Buck didn't become a point of discussion."

In the midst of the discussion, with typical guts and creativity, Martin took a three-month sabbatical. "It was the best thing I could have done," he says in retrospect. "We had talked about my taking one for two years."

"The organization weathered this very, very well. It was good. It got the organization a respite from me, and it got a sense of its own capacity. It got a chance to see some new leadership, and everyone had a chance to catch his or her breath. The changes had occurred fast and furious. My advice to everyone was to treat this sabbatical as though I wasn't coming back. 'I'm not going to replay details of what happened,' I said. 'I am going to get off here and I'm going to get on over there, and your responsibility is to take it from here to there.' "

## CREATING THE FOUNDATION AS A LEARNING COMMUNITY

Martin returned from his sabbatical renewed, and he focused on a new set of goals for himself. He wrote the following list to direct his attention in the months ahead:

1. Assist the Foundation in resisting a tendency toward bureaucracy through effective planning, organization, and management.

2. Maintain strong, positive, visionary leadership at the top.

3. Avoid being drawn into inappropriate day-to-day management issues.

4. Reestablish and strengthen contracts in the local professional community, foundations, agencies, and others.

5. Above all, maintain the sense of mutual trust and confidence between the Director and the Distribution Committee.

"I realized I had all the ingredients to do an extraordinary job. As long as I was in that driver's seat, I would do the best I could. It took me some time to accommodate to pulling away from the bench work, the work on grants, but now I am getting an enormous amount of satisfaction out of seeing the institution take stronger form and shape and move in a coherent fashion toward its future; to see the transition in the Distribution Committee and to see my own transition in terms of a leader-manager working creatively with my colleagues and enriching my relationships with the program people."

Later Martin would come to see this open-ended, adaptive approach as a process that reflected a basic cycle of creativity. He diagrammed it as shown here for a talk reflecting on this period to the National Council on Foundations.

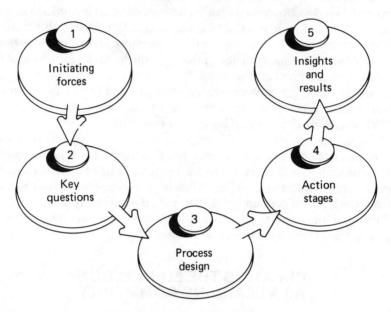

FIGURE 20-1    The San Francisco Planning Process

In 1984 the insights and results of the "Commitment to the Community" process — the purpose, philosophy, and principles statement — was published as the cover and major emphasis of the annual report. It is posted in the conference room as a backdrop to all key meetings, and the dockets — the monthly binders of summaries from which the Distribution Committee makes decisions — carry the three P's in front.

Shortly after Martin's return from sabbatical, the Distribution Committee took the significant step of petitioning the court to modify the Buck will and allow the Foundation to share some of the funds with other communities in the Bay area. The petition was based on the Cy Pres doctrine, historically used to modify charitable trusts when unforeseen circumstances make the donor's stated purpose illegal, impossible, or impracticable to fulfill. This move was perhaps the most dramatic manifestation of an organization that had come to steer itself by principle and values, because the legal action brought about an immediate and angry reaction in Marin County toward the Foundation, and placed the huge pressures involved in complying with the demands of a major law suit on the entire organization.

Martin responded to the Distribution Committee initiative by taking the high road. Trusting more and more in his own staff and management, which were now working as teams to continue clarifying their policies and improving procedures,

Martin extended his community leadership. He initiated a gathering of influential leaders in Marin to begin discussing their countywide values and vision. "A crisis provides an unprecedented type of opportunity," Martin reflects. In spite of the legal climate, in which the County Board of Supervisors was now an opponent, leaders responded with unique enthusiasm, creating Marin Conversations, a project to articulate a countywide values and philosophy statement.

As part of his ongoing interest in developing the Foundation as a learning environment, in 1984 Martin attended the systems dynamics trainings of Innovation Associates led by Peter Senge from M.I.T. He also joined their New Management Styles Project, exchanging ideas with other CEOs of innovative companies who were also focusing on leaders as learners.

In systems dynamics Martin found a powerful approach for appreciating the interrelationships that were key to thinking about the complex issues they were facing at The San Francisco Foundation and in the community at large, such as problems with the Highway 101 Corridor in Marin, or the San Francisco/Bay Delta. As he did with the philosophers, he brought the systems thinking home, beginning with having his own management team attend the Leadership and Mastery seminars run by Innovation Associates and by focusing the 1984 Annual Conference on these themes. He also arranged to have the entire staff experience a two-day session at Monterey Dunes retreat center led by Senge with actual hands-on computer modeling, and then sent two program staff for further training, to see how these ideas might be applied to the exploration of complex problems.

Systems thinking became a guide for his talks inside and outside the Foundation. Martin focused the 1984 Annual Conference on this theme. "We have to understand that the San Francisco Foundation inhabits many worlds, and is itself a system involving donors, Distribution Committee, management program executives, associate staff, intermediary organizations who apply to us for grants, and the ultimate beneficiaries." The diagram shown on page 298 emerged as a focal image for these ideas.

The systems approach allowed the Distribution Committee and program executives to begin to see that their real influence is indirect, through the intermediary organizations who receive and administer grants. Because so much of the decision power rests with the Distribution Committee, inevitably much attention is appropriately directed to the top relationship. Martin is determined to have the relationship with the intermediaries also be a key measure of excellence.

Martin sees listening to the community's ideas as central to maintaining a climate of discovery and learning both within the Foundation and between the Foundation and community. "How do you deal with the problem of renewal in foundations which have no need to renew, and if left to their own devices, might be the least renewed type of organization imaginable?" Martin wonders. "We have to intentionally keep things somewhat unsettled and open. We encourage the wind of new ideas to blow in one window and out another, with some settling in. And we have to do this in a shared way so that it's not just my experience."

"This is why the six 'Commitment to the Community' input sessions we held last summer were so very important—to tell us that this organization doesn't belong to the Distribution Committee and the staff; it belongs to the community. People said,

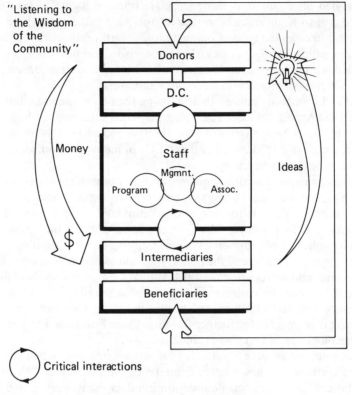

"Listening to the Wisdom of the Community"

Donors

D.C.

Money

Staff

Mgmnt.

Program     Assoc.

$

Ideas

Intermediaries

Beneficiaries

◯ Critical interactions

FIGURE 20-2     The San Francisco Foundation as a System

'this is our organization and take damn good care of it.' That was a powerful message."

Martin began to see that the Foundation had a critical leadership role in the larger system of the private, governmental, and independent sectors. Flying back to the National Council on Foundations annual conference in 1985 he prepared his thoughts. He would be appearing on a program to share his experience with the planning process he had been leading. He would also be attending board meetings of the council and networking with the other larger community foundations. The issues of leadership, power and influence, and ethics were top on his mind.

Martin worked on the plane with David Sibbet, who by this time had become a Senior Fellow at the Foundation, expressly working on implementation of the purpose, philosophy, and principles, and Juanita Brown, who continued as a long-range planning consultant. As an outgrowth of their work at The San Francisco Foundation they had also come to be facilitators of the Program Committee of the National Council on Foundations annual conference, extending the experience of the Foundation in yet another channel.

Martin depicted his latest sense of the Foundation as a system. "I see us moving beyond the traditional view of seeing the Foundation's role as being either *re*-active or *pro*-active. This way of thinking puts things on a continuum. We are building an organization that works from an interactive view, where the relationships between

298

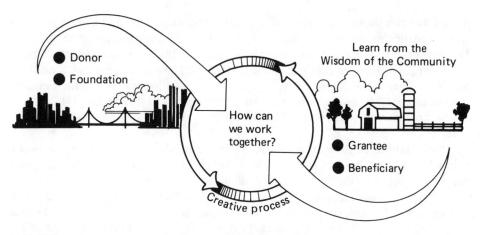

**FIGURE 20-3**     An Interactive View of the
San Francisco Foundation

the elements are seen as interdependent." As Martin coached David's imagery, the earlier systems diagram softened into the following chart.

On the flight Martin also took the time to reflect on his personal observations about his and the Foundation's larger leadership role.

"The approach I have been taking wouldn't in some situations be considered terribly adventurous, but in the Foundation world it is relatively rare. I enjoy doing these kinds of risky things. Besides, the risks you take in philanthropy are very safe. What can happen? A project fails? So it surprises me that people are not eager to take more risks."

"While the closest image I can come to what we are like is a university — in our collegial approach and the sense of being a learning community — we are also somewhere between a bank and a community development organization in terms of the community. We are really a community development bank — but I guess the comparison is not what I am most interested in. I want to say that this whole system is the entity and there are many mutually supportive things we can do."

"I personally have extraordinary freedom within this system. There is nobody I would call who isn't likely to call me back. I can go into a neighborhood with somebody and sit down and chat, or go see the president of the Bank of America. And I have a relationship with the staff, I think, which causes me to have the potential of being very helpful, and I have the respect of the Distribution Committee. Yet I still maintain a pretty low profile. I think people see me as a power figure but I have not really exercised that power."

Juanita asked Martin to look at his role in the process of clarifying the purpose, philosophy and principles of the Foundation as an example of his leadership style.

"First, I had to believe that what we were doing was both right and necessary. I thought it was absolutely essential to the organization to go through the planning process, and I used whatever formal and informal power and authority I had to encourage it."

Martin remains quick to spread the credit when he thinks about his role. "I think I was just early in catching a wave before it reached its crest. I think there are themes that run through society—words, concepts, whatever—and a readiness that causes a particular notion to emerge in several spots. Because it is so timely, because there has been so much unseen force giving rise to this idea, it just emerges almost full-blown. It strikes me that I frequently have the capacity to sense such needs in myself, and in the insitution, early, say, to talk about ethics in 1975 in the Foundation world, to talk about values and a process approach to planning in 1981 or '82, is just an anticipation of a feeling that was already there, and a readiness to be set loose."

"Foundations don't tend to follow easily and it takes leadership. My tendency is, in a lot of things, to lead by example. I find that if I am in a secure position and feel comfortable with my performance I am more open to learning than I might have been when I was seeking recognition, or approval, or both. I think one of the greatest weaknesses in leadership is the lack of personal security. You have to have a sense of identity and a sense of respect for oneself in order to build that sense of respect for others that is critical to the leader's role. If my example can cause others to follow, I get a big kick out of it, but it's not with that intent that I undertake a particular activity. I undertake it because I believe in it for this organization."

## A STEWARDSHIP IN PROGRESS

In June 1985 the Distribution Committee, program staff, and management found themselves south of San Francisco on the Monterrey Bay, checking into a cluster of condominiums dotting the dunes that would be the site of the annual conference.

Peter Haas, chairman of Levi Strauss & Company, was just joining the Distribution Committee—one of four that would come on over two years and yet again influence the character of the organization. He walked with Henry Izumizaki, son of one of the first Salinas Valley farm settlers, a Samurai family, and one of the first to have his land taken away during the Japanese internment in World War II. Henry has been with the Foundation since 1975 and brings a depth of community organizing experience to his job as an urban affairs program executive.

One of Henry's unforgettable laughs cuts through the night to the six other Distribution Committee members and dozen staff winding their way toward the recreation building for the initial meeting—a "State of the Foundation" talk with Martin.

Was Peter testing Henry with a story, sharing some of his wry wit, or was Henry remembering one of the amazing experiences from one of the former retreats? Without knowing, the laugh symbolized for everyone that the annual renewal of the June retreat had begun. The dinner wine had special labels secured by Henry honoring Distribution Committee member Robert Harris, partner of San Francisco's prestigious Heller, Ehrman, White & Maculiffe law firm, who was ending his ten years on the board. The informal dinner led to the beginning conversations and then the walk. In addition to the policy work and review of the staff's new projected annual reports, this conference would also be a rite of passage for this beloved trustee. Perhaps Henry was telling Peter about one of Harris' famous monologues on the celebration evenings at previous annual conferences which, unbeknownst to either of the two now, would this year result in Peter Haas gaining his place in the lore of the Foundation.

The chairs in the recreation building meeting room arced in a semicircle around Martin Paley. His half glasses sat down on his nose as he scanned his notes waiting for everyone to settle. Susan Little, Martin's invaluable assistant, checked in to consult on a logistical question. The laughter and conversation bouncing off the high, dark skylighted ceiling suggested a tough after-dinner audience for a serious address. But Martin does not daunt easily.

He waited to begin, glancing up to his right at the 4' × 8' chart carrying this year's theme, "Developing the Community's Foundation" in foot-high letters. The agenda listed underneath had emerged from several meetings with the management team and staff and individual conversations with each of the Distribution Committee members in the room. But last year the Distribution Committee had substantially modified an equally careful agenda the first night. In this living organization, no one, least of all Martin Paley, takes a planned agenda for granted.

Charles J. Patterson, manager of the Oakland Convention Center, former World Airways senior vice-president and Peace Corps executive gave an encouragement from the back of room. As chairman he would have his turn to manage the next day. Tonight he was in an expansive mood.

Richard B. Madden, chairman of the board and CEO of Potlach Corporation, on boards of many major arts and civic organizations, and recent chairman of the American Enterprise Institute, scanned the agenda. His ability to read and probe the inches thick dockets that summarized the grant requests reviewed at monthly meetings was already legendary. The size of the numbers did not phase him, but the questions of the values and precedents created by Distribution Committee decisions were important in every detail. This meeting had produced the first docket to contain long-range financial projections by grant-making categories, backed up by computer spreadsheets, as distinguished from specific grant summaries—a project led by Mort Raphael, the deputy director and manager of the program executives. Dick had strongly supported this development and would be the first to see opportunities for improvement.

Susan S. Metcalf, chairman designate, nominated by the president of the League of Women Voters, chatted with art program executive John Kreidler. John's new policy recommendations had large implications for the whole arts community, and Sue would be sure to test them thoroughly. The Foundation is one of the most adventurous supporters of middle-sized and ethnic arts organizations in the country, and John is suggesting moving some of the funds away from the major organizations to provide even more support.

In another corner of the room Joan Lane talked with Peter Behr. Joan is new along with Peter Haas, but her sparkling eyes bespeak her relish at this new responsibility. As recent chairman of the board of trustees of Smith College, she is used to complex organizations, but few have the scope of this foundation, with its five Bay Area County reach and its commitments to support the arts and humanities, education, environment, community health, and urban affairs. Christina Cuevas and Janet Ryan Rivera, the two community health program executives, listen in.

Peter Behr shares Joan's relish for the process. His famous gift for language, well practiced as a California legislator and legendary environmentalist, now serves him well as watchdog for Marin County.

Everyone is buzzing. The talented staff Martin has assembled and the older and exceptional Distribution Committee make a powerful chemistry of mutual interest.

"I've been admonished by friend and foe alike to keep these remarks simple," Martin began. The familiar twinkle in his eye told everyone present that he clearly had a plan up his sleeve. "In the past these comments have been totally laden with numbers — how many grants, dollar amounts, how this compares with the past five years."

"But perhaps more important are some of the underlying forces that give rise to the nature of this organization and why we are here and what we are trying to accomplish. It occurred to me it has to do with the enormous obligation that we each bear, staff and Distribution Committee alike, to the hundred or so individuals who have entrusted us with their wealth after they've gone."

By this time everyone was still and listening. Martin's quiet manner was firm. Was this too obvious? Was everyone just being courteous?

"We have to constantly remember what this very special trust implies," Martin continued. "I just don't feel we can recall it too often."

This was Martin's theme, even as he encouraged risks.

"I think our state of health is good," Martin continued. "I think that the Foundation is strong and effective and we have turned the corner on internal organizational and management concerns that have been with us the first years of the Buck money."

"A system of information for management purposes is improving as you can see from the Projected Annual Reports. I think we are learning to implement the purpose, philosophy, and principles. Now, coupled with the Projected Annual Reports, they move us substantially toward our objective of building a complete plan and program for the Foundation. Now the work really begins based on values, purpose, and programs. Now that we have begun to master the 'how' of grant-making we have to emphasize more the 'why'."

Martin went on to list the year's accomplishments:

- Maintain the quality and commitment of the Distribution Committee
- Excellent staff work, reduced complaints, and new praise
- Strong income
- Improved docket quality
- Beginning to listen to the community
- Home-to-home exchange with the Cleveland Foundation
- Systems dynamics work
- Staff leadership activity
- Promotion of independent artists and Art Stabilization Fund
- High school dropout program emulated in N.Y., San Diego
- Child care initiatives

- Minority community programs encouraging citizenship

- BRIDGE program for housing setting a national standard

- Criminal Justice Planning Group work in Marin County

- Water policy and Bay Area water quality network initiatives

- Work with United Way, San Franciscans Seeking Consensus, and Marin Conversations as support for community dialogue on critical issues

- Multicounty transportation studies in Marin

- Social and economic revitalization projects in East Oakland

The core themes of Martin's current work emerge. He wants the Distribution Committee and staff to appreciate the importance of promoting a sense of community interdependence, of sensing the interrelationship of problems, of promoting and understanding the interrelationship between sectors. He is concerned about the immediate problems of where community leadership will come from, and the integrity of the Foundation's own efforts to manage in relation to its principles. And he hopes this year will find a resolution to the Buck Trust law suit and thus opening a more certain future.

"In summary I would like to look at what makes this a successful place," Martin concluded.

"We have the chance to learn so much. That comes through in each of my contacts and discussion I have had with the Distribution Committee and helps contribute to our commitment."

"I think we want to seek to recapture that sense of intimacy, adventure, and curiosity; we'll embrace risk, celebrate tradition, and ultimately learn to trust ourselves and each other. We seek a blend of the intellectual and the intuitive, because it is not what the numbers say or the books say, but what our motives are and our response to ideas and concepts that shape our ability to continue to learn. It is essential to favor the relationship between the institution and the community, ultimately to serve the donors, by serving the community well. Each of us stands in a relation of responsibility to the Foundation for a limited period of time. What came before really is our guide. What follows is our opportunity to leave a legacy."

"I think we must focus on these ideas in our work at this year's annual conference, keeping in mind why we are doing it, what we are trying to evolve, not just how we do it. Thinking back on our work with the philosophers, they helped us to think about the intrinsic values in what we are doing as much if not more than the instrumental values."

"I do not mean to make this somber," Martin finished, noticing the completely quiet room. "I just wanted to express to you the thoughts I had to set the tone for the session, which once again is an opportunity to grapple with tough questions, and also a chance to build that sense of relationship."

The applause broke and conversation bubbled up. Henry's laugh erupted again, joined by Harris. Several weeks later this was to be judged as one of the finest meetings yet.

# NEW DIRECTIONS

Six months later Martin sat in the restaurant in the base of the Transamerica Pyramid thinking ahead. He was excited because the evening before he had invited an unusual group to the Foundation to talk with Robert Bellah, author of *Habits of the Heart,* a new best seller about American community values from the University of California Press. He had sent the book out in advance, and decided on the open discussion format.

"I had the idea of just bringing people together, simply to contemplate some ideas—to take the time to think sideways and in some depth."

Martin had not been sure it would work, but the politician, philosopher, county supervisor, minister, philanthropist, Dean of the Cathedral, lawyer, and agency director he had invited left their status differences at the door. Without roles to play or credentials to establish they talked about their real problems, and shared more deeply than any suspected they would. At the end of the time they didn't want to leave.

"We often tend to look for strategies around and over things, but often the situation itself will inform you," Martin reflected. "We structure too much. With structured learning, someone has to be the teacher. We don't believe people can learn from each other. I'm beginning to think that we must be every bit as interested in understanding as in getting out a solution. People might say, what's the impact? But why does there always have to be impact? There are incremental changes that may ultimately lay down a more solid foundation. Then stimuli like Bellah's book come along and have the effect of liberating this building sense of interest, uncovering truths we already know and showing us that we were not alone with our insights."

"Our assumption of differences may be our major barrier with each other—that others don't have the thoughts we have."

"I'm wrestling now with the competition/cooperation dichotomy for instance. To the extent that our organization is not challenged it atrophies. But if competition goes too far it destroys interdependence and self-regard. How do we discover this balance for ourselves? How can the organizations we fund discover this? How can we ourselves find time for the learning? I'm as busy now as I've ever been with the Buck law suit and all the other challenges—yet I force myself to take the time to expand my thinking. I've made that commitment."

Martin noted that these were just emerging ideas and he hadn't tested them, revealing that his own bias toward clarity and consistency hadn't completely left him. Yet something new was stirring and it wasn't clear yet, for him or his organization. He knows that growing and leading involve uncertainty, courage, and risk, but what does it mean to include heart as well?

It is entirely possible the next few years at the Foundation will see as much organizational change as any yet—depending on the outcome of the Buck case. But the leadership philosophy based on learning that Martin pursues seems to grow more steady each day. To think about the importance of not having clear structures—to consider the importance of heart—to champion taking precious time, not to move forward, but move more deeply—these are the characteristics of Martin's growing edge and his commitment to learning while he leads.

# Glossary

The explorers in every discipline find it necessary to invent language, or borrow it from other disciplines, to describe their experiences and discoveries at the edges of their fields. The pioneers of OT are no different. This glossary is an attempt to help the reader grasp the terms that are used repeatedly by the authors who have contributed to *Transforming Leadership*.

**ALIGNMENT:** The condition wherein people operate freely and fully as an intentional part of a larger whole. It is created when people see their organization's purpose as an extension of their personal purposes.

**ATTUNEMENT:** A resonant, synergistic, and mutually nurturing relationship among the parts of a system; and between the parts and the whole.

**BELIEF:** A subjective judgment or proposition which is accepted as true by an individual without requiring supportive evidence. It is a statement of "fact" one makes to one's self. Although they are only our statements about reality, we usually consider our beliefs to be reality.

**CONSCIOUSNESS:** State of awareness in regard to some thing, sensation, emotion, or thought.

**DISSIPATIVE STRUCTURE:** All structures, including social systems, have been observed to absorb perturbations (Fluctuations, stresses, etc.) up to a certain point, after which a wholly new, more complex structure rapidly arises. This notion is a challenge to the usual ideas about how evolution proceeds.

**EMPOWERMENT:** The creation of an environment in which individuals are encouraged to develop toward their full creative potential.

**EVOLUTION:** Relatively gradual, smooth, uninterrupted change in a system.

**EVOLUTIONARY MANAGER:** A person or team which takes the lead responsibility for the process of transformation in an organization. They hold a metaperspective on the organization and the transformation process and serve a catalytic function. A special application of the fusion team concept.

**FAST-TRACKING:** The conscious acceleration and management of the transformational process in an organization.

**FEAR STATE MANAGEMENT:** Chronically threatened by forces and events, acting to protect self and constrain others. (Contrast with Flow State and Solid State Management.)

**FLOW STATE MANAGEMENT:** Being in harmony with the natural order of things. Working with the human and organizational factors present to accomplish one's larger purpose.

**FUSION TEAM:**   A form of group management that looks after the creative process of large project groups, balancing the needs of members with the requirements of the project, budget, and timetable. Its membership may change at any time, and its leadership generally is shared and resource-oriented.

**HOLOGRAM:**   A three-dimensional image created by laser photography. A unique and intriguing feature of a holographic plate is that every part of it contains all of the information needed to recreate the entire image. That is, the information is distributed generally throughout the plate. As a model and metaphor, the hologram is being used widely today in brain research, astronomy, physics, and organizational psychology.

**INTERVENOR:**   An agent from outside a system, typically a manager in an organization or a staff advisor, who intercedes to solve problems or redirect efforts within the system in question.

**META___:**   A higher-order perspective. Viewing the function and role of a system from the viewpoint of the next larger, encompassing system.

**METANOIC:**   From the Greek word metanoia meaning "a fundamental shift of mind." Used to describe organizations where people operate from the viewpoint that, individually and collectively, they can create the future and shape their destiny. It was used by the early Christians to describe a reawakening of intuition and spirit.

**MORPHOGENETIC FIELDS:**   Fields of resonance, beyond space and time, which are hypothesized to organize the structure of reality into habitual or usual ways of being. If the hypothesis is valid, we may conclude that the reality of the universe is made up of habits (rather than of universal laws) which are subject to change through changed belief systems.

**MYTHS:**   The stories we tell to explain the nature of our realities and indicate what is important. They are the "truths" to which we look in deciding how to conduct our lives. They reflect the collective or consensual beliefs of a group or society.

**NODE POINTS:**   Those critical points in an organization where knowledge, authority, and resources come together. Often good leverage points when facilitating transformational processes.

**ORGANIZATIONAL ENERGY:**   Human potential for action or the accomplishment of work. Also the outcome of tensions generated by polarities in organizations such as long-term/short-term needs or stability/change.

**ORGANIZATIONAL FORM:**   Tangible aspects of organizations such as jobs, tasks, structures, policies, procedures, and results.

**PARADIGM:**   A prevailing worldview or collective belief system. The fundamental set of beliefs or organizing principles which are unquestioned and unexamined assumptions about the nature of reality. New paradigms generally do not replace old ones, but subsume them.

**PERFORMANCE:**   The execution and completion of required or desired functions.

**PROGRAMMING:** The predictable, consistent patterns of perceiving and behaving arising from one's beliefs about the nature of reality.

**REFRAMING:** Changing the context or perspective from which one views the world. Whether reframing is conscious or unconscious, it indicates the invocation of a new belief or attitude.

**RITUAL:** The dramatic reenactment of a myth. An acting out of the central stories of the group. The regularized means by which groups get new members aligned with the old story.

**SLOUGH-OFF STRATEGIES:** Preplanned ways to handle noncontributing operations or persons in an organization.

**SOLID STATE MANAGEMENT:** Skillful at managing the formal aspects of organizational life: the structures, results, tasks, and numbers. Works within set boundaries and maintains set procedures. (Contrast with Fear State and Flow State Management.)

**SYNERGY:** The creative output of various inputs that is greater than any one of the sum of those inputs.

**TRANSITIONS:** Predictable cycles of change within the transformation process. Ideally, the transition cycle describes the change process as that which happens between two stable states. In reality, there are few if any stable states and we experience the cycle of transition on a continuing and multiple basis.

**TRANSFORMATION:** Profound fundamental changes in thought and actions which create an irreversible discontinuity in the experience of a system. Generally the result of the emergence of radically new belief systems (paradigms).

# References and Suggested Readings

Ackerman, L., and D. Whitney. 1982. *The fusion team: A model of organic and shared leadership.* Pending publication.

Adams, John D., ed. 1984. *Transforming work.* Miles River Press, Alexandria, VA.

Agor, Weston. 1984. *The intuitive manager.* Prentice-Hall, Englewood Cliffs, NJ.

Allen, Robert F., and Charlotte Kraft. 1982. *The organizational unconscious: How to create the corporate culture you want and need.* Prentice-Hall, Englewood Cliffs, NJ.

Argyris, Chris, and Donald A. Schon. 1978. *Organizational learning: A theory of active perspective.* Addison-Wesley, Reading, MA.

Axelrod, Robert. 1984. *The evolution of cooperation.* Basic Books, New York.

Beckhard, Richard, and Reuben Harris. 1977. *Organizational transitions: Managing complex change.* Addison-Wesley, Reading, MA.

Beer, Stafford. 1975. *Platform for change.* John Wiley, New York.

Bennis, Warren. 1971. Post-bureaucratic leadership. In Lassey and Fernandez, eds., *Leadership and social change.* University Associates, La Jolla, CA.

Bennis, Warren. 1983. A new definition of success: Personal empowerment, quality, and love. *The Terrytown Letter.* November.

Bennis, Warren, and Burt Nanus. 1985. *Leaders: The strategies of taking charge.* Harper & Row, New York.

Berman, Morris. 1984. *The reenchantment of the world.* Bantam Books, New York.

Best executives know intuition supplements logic. *USA Today.* Aug. 22, 1984.

Blanchard, Kenneth, and Spencer Johnson. 1982. *The one minute manager.* William Morrow, New York.

Bolman, Lee G., and Terrence E. Deal. 1984. *Modern approaches to understanding and managing organizations.* Jossey-Bass, San Francisco.

Bradford, David L., and Allan R. Cohen. 1984. *Managing for excellence.* John Wiley, New York.

Bradley, Marion. 1984. *The mists of Avalon.* Sphere Books, U.K.

Briggs, John, and F. David Peat. 1984. *Looking glass universe.* Simon and Schuster, New York.

Buckley, K. W., and D. Perkins. 1984. Managing the complexity of organizational transformation. In John D. Adams, ed., *Transforming work.* Miles River Press, Alexandria, VA.

Burns, J. M. 1978. *Leadership.* Harper & Row, New York.

Capra, Fritjof. 1982. *The turning point.* Simon and Schuster, New York.

Carroll, Lewis. 1891. *Through the looking glass.* Macmillan, New York.

Cox, Harvey. 1969. *The feast of fools: A theological essay on festivity and fantasy.* Harvard University Press, Cambridge, MA.

Csikszentmehalyi, M. 1975. *Beyond boredom and anxiety.* Jossey-Bass, San Francisco.

Davis, Stanley, and Paul Lawrence. 1977. *Matrix.* Addison-Wesley, Reading, MA.

Deal, Terrence E., and Allan A. Kennedy. 1982. *Corporate cultures: The rites and rituals of corporate life.* Addison-Wesley, Reading, MA.

deVries, Manfred Kets, and Danny Miller. 1984. *The neurotic organization.* Jossey-Bass, San Francisco.

Donaldson, Gordon, and Jay W. Lorsch. 1983. *Decision making at the top.* Basic Books, New York.

Drake, Richard, and Peter Smith. 1973. *Behavioral science in industry.* McGraw-Hill, London.

Drucker, Peter. 1980. *Managing in turbulent times.* William Heinemann, London.

Ferguson, Marilyn. 1980. *The aquarian conspiracy.* J. P. Tarcher, Los Angeles.

Ferruci, Piero. 1982. *What we may be: Techniques for psychological and spiritual growth through psychosynthesis.* J. P. Tarcher, Los Angeles.

Forrester, Jay W. 1968. Market growth as influenced by capital investment. *Industrial Management Review*: 9.

Fritz, Robert. 1984. *The path of least resistance.* DMA, Salem, MA.

Gaffney, Rachel. 1984/85. Systems thinking in business: An interview with Peter Senge. *Revision:*7(2).

Gawain, Shakti. 1978. *Creative visualization.* Whatever Publishing, Mill Valley, CA.

Gawain, Shakti. 1982. *Creative visualization.* Bantam Books, New York.

Golumbiewski, Robert, et al. 1983. Phases of progressive burnout and their work site covariants. *Journal of Applied Behavioral Sciences:*19(4).

Greenleaf, Robert. 1977. *Servant leadership: A journey into the nature of legitimate power and greatness.* Paulist Press, Ramsey, NJ.

Greiner, Larry E. 1972. Evolution and revolution as organizations grow. *Harvard Business Review.* July-August.

Hall, Edward T. 1977. *Beyond culture.* Doubleday & Co., New York.

Hall, Manly. 1923. *The lost keys of freemasonry.* Philosophical Research Society, Los Angeles.

Handy, Charles. 1984. *The future of work.* Pan Books, London.

Harman, Willis, and Howard Rheingold. 1984. *Higher creativity: Liberating the unconscious for breakthrough insights.* J. P. Tarcher, Los Angeles.

Harrison, Roger. 1984. Leadership and strategy for a new age. In John D. Adams, ed., *Transforming work.* Miles River Press, Alexandria, VA.

Hayes, Robert H., and William J. Abernathy. 1980. Managing our way to economic decline. *Harvard Business Review:*58.

Houston, Jean. 1982. *The possible human.* J. P. Tarcher, Los Angeles.

Iglehart, Hallie. 1983. *Woman spirit: A guide to women's wisdom.* Harper & Row, San Francisco.

Ingalls, J. D. 1976. *Human energy.* Addison-Wesley, Reading, MA.

Jampolsky, Harold. 1979. *Love is letting go of fear.* Celestial Arts, Mill Brae, CA.

Jantsch, E. 1975. *Design for evolution.* George Braziller, New York.

Jenkins, Clive, and Barry Sherman. 1979. *The collapse of work.* Eyre Methuen Ltd., London.

Johnson, Robert. 1974. *He.* Religious Publishing Co., King of Prussia, PA.

Joiner, William B. 1984. Experiential learning and the wish for transformation. *Organizational Behavior Teaching Review:*9(1).

Joiner, William B. 1984/85. Waking up in Plato's cave: An ancient vision for transforming contemporary management. *Revision:*7(2).

Joiner, William B. 1985. *The collaboration skills manual.* Action Management Systems, Concord, MA.

Joiner, William B., and Michael J. Sales. Organizational learning: The new priority (brochure). Action Management Systems, Concord, MA.

Kanter, Rosabeth Moss. 1983. *The change masters: Innovation and productivity in the American corporation.* Simon and Schuster, New York.

Kaufman, W., trans. 1970. *I and thou* by Martin Buber. Charles Scribner's Sons, New York.

Kidder, Tracy. 1981. *The soul of a new machine.* Little, Brown, Boston.

Kiefer, Charles, and Peter Senge. 1984. Metanoic organizations. In John D. Adams, ed., *Transforming work.* Miles River Press, Alexandria, VA.

Kimberley, J. R., and R. H. Miles, eds. 1980. *The organizational life cycles: New perspectives for organizational theory and research.* Jossey-Bass, San Francisco.

Kinsman, Francis. 1983. *The new agenda.* Spencer Stuart, London.

Kobasa, Suzanne. 1979. Stressful life events, personality, and health. *Journal of Personality and Social Psychology:*37.

Koestler, Arthur. 1959. *The sleepwalkers.* Macmillan, New York.

Kuhn, Thomas. 1962. *The structure of scientific revolutions.* University of Chicago Press, Chicago.

Kuzela, Lad. Putting Japanese style management to work. *Industry Week.* Sept. 1, 1980.

Lawrence, Paul R., and Davis Dyer. 1983. *Renewing American industry: Organizing for efficiency and innovation.* The Free Press, New York.

Lessem, Ronnie. 1986. *Enterprise/development.* Gower Publishing, London.

Lessem, Ronnie. 1986. *The roots of excellence.* Fontana, London.

Levering, Robert, et al. 1984. *The 100 best companies to work for in America.* Addison-Wesley, Reading, MA.

Levine, S. 1979. *A gradual awakening.* Anchor Books, New York.

Levinson, Daniel J., et al. 1978. *The seasons of a man's life.* Knopf, New York.

Lodge, George C. 1984. *The American disease.* Knopf, New York.

Low, A. 1976. *Zen and creative management.* Anchor Books, New York.

Luttwak, Edward N. 1985. *The pentagon and the art of war: The question of military reform.* Simon and Schuster, New York.

Maccoby, Michael. 1976. *The gamesman.* Bantam Books, New York.

Macrae, Norman. 1976. The coming entrepreneurial revolution: A survey. *The Economist.* December 25.

Maiden, A. H. 1980. Resonance. *Gala* Newsletter:II(2).

Manager's journal. *The Wall Street Journal.* June 21, 1982.

Maslow, Abraham. 1954 (2nd ed., 1970). *Motivation and personality.* Harper and Brothers, New York.

McClosky, Michael. 1983. Intuitive physics. *Scientific American.*

*McGregor, Douglas. 1966. Leadership and motivation.* Massachusetts Institute of Technology Press, Cambridge, MA.

McGregor-Burns, James. 1979. *Leadership.* Harper Torch Books, New York.

Meadows, Donella. 1982. Whole earth models and systems. *Co-Evolution Quarterly.* Summer.

Merritt, William. 1982. *World out of work.* Collins, Glasgow.

Mitchell, Arnold. 1983. *The nine American lifestyles.* Macmillan, New York.

Mushashi, Miyamoto. 1974. *A book of five rings: A guide to strategy.* Victor Harris, trans. The Overlook Press, Woodstock, NY.

Naisbitt, John. 1983. *Megatrends: Ten new directions transforming our lives.* Warner Books, New York.

Noble, Vicki. 1983. *Motherpeace—A way to the goddess through myth, art, and tarot.* Harper & Row, San Francisco.

Nussbaum, Bruce. 1983. *The world after oil.* Simon and Schuster, New York.

Olmae, K. 1982. *The mind of the stategist.* R. R. Donnelly and Sons, Harrisonburg, VA.

Ouchi, William G. 1981. *Theory Z: How American business can meet the Japanese challenge.* Avon, New York.

Owen, Harrison. 1983. *Open space: An introduction to the theory and practice of organizational transformation.* H.H. Owen and Co., Arlington, VA.

Pascale, R. T. 1978. Zen and the act of management. *Harvard Business Review.* March-April.

Pascale, R. T., and A. G. Athos. 1981. *The art of Japanese management: Applications for American executives.* Warner Books, New York.

Pascarella, Perry. 1984. *The new achievers: Creating a modern work ethic.* The Free Press, New York.

Peters, Thomas J., and Nancy Austin. 1985. *A passion for excellence: The leadership difference.* Random House, New York.

Peters, Thomas J., and Robert H. Waterman. 1982. *In search of excellence: Lessons from America's best-run companies.* Harper & Row, New York.

Pinchot, Gifford. 1984. *Intrapreneuring.* Harper & Row, New York.

Quinn, J. B. 1980. Managing strategic change. *Sloan Management Review:*21(4).

Russell, Peter. 1982. *The awakening earth.* Cox and Wyman, Reading, England.

Schein, Edgar H. 1984. Coming to a new awareness of organizational culture. *Sloan Management Review.* Winter.

Schein, Edgar H. 1985. *Organizational culture and leadership: A dynamic view.* Jossey-Bass, San Francisco.

Senge, Peter M. Systems thinking and the new management style. Systems Dynamics Group Working Paper. D-3586-2. Massachusetts Institute of Technology, Cambridge, MA.

Sheridan, Mike. Industrial theatre makes it debut. *Sky Magazine.* April 14, 1985.

Siu, R. G. H. 1980. *The master manager.* John Wiley, Chichester.

Solman, Paul, and Thomas Friedman. 1982. *Life and death on the corporate battlefield.* Simon and Schuster, New York.

Sperry, Roger. 1981. Changing priorities. *Annual Review of Neurosciences:*4.

Starhawk. 1982. *Dreaming the dark: Magic, sex, and politics.* Beacon Press, Boston.

Steele, Fritz, and Stephen Jenks. 1977. *The feel of the workplace.* Addison-Wesley, Reading, MA.

Suzuki, Shunryu. 1976. *Zen mind, beginner's mind.* Weatherhill, New York.

Thomas, Lewis. 1979. *The medusa and the snail.* The Viking Press, New York.

Toffler, Alvin. 1981. *The third wave.* Bantam Books, New York.

Toffler, Alvin. 1983. *Previews and premises.* William Morrow, New York.

Torbert, William R. 1972. *Learning from experience: Toward consciousness.* Columbia University Press, New York.

Torbert, William R. 1976. *Creating a community of inquiry: Conflict, collaboration, transformation.* Wiley, London.

Torbert, William R. 1978. Educating toward shared purpose, self-direction, and quality work: The theory and practice of liberating structure. *Journal of Higher Education:*49(2).

Tregoe, B. B., and J. W. Zimmerman. 1983. *Top management strategy: What it is and how to make it work.* Simon and Schuster, New York.

Vaill, Peter B. 1982. The purpose of high performing systems. *Organizational Dynamics:*11(2).

Vaughan, Frances. 1979. *Awakening intuition.* Anchor Books, New York.

Von Franz, Marie-Louise. 1981 *Puer aeternus.* Sigo Press, Santa Monica, CA.

Watts, A. W. 1968. *The wisdom of insecurity.* Random House, New York.

Wilkins, Alan J. 1984. The creation of company cultures: The role of stories and human resource systems. *Human Resource Management.* Spring.

Yalom, Irvin. 1980. *Existential psychotherapy.* Basic Books, New York.

Yankelovich, Daniel. 1981. *New rules.* Random House, New York.

Zalesnick, Abraham. 1977. Managers and leaders: Are they different? *Harvard Business Review.*